Commercial Property Risk Management and Insurance

Volume II

WILLIAM H. RODDA, CPCU

President, Marine Insurance Handbook, Inc.

JAMES S. TRIESCHMANN, D.B.A., CPCU, CLU

Associate Professor and Acting Head
Department of Risk and Insurance
University of Georgia

BOB A. HEDGES, Ph.D., CPCU, CLU

Professor of Insurance and Risk
Temple University

AMERICAN
INSTITUTE FOR
PROPERTY &
LIABILITY
UNDERWRITERS
INC.

First Edition • 1978

AMERICAN INSTITUTE FOR
PROPERTY AND LIABILITY UNDERWRITERS
Providence and Sugartown Roads, Malvern, Pennsylvania 19355

© 1978
AMERICAN INSTITUTE FOR
PROPERTY AND LIABILITY UNDERWRITERS, INC.
*All rights reserved. This book or any part thereof
may not be reproduced without the written
permission of the publisher.*

Third Printing • *July 1980*

Library of Congress Catalog Number   78-52690
International Standard Book Number   0-89463-005-9

Printed in the United States of America

Table of Contents

Insurance Designed Primarily for Loss of Money and Securities ∽
*Mercantile Robbery Policy; Mercantile Safe Burglary Policy;
Money and Securities Broad Form Policy; Paymaster Robbery
Policy; Safe Deposit Box Policies; Innkeepers' Liability Insurance;
Office Burglary and Robbery Policy; Storekeepers' Burglary and
Robbery Policy; Coverage for Forgery and Counterfeit Money;
Limited Policies for Special Purposes*

Insurance Against Loss of Merchandise ∽ *Mercantile Open Stock
Burglary Policy*

"All-Risks" Coverage of Business Personal Property ∽ *Property Subject
to Limitation or Exclusion; Deductibles in "All-Risks" Coverage;
Crime Losses Covered by "All-Risks" Policies*

Federal Crime Insurance ∽ *Reasons for and Development of the
Program; Policy Coverage and General Provisions*

Noninsurance Techniques ∽ *Protective Devices; Protective Procedures;
Evaluation of Protective Measures Versus Insurance*

Exposure of Property Values to Loss from Employee Dishonesty ∽ *The
Crime of Embezzlement; Characteristics of Embezzlement Losses;
Conditions Conducive to Embezzlement; Types of Embezzlement
Losses; Frequency and Severity of Embezzlement Losses; Evaluat-
ing the Impact of Potential Embezzlement Losses*

Basic Characteristics of Fidelity Bonds ∽ *Principles of Suretyship and
Fidelity Bonds; Common Features in Fidelity Bonds*

Types of Fidelity Bonds ∽ *Individual Bond; Name Schedule Bond;
Position Schedule Bond; Blanket Bonds*

Analysis of Some Important Fidelity Bonds ∽ *Commercial Blanket
Bond; Conditions; Blanket Position Bond; Common Endorsements
and Variations; Bankers Blanket Bond; Other Bankers Bonds;
Excess and Catastrophe Coverages for Banks; Bonds for Other
Financial Institutions; Kidnap-Ransom-Extortion Coverage*

Loss Control Techniques ∽ *Theft of Money; Theft of Merchandise;
Embezzlement of Funds in a Financial Institution; Electronic
Data Processing; Collateral Programs*

Insuring Condominiums ~ *Definitions; Property Forms for Condominiums*

Insuring Buildings Under Construction ~ *SMP Builders' Risk Forms*

Marine Insurance Options Contained in the SMP Program ~ *Radium Floater; Fine Arts Floater; Camera Floater; Musical Instrument Floater; Neon Sign Floater; Physicians' and Surgeons' Equipment Floater (MP-111)*

Insuring Against the Crime Peril in the SMP ~ *Crime Coverages in the Property Section of the SMP; Crime Coverages in Section III of the SMP*

Boiler and Machinery Coverages in the SMP ~ *Boiler and Machinery Forms in the SMP*

Insurance to Value and Deductible Provisions in the SMP Property Program ~ *Insurance to Value; Deductible Provisions in the SMP*

Combination Policies—Single-Line ~ *Commercial Property Form; Office Personal Property Form; Industrial Property Form*

Manufacturers Output Policy ~ *Policy Conditions*

Multiple-Line Policies ~ *Businessowners Policy; Farmowners-Ranchowners (FR) Program; The Electronic Data Processing Exposure*

Multi-Coverage Account Rating ~ *Coverages Available*

Case Studies in Property Exposures and Their Treatment ~ *The Sheltering Arms Case; The White Lightning Case*

CHAPTER 9

Inland Marine Loss Exposures

INTRODUCTION

The exposures to loss or damage during transportation over land were negligible in the United States until the development of the railroad. Overland transportation until about 1850 was slow and laborious, and the bulk of commerce was by the seas or inland waterways. Commerce was so dependent upon water transportation that millions of dollars were spent on the building of canals, some of which are still in use. The Erie Canal across New York State, for example, is still an important avenue of freight transportation. Other canals have long fallen into disuse and some now form the roadbeds for railroads or highways. The hazards of transportation during the days of water transit were similar for inland and overseas risks. Ocean marine insurance with its extension to overland transit through the use of the warehouse-to-warehouse clause was adequate for insurance protection.

The building of railroads from 1825 to 1900 brought about one of the greatest changes in transportation methods ever. Large quantities could be shipped overland at a relatively high speed. Population moved inland with the building of inland cities. Factories were built within easy access to raw materials and to markets. Overland transportation dominated industry in the United States and resulted in new exposures to property in transit.

The development of the motor truck and the airplane further changed the exposures of transportation. The use of the four basic methods of transportation—water, railroad, motor truck, and airplane—present different, although related, chances of loss or damage to goods being carried. The chances of loss or damage differ from one medium to another, not only because of the difference in the threats to property

1

from the different methods of transportation but also because of the different kinds of property that are shipped on the various carriers.

High-value and low-volume property (such as watches) justify a rapid and expensive means of transportation. Coal, ore, gravel, and crude petroleum, on the other hand, are shipped by slower but cheaper means. Inland waterways are used to a great extent for the shipping of bulk materials such as coal, ore, sand, gravel, and fuel oil. The means of transportation chosen by the shipper depends upon the nature and the value of the goods being shipped, the cost of transportation, and the urgency of quick transit. Movable property is subject to virtually all the perils that are common to fixed location property. In addition, it is exposed to perils arising from transportation.

Along with the increased use of modern forms of transportation there developed a new kind of insurance to cover the loss exposures associated with transportation. Inland marine insurance evolved out of ocean marine insurance. In the course of its development, inland marine insurance came to provide coverage for merchandise in transit, bailees, and a variety of "floating" property, as well as other types of property. This chapter will explore some of the loss exposures for which inland marine insurance can provide coverage, and will discuss the origins and development of inland marine insurance. Many of the features common to inland marine policies will be discussed in general. Specific inland marine policy forms will be discussed in Chapter 10.

LOSS EXPOSURES TO PROPERTY IN TRANSIT

In evaluating loss exposures to property in transit, it is necessary to consider the perils which may cause loss to such property, and the potential frequency and severity of such losses. Likewise, it is important to determine which of the parties involved will bear the loss of any property in transit. A number of entities may be involved in a single shipment of goods—the shipper, the consignee, and all parties handling the goods while in transit.

Perils Affecting Property in Transit

Property in transit is subject to virtually all the loss causes that are common to fixed-location property. In addition, it is exposed to perils related to the act of transportation.

Fire may occur in warehouses or while property is enroute in a truck, railroad boxcar, or airplane. Windstorm may affect property at any location. Conveyances may be overturned or upset by a windstorm, with resultant damage to goods being conveyed. Like property at fixed locations, property in transit may be exposed to loss by aircraft damage, vehicle damage, riot and civil commotion, explosion, smoke, vandalism, and so forth.

Property in transit is particularly subject to crime loss, both by theft and by embezzlement. The greatest exposure is faced by property of high value and low bulk, such as a shipment of tobacco products. However, bulky items, such as a load of steel, may also be stolen if an entire shipment is hijacked. Hijackings have also involved property of low unit cost and high marketability, such as one hijacking of a semi-trailer containing $75,000 worth of panty hose. The exposure to crime loss is relatively high for property in transit because tight security is difficult to maintain when property is being moved about. Crime exposures will be discussed more extensively in Chapters 11 and 12.

The chances of flood loss to property in the course of actual movement in transit are perhaps somewhat less than the chances of loss to property at a fixed location in a flood zone. Many floods can be anticipated in advance, giving railroads and truck lines time to move their vehicles out of the flood area.

Earthquakes are not yet predictable, but there have been relatively few serious losses to property actually in transit. There is still an exposure, however. It is possible that a railroad wreck could be caused by the disruption of tracks in an earthquake. Cargo losses have occurred when trucks were being driven or were parked in an area where an earthquake occurred.

Property in transit, because it is in transit, is exposed to loss resulting from the peril of collision or overturn of the conveyance. Trucks, railroad cars, and airplanes may become involved in a collision with a fixed object or other vehicle. Upset or overturn may occur whether a single vehicle or multiple vehicles are involved. Regardless of the mode of transportation, there is a chance of damage or loss to goods being transported when the conveyance is involved in a collision or overturn.

Misdelivery or nondelivery of property are additional perils to which a shipper is exposed. If a parcel is not delivered, or if it is delivered to the wrong party, the shipper, carrier, or consignee faces a loss.

Property in transit is also subject to loss caused by wear and tear, deterioration, loss of refrigeration, excessive heat, and other miscellaneous perils. The potential for loss due to these perils depends in part on the nature of the property. Produce, for example, may be particularly subject to damage caused by loss of refrigeration. On the other hand, liquids or sensitive electronic components may be damaged by freezing temperatures. The exposure to such miscellaneous perils may be increased or decreased depending on the type of packing and mode of transportation utilized.

Frequency and Severity of Transit Losses

The severity exposure of property in transit varies materially with the different kinds of property that are shipped. The mobile television equipment that is sent by motor truck to cover a big event such as a presidential nominating convention may be worth as much as $5 million. In such a case the exposure in a single loss is quite severe, but the equipment may be transported infrequently.

A different situation is presented by an organization that is continuously shipping small quantities of foods. The exposure to loss here is continuous, but any single loss may be relatively small. For example, a retail mail order operation selling men's slacks may ship huge quantities of merchandise direct to consumers, but the maximum value of any single shipment may be less than $100.

In some cases, the continuous exposure may be substantial. A diamond merchant, for example, will frequently carry several hundred thousand dollars worth of diamonds from city to city, and may continuously face a severe theft exposure.

In evaluating the frequency and severity potential of the loss exposure, a number of factors should be considered, including the type of merchandise, the radius of operations, the condition of the equipment carrying the cargo, the caliber of drivers handling the vehicles or merchandise, the terrain and climatic variations where the load will be carried, the past record of the carrier, and the crime rate in areas through which the merchandise will pass.

The frequency or severity potential may be reduced by the application of various loss control measures, discussed in Chapter 10.

Liabilities of Carriers

When property in transit is lost, damaged, or destroyed, there are usually at least two parties involved—the shipper or consignee, and the carrier. The terms of the sale, as well as legal principles and practices, determine at what point ownership of the goods being transported passes from the shipper to the consignee. Regardless of ownership, the carriers having custody of the property bear some legal liability for loss, damage, or destruction of property in their custody.

Property that is in transit from one place to another is in the custody of persons or organizations known as "carriers" who may be classified as either commercial or private carriers. A commercial carrier operates under an authorization to act as a common carrier or under private contract between the shipper and the carrier. Persons or organizations transporting their own goods on their own vehicles are classified as private carriers.

The liability of a carrier for property in its custody varies greatly, depending upon whether the operation is as a common carrier, a contract carrier, or a private carrier. To understand the loss exposures of the various parties involved, it is necessary to understand the liabilities imposed upon the various kinds of carriers.

The Common Carrier It was mentioned in previous chapters that the liability of an ocean carrier for cargo in its custody is limited. The liability of a common carrier on land in the United States, in contrast, is almost complete.

Liability of a Common Carrier. A common carrier is one that undertakes to carry persons or goods of all persons indifferently, or of all who choose to employ it. The common carrier is obligated to carry passengers or property for anyone who applies for passage as long as there is room, there is no legal excuse for refusal, and the carriage is within the authority granted to the carrier. A common carrier in practically all cases in the United States operates under an authority granted by a federal or a state body. The federal authority is the Interstate Commerce Commission (ICC); the states have comparable bodies (known as Commerce Commissions or by other names). The authority granted to a common carrier defines the geographical area of service and the kind of service which the carrier is authorized to perform. Bus companies, for example, have authority to carry passengers between points named in the authorization, and bus companies may also be authorized to carry cargo under certain conditions. Railroads often have authority to carry both passengers and cargo. Truck lines usually are limited to the carrying of cargo between points named in the authorizations. A common carrier might be tempted to arrange dishonestly for the loss of property if it did not have a responsibility for safe carriage and delivery. It developed early as a principle of common law that a firm which makes a business of carrying persons or property for a consideration is responsible for their safe delivery.

This extensive liability of the common carrier makes it probable that the shipper of goods can recover from a common carrier for the value of property that is lost or damaged while in the custody of the common carrier.

Exceptions to Common Carrier Liability. It became clear that a common carrier can do little to control loss due to some calamities. Thus such a carrier is not held responsible for:

1. acts of God
2. acts of the public enemy
3. exercise of public authority
4. fault or neglect on the part of the shipper
5. inherent vice or the nature of the property

An explanation of what is intended by each of these limitations will show that they are generally unusual occurrences.

ACTS OF GOD. Acts of God are occurrences of nature, such as tornadoes, storms, earthquakes, and floods. However, the common carrier might be liable for damage by one of these occurrences if the event could have been foreseen and action by the carrier could have prevented the loss. There was a flood in the Kansas City, Missouri, area some years ago which caused damage to cargo in railroad freight cars in the Kansas City yards. The railroad denied liability for the damage on the ground that the damage resulted from an act of God. The courts decided, however, that the railroad had had sufficient warning in advance that the railroad yard would be flooded and that the railroad was responsible for the loss.

ACTS OF THE PUBLIC ENEMY. The public enemy is a nation or government at war with the nation in which the carrier is domiciled. It does not refer to individual criminals or even groups of criminals not involved in warfare. Although absolved from liability for "acts of the public enemy," a common carrier is responsible for loss resulting from the acts of criminals, even if the criminal is recognized as "public enemy number one."

EXERCISE OF PUBLIC AUTHORITY. An exercise of public authority would be any act that is taken by a public official acting within his or her governmental authority. Examples might include a backfire set by a fire department to stop the spread of a conflagration or the building of a dike which floods some areas to halt rising flood waters in a more critical area. A common carrier's conveyance might be burned or flooded due to such an exercise of public authority, but the common carrier would not be legally liable for such a loss.

FAULT OR NEGLECT ON THE PART OF THE SHIPPER. A shipper may be negligent in packing or shipping some type of property that obviously would be damaged by ordinary handling in transit. The common carrier is not held liable for damage which results directly from such negligence on the part of the shipper.

INHERENT VICE OR THE NATURE OF THE PROPERTY. Inherent vice is a condition within a particular type of property that tends to make the property destroy itself. The natural deterioration of natural rubber over a period of time when it is not in use is often cited as an example of inherent vice. It was decided by a court in one case that injury to cattle when they were stampeded by the passage of a railroad train constituted an inherent vice. The court said that it is in the nature of cattle to stampede, sometimes without apparent reason, so that damage done to the cattle under these circumstances was due to the inherent nature of the cattle.[1]

In summary, a common carrier is liable for almost all loss or damage that occurs to property in the custody of the common carrier. It is only rarely that the common carrier can avoid liability because of loss or damage from one of the five exemptions that have been described.

Limitations on Common Carrier Liability. There are certain limitations on the extent of a common carrier's liability which may be invoked by the common carrier even though the liability seldom can be eliminated entirely. It is well established that a common carrier can limit the dollar amount of its liability where a value or limitation of liability is specified in the contract of carriage, and particularly where the common carrier has in effect a different schedule of charges according to the values declared. One of the extreme examples of this principle is a case where a federal court upheld a $50 limitation on a $4,880 mink coat. The valuation was placed upon the coat by a hotel employee who delivered the coat to an express company on behalf of the owner. The court decided that the hotel employee was the agent of the owner and that the $50 limitation in the express company's receipt was binding.[2]

It is standard practice in connection with many common carrier contracts for a dollar limitation to be put upon the property, or for the contract to specify a dollar limit of liability according to some units of measuring the property shipped. Household goods shipments, for example, usually are limited to a specified dollar amount per pound or per 100 pounds of property.

Another limitation in the liability of a common carrier may occur where the liability is reduced to that of a bailee under certain circumstances. (The comparably limited liability of a bailee will be discussed later in this chapter.) The contract of carriage may provide that the liability of the carrier will become that of a bailee after the property has been delivered to a terminal in the consignee's locality and after the consignee has been notified that the property is there to be picked up. It is considered reasonable for the extreme liability of the common carrier to be mitigated after a reasonable length of time if the consignee neglects to pick up the property after having been notified that it is available for pick up.

Bills of Lading. The bill of lading issued by common carriers serves as a receipt from the carrier for the goods being transported. In addition, it serves as the contract of carriage between the shipper and carrier, setting forth the obligations and responsibilities of each party. The bill of lading may also serve as evidence of title to the goods.

RELEASED BILL OF LADING. On a released bill of lading, the carrier is released of liability above a certain amount which is specified in the contract. This may be a specific number of dollars, or it may be an agreed or declared value according to some unit of measurement. A typical unit is a limitation per 100 pounds of weight. The carrier may have filed tariffs (schedules of charges and conditions of carriage) which specify various charges according to the type of property to be carried and the values to be declared.

STRAIGHT BILL OF LADING. The straight bill of lading is a contract between the shipper and the carrier for the transportation of the property. The carrier is instructed to deliver the goods to the consignee. It is not a negotiable document. Possession of the straight bill of lading by a third party does not convey any title or right to receive the goods. The goods in any case would be delivered to the consignee according to the instructions in the contract. The straight bill of lading does not include any limitation on the value to be paid by the carrier in case of loss. The charges for transporting the property may be paid by the shipper or by the consignee, depending upon the conditions of the contract. The straight bill of lading will specify whether shipment is prepaid by the shipper or whether the charges are to be collected from the consignee.

ORDER BILL OF LADING. The order bill of lading serves as a contract of shipment (the same as a straight bill of lading) and possible limitation on values (as in a released bill of lading) and also as a method of shipping on a cash-on-delivery arrangement. The order bill of lading is used for shipments on land in much the same way that has been described for overseas shipment in connection with ocean marine commerce. The property is shipped under an order bill of lading but the consignee does not receive the goods from the carrier until payment for the goods has been made by the consignee, usually through an arrangement with a bank. Common carriers such as railroads and truck lines often do not want to take the responsibility for handling the money that would be required for a cash-on-delivery arrangement directly through the carrier. The money is handled through banking channels. The carrier delivers the property to the consignee upon receiving instructions from the financial institution that the agreed payment has been made.

SHIPPER'S WEIGHT, LOAD, AND COUNT. There is another possible limitation on the liability of the carrier in cases where the shipper has the facilities to load and seal a railroad car, and the carrier has no opportunity to check the nature, quality, weight, or quantity of the load.

Many industrial organizations that have railroad sidings on their premises ship entire carloads of merchandise to one consignee. The loading is done entirely without checking or observation by the carrier. The bill of lading in such a case is stamped with the words "shipper's weight, load, and count" or words with that intent. The common carrier in this case avoids liability for any loss which results from short load or count unless it can be proved that the car was entered and goods removed en route.

Many well-managed carriers maintain careful records of the seals on cars and trucks. It is possible to enter a car or truck and to reseal it, but this is an unusual occurrence.

MISTAKE ON BILL OF LADING. A mistake on the bill of lading in the description of the goods may bring about a situation similar to that which arises under a shipper's weight, load, and count situation. A carrier might be able to prove that it did not actually receive the goods described in the bill of lading and it might be able to limit its liability to the shipper or the consignee to the value of the goods which actually were received. This situation might arise in the case of sealed packages whose contents are incorrectly described. Or, the carrier might be liable to the consignee as an innocent third party even though it did not actually receive the goods described. These become complicated situations which often have to be resolved in court.

Delivery and Acceptance of Goods. A common carrier's exposure to loss begins when goods have been delivered to and accepted by the carrier. The point at which loss exposure actually is transferred, however, is difficult to define.

DELIVERY TO THE CARRIER. Delivery of goods to the carrier is usually clearly established in the case of package shipments. For example, the shipper may deliver the packages to the carrier at a freight depot. Actual receipt by the carrier of the property under these circumstances constitutes delivery to the carrier, and the property is in the custody of the carrier from that point on. Some carriers provide a pick-up service at the shipper's premises. Here again, actual receipt of the property by the carrier constitutes delivery to the carrier with custody in the hands of the carrier from that point on.

There may be a question as to when delivery is made to the carrier in the case of carload shipments from a railroad siding. The issuance of a bill of lading by the carrier upon notice that the car is ready ordinarily will constitute acknowledgment of delivery to the carrier. This may be true even though the railroad has not yet moved the car. The situation becomes a bit cloudy in cases where the bill of lading is issued before the car is fully loaded. The shipper may be loading the car during the late afternoon and may ask the freight agent to make out the bill of lading so that the car can be moved by the railroad during the night. It would become a question of fact to be determined whether the railroad actually received the goods in a situation where the bill of lading had been issued but the car had not been fully loaded at that time.

DELIVERY BY THE CARRIER. Questions arise regarding whether delivery actually has been made by the carrier to the consignee. Delivery by the carrier to the consignee's premises usually is evidenced by a receipt that the carrier takes from the consignee upon delivery. A question might arise if the carrier's delivery person arrives before the consignee's place of business is open and leaves the goods outside the door. There would be no receipt to evidence delivery in such a case, and the carrier probably would be held liable for nondelivery. There is also the possibility that an imposter at the consignee's premises might receive the goods, sign the delivery receipt and abscond with the goods. Here again there would be a question of fact as to whether the delivery actually was made.

A different situation occurs where the consignee is obligated to pick up the shipment at the carrier's freight depot. The usual arrangement is that the carrier's liability as a carrier continues for forty-eight hours after written notice of arrival has been sent or given to the consignee. The liability of the carrier becomes that of a warehouseman (or bailee) at the expiration of that time. The liability of the carrier as a warehouseman or bailee is limited to negligence liability in contrast to the extensive liability as a carrier. The consignee must make sure that the goods are picked up prior to the expiration of the forty-eight hour limit. The burden of proof of negligence is on the consignee after the liability of the carrier changes to that of a warehouseman.

Railroad shipments may be made on what are called public team tracks. (A public team track is a railroad side track with a driveway alongside that enables consignees to park their trucks at the freight door and unload goods.) The consignee has the obligation to remove goods within the forty-eight hour period after notification has been given that the carload is on the team tracks ready for pick up by the consignee. It is, of course, an obligation of the carrier to provide security for property that is parked on public team tracks.

SIDE TRACK AGREEMENTS. In the case of cars delivered to a private or semiprivate sidetrack, delivery by the carrier is made by placing the railroad car on the side track at a reasonable hour for unloading. The side track agreement between the railroad and the consignee may specify what is to be considered as delivery. There is no forty-eight hour requirement for notice of side track deliveries. The delivery is really the equivalent of the delivery of a package to the premises of the consignee.

The side track agreement may provide that the railroad may place carload freight on the siding at its convenience and that such placing constitutes delivery. The placing of a railroad car on the siding at a late-night hour might make the contents vulnerable to theft—an additional consideration in evaluating loss exposures.

CARLOADING COMPANIES AND FREIGHT FORWARDERS. It is characteristic of shipping rates that the rate for small shipments is higher than for large shipments. This is justified because extra work is necessary in the handling of many small shipments. There are many organizations that operate by consolidating many small shipments into a single large shipment. These organizations are called carloading companies or freight forwarders. Some of them operate not only for railroad freight but also for truck freight and air freight. Such a carloading company, for example, might collect a large number of packages that are destined from New York to Chicago. These would then be combined into a single shipment, perhaps in a container, and the railroad, truck line, or airline would handle the container as a single shipment. The carloading company can make money because of the difference between the rates for many small shipments and the rate for a single large shipment. The carloading company may also provide for pick up and delivery of package freight.

The carloading company usually operates as a common carrier. It issues a bill of lading identical to that issued by the railroads or truck lines. The shipper and consignee have the same rights of claims for lost or damaged merchandise against the carloading company as if the shipment had been placed directly in the hands of a railroad, truck line or airline. There may be some differences between the responsibilities of railroads, truck lines, and airlines under the somewhat different bills of lading used for different types of carriers. This might affect the amount of value that could be recovered from the carloading company in the case of loss or damage. These are questions of fact that have to be determined in any case where a claim is made against the carrier.

Claims Against the Common Carrier. The carrier faces rather severe liability for loss or damage to property in the carrier's custody. However, the claimant against such a carrier must meet conditions which are sometimes difficult in order to recover the value of goods. The paragraph regarding claims in a typical bill of lading reads:

Section 2 (b) As a condition precedent to recovery, claims must be filed in writing with the receiving or delivering carrier, or carrier issuing this bill of lading, or carrier on whose line the loss, damage, injury or delay occurred, within nine months after delivery of the property (or, in the case of export traffic, within nine months after delivery at port of export) or in case of failure to make delivery, then within nine months after a reasonable time for delivery has elapsed: and suits shall be instituted against any carrier only within two years and one day from the day when notice in writing is given by the carrier to the claimant that the carrier has disallowed the claim or any part or parts thereof specified in the notice. Where claims are not filed or suits are not instituted thereon in accordance with the foregoing provisions, no carrier hereunder shall be liable, and such claims will not be paid.

A shipper of goods must realize that common carriers generally enforce strictly the requirements of the bill of lading for making claim against the carrier.

The consignee must note any shortages or damages upon receipt of the goods. Claim must be filed promptly upon the discovery of a loss. The claim must be made clearly as a claim for damages and it must be for a dollar amount.

There are circumstances where the shipper or consignee can collect damages for unreasonable delay if the delay results in a loss. However, a carrier is not permitted to promise expedited service or a definite delivery date unless the carrier has filed a tariff providing the conditions under which such expedited service will be provided.

To collect from carriers for loss or damage, a firm must pursue the claim promptly and in strict accordance with the provisions of the bill of lading. Suit must be filed within the time limit prescribed. Sometimes a claimant may believe that negotiations by the carrier for settlement will act as a waiver of the time limit for filing suit, but this is not the case.

It is important to realize that the interest of the carrier and the interest of the claimant are adverse. The common carrier seeks by strict compliance with the contract conditions to reduce or eliminate its liability. The shipper or consignee who is a claimant against the carrier must pursue the claim with equal vigor.

Shippers and consignees may encounter different situations where goods are shipped in intrastate commerce rather than between states. State statutes and regulations differ in some details from the regulations of the Interstate Commerce Commission. These differences may affect the requirement for notice of arrival to the consignee, or they may affect the liability of the common carrier when an intrastate shipment arrives at the carrier's freight depot at the destination. These possible differences in the exact liability of a common carrier must be determined in any case where they might affect the exposure to loss either for a shipper, consignee, or for the liability for a common carrier.

There may be other details of difference in liability and possibilities of recovery where the shipment may proceed for a certain portion of its journey by water. A barge or lighter used in connection with a rail journey is normally considered as part of the rail journey. Loss or damage occurring during such lighterage would be settled according to the general rules of land transportation and not according to the rules applying to ocean transportation. There may be situations where an ocean carrier operating between ports in the United States is in competition with land carriers. The ocean carrier in that case might assume a liability by contract in order to provide comparable security with that provided by railroads or trucks.

Contract Carriers The discussion of carrier liability up to this point has related to common carriers. A considerable volume of cargo shipment is also handled by contract carrier. The contract carrier does not have an authorized route such as is granted to a common carrier. The contract carrier is relatively free to carry cargo for anybody between any points and is subject to individual contracts of carriage.

The liability of a contract carrier depends to a large extent upon the contract between the shipper and the carrier. The basic liability of a contract carrier is for negligence in the handling of the cargo. It is generally considered to be against public policy for anyone selling a service to contract away his or her entire liability for negligence. Therefore, the contract carrier in general would be liable for any loss or damage that resulted from its negligence in its handling of the cargo. However, the liability may be affected greatly in other respects by the provisions of the contract. The contract carrier may assume complete liability for loss or damage, or on the other hand may put into the contract restrictions or limitations that would greatly reduce the carrier's liability.

Common Carriers Compared with Contract Carriers. It is not always easy to determine who is a common carrier and who is a contract carrier. A few observations will help to identify some of the distinctions in practice. Railroads generally operate as common carriers, and it would be unusual to have a situation where a railroad is operating as a contract carrier. In contrast, a large proportion of motor truck operation is by contract. Many truck lines operate as common carriers with authorization from the Interstate Commerce Commission (ICC) or from state bodies to operate regularly between specified points. However, these same truck lines may also operate as contract carriers in connection with specific shipments. To determine loss exposures, it would be necessary to determine whether a particular shipment is being handled under a motor truck carrier's authorization as a common carrier, or whether this is a situation where the trucker is operating as a contract carrier, because the liability exposures are different.

The scheduled airlines are common carriers operating under authority granted by an agency of the federal government, or in a few cases under authority granted by state bodies. These same airlines also operate as contract carriers in many cases, carrying either passengers on charter trips or special loads of cargo under contract.

Truckers and airlines that operate as contract carriers are subject to safety regulations and certain other regulations of the federal government where they operate across state lines. These restrictions are not material to the question of insurance coverage. The important point to be determined is what obligations are assumed by the carrier under the contract and what restrictions or limitations are placed upon the liability of the carrier. The relative exposure to loss of a carrier, or of a shipper, depends to a large degree upon the liability that is assumed by the carrier or the limitations or restrictions under the contract.

Private Carriers Prior to the enactment of the Motor Carrier Act of 1935, a "private carrier" was generally considered to be a trucker that transported or undertook to transport property in a particular instance for hire or reward. Thus, a contract carrier was considered a "private carrier" before 1935. The Motor Carrier Act of 1935 set up *three* kinds of carriers—common carriers, contract carriers, and private carriers. The Act defines a "private carrier" as one who carries its own goods or goods for which it is the lessee or bailee. The term "private carrier" is now used to indicate those who haul their own goods on their own trucks, which follows the definition in the Motor Carrier Act.

The important point in connection with cargo transported by private carrier—cargo carried by its owner on the owner's trucks—is that there is no chance of recovery for loss or damage from a carrier. It is not possible to transfer the exposure to the carrier. The only chance of recovery from another party would be if some third party were the cause of an accident in which the goods became damaged or lost.

BAILMENT LOSS EXPOSURES

A *bailment* is the legal relation that arises whenever one person delivers possession of personal property to another person under an agreement or contract by which the latter is under a duty to return the identical property to the former or to deliver or dispose of it as agreed.[3] The person receiving the property is the *bailee*. The person who turns over possession of the property is the *bailor*.

Only personal property can be involved in a bailment; real property cannot be bailed. Usually the bailor is also the owner of the property, but ownership is not required for a bailment to exist.

Compensation may or may not be involved with a bailment. When no compensation is involved, it is a *gratuitous bailment*. For example, a person might agree to take care of a neighbor's dog or cat while the neighbor is away on vacation. This would be a gratuitous bailment for the benefit of the animal's owner—the bailor. On the other hand, a person may borrow a neighbor's camera to use on a vacation trip. The bailee in this case is the person who borrows the camera and has custody of it. This is a gratuitous bailment for the benefit of the borrower—the bailee. Laundries, dyers and cleaners, tailors, furriers, and rug and carpet cleaners are paid bailees, or *bailees for hire,* and the care demanded with such a paid bailment is much greater than that of gratuitous bailees.

Bailments may be for the sole benefit of the bailor, for the sole benefit of the bailee, or for the mutual benefit of both parties.

Under a bailment, possession of the bailed property passes to the bailee, but ownership is not transferred.

Liability of Bailees

In most cases, the care required of a bailee is less than that required of a common carrier. The bailee is required to use only the degree of care an ordinarily prudent person would exercise in handling his or her own property. Consequently, the liability of bailees for property in their custody is generally limited to loss or damage that results from the bailee's negligence.

To illustrate the differences in liability of a bailee and a common carrier, consider the liability arising out of loss by fire. A common carrier would generally be legally liable for any damage by fire to property in its custody. This would be true even if the carrier were in no way responsible for the fire. The bailee, in contrast, would be legally liable for fire damage only if the fire is the result of the bailee's negligence.

Although bailees are generally legally liable only for losses caused by their negligence, they may extend their liability by contract. For example, a bailee may agree in the bailment contract to assume responsibility for loss or damage by specific perils, or to assume responsibility for any loss that might occur to bailed property. This contractual extension of the bailee's liability may be so broad as to make the bailee liable for anything that happens to the property. Such an extension of the bailee's liability may also be accomplished by statements of the bailee in advertising, or in other efforts to sell services. For example, an advertisement may state that the bailee assumes all responsibility for the goods, or that the bailee carries insurance for the benefit of the bailor against all losses. Such statements may be interpreted by a court to extend the bailee's liability to the extent stated in the advertising material.

In the absence of any extension of liability by contract, the bailee is liable only for loss or damage that is caused by the bailee's negligence while the property is in the bailee's custody. However, it has developed that there is a presumption of negligence on the part of the bailee. This principle developed because, in most cases, the bailee is the only person who can have any knowledge of what happened to cause the loss or damage. This presumption of negligence against the bailee can be rebutted if the bailee is able to show that the loss or damage occurred without any negligence on his or her part. For example, the occurrence of a fire on the bailee's premises might be presumed to result from the bailee's negligence. However, the bailee might be able to show that the fire occurred without any negligence—for example, if the building had been struck by lightning.

Another variation in the bailee's liability may occur depending upon the nature of the property. A greater degree of security would be demanded in connection with expensive jewelry than would be required for the handling of a package of laundry. The bailee must take appropriate precautions against theft of jewelry or other expensive property.

Absolute liability may be imposed on a bailee who takes some action which is outside of the contract with the bailor. For example, a furrier may send a fur coat to a subcontractor for repairs instead of making them in the bailee's own shop. A court has said in such a case that sending the coat to a subcontractor without the knowledge of the coat's owner terminated the bailment contract to the extent that the bailee was liable for the value of the coat. No negligence was proved against the bailee, but the fact that some action was taken that was outside of the bailment contract extended the bailee's liability to an absolute liability.

Liability of the bailee may be limited to a certain dollar amount, particularly where different charges are made according to the value agreed upon by the owner. This is comparable to the situation in connection with common carrier liability and the use of a released bill of lading.

It is generally considered against public policy for a person to attempt a complete elimination of liability for negligence. Automobile storage garages sometimes attempt to limit or to eliminate their liability by posting signs to the effect that the proprietor (who is a bailee) is not liable for loss by certain perils. It is generally held that such disclaimers of liability are not effective where the bailee has been guilty of negligence.

Types of Commercial Bailees

At some time or another, almost every commercial enterprise becomes involved with bailment, and thus incurs exposures to loss of property. A bailor faces a potential loss if property is damaged by a bailee to whom it is entrusted. Likewise, a bailee faces the exposure to loss of property in its custody, for which it may legally be held liable. A small hardware store, for example, may incur a bailee exposure when a customer's power saw is accepted for repair. The same hardware store may be a bailor when a radio providing background music in the store is sent to a repair shop.

Several types of business enterprises face substantial bailee exposures. Laundries and dry cleaners, for example, are held responsible for loss or damage to customers' goods. Furriers who do cleaning, repairing, or storing of furs are exposed to substantial losses as bailees.

Many other types of business have customers' goods in their custody. Large television and radio repair shops, for example, may have a substantial quantity of customers' goods in their possession at any one time. For the smaller shops, the exposure may be somewhat nominal. The garment-making business likewise involves many bailee-bailor relationships.

Warehouses and other operations in the business of storing customers' goods for a fee, such as cold storage lockers, are bailees as well. These businesses face substantial exposures to loss of bailed property, since their primary business is handling property owned by others.

Indirect Loss Exposures of Bailees

As previously discussed, bailees may be held legally liable for bailors' property in their custody damaged by negligence of the bailee. Bailees are also exposed to indirect losses arising out of loss or damage of customers' property, most notably loss of good will or reputation.

If a dry cleaning plant is destroyed by a fire originating in a neighboring building, the bailee would have no legal liability to the customers for loss of their goods (unless the bailor had extended liability by contract or advertising). It might appear that no loss would then be incurred. But imagine the public image created by a dry cleaner who failed to make good to the customers for the loss of their clothing. The publicity might be so bad that the cleaner would be forced to go out of business. To preserve their good will, many bailees choose to reimburse their customers for losses for which the bailee is not legally liable. Failing this course of action, the bailee suffers a loss of good will. Either way, the bailee is exposed to a loss beyond that created by liability imposed by law.

LOSS EXPOSURES TO "FLOATING" PROPERTY

Many types of property do not fall within neatly defined categories. There are many kinds of property that are exposed to loss because their use is away from any fixed location. For example, contractors' equipment would be of little value if it never left the contractor's premises. It is true that such equipment is subject to loss by fire, windstorm, vandalism, and other perils while at the owner's premises, but the exposure to loss is often greatly increased when such equipment is transported and used away from the premises.

The exposure to loss for such "floating" property is not quite the same as the exposure of property in transit. One difference is that there is usually no carrier from whom recovery might be made if the property is lost while in transit. The owner usually bears all exposure to loss, with little or no chance of recovery from a third party.

Many kinds of business property are exposed to off-premises and transit exposures. Manufacturers and sales organizations send goods and equipment for exhibition to fairs, conventions, and shows. The property is exposed to transit losses while en route, and to unusual hazards during the exhibition. Property may be sent on consignment to a purchaser or prospective purchaser for examination, possible acceptance, and possible return to the purveyor.

Other types of "floating" property exposed to loss include agricultural equipment, livestock, theatrical equipment, morticians' equipment, physicians' and surgeons' equipment, radium, signs, sales samples, patterns and dies, coin operated machines, movies, video tapes, cotton, wool, and other property not necessarily used in a fixed location. Loss exposures vary substantially with the type of "floating" property involved, and will be discussed more specifically in Chapter 10.

DEVELOPMENT OF INLAND MARINE INSURANCE

"Inland Marine" appears to be a contradiction in terms, since the term "marine" usually relates to the sea. As previously discussed, marine insurance originally applied to waterborne commerce. However, as marine insurance developed, it gradually began to apply to inland commerce as well. In the early years of this century, the term "inland marine" was coined to distinguish marine insurance on inland exposures from "ocean marine" insurance. As an outgrowth of ocean marine insurance, inland marine insurance provides coverage for exposures to merchandise in transit, bailee exposures, exposures to "floating" property, and several other types of property loss exposures.

Inland marine insurance is a peculiarity of insurance in the United States. It developed partly because of the division of insurance into "lines" in the United States. It was originally almost a pure transit type of insurance coverage but amendments and extensions developed as the need for broad coverage increased. A general description of these developments will help to develop an understanding of inland marine insurance and make it possible to adapt these ideas to current needs of property owners.

Warehouse-to-Warehouse Coverage

The warehouse-to-warehouse extension of ocean marine policies served to cover the needs of overland transportation as long as most of the transportation was an extension of overseas commerce. However, the development of overland transportation between points in the United States rapidly required insurance coverage of property in transit between land points. The first adaptation that was made by marine underwriters to fit the new demands of overland commerce was merely the use of ocean marine policies with provisions for coverage between land points. The principles inherent in the ocean marine warehouse-to-warehouse coverage were followed. Policies were generally written to meet the specific needs of shippers who had a special need for such coverage.

Responsibility Assumed by the Railroads

The railroads during their early history assumed almost total responsibility for the safe delivery of goods in their custody. The common law principle that a common carrier must be held responsible for loss or damage to goods in its custody was accepted by the railroads. There were many circumstances where the railroads probably went beyond their actual legal responsibility in making settlement for goods that were lost or damaged. As a result, it was relatively easy for a claimant to make a claim against the railroad and secure payment. The railroads had a freight depot and a freight agent in nearly every town and city to which the railroads operated. Settlements of claims were sufficiently prompt and reasonable so that shippers came to depend upon the railroads for settlement of any losses that occurred.

Change in Attitude of the Railroads

Conditions during World War I plus other natural developments changed the attitude of the railroads toward claims for lost or damaged property. The federal government took over the operation of the railroads during World War I. There was considerable question whether claims for lost or damaged property should be made against the railroad corporations or against the government. The railroads were greatly overloaded, with the result that many more claims were being made. It began to take months or even years before claims for lost or damaged property could be cleared. It became increasingly advantageous for shippers to buy insurance on their property. This enabled the shippers to collect immediately for losses. Insurance companies took over the task of collecting from the railroad or the government, depending upon the eventual determination of responsibility. The additional cost of buying insurance was immaterial to shippers at the time because merchandise being processed for the war effort was largely being manufactured on a cost-plus basis. Insurance premiums were merely passed on to the government as part of the cost of manufacture and shipping. Insurance coverages were still provided by ocean marine insurers with whatever adjustments in coverage were needed to fit the overland nature of transportation.

Federal regulation of the railroads began as early as 1887 when the Interstate Commerce Act was enacted by Congress to set up the Interstate Commerce Commission (ICC) with authority to regulate common carriers by railroad operating in interstate commerce. Later amendments to the Interstate Commerce Act extended the authority of the ICC, set forth the specific nature of the regulations that were to be established, and in 1935 included the Motor Carrier Act extending regulation to motor truck operations.

The formalization of governmental regulation of the railroads, the chaotic conditions during World War I, and the natural increase in claims for loss and damage as overland commerce increased led the railroads to examine more carefully the claims that were made against them. The provisions of bills of lading requiring notice of claim, the requirements for filing of suit within specified periods of time, and other restrictions began to be applied by the railroads. This was in contrast to their earlier attitude under which they paid claims largely without examination of technicalities. These changes further encouraged shippers to buy insurance on goods in transit so that they could be assured of quick settlement of their claims, with the problem of collection from the railroads being passed on to the insurance companies.

Advent of the Motor Truck

Motor trucks were not used to any extent for the transportation of goods until after World War I. Motor truck carriage quickly established its advantage over the railroad in hauling less than carload lots of goods between nearby cities. Railroad shipment of freight between New York and Philadelphia, or between Baltimore and Washington, required that the packages be carried to a freight depot or freight yard, loaded onto a freight car, hauled by train over the relatively short distance, and then unloaded and carried to the destination within the consignee's city. All of this handling required from two to four days time even for a short haul of fifty miles. The motor truck quickly established its ability for one day or overnight transportation of property. An increasing proportion of goods came to be handled by motor truck, first for short hauls and later for long distance hauls.

There proved to be disadvantages in the carriage of freight by motor truck. There was little regulation of truck operations, and many truck lines operated under limited capital, with frequent insolvencies. Shippers sometimes found it difficult to locate a trucker into whose custody their property had been placed for shipment. Shippers increasingly turned to insurance for immediate protection against claims for loss or damage to property in transit by motor truck, leaving to the insurance companies the sometimes uncertain possibility of collecting from the trucker.

REGULATION OF MARINE INSURANCE

Many facets of inland marine insurance seem illogical. A brief study of the legal and regulatory aspects of marine insurance development will aid in the understanding of this seemingly illogical line of business.

The statutes of the states define various kinds of insurance. These definitions tend to follow the "lines" of insurance which developed, with divisions between fire insurance, casualty insurance, and marine insurance. Most of the state laws were enacted many years ago. Most of them define "marine insurance" without making any distinction between ocean marine and inland marine.

Encroachment of Marine Insurers into Fire and Casualty Areas

Marine insurers have traditionally been willing to consider the insuring of practically any loss exposure if the conditions of insurance were agreeable to them and if they could secure a premium which they considered commensurate with the exposure to loss. This was in contrast to the attitude of fire insurers and casualty insurers during the 1920s and 1930s. The fire and casualty insurers held rigidly to the concept that coverage must be provided according to the lines of insurance that had been developed historically. Fire insurers, for example, resisted any expansion of their coverage to include the unusual hazards that might be severe in individual cases. Marine insurers, on the other hand, were willing to provide a broad coverage, even to the extent of an "all-risks" type of coverage which would protect against unexpected and unnamed perils. Marine insurers expanded their operations to cover property in warehouses where the transit exposure was negligible or perhaps entirely absent. There were about twenty years of competition between the marine insurers and the insurers for the fire and casualty lines. Fire and casualty insurers made strenuous efforts to limit the growth of the marine insurers.

The Nation-Wide Marine Definition

Development of the Nation-Wide Marine Definition The efforts of the fire and casualty underwriters to restrict the marine underwriters finally brought about an adoption by the National Association of Insurance Commissioners of a document which was known at that time as "The Nation-Wide Definition and Interpretation of the Insuring Powers of Marine and Transportation Underwriters." This was adopted in 1933 by the National Association of Insurance Commissioners and recommended to the states for adoption as a ruling or regulation of the individual states. Eventually, a majority of the states adopted this definition. It should be noted from the title that this was a document which limited the insuring powers of marine insurers. It specified in some detail what were considered to be marine exposures and what could not be covered by marine insurance. Exposures that could not be covered by marine insurers were insured by fire or casualty insurers. Thus the fire and casualty insurance companies were to some extent successful in limiting the further expansion of marine insurers into what the fire and casualty insurers considered to be their territory. A committee of company representatives was empowered by the regulations in many states and by agreements among the companies to penalize insurance companies writing business as marine insurance that was outside the Definition and thus violating it.

Effect of the SEUA Decision and Multiple-Line Underwriting
The South Eastern Underwriters' Association decision in 1944 brought insurance business within the scope of the federal antitrust laws. This made it undesirable or impossible for associations of insurance company representatives to penalize insurance companies for their action. The development of multiple-line insurance around 1950 also made archaic the Nation-Wide Definition as a definition of insuring powers. Insurance companies generally acquired insuring powers that covered the entire scope of property and liability insurance.

This brought about a necessary revision in the concept of the Nation-Wide Marine Definition. The 1953 convention of the National Association of Insurance Commissioners adopted a revised Nation-Wide Marine Definition. The definition includes this statement:

> This instrument shall not be construed to restrict or limit in any way the exercise of any insuring powers granted under charters and license whether used separately, in combination or otherwise.

The Nation-Wide Marine Definition thus became a document for classification purposes rather than a definition of underwriting powers. Its principal function is to determine how an insurer is to report for statistical and annual statement purposes the premiums and losses written as marine business. It has a collateral effect in setting out various forms of insurance policies. These have been used by the rating bureaus and by the state insurance departments in determining what lines of inland marine insurance are subject to rate-filing requirements.

The Nation-Wide Marine Definition does not make any distinction between ocean marine and inland marine. The entire marine business is grouped together as "marine and or transportation policies."

The "Committee on Interpretation of the Nation-Wide Marine Definition" now has no power to determine the insuring powers of an insurance company. It merely recommends to the National Association of Insurance Commissioners (NAIC) and to the states the interpretations of questions that are raised concerning meanings of the various parts of the document.

The principal effect of the definition is on inland marine insurance because ocean marine coverages are so clearly established that questions seldom arise regarding classification of such exposures. The Nation-Wide Marine Definition is generally accepted as a description of what constitutes inland marine insurance. An understanding of the principles upon which the definition is based will help in understanding this sometimes illogical portion of the business. Although inland marine insurance is based upon transit exposures, it includes many situations where the transit exposure is either negligible or absent. These expansions have resulted from historical developments, many of them based upon the willingness of marine underwriters to cover exposures which underwriters in other fields consider to be uninsurable.

Principles of the Nation-Wide Marine Definition The basic principle of the Nation-Wide Marine Definition is that there must be an element of transportation present if property is to be eligible for insurance under an inland marine policy. Of course, bridges and tunnels are not intended to move, but they are held to be insurable under an inland marine policy because they are "instrumentalities of transportation." Some of the "block" policies which will be described later are clearly coverages on stocks of merchandise. Such stocks of merchandise as those in jewelry stores had been insured by marine insurers for many years by the time an effort was made to define marine insurance. The drafters of the original Nation-Wide Definition had no choice but to include jewelers block insurance as a marine coverage because the bulk of jewelery store stocks were then being insured with marine policies. The same justification was accepted for insurance on bridges and tunnels. Thus, it became customary because of historical developments to expand marine insurance beyond what would be a logical demarcation.

The contrary principle which forms a basis for the Nation-Wide Marine Definition is that property located on the premises of an owner is not in transit. There are specific exclusions in the Definition applying to certain situations, such as storage of the insured's merchandise on his or her own premises. It should be noted, however, that these exclusions are overruled by the historical acceptance of certain kinds of mercantile stocks, such as jewelry, as previously stated.

Modification of the Definition The Nation-Wide Marine Definition is modified from time to time. An amended Nation-Wide Marine Definition was adopted by the NAIC in December, 1976, and as of this writing, the amended definition has been adopted in a number of states.

General Effect of the Nation-Wide Marine Definition The Nation-Wide Marine Definition is generally accepted as a classification of what constitutes inland marine insurance in the United States. The Definition is ignored for all practical purposes in relation to ocean marine insurance because ocean marine insurance is related generally to exports, imports, and transportation on inland waters of the United States. There are many situations where an insurer will write an inland marine policy to cover a situation that is not specifically within the Nation-Wide Marine Definition. This is entirely legal as long as the insurer has multiple line insuring powers. There may be a technical violation of regulations if an insurer writes as inland marine coverage a policy that would be under rate regulatory requirements of some other form of insurance. However, the Definition and the practices of the business are so fluid that there is seldom criticism of an insurer for handling a borderline case according to whatever procedures seem best for the situation.

Effect of Multiple-Line Insurance. Many of the multiple-line package insurance policies include some coverage for property away from the insured's premises, and many of them provide a small amount of actual transit insurance. However, most of this fringe transit insurance that is included within package insurance policies is so small in amount and would provide such a small premium that it would not be written as inland marine insurance under separate policies.

The Definition Itself The Nation-Wide Marine Definition is of such consequence in the writing of inland marine insurance in the United States that the student must be familiar with its terms. The text of the Definition adopted in 1953 is presented here.

NATIONAL ASSOCIATION OF INSURANCE COMMISSIONERS

NATION-WIDE MARINE DEFINITION

The purpose of this instrument is to describe the kinds of risks and coverages which may be classified or identified under State Insurance Laws as Marine, Inland Marine or Transportation insurance, but does not include all of the kinds of risks and coverages which may be written, classified or identified under Marine, Inland Marine or Transportation insuring powers, nor shall it be construed to mean that the kinds of risks and coverages are solely Marine, Inland Marine or Transportation insurance in all instances.

This instrument shall not be construed to restrict or limit in any way the exercise of any insuring powers granted under charters and license whether used separately, in combination or otherwise.

I. Marine and/or transportation policies may cover under the following conditions:

A. IMPORTS

1. Imports on consignment may be covered wherever the property may be and without restriction as to time, provided the coverage of the issuing companies includes hazards of transportation.

   A shipment "on consignment" shall mean property consigned and intrusted to a factor or agent to be held in his care, or under his control for sale for account of another or for exhibit or trial or approval or auction, and if not disposed of, to be returned.

2. Imports not on consignment in such places of storage as are usually employed by importers, provided the coverage of the issuing companies includes hazards of transportation.

Such policies may also include the same coverage in respect to property purchased on C. I. F. terms or "spot" purchases for inclusion with or in substitution for bona fide importations.

An import, as a proper subject of marine or transportation insurance, shall be deemed to maintain its character as such so long as the property remains segregated in the original form or package in such a way that it can be identified and has not become incorporated and mixed with the general mass of property in the United States, and shall be deemed to have been completed when such property has been:

(a) sold and delivered by the importer, factor or consignee; or

(b) removed from place of storage as described in paragraph "2" above and placed on sale as part of importer's stock in trade at a point of sale-distribution; or

(c) delivered for manufacture, processing or change in form to premises of the importer or of another used for any such purposes.

B. EXPORTS

1. Exports may be covered wherever the property may be without restriction as to time, provided the coverage of the issuing companies includes hazards of transportation.

An export, as a proper subject of marine or transportation insurance, shall be deemed to acquire its character as such when designated or while being prepared for export and retain that character unless diverted for domestic trade, and when so diverted, the provisions of this Ruling respecting domestic shipments shall apply, provided, however, that this provision shall not apply to long established methods of insuring certain commodities, e.g., cotton.

C. DOMESTIC SHIPMENTS

1. Domestic shipments on consignment, provided the coverage of the issuing companies includes hazards of transportation.

(a) Property shipped on consignment for sale or distribution, while in transit and not exceeding one hundred and twenty (120) days after arrival at consignee's premises or other place of storage or deposit; and

(b) Property shipped on consignment for exhibit; or trial, or approval or auction, while in transit, while in the custody of others and while being returned.

2. Domestic shipments not on consignment, provided the coverage of the issuing companies includes hazards of transportation, beginning and ending within the United States, provided that such shipments shall not be covered at manufacturing premises nor after arrival at premises owned, leased or operated by Assured or purchaser, nor for more than ninety (90) days at other place of storage or deposit, except in premises of transportation companies or freight forwarders, when such storage is incident to transportation.

D. Bridges, tunnels and other instrumentalities of transportation and communication (excluding buildings, their furniture and furnishings, fixed contents and supplies held in storage) unless fire, tornado, sprinkler leakage, hail, explosion, earthquake, riot and/or civil commotion are the only hazards to be covered. Piers, wharves, docks, and slips, excluding the risks of fire, tornado, sprinkler leakage, hail, explosion, earthquake, riot and/or civil commotion. Other aids to navigation and transportation, including dry docks and marine railways, against all risks.

The foregoing includes:

1. Bridges, tunnels, other similar instrumentalities, unless fire, lightning, windstorm, sprinkler leakage, hail, explosion, earthquake, riot or civil commotion are the only perils to be covered.
2. Piers, wharves, docks and slips, but excluding the risks of fire, lightning, windstorm, sprinkler leakage, hail, explosion, earthquake, riot or civil commotion.
3. (a) Pipelines, including on-line propulsion, regulating and other equipment appurtenant to such pipelines, but excluding all property at manufacturing, producing, refining, converting, treating or conditioning plants.

   (b) Power transmission and Telephone and Telegraph lines, excluding all property at generating, converting or transforming stations, sub-stations and exchanges.
4. Radio and Television Communication Equipment in commercial use as such including towers and antennae with auxiliary equipment, and appurtenant electrical operating and control apparatus but excluding buildings, their improvements and betterments, furniture and furnishings and supplies held in storage therein.
5. Outdoor cranes, loading bridges and similar equipment used to load, unload and transport.

E. PERSONAL PROPERTY FLOATER RISKS

1. Covering Individuals.

(a) Tourists Floaters, Personal Effects Floater Policies.

(b) The Personal Property Floater.

(c) Government Service Floaters.

(d) Personal Fur Floaters.

(e) Personal Jewelry Floaters.

(f) Wedding Present Floaters for not exceeding ninety (90) days after the date of the wedding.

(g) Silverware Floaters.

2. Covering Individuals and/or Generally.

(a) Fine Arts Floaters, Stamp and Coin Floaters. To cover objects of art such as pictures, statuary, bronzes and antiques, rare manuscripts and books, articles of virtu, etc.

(b) Musical Instrument Floaters. Radios, televisions, record players and combinations thereof are not deemed musical instruments.

(c) Radium Floaters.

(d) Physicians' and Surgeons' Instrument Floaters. Such policies may include coverage of such furniture, fixtures and tenant Assured's interest in such improvements and betterments of buildings as are located in that portion of the premises occupied by the Assured in the practice of his profession.

(e) Pattern and Die Floaters, excluding coverage on the owner's premises.

(f) Theatrical Floaters, excluding buildings and their improvements and betterments, and furniture and fixtures that do not travel about with theatrical troupes.

(g) Film Floaters, including builders' risk during the production and coverage on completed negatives and positives and sound records.

(h) Salesmen's Samples Floaters.

(i) Jewelers' Block Policies, including tenant Assured's interest in improvements and betterments of buildings, furniture, fixtures, tools, machinery, patterns, molds, and dies.

(j) Exhibition Policies on property while on exhibition and in transit to or from such exhibitions.

(k) Live Animal Floaters, covering wherever animals, wagons and mobile equipment may be.

(l) Installation Risks, covering machinery and equipment including plumbing, heating, cooling and electrical systems (as distinguished from building materials) while in transit to place of installation and during the period of installation and testing. Coverage must cease: (1) where such property is insured for the account of the seller or installer, when the interest of such insured ceases; or (2) in no case later than when such property has been accepted as satisfactory; whichever first occurs, as to (1) or (2).

Building materials (e.g., structural steel, lumber, bricks and mortar), while in transit to place of installation and after arrival thereat but such coverage must terminate when the materials are installed and have become a physical part of the realty or when the seller's interest ceases, whichever first occurs.

(m) Mobile Articles, Machinery and Equipment Floaters, (excluding motor vehicles designed for highway use and auto homes, trailers and semi-trailers except when hauled by tractors not designed for highway use and snow plows constructed exclusively for highway use) covering identified property of a mobile or floating nature, not on sale or consignment, or in course of manufacture, which has come into the custody or control of parties who intend to use such property for the purpose for which it was manufactured or created. Such policies shall not cover furniture and fixtures not customarily used away from premises where such property is usually kept.

(n) Property in transit to or from and in the custody of
   (1) bleacheries, throwsters, fumigatories, dryers, cleaners, laundries and similar bailees:
   (2) needleworkers:
   (3) other bailees (not owned, controlled or operated by the bailor) for the purpose of performing work thereon (as distinguished from the making of a complete article) including the treatment of, or assemblage of property on the premises of bailees.

   Such policies shall not cover bailee's property at his premises.

(o) Installment Sales and Leased Property. Policies covering property sold under conditional contract of sale, partial payment contract, installment sales contract, or leased but excluding motor vehicles designed for highway use. Such policies must cover in transit but shall not extend beyond the termination of the seller's or lessor's interest. This section is not intended to include machinery and equipment under certain "lease-back" contracts.

(p) Garment Contractors Floaters.

(q) Furriers or Fur Storer's Customer's Policies (i.e., policies under which certificates or receipts are issued by furriers or fur storers) covering specified articles the property of customers.

(r) Accounts Receivable Policies, Valuable Papers and Records Policies.

(s) Cold Storage Locker Plant Policies, covering merchandise of customers consisting principally of meats, game, fish, poultry, fruit, vegetables and property of a similar nature.

(t) Floor Plan Policies, covering property for sale while in possession of dealers under a Floor Plan or any similar plan under which the dealer borrows money from a bank or lending institution with which to pay the manufacturer, provided:

1. Such merchandise is specifically identifiable as encumbered to the bank or lending institution.

2. The dealer's right to sell or otherwise dispose of such merchandise is conditioned upon its being released from encumbrance by the bank or lending institution.

3. That such policies cover in transit and do not extend beyond the termination of the dealer's interest.

Provided that such policies shall not cover automobiles or motor vehicles; merchandise for which the dealer's collateral is the stock or inventory as distinguished from merchandise specifically identifiable as encumbered to the lending institution.

(u) Sign and Street Clock Policies, covering neon signs, automatic or mechanical signs, street clocks, while in use as such.

(v) The following policies covering property which, when sold to the ultimate purchaser, may be covered specifically, by the owner, under Inland Marine Policies:

(1) Musical Instrument Dealers Policies, covering property consisting principally of musical instruments and their accessories. Radios, televisions, record players and combinations thereof are not deemed musical instruments.

(2) Camera Dealers Policies, covering property consisting principally of cameras and their accessories.

(3) Furrier's Dealers Policies, covering property consisting principally of furs and fur garments.

(4) Equipment Dealers Policies, covering mobile equipment consisting of binders, reapers, tractors, harvesters, harrows, tedders and other similar agricultural equipment and accessories therefor; construction equipment consisting of bulldozers, road scrapers, tractors, com-

pressors, pneumatic tools and similar equipment and accessories therefor; but excluding motor vehicles designed for highway use.

All such policies shall exclude coverage of monies and securities. Such policies may include coverage of tenant Assured's interest in improvement and betterments of building and of furniture, fixtures, tools, machinery, patterns, molds and dies.

(w) Wool Growers Floaters.

(x) Domestic Bulk Liquids Policies, covering domestic bulk liquids stored in tanks provided the risks of fire and inherent explosion, windstorm, sprinkler leakage, earthquake, hail, explosion, riot or civil commotion are excluded therefrom.

(y) Furniture Shipment Policies, covering furniture, fixtures and equipment in bona fide course of shipment from one location to another location of the owner including in place of deposit incident to such transportation while awaiting determination or availability of final destination, in which event they must cover at time of issuance transportation to or from such place of deposit but may not cover after delivery at destination.

Unless otherwise permitted, nothing in the foregoing shall be construed to permit MARINE OR TRANSPORTATION POLICIES TO COVER:

A. Storage of Assured's merchandise, except as hereinbefore provided.

B. Merchandise in course of manufacture, the property of and on the premises of the manufacturer.

C. Furniture and fixtures and improvements and betterments to buildings.

D. Merchandise in permanent location, sold under partial payment, contract of sale, or installment sales contract, which involves protection of the purchaser's interest after seller's interest ceases.

E. Monies and/or securities in safes, vaults, safety deposit vaults, banks or Assured's premises, except while in course of transportation.

F. Risks of fire, windstorm, sprinkler leakage, earthquake, hail, explosion, riot, and/or civil commotion on buildings, structures, wharves, piers, docks, bulkheads and sheds and other fixed real property on land and/or over water, except as hereinbefore provided.

INLAND MARINE COVERAGE

It should be evident from the previous discussions of loss exposures to property in transit, bailee loss exposures, and loss exposures to "floating" property, that there is a wide range of needs for protection against loss exposures within these categories. It should be evident from the Nation-Wide Marine Definition that marine insurance can be provided to cover a great variety of miscellaneous needs—including not only property in transit, bailee loss exposures, and exposures to "floating" property, but others as well.

Chapter 10 of this text will discuss specific policy forms used to provide protection against many of these inland marine loss exposures. This section will serve as a prelude to the discussion of individual policies.

Inland marine insurance coverage is marked by flexibility and broad coverage. Different approaches to valuation and various limitations on partial loss are found in inland marine policies. Many permissive and restrictive clauses, found in a large number of inland marine policies, will be discussed here.

Flexibility

In terms of forms and rates, inland marine policies can be placed into two categories—*filed* and *nonfiled*. If the rates, rules, and forms of a particular class have become standardized and generally filed by rating bureaus on behalf of the insurance companies with the various state insurance departments, they would be considered filed. A nonfiled class would be one that is not standardized and is simply drawn up and rated in accordance with the underwriting practices of an individual insurance company.

For many filed policies, a standard form (with or without standard endorsements) is available at rates the insurer or rating bureau has filed with the state. These policies are relatively inflexible, in terms of coverage or rates, and are generally those for which a large number of similar exposures exist needing similar coverage.

Many loss exposures covered by inland marine insurance are handled on nonfiled forms. Many insurers have forms that they use for certain common classes of business (such as the contractors' equipment floater discussed in Chapter 10), but the forms in use may vary substantially from one insurer to the next. Depending on company practice, many of these forms may be freely modified at the option of the underwriter, since they are not filed with the state. In many circumstances, it is necessary to design from scratch a "manuscript" policy to cover an unusual or one-of-a-kind exposure.

Because inland marine policies in nonfiled lines may be extensively modified or written from scratch, there is a great deal of flexibility in providing coverages for such exposures. Coverage may be tailored to fit the individual needs of each account. Such flexibility in coverage and the use of judgment rates are not really new concepts. The use of custom-tailored forms and judgment rates goes back to the earliest days of (ocean) marine underwriting. It is only in more recent history that some lines have become more tightly controlled by the regulatory authorities.

Development of Rate and Form Regulation The developers of rate regulatory legislation during the mid-1940s following the SEUA decision found it difficult to specify what portion of the inland marine business should be subject to rate-filing requirements. Most of the inland marine business was still rated individually by company underwriters in accordance with conditions affecting individual exposures. There were two associations of insurance companies that had developed a standardization of rates for certain types of coverage where there were large numbers of accounts with similar exposures. There were, for example, generally accepted rates for personal furs, personal jewelry, fine arts, and the personal property floater. The two associations did not designate themselves as rating bureaus but rather as informal associations of companies for the purpose of setting forth acceptable underwriting standards and suggesting rates for coverages where the law of large numbers could be applied.

Rate regulatory legislation was suggested to the states by an "all-industry" committee. This specified classes of insurance for which rate filings were considered necessary. The final result of these discussions was that rate filing was considered necessary for the lines of insurance that were susceptible to the law of large numbers, but there was an exemption for inland marine lines which by general custom of the business were not rated according to manual rates or rating plans. As it turned out, only about one-fourth of the inland marine business is rated according to manual rates or rating plans and the remaining three-fourths is still rated individually by company underwriters.

The two associations of companies began operating as rating bureaus and became qualified as rating bureaus under the rate regulatory laws that were enacted during the 1940s. The two organizations continued as rating bureaus and eventually were merged into larger organizations. However, the basic situation continued in which rates and rating plans are filed by the bureaus on behalf of their members and subscribers for about one-fourth of the inland marine business with the remaining three-fourths being rated individually by company underwriters.

Broad Coverage

Broad coverage has always been a characteristic of marine insurance. Early ocean marine policies provided coverage for "perils of the seas." As mentioned, "perils of the seas" applied only to fortuitous losses, and did not protect against loss such as ordinary wear and tear. There is no inland marine term that is exactly comparable to "perils of the seas." The words "perils of transportation" have been used but they have never been accorded the kind of definite interpretation that has been given to "perils of the seas." Almost anything that can happen to goods while in transit probably could be considered a "peril of transportation." A similar phrase that has been used in some cases is "other perils of transportation" following a list of specific perils such as collision, overturn, and fire. It might be proper to apply the principle of *ejusdem generis* (of like kind) to a coverage where the phrase "other perils of transportation" follows a list of specified perils. However, it is probable that almost anything that happened to property in the course of transit would be considered as covered by such an insurance phrase.

Inland marine underwriters worked to develop a phrase that would provide broad coverage. The outcome was the phrase "all risks of physical loss and damage." This phrase has subsequently been adopted for use in fire insurance policies.

The term "all-risks" does not encompass everything that can happen to property to cause a loss to the owner. A "risk" in this context is merely a peril or cause of loss. There are several causes of loss or damage that are outside of the term "all-risks." Such causes of loss are not generally considered to be insurable perils. Property wears out in the normal course of use—such wear and tear and deterioration is not a fortuitous loss. Likewise, losses caused by a deliberate act of the property owner are not considered insurable, and are therefore beyond the scope of "all-risks" policies.

No insurance company issues an "all-risks" policy without some modification or exclusions. There are certain exposures that insurance companies are not willing to cover. The usual exclusions and the reasons for them will be discussed later in this chapter. Individual changes may be made by underwriters to fit a particular situation, depending upon insurance company practices and the individual circumstances. "All-risks" insurance covers all causes of loss except those excluded. Inland marine insurance policies may cover on an "all-risks" basis, or may cover only certain specified perils that are named in the policy.

Limitations on Broad Coverage Inland marine policies which provide coverage on an "all-risks" basis always contain some exclusions. Some of these exclusions are common to most inland marine policies, partly to emphasize the nature of the coverage as applying only to fortuitous occurrences, and partly to eliminate coverage for any particular exposure to loss which the insurer does not care to cover.

Perhaps the broadest coverage provided by any inland marine policy is that applicable to jewelry, watches, and furs under a form known as the "personal articles floater" discussed in CPCU 2. This provides coverage against "all risks of loss of or damage to the insured property" except for loss or damage caused by wear and tear, gradual deterioration, insects, vermin, or inherent vice, war damage under a rather lengthy definition, confiscation by order of government or public authority, loss due to contraband or illegal transportation or trade, and nuclear reaction.

Most of these exclusions are for perils which inland marine underwriters generally are not willing to cover. Damage by insects and vermin are in the nature of normal wear and tear and also are to a large degree within the control of the insured.

War risks may be so catastrophic in nature that underwriters generally avoid covering them, unless the circumstances are such that they can be covered specifically and at a premium commensurate with the current exposure.

Loss caused by confiscation by order of government or public authority, and risks of contraband or illegal transportation or trade are perils generally within the control of the insured. A policyholder who was covered against such perils might be willing to take chances on a loss with the idea that insurance would cover any such loss. In addition, it is generally considered to be against public policy for insurance companies to cover the exposures to loss resulting from certain illegal activities.

The exclusion of loss from nuclear reaction is an exclusion of loss from a catastrophic peril. Insurance companies are willing under some circumstances to insure against loss from nuclear reaction, but usually only if the peril can be considered specifically in relation to the particular property. This exclusion is intended to eliminate a catastrophic exposure.

There may be other exclusions of such perils as flood which would involve catastrophic exposure. Flood damage is excluded in many of the policies covering commercial property, but the personal articles floater has no such exclusion. Individual policies, even though extremely broad in their basic coverage, may contain exclusions of certain excessive hazards depending upon individual circumstances. There may be circumstances in which an insurer would be willing to cover a portion of the loss from a catastrophic exposure, but subject to a substantial deductible or participation by the insured.

Certain of the exclusions even in a broad coverage inland marine policy are designed to reinforce the basic nature of the "all-risks" coverage. Wear and tear losses are not covered. An exclusion in the policy serves to emphasize this and to call it to the attention of the insured. Inherent vice is another exclusion inserted for the purposes of clarification and emphasis.

Losses under the control of the insured may be excluded. It has already been pointed out that loss by insects and vermin may be to some extent within the control of the insured. The same applies to contraband or illegal transportation or trade. There may be a question as to whether such losses are actually covered, but specific exclusions are often used to eliminate any possibility of question following a loss.

Many inland marine policies exclude types of property which ordinarily would be covered by other insurance in the normal course of business. For example, many "all-risks" insurance policies exclude automobiles, motorcycles, aircraft, and boats. It is customary to provide coverage on such kinds of personal property under specific policies. Many policies on commercial business will specify rather clearly the kinds of property that are covered and will have exclusions of property that is not intended to be covered under that policy.

Valuation of Insured Property

The determination of property values after a loss has occurred may be substantially more difficult in the case of "floating" property or in transit than for property at a fixed location. Some of these valuation problems have already been discussed in connection with ocean marine insurance.

Valuation of Property in Transit Policies covering property in transit usually provide a method by which the value may be determined for loss adjustment purposes. A typical inland marine clause which is used for this purpose reads:

> The valuation of the property covered hereunder shall be the actual invoice cost, including prepaid freight, together with such costs and charges since shipment as may have accrued and become legally due thereon, and all premiums under this policy shall be paid on this basis. If there is no invoice, the valuation of the property insured hereunder shall be the actual cash market value of the property insured at point of destination on the date of the disaster.

This provision simplifies the determination of value if there is an invoice which sets forth the cost. This is frequently the case where goods are shipped to a purchaser of the property. The insured is obligated to prove the fact of the loss and also the valuation. The insured can do this by producing the invoice under which the goods were shipped, plus evidence of any other charges such as prepaid freight which might be added to the invoice cost to determine the value.

The determination of cash market value of the property may be difficult in the absence of an invoice. Such difficulty would vary according to the nature of the property. It would be relatively easy to determine the value of grain, for example, because there is a constant market for the buying and selling of grain. The cash market value of a shipment of grain could be determined on the basis of the prices quoted on the day of the loss at the grain markets, such as the Board of Trade in Chicago. An appropriate amount could be added or subtracted, depending upon the point of destination. It would be more difficult to determine the cash market value of a load of specially built furniture if the shipper had not determined an invoice value at the time of the shipment.

Actual Cash Value Another clause frequently used to set the value of property reads:

> This company shall not be liable beyond the actual cash value of the property at the time of any loss or damage occurs and the loss or damage shall be ascertained or estimated according to such actual cash value with proper deduction for depreciation, however caused, and shall in no event exceed what it would then cost to repair or replace the same with material of like kind and quality.

"Actual cash value" is a somewhat elusive concept. The conventional method of determining actual cash value for insurance coverages in general is to determine the replacement cost new and then deduct an amount for any depreciation that has occurred. This method has been sustained by the courts in many cases, but not all. There have been cases where a court has said that the actual cash value either is the market value of the property, or that the market value must be taken into account.

Little if any depreciation is involved when the insured property consists of new merchandise that is being shipped.

The two clauses quoted above, one specifying valuation on the basis of invoice cost, and the other specifying valuation as the actual cash value, ordinarily are not used in the same policy. There could be circumstances where valuation produced by these two methods would differ. Policies are written in consideration of the situation relating to a particular shipment or to the shipments ordinarily made by the insured, in order to determine what kind of valuation clause should be used in the policy. Many of the transit policies that cover commercial property in transit are designed specifically for the individual situation. Thus it is necessary to determine what valuation clause is proper.

Replacement Cost Insurance Replacement cost clauses are not usually used in inland marine insurance policies. However, when new merchandise is involved, the actual cash value is often the same as the replacement cost. In certain other cases, it is more appropriate to use a valued policy.

Valued Policies There are many kinds of property for which the values would be particularly difficult or impossible to determine after a total loss. For example, it might be impossible to determine the value of an old painting or an antique chair after it had been totally destroyed by fire. A large proportion of inland marine insurance is written to cover fine arts, antiques, valuable papers, and similar property which could easily be destroyed totally in a fire, and for which it would be impossible to determine values accurately after such destruction. The best answer to this problem has been to determine the value in advance and to provide that the agreed amount will be paid to the insured in case of a total loss. The valuable papers and records policy, for example, provides a blanket amount of coverage on such papers and records on an actual cash value basis, but it also provides for the scheduling of items with the provision that "the amount per article specified therein is the agreed value thereof for the purpose of this insurance."

The valuation provisions relating to fine arts owned by individuals states, "The company shall not be liable for more than the amount set opposite the respective articles covered hereunder, which amounts are agreed to be the value of said articles for the purpose of this insurance."

In the event of a partial loss under most valued policies, the insurance will cover for the actual cash value of the damage, or the cost to repair or replace the damaged property, not to exceed the agreed value.

Limitations on Partial Losses

There may be circumstances in connection with a loss where the insured will claim that the resultant loss or damage exceeds the actual physical loss. For example, the loss of one part of a set may be alleged by the insured to constitute a loss of the full value of the set. Several clauses are used by insurers either to clarify the intent of the policy or to specify how such possible controversies can be resolved.

Pairs and Sets Clause A pairs and sets clause is used in cases where the insured property consists of a pair or set, such as a pair of diamond earrings. A typical clause used for this purpose reads:

> In the event of loss of or damage to any article or articles which are a part of a pair or set, the measure of loss of or damage to such article or articles shall be a reasonable and fair proportion of the total value of the pair or set, giving consideration to the importance of said article or articles, but in no event shall such loss or damage be construed to mean the total loss of the pair or set.

Obviously it becomes necessary for the insurance company adjuster and the insured to agree upon a reasonable and fair proportion of the total value in such a case, but the clause at least makes it clear that the insured does not have the privilege of claiming a total loss of the pair or set where only a part of it is lost.

There are some policyholders who would be dissatisfied with a partial payment for a set, particularly a set of jewelry. The jewelry floater provisions of the rating bureaus provide that the personal jewelry policy can be extended for the payment of an extra premium to cover the value of an entire pair or set, with the insured being obligated to surrender the remaining parts to the insurance company. Such a clause reads:

> It is understood and agreed that in the event of the total loss of any article or articles which are a part of a pair or set, this company agrees to pay the insured the full amount of the value of such pair or set as specified in the schedule listed herein (in accordance with the valuation clause), and the insured agrees to surrender the remaining article or articles of the pair or set to the company.

The use of this clause may avoid dissatisfaction on the part of the policyholder.

Parts or Machinery Clause Many inland marine policies also contain a variation of the pairs and sets clause idea in what may be considered a parts or machinery clause which reads:

> In the event of loss of or damage to any part of property covered consisting, when complete for use, of several parts, the company shall only be liable for the value of the part lost or damaged.

This latter clause may be used where the insured property is part of a machine or a piece of equipment rather than part of a pair or set such as would be the case with jewelry.

Labels Clause Losses of commercial property may involve damage to labels or wrappers of packaged goods without there being any actual damage to the contents. Here again, insureds may attempt to collect for the entire value of the property, contending that the loss of the labels completely destroys the value of the property. Companies frequently use what is called a "labels clause" where the property covered consists of cans, bottles, or similar containers from which the labels might be lost due to a casualty. A typical clause for this purpose reads:

> In case of loss or damage affecting labels, capsules or wrappers, the loss shall be adjusted on the basis of an amount sufficient to pay the cost of new labels, capsules or wrappers, and the cost of reconditioning the goods.

Permissive and Restrictive Clauses
Common to Inland Marine Policies

The clauses discussed here are found in a large number of inland marine policies, sometimes with variations that adapt them to a specific exposure. A study of these clauses will aid in the understanding of specific policy forms to be discussed in Chapter 10.

Sue and Labor Insurance generally carries with it an inherent obligation of the insured to protect property from further damage when a loss occurs. This is reinforced by clauses in most property insurance policies which describe this obligation of the insured. Inland marine underwriters have borrowed from the ocean marine business the "sue and labor" clause. This goes somewhat beyond the mere obligation of the insured to protect property from further loss or damage. It provides that either the insured or the insurance company may take action to preserve the property, that such expenses may be paid to prevent a loss, and that such action will not be considered a waiver of rights on the part of either the insured or the insurance company. These provisions are considered as necessary for property in transit by land as they always have been for property in transit by sea. Current versions of the sue and labor clause that are used in inland marine policies are modernized compared to the ancient language which is still used in many ocean marine policies. One such clause reads as follows:

> In the event of loss to property covered under this policy, the insured, his employees, factors and assigns shall sue labor and travel in efforts to recover, safeguard and defend said property. Such action shall not prejudice this insurance or constitute a waiver of any rights of the insured.

Subrogation The right of an insurer to be subrogated to any recovery that may be made by an insured is recognized under common law. The theory is that any right of recovery should benefit the person who ultimately bears the loss. In the case of an insurance loss this would be the insurance company that paid the loss. However, it is customary in inland marine policies, as well as with many other property loss policies, to state this right of subrogation in the policy and also to obligate the insured to cooperate with the insurer in any recovery attempt. The usual clause gives the insurance company the right to bring suit in the insured's name in cases where a court or jury might be more likely to allow recovery to the insured than to an insurance company. A typical subrogation clause reads as follows:

> In the event of any payment under this policy the Company shall be subrogated to all the Insured's rights of recovery therefore against any person or organization and the Insured shall execute and deliver instruments and papers and do whatever else is necessary to secure such rights. The Insured shall do nothing after loss to prejudice such rights.

No Benefit to Bailee This provision of the insurance policy is a part of the insurer's attempts to preserve the right of subrogation against a carrier or bailee in cases where the carrier or bailee may have primary responsibility for the loss. It has been pointed out that the railroads in the United States during the early years of this century made strenuous efforts to reduce their losses to shippers from merchandise damaged or lost in transit. One of the devices that was established for this purpose by the railroads was a provision in the bill of lading that any insurance carried by the shipper will be for the benefit of the carrier or bailee. An application of this provision in the bill of lading would relieve the carrier of its obligation to make good any loss to the shipper or consignee. Insurance companies countered this move of the carriers with a provision in most inland marine policies that the insurance shall "in no wise inure directly or indirectly to the benefit of any carrier or other bailee." There have been several court cases involving the conflict between the provision in the bill of lading that the carrier shall have the benefit of the shipper's insurance and this provision of the insurance policy that the coverage shall not inure to the benefit of the carrier. In general, the provision of the insurance policy has been upheld by the courts. Some bills of lading may be worded in such a way that any insurer payment of loss to the insured would wipe out the carrier's obligation. Insurance loss adjusters must examine carefully the provisions of the bill of lading and of the insurance policy in such cases in order to determine whether payment of a loss should be made directly to the insured, or whether it should be made ostensibly as a loan, to be repaid if the insured does recover from a carrier.

A "loan receipt" is the device used to pay an insurance claim ostensibly as a loan. The pertinent part of the agreement reads as follows:

Received from _____ the sum of _____ dollars not as a payment of any claim but as a loan and repayable (without interest) only to the extent of any net recovery the undersigned may make from any person or persons, corporation or corporations, or others, on account of loss by _____ to _____ on or about....[4]

With the use of the loan receipt, the insured would immediately receive the amount of the loss and then attempt recovery from the carrier. If recovery is successful, the insurer's loan is repaid.

Territorial Limits Insurance coverage on property at fixed locations usually specifies the location where the property is covered. There may be a certain amount of coverage away from the location named in the policy but the intent is primarily to cover property at a place where hazards and other exposures to loss can be identified. Inland marine policies, in contrast, cover in transit or otherwise wherever the property happens to be, and many inland marine policies cover property anywhere in the world. This is true of most policies covering personal property.

Many of the commercial inland marine policies cover only within territorial limits that are named in the policies. These territorial limitations are comparable to those imposed under the trading warranties that are used in ocean marine insurance. However, the limitations in inland marine policies are not expressed as warranties but as areas within which the coverage applies.

One of the typical limitations in inland marine policies applies to coverage within the "Continental United States." The continental United States includes all of the contiguous forty-eight states, the District of Columbia, and Alaska. (Alaska, being on the North American continent, is a part of the continental United States.) Such a limitation would exclude Hawaii, any of the territories, and Puerto Rico. Inland marine underwriters customarily specifically include Hawaii, Puerto Rico, or any of the territories if it is the intent to cover property within those areas or property going to and from those areas from the continental United States.

The exact meaning of the words continental United States has become increasingly vague during the past few years. For example, the territorial waters of the United States were formerly considered to be 3 miles off-shore, but this has recently been extended to a 200-mile limit.

Commercial inland marine policies may specify coverage within a certain radius or distance from some fixed location. Motor truck cargo policies, for example, often specify coverage within a "radius of operation." Such a radius would ordinarily be the geometric radius ("as the crow flies") rather than a distance by highway. The policy must specify that the radius is the distance by highway if that is the intent.

Deductibles Many inland marine policies have deductibles applying to any loss that may occur. Sometimes the deductibles apply only to the miscellaneous losses and not to certain specified perils such as fire and wind. Deductibles may eliminate the frequency of small claims. There is a tendency to increase the amounts of deductibles because of inflation and its effect in increasing the frequency of claims in larger amounts.

Inland marine policies covering commercial property and mechanical equipment of various kinds may involve considerable amounts. The collision coverage on a piece of contractor's equipment may include a $500 deductible.

There is comparatively little use of franchise clauses in the inland marine field. It will be recalled that ocean marine policies often contain a warranty that coverage is free of average unless the loss reaches a specified amount. Such franchise clauses are unusual in inland marine coverage.

It should also be noted that the deductibles in inland marine policies (as opposed to those in ocean marine policies) are clearly specified as such. They are not worded as warranties.

Warranties in Inland Marine Insurance Warranties are not used in inland marine insurance to nearly the same extent as they are in ocean marine insurance. Where used, their effect is much less severe than it is under an ocean marine policy.

There are no implied warranties affecting inland marine insurance. The only implications are the absence of fraud, concealment, or misrepresentation on the part of the insured.

Inland marine insurance is under about the same limitations as other insurance on land property as far as the effect of warranties is concerned. Courts and legislatures in the United States tend to apply warranties lightly. For example, the courts generally take the position that a breach of warranty under an inland marine policy must have increased the chance of loss in order for it to affect the coverage. It will be recalled that a breach of warranty under an ocean marine policy cancels the insurance from that point on even if the breach of warranty did not affect the chances of loss. The New York State legislature passed a provision which states that: "No breach of warranty shall avoid an insurance contract or defeat recovery thereunder unless such breach materially increased the risk of loss, damage, or injury within the coverage of the contract."

It may be said that property on land, including property in transit, is more easily subject to examination by the insurer than is the case with property at sea. This makes warranties of less importance than is the case with a ship at sea. The net effect of this situation is that inland marine insurers tend to make less use of warranties. It is just as easy in most cases to exclude coverage under certain conditions.

Abandonment The insured under an inland marine insurance policy does not have the privilege of offering abandonment to the insurance company in the way that is customary under an ocean marine insurance policy. Many inland marine policies contain a provision which specifically eliminates any privilege of abandonment. Other policies are silent regarding abandonment. One abandonment clause reads:

> There can be no abandonment to the company of any property. The circumstances in connection with inland marine losses are such that abandonment is not considered to be a necessary or desirable privilege for the insured.

Coinsurance Inland marine insurers generally follow ocean marine insurers in providing for some kind of coinsurance on commercial policies. (Coinsurance is not used to any extent on policies covering the personal property of householders. Policies covering jewelry and furs and the personal property floater ordinarily do not contain any coinsurance provisions. This follows the practices in connection with personal fire insurance and related coverages on property on land.)

Inland marine policies frequently contain the equivalent of a 100 percent coinsurance clause, but this may not be labeled with the word "coinsurance." A typical clause which has the effect of a 100 percent coinsurance reads:

> In no event shall this company be liable for a greater proportion of any loss than the limit of liability under this policy bears to the total value of the property insured under this policy at the time such loss occurs.

Some insurers label such clauses specifically as coinsurance clauses in order to improve understanding on the part of policyholders.

The usual problems with coinsurance and the complications that it introduces into loss settlements are familiar to students of insurance. Coinsurance with inland marine policies has an additional problem. There are many situations involving inland marine coverage where the values exposed to loss are not under the control of the policyholder. The motor carrier, for example, may find at the time of a loss that he or she is carrying values far in excess of the policy limit of liability. It is impossible for a motor carrier to determine with any degree of accuracy the values of the loads that are being carried. The possibility of underinsurance must be taken into account in the negotiations between the insured and the insurer when the limits of liability are set. A similar situation may occur in connection with coverage for bailees. Laundries and dry cleaners, for example, do not ordinarily require any declaration of value when property is submitted for cleaning. A coinsurance clause in a policy might penalize the insured if a severe loss occurs during a peak period when the value of property on the bailee's premises far exceeds what is considered normal.

Other Insurance The practices relating to other insurance under inland marine policies differ from those with ocean marine coverage. Inland marine policies covering the same interest are considered to be contributing insurance in the absence of any provision to the contrary. The dates on which the policies became effective have no effect on their contribution to the loss.

Many inland marine policies have an "other insurance" provision which is intended to make the other insurance the primary coverage, with the policy in question being made excess coverage. Such a clause may provide that the insurance:

> . . . shall not cover to the extent of any other insurance whether prior or subsequent hereto in date and by whomsoever effected, covering the same property. This company shall be liable for loss or damage only for the excess value above the amount of such other insurance.

Several policies on one loss may all have such a provision. Courts generally take the position that all policies shall be considered as contributing insurance if they all contain similar excess clauses.

There may be a provision in an inland marine policy that prohibits other insurance without the consent of the insurer. Such a clause is intended to have the effect of voiding the coverage if there is another policy covering the same interest. This, of course, would not have any effect on a situation where another policy covered a different interest. For example, the existence of a policy written for a motor truck carrier to cover his liability would not have any effect on coverage of a policy that is written for the owner of goods that are being carried by the trucker.

Concealment, Misrepresentation, and Fraud There is a difference between inland marine insurance and ocean marine insurance in the attitude toward concealment, misrepresentation, and fraud. It has been pointed out that any concealment on the part of an ocean marine policyholder usually is considered to void the insurance. This is based on the usual situation where the insurer has little or no opportunity to examine the subject of the insurance at the time the coverage is written. The situation is different with inland marine insurance where the insurer generally has an opportunity to determine the circumstances under which the coverage applies. An examination may be made of the shipper's or the carrier's operations, or other pertinent areas. The usual policy reference to concealment or misrepresentation provides that the insurance shall be void if the insured has concealed or misrepresented any material fact relating to the insurance. The word "material" is understood by the courts in many cases to apply whether or not it actually is used in the policy provisions relating to concealment and misrepresentation. It would be unusual for coverage to be voided under an inland marine policy by any concealment or misrepresentation that was not material to the loss. The same general application would apply to any allegation of fraud. The fraud would have to be material to the loss before a court is likely to sustain a voidance of coverage because of such fraud.

Chapter Notes

1. Texas & P. Rwy. Co. v. Prunty, 233 S.W. 625 (Tex. Civ. App. 1921).
2. Feinberg v. Railway Express Agency, 163 F. 2d 998 (1947); cent. den., 332 U.S. 847 92 L.Ed. 230 (1948).
3. Sullivant v. Penn. Fire Insurance Co., 223 Ark. 721, 268 S.W. 2d 372, cited in Ronald A. Anderson and Walter A. Kumpf, *Business Law, Principles and Cases*, 6th ed. (Cincinnati: Southwestern Publishing Co., 1975), p. 425.
4. Ronald C. Horn, *Subrogation in Insurance Theory and Practice*, published for the S. S. Huebner Foundation for Insurance Education, Univ. of Pennsylvania (Homewood, IL: Richard D. Irwin, 1964), p. 69.

CHAPTER 10

Inland Marine Insurance

INTRODUCTION

The Nation-Wide Marine Definition identifies many types of loss exposures that can be handled by inland marine insurance. These exposures include exposures to merchandise in transit, bailee exposures, exposures to "floating" property, and several other types such as dealer exposures, installment sales or deferred payment exposures, and instrumentalities of transportation.

This chapter will discuss inland marine insurance policies designed for those exposures discussed in Chapter 9. In addition, it will briefly discuss other exposures insurable under inland marine policies together with insurance coverages available to protect against these exposures. Noninsurance techniques for handling the various exposures will also be discussed, where appropriate.

TREATMENT OF PROPERTY IN TRANSIT

There are two basic types of insurance policies on property in transit. The first is that covering loss which may be sustained by the owner of property that is in transit. The second is a form of liability insurance that is written for carriers to cover their liability to the owners for loss of property that is in the custody of the carrier.

Coverage for Owners of Property in Transit—
Transit Insurance

Transit insurance policies are a direct descendant of ocean marine cargo insurance. They cover a property owner for loss that may occur while the property is being transported. Many transit policies follow closely the principles which were first established with the use of the warehouse-to-warehouse clause of ocean marine insurance policies.

There are two types of loss exposures faced by owners of cargo in transit. One exposure involves cargo *in the custody of a carrier* under circumstances where the cargo owner has some chance of recovering from the carrier for any loss that may occur. A different type of exposure is involved when the property is being carried on the owner's vehicles and there is no chance of recovering from a carrier.

Review of Loss Exposures to Property in the Custody of a Carrier Common carriers are legally liable for loss or damage to goods in their custody. Because of this, many owners of cargo feel all loss exposures have been transferred to the carrier, and no further treatment is necessary.

There are several reasons why transfer of the exposure to the carrier is inadequate to cover all losses. These reasons are also given as reasons to purchase transit insurance, although some owners may consciously choose to retain the exposure. Insurance guarantees prompt payment of a loss even though a carrier may ultimately be held liable. Transit insurance will indemnify the owner for any loss exceeding the liability of the carrier. Recall that the liability of the carrier may be limited to a certain amount in total, or a certain amount per pound. Transit insurance may protect the insured against losses for which the carrier is not legally liable, such as acts of God. In addition, the use of insurance greatly facilitates the filing of claims by cargo owners and eliminates the problems faced when a carrier is found legally liable, but is unable to pay for the loss.

Characteristics of Transit Coverage It is characteristic of transit insurance policies that they provide very broad coverage. Many such policies are written on an "all-risks" basis although specified perils policies are also written. Some policies are written to cover essentially for nondelivery of the property regardless of the reasons. Such broad coverage generally would be written only where there is a probability that the cargo owner (or the insurer) has the reasonable chance of recovering the full loss from the carrier. This apparent double treatment of the exposure is not unreasonable, because one of the purposes of transit insurance is to permit the cargo owner to recover immediately for any loss that may occur, with the insurer taking over the task of collecting from the carrier. There are many situations where the principal purpose of the insurance is to shift from the owner of the cargo to the insurer the burden of collecting from the carrier. The rates for coverage under these circumstances usually are just enough to cover the expenses incurred by the insurer in making the collections, plus enough premium to cover those unusual circumstances where the carrier may not be liable for the loss.

There may be circumstances where a loss might be in excess of the carrier's liability. This occurs frequently in connection with cargo that is carried under a released bill of lading. There may be circumstances where the cargo value generally is within the limited values specified in the bill of lading but where an occasional shipment will exceed the released value. The transit insurance generally is written to cover any such excess value above the released amount.

It has already been pointed out that there are certain losses for which a common carrier is not liable and for which a contract carrier may exclude liability by contract. For example, the carrier is not liable for acts of God, and this category may include such insurable perils as windstorm and earthquake. The cargo owner may be protected against loss from such unusual circumstances by purchasing a transit insurance policy.

Transit insurance premiums generally are based upon the value of the property shipped rather than upon a limit of liability. This contrasts with most fire insurance policies where the premium is based upon the limit shown in the policy. A transit policy covering various shipments of property over a period of time usually would require that premium be based upon the total value of all property shipped during the term of the policy.

The rating bureaus have not made filings of rates or forms for most of the transit insurance policies. Such policies are tailored to fit the circumstances of individual policyholders, depending upon the type of cargo shipped, the frequency and value of shipments, and the method and distance over which shipments are made. Coverage may be limited to certain territorial areas or may be worldwide, depending upon the insured's needs. Several specific types of transit insurance policies will be discussed here. Because nonstandard forms are involved, discussion here is general.

These policies are written on an ongoing basis to cover incoming shipments, or outgoing shipments, or both, during the policy period. They may be written for a specified term such as one year, or may be written on an ongoing basis with periodic reports of the values required. Some reporting form policies require that premium be paid with each report of values.

Annual Transit Policies   An annual transit policy that is written on an "all-risks" basis may be written with a deductible in order to eliminate frequent small claims. In some instances, the coverage of such a policy may be limited to shipments that are sent by regular bill of lading and not subject to any of the limitations of a released bill of lading.

Policies that cover the full value of property shipped under a released bill of lading, or other means of transit where the carrier may not be liable for the full value, are often written on a specified perils basis. The perils covered would often include fire, lightning, windstorm, flood, earthquake, landslide and the perils of transportation. The "perils of transportation" may be replaced by specific coverage of collision, derailment, or overturn of the transporting conveyance. Theft coverage may be subject to restrictions or may be omitted entirely, depending upon the nature of the property and the exposure to theft. It should be noted that loss due to nondelivery ordinarily would not be included as a specified peril. A very broad coverage including loss from nondelivery might be provided if property is being shipped by common carrier and the carrier's liability would be complete except for the few perils for which the common carrier is not liable.

An insured who is shipping property between domestic locations by coastal shiplines may have coverage included for waterborne shipments. However, such coverage would not apply to exports or imports, which are customarily insured by ocean marine policies.

Custody of a Carrier.   Many transit insurance policies, including the annual transit policy, often cover only while the insured property "is in the custody" of the named carrier or class of carrier such as a common carrier. (It is possible to write an annual transit policy to cover the property while it is on the insured's own vehicles en route to the carrier's location, but this coverage must be spelled out specifically in the policy.)

A question has arisen in many cases regarding the time when property actually comes within the custody of the carrier and when it is removed from custody. Such a policy ordinarily does not cover while the property is on the insured's own trucks being taken to a railroad or truck station. The property is not in the custody of the carrier until it is actually at the carrier's location or accepted by the carrier to be placed on the carrier's vehicles. An interesting situation arose in one case in which the cargo owner put cargo into the hands of an imposter under the mistaken belief that this trucker was a representative of the carrier. A court ruled that delivery to this imposter did not constitute delivery to the carrier, and the insurance policy did not cover the loss. The goods never were in the custody of a carrier and consequently never were covered by the policy.

Another question has arisen regarding coverage during a period of storage. A common policy phrase applies to property that is in depots or warehouses, but only while *in due course of transit*, and not if such property is in storage. It becomes a question of fact whether a situation involves temporary storage in due course of transit or whether it is a storage situation. One of the pertinent facts in such a case is whether there is a continuing order for the goods to be moved at some time and to a specified destination, or whether the property is in storage awaiting a future determination as to its further shipment.

Trip Transit Policies The trip transit policy covers specified cargo on a specified trip. It is commonly used to cover property such as a valuable piece of machinery that is being moved from its place of manufacture to its place of use. An electrical transformer, for example, built in an eastern factory may be shipped to a utility company in the midwest. Such a transformer may be worth many thousands of dollars and quite possibly may exceed any limited liability provided by the carrier. Loss exposures (and insurance rates) are affected by the value and the chances of loss under the method of shipment chosen, as well as other factors.

An interesting and unusual example of a short term trip transit policy involved a computer segment worth $1 million that was being carried from a delivery truck to the twentieth floor of an office building. The only way that this particular machine could be transported to the twentieth floor was up the outside of the building and through a window. The elevators were not large enough to accommodate it. A trip transit policy was issued to cover the $1 million value from the time it left the bed of the truck at curbside until it was set onto its foundation on the twentieth floor. Although this is not the primary purpose of trip transit insurance, it illustrates how inland marine coverages can be adapted to peculiar situations.

A more common form of trip transit policy is issued for the owner of household goods that are being shipped. Such coverage for household furniture frequently applies also to property that is temporarily in storage in due course of transit while awaiting instructions for final delivery.

An exhibition policy is one variation of the trip transit policy. Such a policy would cover during transit from the original location to the place of exhibit, while the property is on exhibition, and during the return trip to the original location. It is a customary practice for art museums to lend valuable works of art to other museums for display. For example, an exhibition of Rembrandt paintings in Chicago a few years ago involved the exhibition of Rembrandts from all over the world. The borrowing museum in such a case ordinarily will buy insurance on the work of art to cover from the time each piece leaves its owner's premises, during transit, while on exhibition at the borrower's premises, and during return to the owner's premises. The extent of coverage of such an exhibition policy would depend upon the values involved, the time involved and the methods of transportation and the exposures to loss while the property is on exhibition. The coverage for an irreplaceable Rembrandt painting, for example, would need to be extremely broad, whereas the coverage of a commercial exhibit that could be rebuilt might be much more limited. Any such policy might be designed to fit the exposures of the case.

Parcel Post Policies Parcel post shipments may be insured through the Postal Service. However, insurance is also available through private insurance companies. Many of those who are aware of its availability favor the use of private insurance because it eliminates the necessity of standing in line at the post office, the cost is frequently lower than that of government insurance, the amount of insurance available from the Postal Service is limited, and private insurance provides for faster claim settlements.

Parcel post insurance is easy to use. The insured merely keeps an accurate record of the value of all shipments sent through parcel post and reports these values periodically to the insurer. A rate per $100 of values is applied to determine the earned premium. Annual transit policies other than parcel post policies frequently exclude coverage on property in the custody of the United States Postal Service under a parcel post shipment. The Postal Service is not a common carrier. It does not incur any liability for property it carries unless insured under the Postal Service arrangements. Annual transit and trip policies ordinarily exclude coverage of parcel post shipments because the Postal Service does not have the liability of a common carrier.

Coverage on shipments by ordinary parcel post generally is written on a parcel post policy. The coverage usually is extremely broad, often including nondelivery. This is feasible because of the excellent record of the Postal Service in handling parcel post shipments. The insurance policy generally specifies how the property is to be packaged and labeled because a large number of the losses that occur to parcel post shipments are the result of improper packing and improper labeling.

Coverage applies while the property is in the custody of the Postal Service. This generally means that the property has to be actually deposited with the Postal Service before it is in their custody. There may be some question regarding small parcels that are being shipped by first class mail and that may be placed on or near collection boxes. The Postal Service is not required to pick up mail that is deposited outside of a mailbox but it is a federal offense to steal mail so deposited. This is a peculiar situation because the person who steals such mail is subject to prosecution for stealing from the United States mails, but the postal employees are not required to pick up such property.

Usually, limits per package shipped by ordinary parcel post are low—say $100—and parcel post policies do not cover valuable articles such as currency or securities. Such property would be better shipped by registered mail and covered under registered mail policies.

The parcel post policy is in effect a special type of annual transit policy which covers only during shipment by United States Parcel Post. A comparable policy could be written to cover shipments by commercial parcel carriers, but this would not ordinarily be included in the parcel post policy coverage.

Registered Mail Policies These are special forms of transit policies, usually written annually or on a continuous basis with periodic reports of the values shipped with premium payments accordingly.

The various types of registered mail policies are standard contracts filed by the rating bureaus. However, the bureau rules apply only to policies issued to banks, bankers trust companies, insurance companies, security brokers, investment corporations, and other fiduciaries. If an insurance company were to issue a registered mail policy to some firm not of a fiduciary nature, the rules would not apply, and the insurer can use any rates, rules, or forms agreeable to the insured. This would be a nonfiled inland marine policy.

The property covered under policies filed by the rating bureaus include the following:

1. bonds, coupons, stock certificates and other securities; postage and revenue stamps; postal, express and other money orders; certificates of deposit, checks, drafts, notes, bills of lading, warehouse receipts, and other commercial papers, and other documents and papers of value
2. bullion, platinum and other precious metals
3. currency (whether coin or paper), jewelry, watches, necklaces, bracelets, gems, precious and semiprecious stones; and other valuables of like kind

Extremely high values may be involved in a single shipment, and the property may be such that there is a great temptation for theft. The amount recoverable from the Postal Service under a registered mail shipment is relatively small compared to the value of the property which may be shipped. Some insurance companies have automatic arrangements for protection up to $5 million in one shipment, and there are occasions where values in excess of this amount are shipped and must be covered by insurance. Policies frequently provide for limits of $5 million to any one addressee in any one day, and there may be a limit of $250,000 in any one package applying to shipments of currency or jewelry.

It is intended that the coverage apply primarily to shipments by registered mail but the rating bureau filings permit coverage of shipments of negotiable securities under air bills of airline carriers which have been approved by the bureau. This extension of coverage ordinarily would not be made to property such as money, gems, or jewelry. It is also permissible for an insured to include coverage for valuable articles which the insured is shipping on behalf of customers of the bank or investment house. Incoming as well as outgoing shipments may be covered.

Coverage is against "all-risks" of physical loss or damage or destruction of the property, subject to only two exclusions. These exclusions relate to war damage and to loss or damage resulting from civil war or the exposures involving piracy, contraband, or illegal transportation or trade, and seizure or destruction under quarantine or customs regulations. This policy, therefore, provides just about the broadest coverage of any insurance policy written in the United States. Coverage applies to shipments within the states of the United States, or to or from places in North America, depending upon the needs of the insured and the willingness of the insurer to accept the exposures. Arrangements may also be made if acceptable to the insurer for coverage to or from North American points to other places in the world.

Theft losses perpetrated by employees of a sender or addressee are covered, but the registered mail policy is excess insurance above any other fidelity coverage that may apply to the loss. (Fidelity bonds are discussed in Chapter 12.) The registered mail policy may be issued for an amount in excess of the value at the time of shipment. This provision recognizes that security values may fluctuate within short periods of time. The intent is to cover the actual value at the time of the loss. Losses are payable within seven days after receipt of proof of the loss. This is an unusually short period of time which is intended to recognize the fluctuations in value that may occur within short periods of time.

First Class Mail Policies First class mail insurance is intended to serve somewhat the same market as registered mail insurance, but it is used primarily for nonnegotiable securities or other property not subject to as severe a hazard of loss as negotiable securities, money, or jewelry. The property covered is much the same as that covered under a registered mail policy except that checks and currency, bullion, precious metals, gems, jewelry, and watches are not covered.

Coverage applies to shipment by first class mail by fiduciary organizations of the same types to which registered mail policies may be issued.

It is an interesting commentary on the safety of the mails that the loss ratios for registered mail and first class mail insurance are generally good. The Postal Service takes special precautions with registered mail, and the precautions are related to the declared value of a shipment. Special safety measures are taken where large values are involved.

Similar policies may be issued to cover shipments by armored car or armed messenger service. However, these policies have not been formalized by the rating bureaus as have the registered mail and first class mail policies. Armored car and messenger policies are devised to fit the individual needs of the policyholders. These policies may cover, for example, the liability of a bank which has a contract to deliver payrolls to its clients.

Department Store Floaters This is another form of an annual transit policy. It is issued to cover the particular needs of a department or general store. The coverage usually applies to property that is being delivered to customers, and may also cover incoming shipments. Coverage may apply while the property is in the custody of common carriers and also while on the insured's own trucks or in the hands of parcel delivery services.

The policy as ordinarily written excludes property of customers that is intended for storage or repair. The store that does a large amount of repair work for customers would be expected to buy a policy in the nature of a bailees' customers coverage to cover property that is in its custody for repair or service.

Other Variations of Transit Insurance Policies We have mentioned a few of the special forms of annual or trip transit insurance policies that may be devised to cover the special needs of persons or organizations that regularly ship property. Many unique exposures develop where property is being shipped, such as the shipment of an occasional valuable piece of machinery, shipments of cancelled checks between banks, or any one of hundreds of other types of property. The chances of loss vary based upon the type of property, the method of shipment, and other factors. There is almost no kind of shipping exposure that cannot be covered by an inland marine policy.

Coverage for Carriers of Property in Transit— Cargo Liability Policies

The various forms of annual transit and trip transit policies that have been discussed apply to the property of *shippers*. The insurance is written to protect the owners of such property from loss which may occur in transit. The *carrier* who is transporting the property from one place to another also has an insurable interest in the property because of the carrier's legal liability to the owner of the property. A loss of cargo may require that the carrier pay the owner for the value of the property, thus giving the carrier an insurable interest. This insurable interest is generally covered by, for example, a motor truck cargo policy purchased by the carrier.

Railroads generally do not carry cargo liability insurance. The operations of a large railroad are so extensive that the railroad can afford to handle its own claims for loss or damage to cargo. Airlines may or may not carry cargo liability insurance, depending upon the size of the airline and the extent of its cargo hauling activities. Many motor truck cargo carriers, however, carry motor truck cargo insurance. Therefore, this discussion will relate primarily to motor truck cargo insurance. A small railroad or an airline that carries cargo liability insurance would secure coverage similar to that which would be provided for a truck line. Very large truck lines may retain their cargo liability exposure, possibly with some kind of a deductible or excess insurance coverage that would apply to losses above the amount which the truck line could afford to retain. One of the most important exposures to catastrophe loss would be the destruction by fire of a truck terminal. A truck line that decides to retain ordinary losses may find it desirable to carry a catastrophe policy to protect itself from loss by the total destruction of a cargo terminal.

Limitations of Insurance Coverage on Carriers' Liability The insurance coverage on a carrier's liability is subject to two basic limitations. The primary limitation is that of the carrier's liability. There is no coverage under a motor truck cargo policy for the benefit of the shipper or property owner. The insurance coverage is effective only as it applies to the liability of the *carrier* for damage. For example, it may be determined that a particular loss is due to the fault of the shipper (for example, due to improper packing). The carrier would not be liable under such circumstances and the insurance would not cover the loss.

Coverage is also limited to loss caused by the perils named in the insurance policy. It is unusual for an insurance policy to cover all of the occurrences which might cause loss to cargo and liability on the part of the carrier. For example, many motor truck cargo policies cover only loss from such specified perils as fire, windstorm, collision and overturn of the transporting conveyance, and flood. Coverage for loss by theft usually is subject to negotiation between the carrier and the insurer, depending upon the nature of the goods carried, the hazards of theft, and the willingness of the carrier to pay the rate required by the insurer. Noninsurance techniques can greatly reduce crime exposures.

Many parcels are lost, with no evidence as to what happened to them. There is a substantial number of what is called in the trade "overages, shortages, and disappearances," colloquially called "OS&Ds." A package that loses its labeling and identification becomes an overage. Packages that disappear and cannot be found are shortages or disappearances, and there is a nondelivery as far as the consignee is concerned. Insurance is not ordinarily written to cover these ordinary, every day losses—such losses are retained by the carrier and are considered a normal business expense.

There are circumstances where an insurer will cover the entire liability of the motor carrier for loss or damage, subject to a substantial deductible per loss ranging from $500 to $10,000 per occurrence. Such coverage is written because the motor carrier needs protection against all large losses that occur but is willing to retain the smaller losses.

A large proportion of motor cargo is subject to released bills of lading. The insurance then would ordinarily cover only up to the liability of the carrier under a released bill of lading. The owner or shipper of the property would not be able to recover for any actual value in excess of the limitation specified in the bill of lading.

Contract Carriers It has already been pointed out that the liability of a contract motor carrier is determined by the terms of the contract of carriage. This may be greater or less than the liability of a common carrier. A contract carrier should examine the contracts to see what liability may be assumed or excluded. It is not ordinarily permissible under court interpretations for a common carrier to exclude entirely its liability for negligence, but the liability may be limited by contract. The contract carrier, on the other hand, may assume complete responsibility for the property, even beyond that which is required of a common carrier. These are all factors that affect the exposures which can then be insured or retained. Insurance coverage can be adapted to meet a contract carrier's specific needs.

Federal and State Regulations Affecting Cargo Liability Insurance Motor carriers operate under a variety of federal and state regulations. Common carriers are permitted to operate only after they prove that their service is necessary for a particular area or route. Such carriers are provided with certificates of convenience and necessity which define their routes and the types of property that they are permitted to carry. It is also considered desirable for carriers to be required to provide insurance coverage according to certain minimums. Insurance policies covering interstate common carriers must contain an endorsement which is required by the ICC. This endorsement extends the coverage of the policy to any loss for which the carrier is liable up to certain minimum amounts specified in the endorsement. Thus the insurer becomes the guarantor of payment by the trucker for any loss that may occur and for which the trucker is liable. However, the endorsement also contains a clause which provides for reimbursement by the trucker to the insurance company for any loss for which the insurance company is not liable to the insured under the terms of the policy. For example, a loss might be caused by theft but the insurance policy may not cover theft losses. The insurer guarantees the payment of such a theft loss but the trucker is obligated to reimburse the insurer for any such loss paid because the insurance policy does not cover theft.

The general practice is for the trucker to report losses to the insurance company only when a loss is covered by the policy. The carrier pays other losses directly to the customers. An insurance company seldom is called upon to pay a loss to a trucker's customer under the liability imposed by the ICC endorsement. The question then is, what purpose does the ICC endorsement serve?

A trucker that gets into financial difficulty may delay the payment of claims to customers. The insurance company would then be called upon to pay all claims to customers up to the limits specified in the ICC endorsement. There have been several cases where truckers have become bankrupt, with the insurance company being obligated to pay many thousands of dollars in claims to shippers.

Regulations Affecting Household Furniture Movers. Special regulations of the ICC apply to household furniture movers. It is obvious that such truckers cannot operate according to regular routes. They must carry the household goods from the original domicile of the property owner to the new location, wherever it may be. Such movers operate under bills of lading which spell out their responsibilities.

Household furniture movers under ICC regulations are required to provide three levels of responsibility for loss or damage to property in their custody. The basic value under the released bill of lading is $.60 per pound. This is a minimal amount which is insufficient to cover the value of most household goods shipments. A second layer of responsibility provides for an amount of $1.25 for each pound of weight in the shipment. The shipper is also permitted to declare a lump sum value to the carrier. Different charges are made for transporting household goods according to which level of value is provided in the bill of lading. However, the declaration of the full value of the shipment would still leave the owner unprotected if a loss resulted from some rare cause for which the common carrier is not responsible. The owner of household goods being shipped may find it advantageous to buy a trip transit policy from an insurance company rather than to depend upon recovery from the household goods carrier or its insurer.

The household goods carrier may carry a motor truck cargo insurance policy to protect against loss because of the liability to customers. Such a motor truck cargo policy would be similar to those already discussed.

Coverage for Owners' Goods on Owners' Trucks

The preceding discussion has related to the liability of motor carriers for goods of others in their custody. Another form of motor truck cargo policy, owners' goods on owners' trucks, is issued to firms who carry their own property on their own trucks. The essential difference between a motor truck cargo policy covering a trucker for liability to customers and a policy issued to an owner of goods is that the policy issued to an owner is primary insurance. There is no possibility of recovery from a third party who is the carrier of goods. The expectation would be that greater losses would result from covering owners' goods on owners' trucks because there is an absence of liability under which collection might be made from a carrier. However, the general loss experience in connection with insurance for owners' goods on owners' trucks is better than for motor truck cargo written for truckers. The reason perhaps is that owners of property who are operating their own trucks do not have schedules to meet the needs of their customers. Many of the motor carriers operate on regular schedules, and this pressure of maintaining schedules may be one of the reasons for a higher incidence of losses as compared to the operators of their own trucks. Moreover, owned trucks generally are not used to transport property over the long distances that motor carriers often travel, and it is doubtful that owned vehicles are usually subject to extensive and continuous use as are the vehicles of common carriers.

Coverage for Carloading Companies or Freight Consolidators

A carloading company or freight consolidator may operate in the field of motor cargo as well as railroad or air freight. The function of the carloading company is to combine many small packages into a single shipment. This frequently is done by way of container. The consolidator may pick up many packages which must travel, for example, from New York to Chicago, and put them all in a container which is then delivered to Chicago by the truckline, the railroad, or the airline. The consolidators' Chicago office then distributes the individual packages to their destination.

The freight consolidator usually operates as a common carrier and is one of the carriers in the chain of operations from the time the cargo leaves its originating point to its destination. A freight consolidator may buy a motor truck cargo policy to protect against liability to customers in much the same way that a trucker would buy such a policy to protect against liability to customers.

Noninsurance Techniques for Treatment of Property in Transit

Property may be shipped by many different methods. Sound risk management practices would require an analysis of the type of property being shipped, a comparison of alternative types of shipment, and selection of the best method. Alternatives that could be considered include shipment by common carrier (truck, rail, barge, or air), shipment by contract carrier, shipment on owned vehicles, or the use of parcel post, registered mail, or first class mail. In selecting a mode of shipment, of course, it would be necessary for a business to consider other factors in addition to the varying loss exposures, such as time and expense.

Loss exposures can be transferred, in whole or in part, depending on the liability of a common carrier or the contract with a contract carrier. When common or contract carriers are used, exposures may be reduced by careful selection of carriers to be used. Risk managers should, where feasible, consider past experience of the carrier, quality of personnel, adequacy of equipment and security measures, among other things.

Losses caused by improper packing or labeling can be reduced by the use of good packing and shipping procedures.

TREATMENT OF BAILEE EXPOSURES— BAILEES' CUSTOMERS INSURANCE

There is a difference between the extensive legal liability of the common carrier and the more limited legal liability of an ordinary bailee. The bailee is liable under common law only for loss due to the bailee's negligence for property in the bailee's custody.

Many business firms that have a large amount of customers' property in their custody find it advantageous to provide insurance for the benefit of the customers and also to cover their own legal liability for damage to customers' property. This is generally true of such operations as laundries, dry cleaning plants, and fur storage facilities.

The customers of such businesses expect their property to be returned intact or to be paid for any loss or damage that might occur. Small losses occur with high frequency and large losses may be severe. Most such business firms find it desirable to buy insurance. The customary way of covering such situations is by means of a bailees' customers policy. This is a dual interest insurance which covers the value of the property for the customer and also covers the interest of the business operator because of potential liability for loss or damage to customers' property. Different kinds of bailees' customers policies are written to cover the peculiar exposures of each business.

Laundries and Dry Cleaners

Laundries and dry cleaners face two types of loss exposures. They are exposed to the loss of customers' goods for which they may be legally liable. There is also a chance of loss to customers' goods for which the bailee may not be legally obligated to reimburse the customer. However, it is common business practice to pay for such losses even though there is no legal obligation to do so, in order to retain customer good will. Most laundries and dry cleaners purchase insurance to cover loss of customers' goods regardless of legal liability.

Insurance relating to customers' goods as carried by laundries and dry cleaners usually is a dual interest policy called bailees' customers insurance. Coverage of the policy usually is on a specified perils basis although "all-risks" coverage is sometimes provided. Specified peril policies usually provide coverage against loss by fire and the extended coverage perils, burglary and robbery, transit perils, and confusion of goods. Coverage applying to fire and the extended coverage perils and to the transit perils usually applies anywhere that the customers' goods may be in the custody of the insured. It is interesting to note that the explosion peril usually includes any explosion, including boiler explosion. This is important because most laundries and dry cleaners have boilers to provide steam for heating and processing, and face a significant exposure to loss caused by boiler explosion.

Limitations usually apply to theft, burglary, and robbery coverage. Burglary and robbery usually are covered without significant limitations when the burglary or robbery occurs on the premises of the insured. However, coverage with respect to theft or robbery from one of the insured's vehicles may apply only if an entire truckload is stolen, or may be subject to other restrictions. Some insurers tend to exclude loss of individual packages of laundry or dry cleaning. Such frequent but small losses are generally within the control of the insured to some extent by the use of noninsurance techniques including locking devices on the trucks and other precautions. The transit exposure may be considerable—an entire truckload of goods may be lost due to a traffic accident.

Some dry cleaners do not have their own facilities for the cleaning of leather goods, and may send them to a specialist for such service. Coverage for goods in the hands of the Postal Service or a parcel delivery service would be important for such a processor. Some policies are extended to cover property shipped by mail or in the hands of parcel delivery services.

It was mentioned that the usual bailees' customers policy covers loss due to confusion of goods. It is likely when a fire or other loss occurs at the premises, or when an entire truckload of goods is damaged, that the identification of customers' property will be destroyed. The loss which results from the inability to identify customers' property following an insured peril is a type of consequential loss usually covered by the policy.

Several exclusions usually appear in the policy. There is usually an exclusion of theft of goods left on delivery vehicles overnight unless the vehicles are locked within a garage or other building. Shortages of individal pieces would be excluded. Loss to goods in the custody of other processors would be excluded unless there is specific provision for such coverage. Also generally excluded are misdelivery, careless destruction of goods, or unaccountable loss for which there is no evidence that loss was caused by a specifically insured peril.

Property that is in storage on the premises of the insured is ordinarily excluded from the bailees' customers policy. The insured who also provides storage facilities can secure coverage for such property under a furriers' customers policy (discussed later).

The bailees' customers policy usually permits the insured to handle claims for small losses. It is a convenience in many cases for the insured to handle small losses directly without bringing an insurance company adjuster into the negotiations. Such direct loss handling may be limited to losses below $100, or some other modest amount. Larger losses are customarily handled by an insurance company adjuster. Loss payments are then made to the insured for the benefit of the customer or directly to the customer. It is a valuable service to the insured for the insurance company to take on the problem of handling the large number of losses that might occur as a result of fire or other catastrophe at the plant.

Many policies are subject to a deductible applying to each occurrence. The laundry or dry cleaner may find it advantageous to handle small losses as business expense, thus cutting down the insurance premium. Although small deductibles (such as $50.00) are common, the deductible may be substantial (several hundred dollars or more) in some cases.

Limits of Liability It is difficult for laundries and dry cleaners to determine the values exposed to loss. Customers who drop off clothing (or other items) for processing are usually not required to make any declaration of value. As a result, the bailee finds it difficult to estimate with any accuracy the values in customers' goods on the premises. This contrasts with the situation faced by a storekeeper who can more accurately estimate the value of merchandise in stock, based on inventory records.

Some bailee policies for laundries and dry cleaners are written for a fixed limit. This can present problems, following a loss, if the bailee has underestimated the value of customers' goods on the premises. This can be particularly crucial because the values are constantly changing, and the value of goods in process may increase dramatically right before Easter or Christmas, before school opens, or at other times. Coverage written for a fixed limit may be adequate most of the year, but inadequate to cover a loss during such peak periods.

To overcome this problem, some bailee policies are written with no limit of liability. That is, any loss to customers' goods is covered in full. Premiums are based on the gross receipts of the laundry or dry cleaner, under the assumption that there is a direct relationship between gross receipts and the degree of exposure.

Furriers' Customers Policies

The furriers' customers policy is a special form of bailees' customers insurance. The furrier or the warehouse that stores furs is a bailee. Such bailees would be legally responsible to the owners of property in their custody for any damage that occurs as a result of the bailee's negligence. However, a fur storer has the same customer relations problems as a laundry or dry cleaner. Customers expect their furs to be returned in good condition regardless of possible negligence liability on the part of the fur storer. The fur storers, therefore, have assumed the liability for providing a broad coverage fur insurance on the furs that are left for safekeeping.

Furriers' customers insurance differs from bailees' customers insurance for laundries and dry cleaners in several important respects. This is a filed form, and forms and rates are filed with state insurance departments. The "all-risks" coverage of the furriers' customers policy is very broad.

Furriers' customers insurance also differs from bailees' customers insurance for laundries and dry cleaners in that the furrier commonly issues a receipt for each garment and a limitaton of liability is stated in the receipt. The fur storer asks the customer what value the customer wishes to place upon the garment. This amount is all that the customer ordinarily can recover if the coat is lost or damaged. We have already pointed out that it is generally considered against public policy to permit bailees or common carriers to secure complete exemption from their liability for negligence, but that dollar limitations on the amount of liability have generally been upheld by the courts where the charge for service is adjusted according to the amount of such liability.

It is a characteristic of furriers' customers insurance that the form of the receipt which is given by the fur storer to the customer is specified in the furriers' customers policy. The policy covers only the property which is owned by customers or under contract of sale to customers and for which the insured fur storer issues a receipt in the required form. There is no coverage of any fur garment for which a receipt is not issued.

Furriers face a catastrophe exposure that must be considered. A fire in one fur storage warehouse a few years ago actually caused a loss of several millions of dollars. The total value of furs stored in a large warehouse in an eastern city is reported to be in excess of $30 million. Some fur storers maintain their own vaults; with others, furs are actually stored in some other warehouse.

Excess Legal Liability The liability of the fur storer ordinarily is limited to the amount specified in the receipt. However, there can be special circumstances under which the fur storer would be liable for the full value of a garment even if this exceeds the value stated in the receipt. This might occur if the fur storer has taken some action which is tantamount to conversion of the garment. There was one case where a furrier had put up several garments of customers as security for a loan. The garments were destroyed while they were outside the custody of the furrier. The furrier was held liable for the full value of these garments because the action in putting them up as security for a loan was tantamount to conversion. Another situation which resulted in the furrier's being held liable for the full value of a garment involved the sending of the garment to another furrier for certain work on the garment without the customer being informed that the garment was to be sent outside of the furrier's own place of business. There is always this remote chance that the furrier may be held liable for the full value of the garment in spite of the limitation of liability on the receipt. This exposure to loss is met by excess legal liability coverage. The insurance usually is provided by an endorsement to the furriers' customers policy. This excess legal liability coverage applies to any loss that the insured is obligated to pay in excess of the amount stated in the receipt which is issued to the customer. The endorsement usually includes a limit of liability per article and an aggregate limit that the insurer would be obligated to pay as a result of any one occurrence. The extra premium for the excess legal liability endorsement usually is nominal because the chance of loss is not great.

Certificates Issued by the Furrier The bureau filings of the furriers' customers policy provide for issuance of certificates of insurance by the furrier to customers. It should be noted that the furriers' customers policy itself covers the property only while it is in the custody of the fur storer. However, the certificates are actually individual policies of insurance on the fur garments. These certificates cover the property in all circumstances and really are individual fur garment policies comparable to those which the owner of a fur garment can privately purchase from an insurance company. The rate for the certificate usually is less than the rate for an individual fur coat policy. This is possible because the furrier already has paid a premium for insurance on the property while it is in storage. There is some additional saving to the insurance company in that a volume of business is generated from a single source with a minimum of processing expense, which allows them to apply a lower premium.

Rating Procedure The inland marine rating bureaus compute the rates for furriers' customers policies for their members and subscribers. The rating procedure is complicated. The agent and the submitting company are required to supply the rating bureau with a detailed proposal which includes a description of the storage enclosure and other information regarding the storage and handling of the fur garments. The usual arrangement is for a monthly or other periodical report of values covered by the receipts and the payment of a premium according to the rate calculated by the rating bureaus.

Other Bailees' Customers Policies

A variation of the bailees' customers policy is a "pressing or tailor shop" form. Such a policy may be written for a small shop that acts as an agent for a laundry or dry cleaner. This is usually written as a simplified bailees' customers policy applying to property that is in the custody of the tailor shop or laundry agency. The small amount of premium that would be involved usually requires that this be written on an annual basis. The amount of premium would not justify the monthly payment that would be justified in the case of a larger operation.

A special form may also be written to cover rug and carpet cleaning establishments. Limits of liability usually would be established according to the types of carpets or rugs that are handled and the volume of the insured's business, including the amount of property that might be in the insured's custody at any one time.

Bailee Coverage for Miscellaneous Situations

The bailees' customers insurance policies just discussed have been well established as inland marine coverages for many years. Other situations have developed under which a bailee needs coverage to protect against the liability to customers, or where a bailees' customers coverage is justified.

One such situation is that of the television and radio repair shop. Such a shop may have property worth many thousands of dollars in the custody of the shop for repairs. Customers would expect the replacement of television sets that are destroyed in a catastrophe regardless of whether the shopkeeper is legally liable for the loss. Television and radio repair shops which have large amounts of customers' property in their custody may buy a bailees' customers type of insurance policy which would cover their liability and also would cover for the benefit of the customer. Such a policy would be written to cover the particular needs of the shop. There is no bureau or standard form but the coverage would follow generally the pattern of the bailees' customers policy that is written for laundries and dry cleaners. It would generally be true that the coverage would be on a specified perils basis rather than on an "all-risks" basis, but either type of coverage could be written.

Department stores and furniture stores that repair customers' property may find it advantageous to buy bailees' customers insurance. The need for such coverage on the part of a merchant depends primarily upon the value of customers' goods that are in the custody of the merchant. The store that has only a small amount of customers' goods on hand may consider it more advantageous to retain any losses and treat them as a business expense. However, the loss of a large amount of customers' goods might seriously impair the future prospects of the merchant. The merchant would be certain to lose a great deal of future trade if payment to the customers were refused. Yet the financial loss could be substantial if the merchant decides to pay for the property regardless of liability.

Still another situation in which bailee liability or bailees' customers insurance may be justified is where a business organization regularly accepts property on consignment for sale or distribution. Art galleries, for example, often accept the work of various artists for display and sale. These are handled on a consignment basis, and the proprietor gets a commission for any works of art that are sold. A large proportion of the art galleries stock, or even the entire stock, may be on consignment from artists or from other dealers. The art gallery in such a case is a bailee, with the bailee's usual liability. There may be a contract between the art gallery and the owners of the property, or the art gallery may depend upon the customs of the trade to determine liability for any property that might be lost. The determination of what exposure exists, and the decision whether to purchase a bailee liability insurance or a bailees' customers insurance, would depend largely upon the terms of any contract between the art gallery, the artist, or other dealers from whom the gallery accepts property on consignment, as well as the length of time of consignment.

The auctioneers conduct yet another type of business where property is accepted on consignment for sale at auctions. Here again, the need of auctioneers for insurance coverage on property in their custody will depend largely upon the terms of any contract between the auctioneers and the property owners, or upon the practices of the trade.

There are many other situations in which a bailee liability or a bailees' customers type of insurance may be advantageous to a business organization that has the property of others in its custody. An inland marine coverage generally can be written to cover such property because it is away from the premises of the property owner and is subject to a transit exposure during at least a part of the time. Coverage for such situations would follow the patterns that have been described. The rates for the coverage would be an important consideration in any decision to insure or retain such a bailee loss exposure.

Morticians' Liability Policy   Morticians' liability insurance is a curious variation of the bailee liability coverages which can provide some idea of the diversity of insurance coverages available to meet special needs. This policy covers the legal liability of a mortician for damage to a corpse, or to caskets and fittings that have been purchased by a relative or friend of the deceased. The corpse may be damaged because of improper handling during transit, or as a result of a traffic accident. A morticians' liability policy can be obtained to protect morticians against possible liability for damage to a corpse and accompanying equipment. This is a type of bailee liability. It may be written as a separate inland marine or casualty policy, and sometimes is added by endorsement to a policy covering morticians' equipment.

Warehousemen and Innkeepers   Warehousemen's liability coverage and innkeepers' liability coverage are sometimes written as marine insurance, and sometimes as miscellaneous casualty coverages. For warehouses and inns, the primary exposure to loss of customers' property is that of theft. Innkeepers' coverage is discussed in Chapter 11.

Noninsurance Techniques

In some cases, a decision may be made to retain the loss exposure, or adequate coverage may be extended under another type of property insurance policy. Any decision to retain a bailee exposure should be made only after analyzing the potential frequency and severity of the losses that might occur. Noninsurance techniques relative to fire protection (as discussed in previous chapters), or crime protection (as discussed in Chapter 11) may reduce the exposure to loss. Such loss control measures may reduce the cost of insurance, or may reduce the exposure to the point where it can be retained.

EQUIPMENT FLOATERS

The Nation-Wide Marine Definition provides for marine insurance policies on mobile articles, machinery, and mobile equipment. Such property is considered to be identified property of a mobile or floating nature, not on sale or consignment, or in the course of manufacture, which has come into the custody or control of parties who intend to use such property for the purpose for which it was manufactured. The usual insurance policy for such property covers it under all circumstances, including while the property may be in temporary storage incidental to its regular use at other locations.

The bureaus have not filed rates or forms applicable to most types of equipment that can be covered by equipment floaters. The perils to be covered by a policy, deductibles, and limits of liability are all subject to negotiation between the insured and the insurer. The commonly used conditions for the insuring of several principal types of mobile equipment will be discussed here. It should be remembered that practically any type of floating equipment can be covered by an inland marine policy, subject to conditions and premiums which are agreed upon by the insurance company and the property owner.

Contractors' Equipment Floaters

The equipment used by contractors in constructing buildings, highways, dams, tunnels, and bridges ranges from small hand tools to large machines that may be worth hundreds of thousands of dollars. Such equipment may include cranes, earthmovers, tractors, stone crushers, bulldozers, portable tool houses, and scaffolding. Municipalities may own substantial values of mobile equipment used for snow removal, road building, and maintenance.

It should be noted that inland marine policies are not ordinarily written to cover automobiles, trucks, or concrete mixing units designed to be driven on the highways. These customarily are insured under automobile type policies.

A contractors' equipment insurance policy written for a small- or medium-sized contractor with perhaps two or three dozen pieces of equipment would list each piece of equipment with its own limit of liability. It would not be necessary to have any coinsurance applicable to such a policy if the amount of insurance for each piece is approximately the actual cash value of that equipment. However, a policy may include a blanket item to cover such small pieces of equipment as wheelbarrows and shovels. It is customary to use the equivalent of a 100 percent coinsurance clause applying to any such blanket coverage.

It is obviously difficult or impossible to keep an up-to-date list of all items where several hundred pieces of equipment may be used by an insured. A large contractor may want to have blanket coverage applying to all of the equipment that is owned and used. Such blanket coverage will usually include a coinsurance clause in order to make certain that the insurance company will get a premium commensurate with the large amount of exposure that would be brought about by such a situation.

Contractors' equipment policies may specify territorial limits, because exposures vary in different territories. There would be less danger of collision and overturn, for example, in the midwestern plains states than in mountainous areas. The hazards of collision and overturn in such operations as highway building through mountainous areas should be considered in determining the loss potential. "All-risks" coverage may be available subject to underwriters' judgment. Coverage usually is for specified perils such as fire, lightning, explosion, windstorm, earthquake, collapse of bridges and culverts, flood, collision, and overturn. Theft coverage usually is subject to a deductible in order to eliminate small claims for pilferage of parts from equipment. However, theft of entire machines, or theft of huge tires from large pieces of equipment occasionally occur. One of the factors to be considered in underwriting this class of business is whether the equipment is left unattended over weekends and otherwise when not in use, or whether adequate guard service is provided to help prevent theft and vandalism. Losses from fire, flood, or landslide may be catastrophic in certain areas.

Rental of contractors' equipment to others, or the rental of equipment from others by a contractor may create additional exposures to be insured or retained.

Farm Equipment Floaters

The bureaus have filed rates and forms for farm equipment floaters. This is contrary to the practice in connection with contractors' equipment floaters. There is a considerable degree of homogeneity in the types of equipment used for farming operations. Filings of rates and forms by the bureaus is feasible.

Coverage of farm equipment may include practically any equipment that is used in farming operations except motor vehicles, aircraft, and watercraft. Feed, hay, grain, or crops of any nature cannot be insured under a farm equipment floater.

"All-risks" coverage is available for farm equipment. Exclusions under the farm equipment floater, comparable to exclusions in other inland marine policies, exclude losses due to wear and tear types of damage, mechanical or electrical breakdown, and the war damage and nuclear damage exclusions. Misappropriation and infidelity or dishonest acts of the insured, the insured's employees, or others to whom the property is entrusted are excluded. Tires or tubes are excluded unless the damage is caused by fire, windstorm or theft, or is coincidental with other loss covered by the policy. A tire explosion resulting from overinflation, or a puncture, would therefore not be covered.

The values of some modern types of farm machinery may approach or exceed $50,000 per item, and the scheduling of each item reduces problems of determining the amount of applicable insurance in case a loss occurs. However, it should be understood that the amount of insurance shown on the policy for each item is simply the limit of an insurance company's liability. Stipulating an amount does not mean that such an amount must be paid in the event of a total loss. Under the basic policy, the company has the right to repair, rebuild, or replace equipment destroyed or damaged.

Deductibles ordinarily apply to the coverages that might engender a frequency of losses. The farm equipment floater contains an 80 percent coinsurance clause applicable to both blanket and scheduled property.

Pattern and Die Floaters

Manufacturing operations often require the use of patterns and dies. It is customary in manufacturing for portions of the work to be subcontracted to other factories. This may require that the manufacturer send the patterns and dies to the subcontractor's premises for that part of the operation. There may be other reasons for shipping patterns and dies from one place to another, or perhaps to have the patterns and dies customarily subject to frequent transit between locations.

While at the owners' premises, patterns and dies are insurable under fire and allied lines forms. A floater policy protecting such patterns and dies against loss may include coverage against fire, lightning, windstorm, explosion, smoke damage, falling aircraft, collision, and overturn during transportation. Theft coverage may be needed if the property would be valuable to others. A deductible may be used in cases where a frequency of small losses could be anticipated.

There may be a catastrophic exposure to loss if large values are subject to a fire loss at any single location. Coverage is usually written for the largest amount that would be away from the insured's own premises at any one time. Rate and premium would be dependent upon the fire insurance rates where the property may be located, plus an allowance to cover the transportation exposure. Reporting form policies may be written for larger operations.

Floaters for Rental Equipment

Some firms are in the equipment rental business. They rent all kinds of furniture and equipment for social functions, community affairs, and may rent hospital and similar equipment to those recuperating at home. Equipment rental companies can provide almost any kind of furniture, tools, or equipment that may be needed temporarily in homes or businesses.

Floater coverage that is provided for equipment rented to others usually is on a specified perils basis with coverage against fire and lightning, windstorm, earthquake, the hazards of transportation, and theft. A deductible often applies for the theft coverage. Such property is subject to miscellaneous hazards such as breakage and excessive wear and tear, and the practice of underwriters in most cases is to exclude such damage from the insurance coverage. There are no bureau filings for equipment rental policies. Coverage and rates are subject to determination by the underwriters and agreement between the insurer and the insured.

Installation Floaters

The installation floater covers loss to materials and equipment that are in transit to a construction site and while at the construction site prior to their being incorporated into the building. This is comparable to a transit floater coverage. In addition, the installation floater covers the value of equipment that has been installed in a structure until such time as the installation is complete and has been accepted by the owner of the property.

The Nation-Wide Marine Definition specifies certain conditions regarding coverage of installation floaters. The type of property that may be covered includes machinery and equipment such as plumbing, heating, cooling, and electrical systems. Such property may be covered while in transit and during the period of installation and testing.

The type of property that may be covered by an installation floater varies from such small values as grain dryers that may be installed on a farmer's premises to a multi-million dollar elevator installation in a high-rise office building. Coverage usually is on a specified perils basis with the coverage of perils such as fire, windstorm, explosion, riot and civil commotion, and perhaps against loss by earthquake and flood. The policy usually is written along the same lines as a transportation policy, with additional provisions to meet the exact circumstances at the place of installation.

Insurance on a large installation usually is written on a reporting basis. The insured reports the progress of the work with the value that has been installed up to the time of the report. It is customary to use a 100 percent coinsurance clause so that the insured will report full values.

A separate policy may be written on specific job sites, or a blanket policy may be written for a contractor who has many jobs in progress at the same time. The values to be reported by the insured include labor and materials that have been installed up to the time of the report.

Animal Floaters

Inland marine coverage on animals usually protects against loss because of some accident to the animal. Mortality insurance on animals which protects against death from natural causes ordinarily is not written as an inland marine coverage. Livestock mortality coverage is a separate kind of insurance, somewhat equivalent to life insurance on humans.

Purebred livestock of many kinds is shipped internationally. It was customary for such shipments to be made by sea. However, most shipments of purebred livestock now are being made by airplane. A shipment to South America, for example, can be made within a matter of hours instead of the weeks that would be necessary for shipment by sea. A large jet aircraft may fly cattle to South America, Africa, or Japan. Bulls have been imported into the United States from Great Britain with values in excess of $200,000 per animal. Insurance coverage of such shipments is on the basis of actual delivery to the consignee's site. Practically any accident that could occur in transit would be covered by the insurance.

Insurance is also extensively used to cover livestock at stockyards or en route to stockyards or during breeding.

Insurance on farm animals is subject to rates and coverages filed by the rating bureaus. The bureau filings apply to farm animals, horses used for riding, and related activities. The filings exclude livestock that is used for racing, show purposes or delivery work.

Farm animal insurance policies cover loss due to death or destruction of animals made necessary by fire, lightning, windstorm, riot, strike, aircraft, hail, earthquake, flood, collapse of bridges or culverts, and collision or derailment of a conveyance on which the animals are being carried. There is an optional coverage at an extra rate for loss from accidental shooting, drowning, artificial electricity, or attack by dogs or wild animals. It should be emphasized that this coverage is against death or destruction made necessary by some accidental occurrence and there is no coverage against death from natural causes.

The provisions for coverage of farm animals are coordinated with the provision for coverage of farm equipment. Policies frequently are written so that the farm equipment and the livestock are covered under the same policy, with appropriate modifications to provide the exact coverage needed for the two kinds of property.

Processing Floaters

Property that is being processed for the owner by a contractor or subcontractor is similar in its exposure to that of equipment that may be away from the owner's premises. There are two kinds of insurable interests in property that is being processed. The first is the interest of the owner who needs protection from loss if the property is damaged while it is away from the owner's premises. The second interest is the legal liability of the contractor or subcontractor as a bailee for loss or damage to the goods.

Exposure to loss on the part of the owner of property or on the part of the processor because of legal liability are related to bailee liability. Many types of processors purchase inland marine coverage. A representative type of policy has been developed in the garment manufacturing trade to cover property that may be away from the owner's premises while being processed by a contractor or subcontractor.

Garment Contractors Floaters The garment contractors floater is so designed that it can cover for the owner of the property or for the garment contractor who may be a bailee with the property of others in his or her custody. Policy forms, rules, and rates for garment contractors floaters have been standardized and filings of them have been made by the rating bureaus. The property which may be covered under a garment contractors floater is essentially men's, women's and children's clothing. Excluded from the filings are certain types of property which are related to clothing, but which are not usually subject to the same exposures to loss as clothing. Such items as headwear, bedding, footwear, umbrellas, and jewelry are excluded from the filings applicable to the garment contractors floater. It is considered that such property is subject to different exposures so the bureau rules are not applicable.

It is customary in the clothing business for a manufacturer to send goods out to other plants for much of the work. This may include dyeing and bleaching cloth in preparation for further manufacture, and it may also include specialty work such as cutting, embroidering, or sewing on buttonholes or trimmings. Most states permit coverage of the property on the premises of the owner as well as while in transit and while on the premises of a contractor or subcontractor. Insurance coverage on property in transit is very broad and of the "all-risks" type, but coverage on the premises of the contractor or subcontractor or on the owner's premises, usually is limited to named perils.

One of the peculiarities of the garment business is that loss or destruction of one part of a suit or garment may result in a consequential loss to the other part. For example, the trousers of men's suits might be sent out to a contractor to have zippers installed. Loss of the trousers would make the jackets of the suits worth considerably less. The coverage of the garment contractors floater can be extended to cover the consequential loss to portions of garments resulting from damage or destruction of other portions of the garments. The insured is obligated to attempt a replacement of the lost or damaged portions, but the insurance company pays the difference between the resulting value and the value of the completed garments if the damaged portions cannot be replaced.

The garment contractors floater is one type of inland marine policy for which the rating bureaus provide specific rates. The insurance company that is a bureau member or subscriber is required to submit a detailed and completed application to the bureau. The bureau then calculates the rate in accordance with a formula that has been filed with the state insurance departments. Important as a factor in the development of this rate is the average fire insurance contents rate for premises where the property is likely to be located.

DEALERS POLICIES

It has been evident in our discussions up to this point that marine and inland marine insurance pertain basically to property which is subject to a transit exposure or is mobile in nature. Customs of the business, and particularly those customs as expressed in the Nation-Wide Marine Definition, generally exclude stocks of merchandise on the owne.'s premises from eligibility for inland marine insurance. However, some exceptions to this general rule have developed through the years. Inland marine policies are written to cover stocks of certain kinds of merchandise even while such stocks are on the owner's premises.

Some kinds of mercantile stocks have characteristics that make desirable the type of insurance that traditionally has been written by inland marine underwriters. These characteristics are as follows:

1. Individual items, though small in size, have a high value.
2. There is frequently an off-premises exposure to loss because the property may be loaned, sold on approval, or sent out on consignment.
3. The property, because of its value and comparatively small size per item, is subject to a broad spectrum of perils.

Jewelers, especially, felt the need for broad coverage and a floater type of insurance policy on stock. Jewelry stocks are subject to loss from fire and the extended coverage perils but they are also particularly susceptible to loss from burglary and theft, and from unexplained loss where theft was the probable cause.

Years ago, the separation of underwriting powers between fire insurance and casualty insurance in the United States made it difficult and in many states impossible for insurance companies to write a single policy covering all of the exposures to which a jewelry stock is subject.

Lloyd's of London began to write a broad form of jewelry policy about 1900. It was called a jewelers' block policy, probably taking its name from the French words *en bloc*, meaning "all together." Lloyd's of London were the principal writers of jewelers' block insurance for the first twenty years or so of this century. However, they restricted their writing after World War I because of unfavorable loss experience due to increased crime. Inland marine underwriters of American insurance companies were willing to write the coverage. Laws were changed in many states so that jewelers' block insurance could be written either by inland marine insurers or by casualty companies. It developed that most of the jewelers' block business has been written as inland marine coverage. Casualty companies never did write any substantial amount of jewelers' block insurance. This precedent of permitting inland marine underwriters to write jewelers' block insurance provided the basis for inland marine coverage on several kinds of dealers' stocks of merchandise.

The exposure to loss under a dealers policy is principally at the business premises but it is customary to write the coverage as a floater policy. Originally there were two reasons for this practice which developed into a general custom. The first reason was an effort by inland marine insurers to give an appearance of a floater coverage in order to meet the objections of fire and casualty insurers who felt that inland marine underwriters were invading their domain. The second and more important reason was that property of dealers such as jewelers is more frequently subject to a substantial off-premises exposure than is the case with ordinary merchandise. The proportion of coverage that may be provided for the off-premises exposure may be less than the total amount of coverage. For example, a policy covering a stock of merchandise in the amount of $100,000 might provide only a $10,000 off-premises coverage. The amount of off-premises coverage would be adjusted to meet the actual needs of the insured so as to cover the values which might ordinarily be away from the business premises.

It is customary to use deductibles in connection with dealers policies in order to avoid a frequency of small losses that can result under a broad coverage. The coverage typically is of an "all-risks" type. Deductibles may apply to all losses rather than being limited to certain types of perils.

There are also exclusions of certain perils which may result in a catastrophic loss or which the underwriter may consider as uninsurable. Many policies, for example, exclude loss from flood or earthquake, particularly if the business premises are located in a flood plain or in an earthquake prone area. Provisions are made for addition of flood and earthquake coverage where the loss potential is such that insurance coverage may be provided without exposing the insurer to an excessive chance of loss.

The inland marine rating bureaus have filed rules, rates and forms for the principal kinds of dealers' inland marine policies which are shown in the Nation-Wide Marine Definition. The principal forms of dealers' policies and their peculiarities will be discussed here.

The Jewelers' Block Policy

The fact that the jewelers' block policy was developed largely by Lloyd's of London and independently of other inland marine policies at that time resulted in several differences between this policy and inland marine coverages in general. The terms of the policy make it appear to be a floater coverage.

The jewelers' block policy covers property while within, or in transit between, the states of the United States, District of Columbia, Puerto Rico, and Canada, but subject to limitations of liability in various circumstances. There are five limitations of liability applying to property in various circumstances. The first is a dollar limitation at the insured's business premises. The second dollar limitation applies to property in transit by first class registered mail and other specified highly protected transit means, or deposited for safekeeping under certain specified circumstances. A third limitation applies to property in transit to any one addressee at any one address during any one day. The fourth limitation applies to property in transit by customer parcel delivery service and other transportation services which are not considered to be quite as safe as first class registered mail and the other means of transportation specified in the second limitation. The fifth limitation applies to property situated elsewhere than under the four previous situations.

The policy provides blank spaces for these five limitations so that the dollar amounts can be inserted according to the insured's needs. The amount of coverage at the insured's business premises usually would be the maximum amount of the stock of merchandise during the policy term. The other limitations would depend upon whether the insured has sales personnel who carry property with them for display and sale, how much merchandise the insured ships and the valuations of shipments, and other circumstances applying to property away from the business premises.

The property insured is described in general terms and includes that usual to a jewelry store. Specifically mentioned are pearls, precious and semi-precious stones, jewels, jewelry, watches and watch movements, gold, silver, platinum, other precious metals, and alloys and other stock usual to the conduct of the insured's business. It is customary in the case of a department store or general store for the jewelers' block policy to apply only to the jewelry stock.

Coverage of the jewelers' block policy differs in an important respect from many mercantile property coverages. The jewelers' block policy has specific provisions applying to the property of others in the custody of the insured. Complete coverage is provided for property that is delivered or entrusted to the insured by others who are not dealers in jewelry or otherwise engaged in the jewelry trade. This is to take care of customers' property that may be entrusted to the jeweler for repair, safekeeping, or some other purpose. This has the effect of a bailees' customers coverage—it covers the interest of the jeweler because of liability for property in his or her custody, and it also provides coverage for the benefit of the property owner.

Coverage is different on property that is delivered or entrusted to the insured by others who are in the jewelry trade. This coverage is limited to the extent of the insured's own actual interest in the property because of money actually advanced thereon or legal liability for loss of or damage thereto. (It is presumed that other members of the jewelry trade will have their own insurance. They should look to their insurers for protection of their interests.) The insured is protected against loss that might occur because of any interest in the property or because of legal liability for loss or damage to the property but no coverage is provided for the owner of such property which may be entrusted to the insured.

Exclusions The exclusions of the jewelers' block policy deserve special consideration because they differ in many respects from those of other inland marine policies and they are particularly applicable to coverage of jewelers and the jewelry trade. The standard exclusions apply to war damage, to confiscation by order of any government or public authority or risks of contraband or illegal transportation or trade, and to nuclear losses in the same terms as those applicable to most inland marine policies. There is also an exclusion of delay, loss of market, gradual deterioration, insect, vermin, inherent vice, and other wear and tear losses in language similar to that of inland marine policies generally.

Loss by earthquake and flood are also excluded, but the policy specifically provides that fire damage occurring during or resulting from earthquake or flood would be covered if the policy covers fire damage. There is provision in the rules for the exclusion of fire coverage where the insured wishes to cover fire insurance separately from the jewelers' block policy. Losses due to infidelity or other act or omission of a dishonest character by the insured, the insured's employees, or on the part of any person to whom the property is entrusted are excluded, with the exception of property that is in the custody of the Postal Service or a person serving as a porter or helper not on the payroll of the insured. This last phrase recognizes the fact that jewelry sales personnel at times find it necessary to hire porters to help them transport their samples from place to place. Likewise, employees of common carriers and employees of the Postal Service are not within the control of the insured so that infidelity on their part could not be prevented by any act of the insured. The intention here is to exclude loss resulting from dishonesty of any person who is under the control of the insured.

Another exclusion defines the methods by which property may be transported and be covered. This essentially permits coverage by first class registered mail and comparable security operations.

Ordinary breakage of articles of a fragile or brittle nature is excluded unless the breakage is caused by certain specified perils. Goods sold on an installment plan are not covered after they leave the insured's custody.

One of the interesting exclusions directly applicable to the jewelry trade is that applying to property which is being worn by the insured; an officer of the corporation; a member of the firm; director, agent, employee, servant, or messenger of the insured; by any dealer or other person, firm, or corporation engaged in the jewelry trade; or by family members or relatives of the insured. Some jewelers permit their family members and friends to wear jewelry from their stock, and this obviously increases the chances of loss. The clause is so worded that it also excludes coverage on jewelry displayed by models. There are occasions when a jeweler will permit models at a fashion show to wear jewelry from the jeweler's stock. Since this exposure greatly adds to the chances of theft or other loss, and since it is somewhat within the control of the insured, the policy excludes such jewelry from coverage. The exposure may be avoided or retained, or an insurance company could provide coverage for jewelry that is being shown at a fashion show, but an extra premium would have to be charged to cover the additional exposure.

An exclusion also applies to property that is being shown at an exhibition promoted or financially assisted by any public authority or by any trade association. The provisions applying to property within a motor vehicle are different from those in most inland marine policies. Loss from an automobile, motorcycle, or other vehicle is excluded unless at the time the loss occurs there is actually in or upon such vehicle the insured or a permanent employee of the insured, or a person whose sole duty it is to attend the vehicle. Loss is excluded even from a locked motor vehicle unless there is someone actually in or on the vehicle whose duty it is to prevent theft. This is a very stringent exclusion which is specifically designed to eliminate losses of valuable property such as jewelry. There has been a question as to whether a car that has been left locked and in the custody of a garage or parking lot is attended within the meaning of the policy. It has been held that the parking of a car in a garage or parking lot does not meet the requirements of this provision in the policy. There must be some person whose actual duty is to watch that particular car.

There is no coverage for mysterious disappearance, unexplained loss, or shortages disclosed upon taking inventory. Loss from shoplifters and pilferage by employees can be treated by noninsurance techniques. However, it is not the intention to exclude losses by trickery where there is reasonable evidence that an actual theft occurred at a specific time and place.

Special provisions apply to losses from show windows. The rules provide for coverage of property in show windows but only under specified conditions and usually upon the payment of an additional premium to cover the added exposure to loss.

The rules also recognize the fact that some jewelers act as pawnbrokers. Claims for loss or damage to pledged articles on which loans have been made are limited to the amount actually loaned and unpaid, plus the accrued interest at the legal rate.

Other Policy Provisions The insured is required to keep a detailed inventory of all property in such a manner that the exact amount of any loss can be determined accurately. There is the usual inland marine provision that the insurance will not inure directly or indirectly to the benefit of any carrier or other bailee. The policy amount is not reduced by loss payment.

The policy also recognizes that merchants adjust their selling prices from time to time. The policy provides that the value of any particular item shall not exceed the *lowest* figure put upon the property in the insured's inventories, stock books, stock papers or other lists existing at the time the loss occurred. The policy also excludes from valuation any antiquarian or historical value attaching to the property.

It is customary for the insured to complete a detailed proposal form which gives pertinent facts regarding the business operation. This signed proposal customarily is attached to the jewelers' block policy. The intent of the insurance company is to have this proposal be a warranty as to the conditions governing the issuance of the policy. Protection services that are maintained by the insured are usually described in the application and the insured is obligated to maintain such protective services as far as is within the insured's control. The fact that the signed application form is attached to the policy helps to make this effective as a warranty. This is one instance in which inland marine underwriters attempt to make a warranty effective as to the insured's representations. Inaccurate statements on the proposal may be cited by the insurer as misrepresentations.

It is customary for the bureaus to rate specifically each jewelers' block policy on the basis of the application form that is submitted by the insured. This is a filed inland marine form.

Other Dealers Policies

The jewelers' block policy had been recognized as an inland marine coverage by the original Nation-Wide Marine Definition. By 1953, it became obvious that certain other types of merchandise were of similar character in that a broad insurance coverage was desirable, with a floater type of coverage for property away from the business premises of the insured. The 1953 Nation-Wide Marine Definition, therefore, recognized several additional types of dealers policies as classifiable under the inland marine type. These will be discussed here with particular attention to the differences between them and jewelers' block coverage, plus attention to any particular features that should be noted.

Furriers' Block Policy It will be recalled that the furriers' customers policy applies only to property of customers that is stored in the custody of the insured furrier. The furriers' block policy is designed to cover the stock of furs, fur garments, garments trimmed with fur and accessories pertaining thereto which are the property of the insured or sold but not delivered. The values and susceptibility to loss pertaining to fur garments are similar to those affecting jewelry. The design, coverage and exclusions of the furriers' block policy are similar to those of the jewelers' block policy.

Somewhat more leeway is given to the furrier for the shipment of low-valued merchandise. Shipments valued at less than $200 are covered when shipped by rail, water, air, motor carrier, or freight forwarders if a full value declaration is made to the carrier. Certain other types of shipments are covered with values in excess of $200 under conditions specified in the policy.

Exclusions are similar to those in the jewelers' block policy. It is interesting to note that the exclusion of property in a vehicle applies unless there is someone in attendance at the vehicle.

The bureaus provide for the rating of each account by the bureau for their members and subscribers. The insured is required to sign a proposal which gives details concerning the property to be covered, the limits of liability desired, loss protection services, the amount of property outside of the insured's premises during the preceding twelve months, the coverage desired for property in show windows, and other pertinent information. It is the practice in connection with furriers' block policies, as with jewelers' block policies, for a copy of the signed proposal to be attached to the policy. Certain warranties are specified in the proposal relating to coverage and protection.

Furriers' block policies may be written subject to deductibles of $500 to $5,000. Underwriters may require a deductible of sufficient size to eliminate losses from individual fur garment thefts in order to make the risk acceptable for insurance. It is interesting to note that this policy contains an exclusion comparable to that in the jewelers' block policy applying to property that is being worn by insureds, their representatives, or family members. However, the exclusion does not apply to property while being modeled on the premises of the insured or another dealer. An exclusion does apply to property on exhibition at an exhibit promoted or financially assisted by any public authority or any trade association.

Camera and Musical Instruments Dealers Policies Musical instruments and photographic equipment have substantial values in small items. A camera and musical instrument dealers policy is provided for in the bureau manuals. This policy is patterned after the jewelers' block policy but does not follow it quite as closely as the furriers' block policy. The coverage is on an "all-risks" basis with appropriate exclusions. Exclusions particularly appropriate to these types of properties apply to corrosion, rust, dampness of atmosphere, or extremes of temperature. Another exclusion appropriate to this type of property is that applying to short circuit, blowout, or other electrical disturbance within any article insured unless fire or explosion ensues. There is also an exclusion of loss applying to breakage of tubes, bulbs, lamps, or articles made principally of glass, although breakage of photographic lenses is covered. It is interesting to note that there is an exclusion applying to theft from a motor vehicle while unattended unless the vehicle is locked and there is evidence of forcible entry. This policy does not require the attendance on the vehicle of a person in the manner required by the jewelers' block and furriers' block policies. It merely requires that the property be within a locked vehicle and that there be physical evidence of forceable entry if the theft loss is to be covered.

Like the other block policies, there is provision for differing limitations of liability in different situations. The first applies to property at the premises of the insured, the second to property in due course of transit, the third to property away from the insured's premises in the custody of the insured or employees, and the fourth limitation on property located elsewhere. The amounts to be inserted in these items would depend upon the business of the insured, to what extent property is carried by employees or the insured, and to what extent shipments are made to and from suppliers and customers.

The Nation-Wide Marine Definition in its provision for musical instrument dealers policies states that radios, televisions, record players, and combinations thereof are not deemed musical instruments. Therefore, a radio and television dealer would not be considered eligible for a musical instruments dealers policy. The intent is to cover actual musical instruments and accessories. This would, however, include audio reproduction equipment that is used in connection with a musical instrument like an electric guitar.

Many camera or musical instruments dealers carry substantial amounts of other merchandise, which may be more or less related to the camera or musical instruments business. The committee on Interpretation of the Nation-Wide Marine Definition decided that the proportion of other stock should not exceed 25 percent if this stock is to be insured under the camera and musical instruments dealers form. Provision is made for coverage of a camera or musical instruments department separate from other stock in a store that operates with large amounts of general merchandise. This is comparable to the provision which permits the jewelry department of a department store to be insured under a jewelers' block policy while the other merchandise is insured under another type of policy.

Requirements of the rating bureaus differ. One bureau requires submission to the bureau for rating for its members and subscribers. The other bureau provides a rather elaborate rating schedule which is used by the companies. It is customary to have the insured or prospective insured sign an application form for a musical or camera dealers policy, but the signed application form is not required to be attached to the policy unlike the jewelers' block and furriers' block policies.

Equipment Dealers The equipment dealers policy is used to cover the stock of dealers in mobile agricultural and construction equipment. The provision for this type of policy in the Nation-Wide Marine Definition recognizes the fact that agricultural equipment and construction equipment may be stored out of doors, may be stored away from the premises of the insured, and frequently used away from the insured's premises for demonstration purposes. There is a real need for a broad and off-premises coverage for such items of mobile equipment.

The rules concerning the equipment dealers policies in the bureau manuals as well as the Nation-Wide Marine Definition specifically exclude motor vehicles designed for highway use. The intent is to provide coverage for types of mobile equipment which are not designed for highway use.

This, like the other dealers policies, insures on an "all-risks" basis with pertinent exclusions. Loss or damage to electrical appliances or devices are excluded when the loss occurs from artificially generated electricity. Loss by infidelity is also excluded.

Other exclusions apply to delay, loss of market, and indirect or consequential loss of any kind. Loss disclosed upon taking inventory is excluded. There is also the customary wear and tear or mechanical breakdown exclusion and also an exclusion of damage caused by corrosion, rust, dampness of atmosphere, freezing or extremes of temperature. Another exclusion applies to loss or damage to tires or tubes unless the loss or damage is caused by fire, windstorm, or theft or is coincident with other loss or damage insured by the policy. It will be noted that the list of exclusions is not as lengthy as is the case with the other types of dealers policies already described. Mobile agricultural and construction equipment is not subject to the high proportion of loss that would apply to the valuable property and small items typical of jewelry, furs, cameras or musical instruments.

There customarily is a coinsurance clause applying to this property. Because inventories change constantly, it is not feasible for a dealer to list items specifically for coverage, and a coinsurance clause is considered necessary in order to make certain that the insured will carry an amount of insurance commensurate with the value of the property.

The rating bureaus differ as far as deductibles are concerned. One bureau provides for a deductible in the filing, whereas the other bureau does not have any such provision. The deductible is not considered by some to be quite as important with this type of property because of its substantial physical nature. However, many insurers feel that a deductible is desirable where the property is stored out of doors and pilferage is likely.

The form provides for insertion of limits of liability applying to any one loss, and a separate limit of liability applying to property in transit or at a location elsewhere than the premises of the insured.

Many states permit the equipment dealer to include in the coverage of the policy other types of merchandise. This has the effect of permitting the coverage of large amounts of other stock such as hardware under the very favorable conditions of the equipment dealers policy. Some states limit the proportion of other stock to 15 percent in order to make this policy truly an equipment coverage policy.

Rates and premiums ordinarily are calculated by the company in accordance with filings of the bureaus. A substantial credit from the fire insurance rate is provided because a large proportion of the mobile equipment may be outside of buildings where it is not subject to the building fire hazard.

Floor Plan Policies There are many cases in which equipment is financed by dealers under what is called a "floor plan." The manufacturer or wholesaler places the merchandise or equipment in the hands of a dealer. Money to pay for the goods is loaned to the dealer by a bank or other financial institution. This type of financing may be done in connection with individual units which may be specifically identified, such as mobile agricultural or contractors equipment.

The Nation-Wide Marine Definition provides for inland marine policies on property under a floor plan. The requirements of the Definition are that the merchandise be specifically identifiable as encumbered, that the dealer's right to sell the merchandise is conditioned upon its being released from encumbrance by the bank, and that such policies cover in transit and do not extend beyond the termination of the dealer's interest. Also excluded under the provisions of the Definition are motor vehicles and a general stock of merchandise where the items are not specifically identifiable. The rating bureau rules further provide that general merchandise may not be indicated as the property to be covered.

A floor plan policy may be issued to cover the single interest of the merchant or may be issued to cover the dual interests of the merchant and of the lending institution.

Coverage of the policies is similar to that of the other dealers policies, being closest to that of the equipment dealers policy.

The exclusion applying to loss or damage resulting from delay or loss of market adds the further exclusion of loss or damage due to bankruptcy, foreclosure, or similar proceedings. The dealer, therefore, is not protected under this policy for loss that might occur because of foreclosure by some other party.

Flood damage is excluded but this exclusion may be deleted for an additional charge if the insurer is willing. This would be subject to individual underwriting depending upon the location of the insured's premises.

Valuation in case of loss may not exceed the purchase price plus transportation charges. The value of property that has been sold, however, is the net selling price of the dealer after all allowances and discounts. These valuation clauses are subject to a further restriction that the amount of loss shall not exceed the cost to repair or replace the merchandise with material of like kind and quality.

The policy very often is written on a reporting form, particularly if the insured is operating with substantial amounts of property subject to the policy.

INSTALLMENT SALES OR DEFERRED PAYMENT POLICIES

A large proportion of business is conducted on a deferred payment basis. There are many variations in the details of installment payment or deferred payment arrangements, but they fall basically into two principal groups. One method is the purchase of property under an installment payment contract applying to a specific piece of property or group of items. This is the method that is commonly used in connection with the purchase of more expensive pieces of household equipment such as refrigerators, or the purchase of industrial equipment by manufacturing or merchandising firms. A typical installment contract uses a conditional bill of sale under which the purchaser does not acquire title to the property until the final installment has been paid. The seller has the right to repossess the property if payments are not made as required.

Property is also purchased under revolving charge accounts. The purchaser establishes credit with the merchant and has the right to buy property which is charged to the account. Additional items are charged to the account from time to time as purchases are made, and the purchaser makes installment payments which may vary in amount according to the dollar values which are currently owed by the purchaser.

Larger mercantile firms may provide the credit to customers on their own account. However, many merchants sell the notes in connection with an installment payment contract to a bank or other lending institutions. Therefore, the financial institution which buys such commercial paper has a financial interest in the property for which payment is being made.

It had developed over a period of years that the sale of the finance contract by the merchant to a financing organization effectively cut off the purchaser from any recourse in case the merchandise purchased was not as represented or developed defects. The financing organization could enforce the contract against the purchaser regardless of the condition of the merchandise, and the merchant who sold the property was entirely out of the transaction and could not be forced to make good any defect or fault in the property. This has been changed by federal legislation making the organization which holds the financing contract responsible for any defects that may develop subsequent to the sale.

The Nation-Wide Marine Definition sets forth the conditions under which property being purchased under a deferred payment plan may be covered by a policy of inland marine insurance. An inland marine policy may be written to cover property sold under conditional contract of sale, partial payment contract, installment sales contract, or leased property, but excluding motor vehicles designed for highway use. These provisions are sufficiently broad that an inland marine policy may be issued on property that is encumbered under many kinds of deferred payment or installment sales arrangement. This would apply regardless of whether the property is specifically encumbered under an installment sales contract applying to the specific item, or whether it is property purchased under a revolving charge account.

It is further provided that inland marine policies covering such property must cover in transit but shall not extend beyond the termination of the seller's or lessor's interest.

It should be noted that leased property is also included as subject to coverage under an inland marine policy. There are many situations where industrial and commercial firms will lease equipment on a long-term basis rather than buy the equipment. Many computers, for example, are leased rather than purchased by the users. Such property that is away from the premises of the owners and on the premises of customers under a lease arrangement may also be covered by inland marine policies.

There are three parties to an installment sales transaction who may have an interest in the insuring of the merchandise. The dealer who sells the merchandise and provides the financing for the property has an interest as long as some other organization has not taken over the financing operation. The financing company that purchases the obligation may also have an interest in the property. This finance company may take over completely the interest of the dealer in cases where the dealer sells the obligation to the finance organization, and is absolved of any recourse under the contract between the dealer and the finance organization. The third person with an interest in the property is the purchaser. The typical installment sales or deferred payment contract protects the dealer or the finance company that takes over the obligation. The policy may be a single interest policy covering only the interest of the dealer or finance company, or it may be a dual interest policy which also provides coverage for the benefit of the purchaser.

The interest of a bank or other lender in personal property pledged as security for a loan may only be covered if the property itself falls within the marine definition. The exposures involved with transit coverage, which is required to be included as a part of inland marine coverage, may be incidental. The policy usually covers in transit from the time the property leaves the premises of the dealer until it is delivered to the purchaser. As a practical matter, this may be the only transit exposure in the case where the property stays on the premises of the purchaser until payment is completed. However, the transit coverage may also apply to any move that is made by the purchaser during the term of the contract.

Many inland marine installment sales policies are issued in connection with other types of insurance. It is customary for a dealer to arrange a complete package of credit insurance for the benefit of a purchaser. This may include accident, hospitalization, and other health or life insurance coverage which would pick up the payment installments if the insured died or became disabled during the term of the contract. This, of course, is not inland marine insurance but is written as a health, accident, or life insurance coverage as the case may be. The property coverage which would be written as part of such a package would be provided as an inland marine coverage.

The bureaus have not taken jurisdiction over installment sales or deferred payment coverages. The rates, underwriting rules, and forms for these coverages are developed independently by companies wishing to provide the coverage. A few states have required that filings of forms or rates be made with the state insurance departments. Some states have established minimum standards for coverage and rates but the minimum standards apply particularly to the health, accident, and life insurance coverages. The property insurance coverage under the inland marine provisions are not subject to specific regulations in most states.

Exposures vary according to the type of property, the locations in which property is sold by the merchants, and any likelihood of catastrophe losses. Flood coverage has resulted in castastrophe losses in certain areas. The potential for widespread flooding in the merchants' sales area would have to be taken into account in arranging coverage. In other respects, the probabilities of loss depend largely upon the integrity of the merchants insured and their care in selecting customers with whom conditional sales contracts or leases will be issued.

INSTRUMENTALITIES OF TRANSPORTATION AND COMMUNICATION

It has become customary for inland marine policies to be issued on certain types of property such as bridges, tunnels, pipelines, power transmission lines, telephone and telegraph lines, and radio and television equipment. This is to a large extent an artificial grouping as far as transportation exposure is concerned. This practice developed many years ago during a time when marine underwriters were the only ones who were willing to write insurance on bridges. The division of insurance in the United States between fire insurance and casualty insurance made it difficult, if not impossible, for a single insurer to provide the broad coverage a bridge or tunnel would need. Marine underwriters were willing to provide the coverage. This became firmly established by the time the original Nation-Wide Marine Definition was developed so that it was considered proper for a marine policy to be issued on a bridge or tunnel. This was later expanded to include coverage on other types of what came to be designated as "instrumentalities of transportation."

There was some practical justification for marine coverage on bridges and tunnels because they are subject to damage by ships passing underneath the bridge or above the tunnel on a waterway. The bridge and tunnel system across the mouth of Chesapeake Bay, for example, has been seriously damaged several times by ship collisions.

Bridges and Tunnels Insurance

Bridges and tunnels are exposed to a wide variety of perils. Most of the older bridges in the United States were mainly built of wood and were subject to a severe fire hazard. Bridges are also subject to loss from windstorms, ice jams, flood waters, as well as ship collisions. Modern bridges are constructed of steel which may appear to eliminate fire as a serious peril. However, severe damage may occur because of the transportation of gasoline and explosives by motor truck. An accident involving a gasoline transport with resulting fire might create sufficient heat to weaken the suspension cables and cause the entire bridge to fall into the river. A serious fire occurred in the Holland Tunnel between New Jersey and New York City a few years ago as a result of a fire in a truckload of a flammable liquid.

Insurers have been willing to provide a very broad type of coverage for bridges and tunnels in spite of the severe hazards to which they are subject. Coverage is against "direct physical loss or damage however caused" except as otherwise provided. There is a war and governmental action exclusion which is worded essentially the same as that appearing in many inland marine policies.

There is also an exclusion of loss from inherent defect, wear and tear, gradual deterioration, or expansion or contraction due to changes of temperature. However, this exclusion is applicable only if there is not a resulting collapse of the property or a material part thereof. In other words, actual collapse of the bridge is covered even though it might result from inherent defect, wear and tear or gradual deterioration, or from expansion or contraction due to changes of temperature. The exclusion is intended to apply to partial loss and does not apply to total collapse.

There is also an exclusion of loss resulting from failure of the insured to maintain the property or to use reasonable means to save and preserve the property at the time and after a loss. There is also a nuclear exclusion comparable to that which appears in other inland marine policies.

It can be seen that the coverage is one of the broadest that is provided by any inland marine policy, particularly as far as collapse of the bridge is concerned. Practically any collapse is covered with the exception of that due to a war or a nuclear exposure.

Toll Bridges

Many bridges are financially supported by tolls collected from motorists crossing the bridge. An interruption of use due to an accident would result in a large financial loss to the bridge authority or owner. A "bridge use and occupancy form" is used to cover loss of revenue resulting from necessary interruption of use because of direct physical loss or damage to the bridge.

Builders' Risk

Many bridges under construction are covered by inland marine policies. The coverage usually provided under a bridge builders' risk form is against direct physical loss or damage caused by fire, lightning, flood, rising waters, ice, explosion, windstorm, earthquake, and collision. This is a much narrower coverage than is provided for completed bridges. The designer and contractor in connection with the building of a bridge are expected to use acceptable designs and necessary precautions to prevent the collapse of a bridge or other miscellaneous damage such as would be covered under a bridge policy for a completed bridge.

Other Instrumentalities of Transportation and Communication

Inland marine coverage is also provided at times for pipelines and power transmission lines. However, these are not insured as frequently as bridges or tunnels because the value usually is distributed over a wide geographical area. The low concentration of value in one location reduces potential loss severity. Therefore, many utilities having pipelines or transmission lines retain their loss exposures.

Television and radio towers and transmission equipment may be insured under an inland marine policy. There may be a concentration of value amounting to several millions of dollars at one location in a television transmitting tower and equipment. It is customary, therefore, for insurance to be written on such equipment. The principal exposures are from windstorm and collapse, but losses also have occurred from forest fires and from vandalism. Such towers may be destroyed if the supporting cables are cut.

Rates and special conditions for bridge and tunnel insurance are provided to bureau members and subscribers by a bridge committee. The values of some of the larger bridges are so great that the entire world's insurance capacity is needed in order to provide adequate coverage. The rate developed by the rating bureau generally is accepted by all of the other insurers that might agree to provide coverage for the particular bridge. Each is rated and underwritten specifically, in many cases after consultation with the insurers that might be providing the coverage.

Rates and coverages for such equipment as television and radio towers and equipment, or other instrumentalities of transportation are determined by the insurance company or by a group of companies where the values are such that several insurers must be used. An "all-risks" form might be used if agreeable to the insurers. Actual coverage would be comparable to that provided for a bridge under the bridge forms. Important consideration is given to the catastrophic potentials because wind and icing conditions may cause collapse of the tower with a resulting catastrophic loss.

MISCELLANEOUS INLAND MARINE COVERAGES

A characteristic of marine coverage, including inland marine, is the willingness of insurers to meet whatever unusual conditions may face a property owner. Broad insurance coverage is provided where demanded by circumstances. Flexibility of coverage and flexibility of rates are necessary in order to meet special or unusual conditions. The following material covers some of the inland marine policies that have been developed to meet these special situations. There are many others, depending upon the types of property and the ingenuity of insurers in meeting the needs of property owners.

Neon Sign Policies

Inland marine insurance for neon signs and automatic or mechanical electrical signs and street clocks is another example of allocation to the marine classification of a coverage which fire insurers were unable or unwilling to provide. It should be noted that the inland marine classification for signs does not apply to billboards even if they are electrically lighted. There must be a neon tube or mechanical feature to justify the inland marine coverage. Neon and mechanical signs are often expensive. Some of the elaborate signs that are erected at motel and hotel sites may approach $100,000 in value. The tubing that is an essential part of the neon sign is subject to breakage and other types of loss which do not affect billboards.

Coverage for neon signs and mechanical signs has been filed by the rating bureaus. It is of an "all-risks" type with exclusions applying to wear and tear, gradual deterioration, breakage during installation and transportation, mechanical breakdown, and loss due to faulty manufacture or installation. There are also the usual exclusions of war damage and nuclear damage. The bureau filings provide for a full coverage policy but a large proportion of these policies are written subject to deductibles in order to eliminate a frequency of small claims. It is required that each sign be listed specifically with a limit of liability applying to each sign.

Provisions are made for insuring sign dealers for their interest in signs that are being paid for under an installment payment plan or sold under a maintenance contract.

Accounts Receivable

The assets of commercial establishments may include a high proportion of accounts receivable. Destruction of the accounts receivable records might make it difficult or impossible for the organization to collect the accounts.

Accounts receivable insurance is a consequential loss type of insurance. It covers the amount of money the insured would be unable to collect if the records were destroyed. It is particularly desirable for merchants who have large numbers of accounts receivable which could not be reconstructed following destruction of the records. It is not intended to cover the actual physical value of the records themselves, because fire forms will replace the blank books of account and so forth. The Nation-Wide Marine Definition recognizes accounts receivable as an inland marine coverage but this is also recognized as a casualty coverage.

The perils insured against are "all-risks" of loss and damage except as excluded. There are the usual war damage and nuclear exclusions. There are also exclusions of loss or damage due to fraudulent, dishonest, or criminal acts by an insured or certain officers or directors of the insured. Also excluded are losses due to bookkeeping or accounting errors.

Insurance rates usually are less than the insurance rates for other property. It is considered that some debtors would pay their accounts even though the insured was unable to bill them. There may be other circumstances that would permit some salvage or reconstruction of the records. Policies usually are written on a reporting basis depending upon the outstanding accounts at the end of each reporting period. However, nonreporting forms subject to limits not exceeding $100,000 are available.

Accounts receivable loss exposures are particularly susceptible to loss control measures. Where duplicate records are kept at remote locations, the chance of loss is virtually eliminated. Loss exposures can be reduced if records are kept in fire-resistive safes or vaults. Even a metal desk or filing cabinet provides some protection against loss in a minor fire.

Valuable Papers and Records

Many documents are difficult or impossible to replace. The valuable papers and records policy provides coverage for such property on an agreed value basis, with a specific amount of insurance allotted for each item. This type of coverage is used for historical documents and similar papers and records.

The other type of property which may be covered under this policy consists of such property as blueprints, architectural plans, manuscripts, deeds, maps, and such documents that can be replaced or reconstructed. Replaceable documents are covered on a blanket basis. The policy may specify a limit of liability, or a value per item, subject to a limit of liability for all of the documents covered by the policy.

The principal chances of loss to valuable documents and records are those of fire and the extended coverage perils. There may be circumstances where the documents would also be subject to damage by vandals. The coverage is written for engineering and architectural firms which may have large investments in plans and specifications for buildings under construction or proposed, for museums that have historical documents, and for governmental offices which are repositories for legal documents, deeds and similar records. Coverage applies primarily to the premises where the documents are located but may be extended to cover during transit and to other locations, depending upon the use to which the documents are placed and the needs of the insured.

The exclusions from the "all-risks" type of coverage are those usual to inland marine policies. Exclusions which are specially applicable to this coverage are those applying to property held as samples, for sale, or for delivery after sale; for errors or omissions in processing or copying; and for electrical or magnetic injury.

Valuable papers and records can also be protected with noninsurance techniques similar to those discussed for accounts receivable.

In evaluating the exposure arising out of loss or destruction of valuable papers, a risk manager should ask what the firm would do if the records were destroyed (assuming there was no insurance). Would there be a tangible monetary loss? Would expenses be incurred in reconstructing the papers, or are the papers irreplaceable?

Doctors' or hospitals' patient records are an example of an exposure that, in the opinion of some risk managers, should not be insured. Such records provide valuable historical information on a patient's previous health. For example, an electrocardiogram taken five years ago might be of immense help in diagnosing a heart patient's current condition. But, if that electrocardiogram is destroyed, there is no way that it can be recreated. Therefore, no expense will be incurred in replacing the lost record, and there may be no measurable damages. For exposures of this type, noninsurance techniques (to prevent the loss) may be more appropriate than insurance techniques, which merely provide some payment following a loss.

Fine Arts Floaters

Fine arts objects have a quality that make them worth more than their utility value; they may be of rare or historical value. Antique furniture may also be classifiable as fine arts because antiques have commercial value in excess of the utility value.

Fine arts came to be covered by inland marine insurance because many objects of art are more easily damaged than ordinary items, and are often subject to transit exposures. Marine insurers were able to provide broader coverage than fire insurers.

According to the Nation-Wide Marine Definition, fine arts floaters can be written to cover "objects of art such as pictures, statuary, bronzes and antiques, rare manuscripts and books, articles of virtu, etc." Art glass windows of the character of fine arts are considered insurable under an inland marine policy even if they are permanently installed in a building, such as a church or library.

Fine arts coverage is written on an "all-risks" basis. Special exclusions exclude damage sustained from any repairing, restoration, or retouching process. Likewise, breakage of art glass windows, statuary, marbles, glassware, bric-a-brac, porcelains, and similar fragile articles is excluded unless coverage is caused by one of the named perils. This exclusion can often by deleted by agreement of the insurer and the insured. Property on the premises of fairgrounds or the premises of any national or international exposition is excluded from coverage, unless specific permission is given by the insurer.

It is customary to issue fine arts policies on a valued basis. The insurer agrees to the value of each item as listed in a schedule, and, in case of loss, the amount listed is paid. Such valued coverage is desirable in most cases, because it is often difficult to determine the value of a work of art after it has been damaged or destroyed. It may be extremely difficult to establish the value of a one-of-a-kind item, unless the insurer and the insured agree on a value before the policy is issued.

Museums and Dealers in Fine Arts The fine arts in the possession of a museum or dealer are in effect a large private collection.

Bureau rules, rates and forms do not apply to fine arts museums and dealers. It is not feasible for a dealer, and many times is not feasible for a museum, to list each individual work of art as is done with smaller private collections, so such exposures are usually insured on a blanket basis.

Many large museums do not insure their permanent collections. They rely on noninsurance techniques includng superior protection and guard systems. As with valuable papers, insurance may not be appropriate in the case of irreplaceable items.

One of the most important exposures on the part of museums involves property that is borrowed from other museums. It is customary for museums to carry insurance on the property of others in their custody. Coverage is effective from the time the property leaves the premises of the owner, while it is on exhibition in the borrowing museum, and until returned safely to the owner. This is similar to floater policies that are written on exhibitions as previously described.

Fine arts policies that are written for dealers must include carefully drawn provisions for the valuation of such merchandise. The values of fine arts fluctuate substantially according to the whims and desires of people who buy such property. The price paid by a dealer may be far below its actual value, or occasionally may be in excess of the actual value in cases where the dealer has misjudged the market.

CHAPTER 11

Property Crime Exposures and Their Treatment

INTRODUCTION

Exposures to loss from crime may be classified in various ways. A business may have an exposure to loss from crimes committed by employees or by outsiders. This chapter will not deal with employee dishonesty, as that is the topic of Chapter 12.

The crime exposure includes both crimes against the person and crimes resulting in property loss or damage. This chapter will concentrate on property crime exposures, although crimes against the person may be an additional source of loss. For example, the proprietor of a liquor store who is wounded by a shotgun blast during a robbery would suffer from a crime against the person, in addition to loss or damage to property.

Property crime exposures are substantial. In 1976, property losses from robbery, burglary, and larceny-theft in the United States amounted to over $2.7 billion dollars, based on crimes reported to the FBI. These figures exclude auto theft (see Table 11-1). Other sources place the cost of crime much higher.

In another report published early in 1976, the total cost of crime in the U.S. was estimated at $97 billion, including $25 billion in losses resulting from crime against property and business.[1] It is impossible to determine accurately the total of property losses from crime, because many instances of crime are not reported. For example, much of the loss from shoplifting is undetected and shows up only as an inventory shortage. It is certain, however, that the total loss from all crime creates a serious drain on the economy and is a threat to the solvency of many businesses.

Table 11-1

Crimes Against Property—1967-1976*

Year	Robbery	Burglary	Larceny-Theft
1967	202,100	1,616,500	3,080,500
1968	261,780	1,841,100	3,447,800
1969	297,650	1,962,900	3,849,700
1970	348,460	2,183,800	4,183,500
1971	386,150	2,376,300	4,379,900
1972	374,790	2,352,800	4,109,600
1973	383,260	2,549,938	4,319,118
1974	442,397	3,039,159	5,262,505
1975	464,973	3,252,129	5,977,698
1976	420,214	3,089,789	6,270,822

*Reprinted with permission from *Insurance Facts* (New York: Insurance Information Institute, 1977), p. 61.

IDENTIFYING PROPERTY CRIME EXPOSURES

A *crime* is a violation of the law that is punished as an offense against the state or government.[2] In order to identify crime exposures to property, it is necessary to examine those types of crime which may result in a property loss. This section will examine the subject of crime exposures. A later section of this chapter will discuss crime insurance coverages (excluding employee dishonesty).

Degrees of Crime

Statutes in the United States relating to crime generally classify crimes by their degree of seriousness.

Felonies and Misdemeanors A *felony* is a serious crime such as murder, assault, burglary, robbery, or arson. It is usually defined as such in the laws applicable to crime and generally is an offense punishable by death or by imprisonment.

A *misdemeanor* is an offense of a less serious nature than a felony. Vandalism that produces damages of less than $100 is an example of a misdemeanor under the statutes of some states. Note, however, that an act may be a felony in one state and a misdemeanor in another, depending on each state's statutes.

Grand Larceny and Petit Larceny Larceny is any unlawful taking of the personal goods of another. Some state statutes distinguish between *grand larceny* and *petit larceny* (or "petty" larceny, meaning small). The distinction, based on the value of the property stolen, has been abolished in most of the United States, and varies from state to state where still used.

These distinctions notwithstanding, in any case of crime against property there is a property loss, and it is this fact that is of prime importance to the student of insurance.

Relationship Between Crimes and Torts

A tort is a private or civil wrong against one or more individuals; a crime is a wrong against the people generally. A tort involves a violation of some duty that is owed to the injured person. The duty must be something that arises by operation of the laws rather than a violation of a contract. A property tort involves injury or damage to real or personal property. Generally, a tort which results in damage to the property of another is the result of unintentional negligence of the tortfeasor. The criminal, however, intends to take or injure the person or property of another. It is this element of intent that generally distinguishes a tort from a crime.

There may be circumstances where a tort may approach the status of a crime, or it might actually constitute a crime. This could occur in the case of what is called a willful tort. The commission of a willful tort implies the intent to injure or, in the absence of an actual intent to commit injury, a reckless disregard for the safety of people or property. Willful torts, however, are not a major part of the threat to property from loss by crime. The vast majority of property losses from crime are the result of deliberate intent on the part of the criminal to deprive a property owner of his or her property.

Types of Crimes Against Property

Crimes differ in their method of accomplishment and in their effect upon the owner of the property. The various types of crime, their legal definitions, and the ways in which they threaten loss to property are described in the following paragraphs. In many cases these legal definitions differ somewhat from the definitions used in insurance policies.

The Uniform Crime Reporting Program provides a great deal of information on the extent of crime losses. For this reason, it is also necessary to examine the definitions used in that program. (The Uniform Crime Reporting Program was initiated in 1930 by the Committee on Uniform Crime Records of The International Association of Chiefs of Police. Reports from law enforcement agencies throughout the United States are consolidated each year by the FBI in the "Uniform Crime Reports" under the title of "Crime in the United States.")

The terms discussed in this section are not mutually exclusive— several of the following definitions might be applicable to any given crime.

Burglary The common law definition of burglary was the breaking and entering of the dwelling house of another at night with the intention of committing a felony, whether or not the felonious purpose was accomplished. The crime was not designated as burglary under the common law if there was enough daylight to discern a person's face.

The statutory definitions of burglary in many states as well as court decisions have expanded the term beyond the common law definition. The breaking and entering of any premises (not merely dwellings), any time of the day or night, generally constitutes burglary. At least one state includes in its statutory definition the burglarizing of an automobile.

Very little force is required to constitute breaking within the legal definition. Even the turning of a doorknob, the lifting of a latch, or the opening of an unlocked window have been considered breaking.

The Uniform Crime Reporting Program defines burglary as the unlawful entry of a structure to commit a felony even though no force is used to gain entry. This is a practical recognition of the fact that unlawful entry onto the premises of another constitutes a crime even if the burglar is fortunate enough to find an open door or window through which to make entry.

It follows, therefore, that a burglary is committed when one or more persons enter the premises of another with the intent to steal property. Any type of business operation that keeps or appears to have on its premises money, merchandise, stock finished or unfinished, plans or drawings, or any commodity that may be carried away and used by the thief or converted into money may be victimized by burglary.

Robbery Robbery is the taking of the property of another with the intention of stealing it *by means of violence* or by putting the lawful custodian of the property in fear of violence. A "holdup," for example, would be a robbery. Awareness of the theft by the owner or lawful custodian is necessary for a crime to be considered robbery, except that awareness of the victim that a theft is taking place is not required if the victim has been knocked unconscious in the commission of the crime. The victim must be attacked by violence, be threatened with violence, or be put in fear of violence, and the theft must be without the consent of the victim. Statistics concerning robbery are collected on the basis of any forcible taking of property regardless of the weapon that may be used, or "strong-arm" robbery where the only weapon is the physical body of the robber.

All businesses are potential robbery victims. A retail store may attract persons who attempt to obtain merchandise or money by threatening bodily harm to the owner, clerks, or customers in the store. Outside of the premises, bank messengers, sales persons carrying samples or collections, or people delivering merchandise to the premises of a business or its customers are also potential victims.

Larceny or Theft   By definition, larceny or theft is the unlawful taking or stealing of property or articles of value without the use of force, violence, or fraud. In a broad sense, burglary and robbery for the purpose of taking property are included within the definition of larceny and theft. For statistical purposes, however, the Uniform Crime Reporting Program uses the term *larceny-theft* to include such crimes as shoplifting, pocket-picking, thefts of property from automobiles, theft of automobile parts and accessories, bicycle thefts, and similar acts. Theft of automobiles is separated statistically, as are embezzlement, confidence games, forgery, and worthless checks.

The words larceny and theft commonly are used to indicate a *theft by stealth* as contrasted to a theft by violence. The stealing of money from a pocket or purse without the owner's awareness of the theft is considered larceny or theft. This is contrasted to a purse snatching, which is usually considered robbery because it is a crime of violence. For example, consider the club owner who removed most of the money from the cash register, put it in his jacket pocket to transport it to his office for safekeeping only to discover when he reached the office that he had been the victim of a pickpocket along the way. This would be categorized as a larceny or theft.

Shoplifting is another act that is considered theft because it is accomplished by stealth without any intended violence. Crime statistics indicate that shoplifting is a major source of loss to all retail stores, regardless of type of merchandise. Shoplifting losses include the single item taken by a teenager on a dare, the constant taking of a number of fairly valuable items by the compulsive thief, and the skilled shoplifter who arrives at a department or discount store in attire designed to secrete a number of items and who leaves carrying thousands of dollars of the store's merchandise.

Statutes and courts are tending more and more to include the obtaining of property by false pretenses within the meaning of larceny or theft. False pretense involves an intended misrepresentation of facts or conditions whereby a person obtains the money or property of another.

Larceny by trick occurs when a victim parts with the property voluntarily, but is persuaded to do so by some trick, device, or swindle. The victim understands that something of value is to be received in return, but the perpetrator of the fraud has no intention of making good on the agreement. Among the perpetrators of larceny by trick is the "new" delivery person who arrives at the retail or wholesale distributor and departs with valuable merchandise which never reaches its intended destination.

Extortion or Blackmail Extortion, a special form of theft involving the unlawful obtaining of money from another, is similar to robbery in that the money is obtained through violence or threat. The force may be a threat to injure the victim or the victim's relatives, or it may be a threat to destroy property. The placing or alleged placing of a bomb or destructive device which will be detonated unless money or property is given to the persons making the threats is a form of extortion. Kidnapping of a person or of a person's family is often another form of extortion.

Worthless Checks A worthless or bad check is one which is drawn on a nonexistent account or on an account with funds insufficient to meet the amount of the check. The drawing of a worthless check is a crime when the intent is to defraud the payee. There can be questionable circumstances as to whether a crime is committed in cases where the drawer of the check is negligent in determining whether there are sufficient funds to cover the amount of the check or where the check is drawn in advance with the anticipation that sufficient funds will be in the account by the time the check is presented for payment. There is a substantial loss each year, particularly to merchants, from the intentional drawing of worthless checks. Such loss is the result of a crime because it is a form of theft by deception. The United States Department of Commerce estimated that bad check losses for food stores amounted to $450 million in 1974 alone.[3] Estimates are not available for other kinds of retailers but the totals of such losses are staggering.

It is important to note that there are several types of documents that fall within the general category of checks. Some of these are bank payment orders, bank money orders, and similar negotiable forms.

Forgery Forgery is the false making or alteration of writing with intent to defraud. This includes falsely endorsing a check with the name of the payor or the payee, the alteration of a check or other document by changing the name of the owner or payee, or by changing the amount of the instrument.

A form of forgery that has been costly to merchants is the theft and forging of payee's names on government-issued checks such as social security or other benefit checks. The merchant or other person who initially cashes the check ultimately stands the loss.

Frequently, blank checks are taken in a burglary. The business owner often becomes aware of this only after the checks have been forged and presented to the bank for payment. If warehouse receipts are stolen, a merchant may discover valuable merchandise has been delivered from the warehouse in exchange for forged receipts.

Credit Card Fraud   The fraudulent use of credit cards is a special form of forgery. A stolen credit card is used by forging the name of the credit card owner in order to secure articles of value. Federal statutes (Public Law 91-508) limit to $50 per card the amount which the card owner can lose in the case of fraudulent use. However, the amount of the fraudulent purchase is a loss to the merchant or to the credit card company or bank, depending upon the agreement between the merchant and the credit card company. The federal law which limits the amount which the card holder can lose does not reduce the loss from this crime. It merely passes the loss to others who must, in turn, recoup this amount by upward adjustment in the sale price of their merchandise or services. Merchants lose many millions of dollars each year through the fraudulent use of credit cards. A card-holder's total exposure is not limited to $50. For the business person who carries or gives to various employees a number of credit cards, all of which may be stolen at the same time, the loss can be much more. The business that keeps a number of credit cards on the company's premises may sustain an even more substantial loss if these cards are stolen.

Counterfeit Money   A special form of forgery is the making of counterfeit money. Two crimes are involved here—the making of counterfeit money and the intentional passing of counterfeit money. The counterfeit money usually is sold at a fraction of its face value to passers who use various devices to secure genuine money in place of the counterfeit, such as buying a small amount of merchandise in order to get change in genuine money. Supermarkets and similar merchants are frequently victims because the checkout clerks are rushed at certain times of the day and do not take the time to examine the money carefully.

Counterfeit money is subject to confiscation when it is discovered. The person who holds a counterfeit bill bears the loss even though the money may have been accepted in good faith. The passing of money known to be counterfeit is a crime even if the passer received the money innocently.

Unexplained Loss—Mysterious Disappearance Many losses of merchandise in a commercial establishment are discovered only upon taking inventory or making a search for the article. It may be impossible for the owner of the property to determine whether an actual theft occurred or whether the property was lost due to some accidental occurrence. The property may have been thrown out or otherwise unintentionally disposed of, or a sale may have been improperly recorded. A pattern of continued inventory shortage in a commercial operation may indicate poor inventory records, or may be evidence that criminal theft has occurred.

Industrial Espionage Theft is involved in industrial espionage, usually in the form of burglary or embezzlement. The theft may consist of taking documents, ideas, or devices that have been developed. It may be accomplished entirely by outsiders who gain access to the premises, by employees, or by a combination of both.

One form of industrial espionage is the stealing of trade secrets from a manufacturer or research organization. This may be accomplished by burglary of the premises where the information is located, or in many cases, in collusion with employees. An important development by research facilities of a manufacturer or laboratory may have to be kept secret until the development is completed. This may cover a period of years in some cases. The organization may refrain from securing a patent on some new device or drug or other product until the research and development are completed. In the meantime, loss of the information to a competitor may cost the developer an important competitive advantage. Some manufacturers are dishonest enough to pay substantial amounts of money to persons who secure access to such trade secrets. It is alleged that some foreign governments or foreign businesses are eager to take advantage of any information that can be stolen from American developers.

Computer Crime Crimes committed with the aid of computers are on the increase. According to a study in 1976 by the Stanford Research Institute, reported U. S. cases of computer abuse rose from two in 1966 to sixty-six in 1973, the latest year for which figures were available. Losses running into millions of dollars were involved, although no single loss approached the Equity Funding fraud of 1973, in which sixty-three thousand fake insurance policies were produced through company computers.[4]

Computer crime includes cases where the computer may be damaged or destroyed for purposes of revenge or vandalism, or to eliminate information held in the computer. One example involved a discharged computer room employee who cleared all the payroll records from the system before leaving the premises. Sometimes damage to records is accomplished by magnetic devices that impair or destroy magnetic records.

A second form of computer crime is theft of information for industrial espionage such as has been described above. The theft is accomplished by gaining access to the information stored in the computer. This may be done by an employee from within the organization. It also has been accomplished by outsiders securing secret code numbers which instruct the computer to give out information through telephone connections.

A third kind of computer crime consists of securing money, credit, or merchandise, by instructing the computer to issue orders for delivery of such property. Many organizations such as banks, stockbrokers, large distributors, and commercial entities with widespread facilities maintain a number of computer terminals in different locations. Access to these terminals may be accomplished by means of special code numbers and the use of special equipment which can be attached to a telephone, or in some instances, by telephone alone. Orders are given to the computer to transfer a credit to a bank account that has been set up by the criminal. Money is then withdrawn by the criminal from the account into which the credit has been transferred. Some industrial organizations have all of their ordering and delivery procedures on their computer. A person who gains access to this computer may order the delivery of material to a location that has been set up for this purpose. This transaction appears to stockroom personnel to be a normal order for delivery. Then the material may be sold to some other buyer. The buyer may or may not be a party to the theft. Here again, the actual crime is that of theft. The computer merely is used as a device or conduit through which the theft is accomplished.

Embezzlement   Embezzlement is the fraudulent appropriation of property or money by a person to whom the property or money has been entrusted in one way or another. An analysis of embezzlement is presented in the next chapter on employee dishonesty. It is mentioned here in order to complete the list of crimes affecting property, and also to point out that there are cases where collusion may exist between employees and nonemployees in connection with a particular embezzlement.

Other Forms of Crime Against Property   Vandalism is a crime which results in damage or destruction to property. Much vandalism is unrelated to other forms of crime, but it may be committed in connection with extortion or burglary.

A particular form of vandalism that affects many businesses is the damaging of merchandise. The potential thief who fails to find money or valuable merchandise in an appreciable quantity may damage whatever contents are available. Sometimes, the vandals may believe there has been a wrong committed by the person whose property is damaged.

Arson is also a very important crime against property. The Federal Bureau of Investigation estimates that 50 percent of fires of unknown origin result from arson. Arson may be committed by the owner of property for financial gain, it may be for the purpose of revenge against someone for a real or imagined wrong, it may be to cover evidence of other crimes such as burglary, or it may be committed by a person whose object is the thrill of the fire. Some of the fires that were set in mercantile establishments during periods of rioting appear to have been set partly in an effort to destroy records of time payments that were due from people in the neighborhoods.

Losses Resulting from Crimes Against Property

Crimes against property involve much more than loss of the property itself. A firm is also exposed to collateral property losses and indirect and consequential losses.

Loss of the Property Taken The loss of the property which is taken in a crime is the obvious loss. This consists of money or other tangible property in most cases, although industrial espionage may involve the theft of ideas, formulas, or information. Statistics of losses from crime against property ordinarily include only the value of the tangible property taken. These statistics are, therefore, somewhat misleading in determining the true exposure to crime loss.

Collateral Property Losses from Crime There are many cases where, in addition to the value of the property which is taken, there is other property loss resulting from a crime. The breaking and entering by a burglar usually causes some damage to the premises. A frequent type of crime is the smash-and-run theft from show windows. The object of such a theft usually is a high-value item in the show window, but there are many incidents where the value of the smashed window will exceed the value of the property taken.

Safe burglary almost always results in serious damage to the safe. In many cases, the safe is damaged to a degree that prevents its further use for the keeping of valuable property. The building containing the safe and fixtures adjacent to the safe may be damaged if the safe is opened by means of explosives.

Vandalism often accompanies burglary or robbery. Some criminals wish to express their resentment to society or to a business organization by vandalizing the premises in addition to taking property.

A serious type of damage that may accompany burglary is arson perpetrated in an effort to conceal the crime. This may involve only a portion of the premises, contents, or stock, or may ultimately destroy the entire property.

Indirect and Consequential Losses from Crime There can be many indirect and consequential losses from the commission of a crime against property. One of the most important is the loss from disruption of business. A store that handles high-value merchandise such as jewelry may have a substantial portion of its stock taken in a burglary, and may lose sales until the stock can be replenished. The profit that would have been made on the lost sales constitutes an important part of the loss to the business. Depending on the nature of the stock and the length of time required for replacement, a business could lose its entire trade to competitors. Tools or equipment taken may be difficult or impossible to replace, necessitating a cutback or cessation of all or part of a manufacturing or service business.

A burglary or robbery almost always interferes with normal operations. Employees may spend a considerable amount of time in answering the questions of police and in determining the amount and nature of the property taken for purposes of preparing insurance claims.

Loss of business may also result from unfavorable publicity from crime. Repeated robberies during business hours may frighten customers away and discourage employees from working for the business.

The cost of doing business may be increased substantially by the need for crime preventive measures. Guards, burglar alarms, and special locking devices can be expensive. This extra expense must be recognized as a part of the indirect loss from crime.

Another part of the indirect cost of crime to society in general is the closing or abandonment of businesses as a result of specific crimes or the threat of crimes. In some cases, the loss from a burglary or robbery may be sufficient to result in bankruptcy of a business. The killing of a business proprietor generally is considered as a crime against a person rather than a crime against property, but a business may be forced to close because of the proprietor's murder. This is an indirect loss to the community and to the proprietor's family or employees. There are many cases where businesses abandon a neighborhood because of repeated crimes or because of the continuing threat of crime in the neighborhood. Thus, crime may cause a deterioration of property values in a neighborhood and a loss of business revenue and wages. Unemployment in some areas has been accelerated by the exodus of businesses because of repeated crime.

Frequency and Severity of Crime Losses

What are the chances that a person or a firm will suffer a loss from crime in any one year? How much do the chances differ between the city, the suburbs, and the country? This section will explore these and other questions concerning the frequency and severity of crime losses. Automobile crime losses are not discussed here.

Aggregate Crime Losses How important are potential losses from crime in determining the potential success of a business operation? More than $20 billion worth of property is lost to criminals each year.[5] This figure becomes more meaningful when it is realized that mercantile operations in many types of business lose *more* to criminals each year than they make in profits. It is estimated that some mercantile operations lose more than 3 percent of their gross sales due to inventory shortages and from burglary and robbery losses. A store that makes more than 3 percent of its gross sales as a profit is considered to be doing well.

Crime-related losses for food stores are estimated at 1 percent or more of gross sales. The difference between the percentage of losses for food stores and general merchandise stores may be explained by the fact that general merchandise stores carry a greater proportion of merchandise that can be turned into cash by the criminal. Theft of property is seldom related to hunger needs of the thief. Most crime losses are thefts of money, or of merchandise that can be converted to money by sale to a "fence" or to someone else who is willing to buy stolen merchandise at a cheap price. The primary targets of food store thieves, for example, are cigarettes and meat, both of which have a high value-to-weight ratio and are readily saleable. A profit ratio of 2 percent of sales is often quoted as a typical figure for food stores, so that the loss from crime of 1 percent of sales is an important factor in reducing the profits of food stores.

Losses from Specific Perils Crime losses to businesses, and particularly to retail businesses, are the result of a wide range of criminal incidents. Shoplifting is considered the most widespread crime as far as retail merchants are concerned. A retail chain in New York City, for example, closely observed 500 shoppers and found that 42 of the 500 shoppers (or 1 in 12) stole something. Approximately 55,000 shoplifters are apprehended each year in New York City. Other stores throughout the country report comparable losses from shoplifting. One survey indicated that 1 million or more shoplifters are apprehended for theft countrywide in each year.[6]

Worthless checks account for a substantial loss by retail merchants.

One estimate has been that 10 percent of the crime-related losses to business are from bad checks.

Burglary and robbery loss occurrences tend to be more severe than pilferage loss occurrences. Robbery typically is an attempt to steal money, although high-value items such as jewelry also may be taken. Burglary losses to mercantile operations may involve almost any type of property which has a high value-to-weight ratio. This may include men's and women's clothing, as well as jewelry, meat, furs, cosmetics, electronic equipment, and tobacco products. Burglars may steal almost any type of property that may be ordered by a dealer in stolen property, known colloquially as a "fence," who has a ready market for a particular kind of property. It is interesting to note that a large proportion of the burglaries and truck hijackings are committed on order for a particular kind of merchandise or even a particular load of merchandise that is known to be shipped at a particular time.

Geographical Incidence of Crime Losses There is a considerable difference in the rate of crime by location, although the person who lives or works in a rural or suburban area is subject to the city crime rate whenever a visit is made to the city. Geographical variations in crime rates, therefore, are a valid consideration only as to location crimes, such as burglary. The chances of being involved in a crime other than burglary are generally related to the location of a person's daily activities rather than to the person's residence.

The crime rate is considerably higher in larger cities than in suburban and rural areas. According to the Uniform Crime Report issued by the FBI, the rate of crime in relation to population is highest in cities of more than 250,000. Crime in suburban areas is about half the rate in cities of more than 250,000 population. Crimes in rural areas are at the rate of one quarter of that for cities of more than 250,000 population. (Crimes are recorded according to the location of the crime, not the residence of the victim.)

Geographical location of a business is an important factor in determining the probable exposure to a crime loss from burglary. The building of interstate highways has increased the incidence of suburban and rural burglaries. Location near a highway entrance permits a criminal to get away from the scene of the crime and become lost in the stream of traffic on the highway, which greatly lessens the chances of apprehension. This has been particularly true where belt highways have been constructed around a large city.

There also are substantial variations in the crime rates by geographical region and by state. The United States is divided into four regions for statistical purposes in reporting crimes. The lowest rate of crime against property is in the southern states, with intermediate rates in the northeastern and the north central states, and with the highest rate of crime against property in the western states. The incidence of crime within individual states varies even more than the variation by region. The rate of crime against property varies all the way from approximately 2,000 incidents per 100,000 population annually in one state to a high of almost 8,000 incidents per 100,000 population in another state.[7] The average rate of crimes against property in a region, state or locality could be an important consideration in establishing the location for a business operation.

There are factors other than geography that affect the rate of crime in a particular locality. Many of the smaller and medium-sized cities in the United States have a higher crime rate against property on a population basis than those for such large cities as New York or Chicago. The relative effectiveness of law enforcement, the attitude of the courts which hear criminal cases, and the general attitude of the local populace regarding crime prevention and law enforcement affect the incidence and seriousness of crime in different localities.

Crime Losses by Size of Company In relation to their assets, small businesses suffer more from crime against property than large businesses. Retailers suffer more than any other segment of business, and losses in the retailing sector are a quarter of all the business losses from crime. The service businesses are next in size, and a large proportion of these are also small businesses. The manufacturing and wholesale sectors suffer from property crime to only half the extent suffered by retailing and servicing businesses.

The index of losses from crime in relation to the gross receipts of the businesses shows an even more startling effect on the small business. This index shows that the rate of crime against businesses with less than $100,000 of gross receipts is three times the rate of loss for all businesses in the United States.[8] The loss from crime for businesses with gross receipts from $1 million to $5 million annually is only one-third of the loss for the small businesses. The incidence of crime against businesses having gross receipts of more than $5 million annually actually is negligible. Thus, small businesses suffer an impact from crime losses of more than three times the average, and thirty-five times that of businesses with receipts of more than $5 million. It is an unfortunate fact that the small businesses which are hit most often by crime are also often the ones that are least able to afford protective measures or to absorb the losses as a business expense.

There are two important reasons why the impact of crime is greater against the small business than the large ones. First, small business consists principally of retailers and the service operations which are accessible to the public. The criminal has access to the premises in the guise of a customer. Manufacturers and the wholesalers, in contrast, ordinarily do not permit access by the public to their business premises. Security measures are more easily established to prevent access by strangers who may have criminal intent. The second factor is that a small business usually suffers a greater loss in relation to its total assets than a large firm. A manufacturer or wholesaler, on the average, would have a larger stock of merchandise and greater general assets in relation to the amount that could be taken in a burglary or robbery. Thus the financial impact is likely to be greater on the small business than on the large business.

Evaluating the Impact of Crime Losses

Estimating Loss Potentials Frequency and probable severity must both be taken into account in estimating the probable loss from crime. An individual must consider the possibility of loss as a result of a particular lifestyle. The business firm must take into account the factors that affect the probability and possibility of loss.

Money is the objective of a large proportion of robbers and burglars. Accessibility of the money to a criminal and the amount of money available are the two most important factors in determining whether a crime will be committed in an effort to get the money. As pointed out previously, the criminal determines in advance the probable success of the criminal act. Keeping cash on hand to a minimum is a deterrent. For example, a high proportion of robberies in supermarkets occurs near the end of a busy period when large amounts of cash are in the registers. Frequent collections of the cash from the registers and frequent deposits of cash in banks will serve as a deterrent to robbers.

Frequent deposits also reduce the amount of cash that is in the hands of messengers on their way to a bank. A variation of the time of day for deposits and a variation in the route of the messenger also will reduce the probability of loss from robbery of a messenger. The individual who has occasion to make large purchases will reduce the probable loss from robbery by using credit cards or travelers checks to reduce the necessity for carrying large amounts of cash.

Since loss of merchandise by burglary or robbery is related to the value of the property in comparison to the weight or volume, loss potential is increased when there is a concentration of high value, low bulk items. A men's clothing store, for example, may be vulnerable if the burglars are able to remove all of the high-value clothing from one section of the store because it is easily accessible.

The hijacking of a truckload of merchandise occurs most frequently when the truck is loaded with a valuable cargo of especially marketable merchandise. A truckload of cigarettes or of furs, for example, is more likely to be hijacked than a load of general merchandise which includes items of less value per unit.

The loss potential faced by an individual or merchant depends primarily upon the amount of value that is accessible to the burglar or robber. Accessibility of the property to the criminal determines to a large extent the probability that a crime loss will occur. These factors must be evaluated by the property owner in estimating the probable impact of the crime.

Impact of Crime on Financial Stability As has already been pointed out, the impact of crime is greater on small firms than on large ones. This greater impact on small business results not only from a greater chance that a crime will occur to a small business because of greater accessibility but also from a greater impact on the financial condition of the small business. A retail operation that has a gross income of about $100,000 annually may have a net profit of less than $10,000 a year. A crime loss of several thousand dollars could wipe out the entire profit for the year and may actually make future business operations unprofitable. The potential effect of a crime on a business may be evaluated by comparing the probable loss from a burglary or robbery to the working capital of the firm. A loss from crime that equals or exceeds the working capital may actually throw the operation into bankruptcy.

The business person, in trying to estimate the probable effect of crime, must evaluate not only the probable severity of a crime but also the probable frequency in relation to the particular business and the neighborhood. A high frequency of crime in the neighborhood should impel the institution of measures to reduce the probable frequency and severity. Reduction in the value situated in one location and reduction of the accessibility to valuable property are measures that need to be taken in order to reduce the probable impact of crime on the business operation.

CLASSIFICATION OF CRIME COVERAGES

As one might expect from the many types of crime loss described, crime insurance takes many forms. While some crime insurance forms are quite broad, it has not proved practical to insure all crime loss under a single insuring agreement.

There are two primary reasons for providing different policies to cover different kinds of crime. First, few business firms would want to insure against every kind of crime. A broad policy covering the full spectrum of crime losses would be prohibitively expensive. Also, some crime losses, such as shoplifting, are likely to be relatively constant and predictable, and are best handled as a normal cost of doing business. In addition, it frequently is difficult to be sure that a particular loss resulted from crime. As mentioned earlier, an inventory shortage could be the result of crime, but it also could result from a wide variety of innocent errors, some of them involving no actual loss at all to the firm.

In spite of the wide variety of coverages, crime policies can be divided into a relatively small number of categories. The paragraphs that follow will discuss the nature of the categories and the reasons for classification.

Purposes of Classification

The classification of crime coverages is important for two reasons. Classification will serve an educational purpose in facilitating the understanding of the coverages provided under the various policies, and it will assist risk managers in identifying crime exposures and designing programs to cope with those exposures.

Risk Management An important function of risk management is to determine the probable exposures to loss and then to match the available insurance coverages to these exposures. The risk manager must determine whether the probable exposure is from burglary, robbery, or from one of the more indefinite types of criminal act, such as shoplifting. The available insurance coverages can then be matched to these exposures, the cost compared with the probable severity and frequency of loss, and a determination made as to whether insurance should be purchased or whether the losses can be absorbed as a business expense. A classification of crime insurance coverages is helpful to the risk manager in determining what protection is available and whether it is worthwhile in the individual circumstance.

Education The classification of crime insurance coverages into groups will help one to understand what protection is available. There is a wide variety of crime insurance policies, and there are many overlapping provisions between different policies. In so far as possible, these coverages will be related to one another in such a way that some order will be brought out of what otherwise might appear to be a somewhat chaotic group of insurance policies.

Types of Crime Policies

A rough classification of crime insurance policies can be made according to: (1) the perils covered by the policies; (2) the property covered; (3) whether coverage is provided merely for the insured's property or also extends to property of customers; and (4) a grouping according to the relationship of the criminal to the insured: that is, whether the criminal is an outsider who is totally unrelated to the insured or an employee or other person in a position of trust. Many combinations of these circumstances are covered by the policies, so that classifications are general and, in many cases, overlapping.

Perils Covered Burglary and robbery are two identifiable perils for which coverage is provided by many crime insurance policies. However, the coverage may be limited to specified situations. The safe burglary policy, for example, covers only the breaking and entering of a safe. This policy does not provide any coverage for the peril of robbery. A paymaster robbery policy, on the other hand, covers only loss of payroll funds by robbery. It does not provide any burglary coverage and only very limited robbery coverage for property other than payrolls. Other policies provide combinations of coverages. Some of the broader forms combine coverage for burglary, robbery, and for theft or larceny under certain conditions. A few policies that are classified as crime policies provide "all-risks" coverage, including crime perils, for some classes of property, such as money and securities. It is generally true of crime insurance policies, however, that the crime must be identifiable as such in order for coverage to apply. Most policies, even the very broad forms, exclude loss which is discovered by an inventory computation, or any other disappearance for which there is no evidence that a crime has been committed.

Property Covered Insurance policies also may be classified broadly as to coverage against loss of money and securities and coverage against loss of merchandise. Some policies, such as the safe burglary policy, may be written to cover highly valued merchandise, such as jewelry, as well as money. A policy may cover theft of money and securities as well as theft of merchandise, but such coverage probably would be provided by two separate sections in the policy, one applying to money and securities and the other applying to merchandise.

Policies Extending Coverage to Customers Some crime insurance policies do cover the property of customers as well as the property of the insured. Such coverage generally would be limited to property that has been placed in the custody of the merchant for sale or repair. This is comparable in some respects to the bailees' customers' coverage that is written as inland marine insurance for laundries and dry cleaners. However, the principal objective of crime insurance policies is to provide coverage for the property of the insured.

Relation of Criminal to Insured Crime insurance policies also may be categorized according to the broad classifications of employee dishonesty and other crime, as previously described. Employee dishonesty will be discussed in Chapter 12.

INSURANCE DESIGNED PRIMARILY FOR LOSS OF MONEY AND SECURITIES

The following sections describe the more commonly used insurance policies. Combinations or variations of these policies are used by different insurance companies to meet their marketing requirements or to provide coverage for special exposures of their policyholders. The definitions may vary in detail from those described here, but it is characteristic of crime insurance policies that terms are defined in the policies rather than placing dependence on the common law or statutory definitions of particular crimes or situations.

Mercantile Robbery Policy

This policy is popularly known as an "inside and outside holdup" insurance policy. It is called a mercantile policy, but it can be written for any kind of business. The policy can be written to cover robbery inside the premises, robbery outside the premises, or both. Coverage applies to loss of money, securities, and other property. There is no limitation on the kind of property other than money and securities, so that loss of mercantile stocks would be covered. However, most robbery losses involve money or securities rather than merchandise.

Money is defined as: (1) currency, coins, bank notes, and bullion; and (2) travelers checks, registered checks, and money orders held for sale to the public. Securities are defined as all negotiable and nonnegotiable instruments or contracts representing either money or other property, including revenue and other stamps in current use, tokens and tickets, other than money.

The policy definition of robbery is rather lengthy. The definition, summarized here, is typical of the definitions of robbery found in crime insurance policies. Robbery means the taking of insured property by violence inflicted upon a messenger or custodian, by putting him or her in fear of violence; by any other overt felonious act committed in the presence of a messenger or custodian and of which he or she was actually cognizant, provided such other act is not committed by an officer, partner, or employee of the insured. Coverage also applies to the taking of property from a person who has been killed or rendered unconscious and to loss within the premises by means of compelling a messenger or custodian by violence or threat of violence while outside the premises to admit a person into the premises or to furnish the means of ingress into the premises. Coverage also applies to the taking of property from a showcase or show window within the premises while regularly opened for business by a person who has broken the glass thereof from outside the premises.

This definition may differ in minor details from the common law or statutory definition of robbery. This is considered necessary in order to specify the exact extent of the coverage that is provided. Also, it is necessary in order to provide uniform coverage in all states, since the statutory or common law definition may vary from state to state. For example, theft from a show window by means of breaking the glass and grabbing the property would ordinarily be closer to a burglary loss than a robbery loss under statutory definitions of burglary and robbery. However, insurers are willing to provide the show window coverage as part of the mercantile robbery insurance, so the definition is made accordingly.

Coverage is also divided between robbery that occurs inside the premises and robbery that occurs outside the premises. Provision is made for covering either or both of these circumstances. Premises is defined as the interior of that portion of any building at a location designated in the policy which is occupied by the insured in conducting the business as stated therein. A tenant in a multiple occupancy building, therefore, would be protected against robbery inside the premises only if the robbery occurred within that portion of the building which the insured occupies.

Robbery outside the premises applies to loss of money, securities, and other property by robbery or attempt thereat outside the insured's premises while the property is being conveyed by a messenger. It should be noted that the coverage does not apply if the property is not being conveyed by a messenger at the time of the loss. A messenger is defined as the insured, a partner or an officer of the insured, or any employee who is in the regular service of and duly authorized by the insured to have the care and custody of the property outside the premises.

It should be noted that robbery is defined to include violence inflicted upon or threatened to a messenger or a custodian. The definitions of messenger and custodian in the policy are so worded that they exclude a watchman, porter, or janitor. Therefore, theft from a watchman, porter, or janitor would not be a robbery under the terms of the policy unless the policy had been endorsed to include them within the definition of messenger or custodian. There could be a fine line of distinction as to whether the person involved in the robbery is actually a custodian or whether his or her duties were merely that of watchman, porter, or janitor. This would be a question of fact that would have to be determined in case of questionable circumstances.

A policy also may be written with a requirement that a guard accompany a messenger when outside of the premises. This would be likely in a case where large values are carried frequently on behalf of the insured outside the premises. A guard is defined in the policy as "any male person not less than seventeen nor more than sixty-five years of age who accompanies a messenger by direction of the insured but who is not a driver of a public conveyance." A taxi driver, for example, would be excluded by this definition of a guard.

There is an extension of coverage to pay for damage to premises by robbery or attempted robbery if the insured is the owner of the premises or is liable for damage. Several other extensions of coverage are available, depending upon the rates to be paid. Coverage may be extended so that a watchman, porter, or janitor would be considered a custodian. Coverage also may be extended to the home of a custodian in cases where it is necessary or desirable for the custodian to take the money home overnight or for some other period en route to deposit it.

Credits are allowed for certain protective features, such as alarm systems, or for limitation of the coverage to apply to securities only, excluding money. It is an interesting feature of the rating system for this and some other crime insurance policies that absence of a protective feature for which a rate credit is given does not void the coverage. The amount payable by the insurance company for loss occurring during the absence of such protective devices usually is reduced in proportion to the rate credit which was given for the protective feature.

Mercantile Safe Burglary Policy

Insurance against safe burglary may be written under a separate policy, but it frequently is included under a separate insuring clause in the mercantile robbery policy just described. The hazards of safe burglary are different from the hazards of robbery, and different rates and conditions apply.

Safe burglary is defined as:

> ... the felonious abstraction of insured property from within a vault or safe described in the policy and located within the premises by a person making felonious entry into such vault or such safe and any vault containing the safe, when all doors thereof are duly closed and

locked by all combination locks thereon, provided such entrance shall be made by actual force and violence of which force and violence there are visible marks made by tools, explosives, electricity, or chemicals upon the exterior of all said doors of such vault or such safe and any vault containing the safe, if entry is made through such doors or the top, bottom or walls of such vault or such safe and any vault containing the safe through which entry is made if not made through such doors, or the felonious abstraction of such safe from within the premises.

This definition of safe burglary means, in brief, that the safe or the vault must be broken into and that there must be physical evidence of the break in. There is no coverage if entry is accomplished by manipulation of the combination or if the safe or vault is left unlocked or partially unlocked. However, the complete removal of the safe from the premises is covered.

It should also be noted that the definition does not require forcible entry into the premises; it merely requires that there be a breaking and entering of the safe or vault. The burglar may have hidden within the premises, or might be able to enter the premises without any evident force or violence, but that does not affect the coverage as long as there is a violent entry into the safe or vault itself.

This policy, like the mercantile robbery policy, also covers damage to property, including the premises, by such safe burglary or attempted safe burglary. This would include damage to the safe or vault, stock, furniture and fixtures and to the building if the insured is the owner of the building or is legally responsible for such damage.

The mercantile safe burglary policy is an appropriate coverage for businesses that have valuable stock as well as for the coverage for money and securities. This would apply to manufacturers with substantial values of precious metals or for a druggist who keeps narcotics in a safe. It is likely that those in the jewelry trade would have a jewelers' block policy because of its broad coverage for all phases of the business, but a mercantile safe burglary policy could be written for a jeweler or a manufacturing jeweler if the only coverage desired was that applying to safe burglary.

Many insurance companies use a combination mercantile robbery and safe burglary policy, with appropriate space to indicate which coverages are to be provided. This saves the expense of preparing more than one policy form and also permits a combination of coverages where the insured desires both robbery and burglary coverage.

Money and Securities Broad Form Policy

This policy provides broader coverage on money and securities than is provided by the mercantile robbery and safe burglary policy. Like the mercantile robbery and safe burglary policies, there are separate insuring agreements applying to losses inside the premises and to losses outside the premises. Insurance may be purchased under either one or both of these insuring agreements.

Coverage applying to loss of money and securities within the premises includes loss from actual destruction, disappearance or wrongful abstraction from within the premises or from within any banking premises or similar recognized places of safe deposit. This means that any destruction, disappearance or wrongful taking of money and securities from within the premises or banking premises is covered even though there is no actual burglary or robbery responsible for the destruction or disappearance. Thus, the policy provides "all-risks" coverage on money and securities. A classic example of the breadth of this coverage is the stack of money blown out an open window by a gust of wind.

Loss of property other than money or securities from within the premises is restricted to loss by safe burglary or by robbery within the premises or attempts thereat, or from within a locked cash drawer, cash box, or cash register by felonious entry into such container within the premises or attempt thereat. Destruction or disappearance of property other than money or securities is not covered. The policy also covers damage to the premises only if caused by safe burglary, robbery, or felonious abstraction, similar to the coverage of the mercantile robbery and safe burglary policies.

The coverage outside of premises applies to loss of money and securities by actual destruction, disappearance, or wrongful abstraction outside the premises while being conveyed by a messenger or any armored motor vehicle company or while within the living quarters in the home of any messenger. Loss of property other than money and securities is covered only for robbery or an attempt thereat outside the premises while conveyed by a messenger or any armored motor vehicle company or by theft from within the living quarters in the home of any messenger. Here again, it will be seen that coverage for loss of money and securities is extremely broad, but loss of property other than money and securities is restricted to robbery, or to theft if it occurs within the living quarters of a messenger. This policy does not provide adequate coverage for loss of mercantile stock.

The exclusions and limitations further limit the application of this policy in several important respects. There is no coverage of manuscripts, books of account or records. There is no coverage for loss due to giving or surrendering money or securities in any exchange or purchase or of accounting errors or omissions. Thus, a fraudulent transaction involving the sale or surrendering of money or securities would not be covered. Neither is there any coverage for a fraudulent, dishonest, or criminal act on the part of any insured, partner, officer, or employee.

It is interesting to note also that special limitations apply to destruction by fire of property other than money or securities. The exclusion is so worded as to provide coverage for loss or damage to money or securities by fire but not for the destruction of any other property by fire. It is expected that an insured would have fire insurance coverage applying to loss of mercantile stocks from fire.

The coverage of this policy may be summarized by pointing out that it provides the coverage of the mercantile robbery and mercantile safe burglary policies, plus a broad form of coverage for destruction, disappearance or wrongful abstraction of money and securities. The coverage on property other than money and securities is essentially the same as that of the mercantile robbery and the mercantile safe burglary policies.

Paymaster Robbery Policy

This policy is intended to provide a special type of robbery coverage for payroll funds either inside or outside the insured premises. The limited form of the policy covers loss from robbery of the payroll from a custodian and kidnapping, which includes the stealing of the payroll from within the premises by compelling a custodian to admit the thief to the premises. There is also coverage of robbery from employees on the day on which they are paid provided that at the same time there is a robbery or attempted robbery from a custodian. A broader form is written to cover payroll funds against actual destruction, disappearance, or wrongful abstraction. Definitions of robbery, of money and securities, and of the premises are all similar to those which have been described for other policies.

The policy is written to cover the amount that might be lost in a payroll robbery. There is also coverage for other money and securities up to 10 percent of the policy amount provided the other money or securities are taken in connection with a payroll robbery.

Coverage may be limited to the insured's premises if the payroll funds are brought to the premises in the custody of an outside messenger service so that the insured would not lose if a robbery occurred before the funds reached the insured premises. Sometimes a bank makes up a payroll under circumstances where the insured would sustain a loss from a bank robbery of such payroll funds. A policy may be written to include the bank premises under those circumstances.

Safe Deposit Box Policies

Banks and other organizations may maintain safe depository boxes for the use of their customers. Several policies are available to cover crime losses to property stored in such boxes.

Combination Safe Depository Policy Policies written to cover a bank or other operator of a safe depository may cover merely the legal liability of the bank, or they may be written to cover the interests of customers regardless of the bank's liability. A policy which covers only the liability of the depository usually is written as a broad form of coverage applying to all sums which the insured depository operator becomes legally obligated to pay by reason of liability for loss of customers' property. There are few exclusions usually applying only to wear and tear, damage by fire, loss of property due to a fraudulent, dishonest, or criminal act by an insured or partner, nuclear energy or war damage.

Spectacular losses from safe depositories have occurred from time to time. Coverage of the depository's liability is similar to that of a warehousemen's legal liability coverage and liability occurs only if negligence on the part of the depository can be proved.

A policy also may be written to cover the interests of customers. This is a bailees' customers type of insurance similar to that which would be provided for a furrier under an inland marine policy. The perils covered usually are more restricted than those in a policy covering the insured's liability only. Coverage is restricted to loss from burglary or robbery or attempt thereat, or for damage to or destruction of customers' property from burglary or robbery or attempt thereat. Burglary and robbery are defined in terms similar to those which have already been described for other policies, with specific reference to felonious abstraction of customers' property from within a safe deposit box.

Safe Deposit Box Burglary and Robbery Policy (Individuals) This policy is written to cover the renter of a safe deposit box deposit box against loss from burglary or robbery. It applies to all property except money. There are practical underwriting reasons why insurance companies ordinarily do not find it feasible to provide safe deposit box coverage against loss of money. There would be the difficulty of proving the amount of money that had been stolen. This might be complicated further by the possibility that money in a safe deposit box has been placed there for questionable purposes, such as the evasion of taxes. Money held for lawful purposes is usually invested. The property covered, therefore, includes any type of property other than money that might be placed in the box, such as securities, jewelry, or other valuable articles. The property covered may include that held in trust or for safekeeping by the insured, or property held by the insured as a bailee or in any capacity which would make the insured liable to the owner for a loss.

Perils covered are limited to a burglary and robbery. The definitions of those terms are similar to those already described.

Policies of this nature may be issued to public officials who have securities of other persons or organizations in their custody. These policies are examples of burglary and robbery insurance policies which are written to cover special circumstances. Coverage and restrictions follow the definitions that have already been described for other burglary and robbery policies.

Hotel Safe Deposit Box Legal Liability Policy   Many hotels have a safe deposit section in which guests may deposit their valuables. The hotel may be liable for loss from the safe deposit box if the owner can prove negligence on the part of the hotel. The purpose of this policy is to cover the legal liability of the hotel for loss of property. The most likely occurrence is that of burglary or robbery but the policy is written to cover most losses that could occur to property in the hotel's safe deposit section. The policy is similar in its intent and effect to the safe deposit liability policy that would be written for a bank.

Innkeepers' Liability Insurance

The innkeepers' liability policy must be distinguished from the hotel safe deposit box legal liability coverage just described. The purpose of the innkeepers' liability policy is to protect the innkeeper or hotel operator from legal liability for damages to property belonging to guests while such property is within the hotel premises or in the possession or custody of the hotel. The probability of an innkeeper being liable for damage to a customer's property is largely related to crime, but there are many other circumstances under which the hotel might be liable for damage. The insuring agreement obligates the insurance company to pay on behalf of the insured all sums for which the insured becomes legally liable for damages because of injury, destruction or loss of property belonging to a guest at the premises while the property is on the premises or in the custody of the insured. There is no coverage of the customer's interest if the hotel is not liable for the damage.

An exclusion applies to any liability that is assumed under contract by the insured. There may be provision for a limited amount of coverage up to a specified dollar amount if there is a written agreement between the owner and the hotel operator prior to a loss. A deductible of some nominal amount usually applies; it usually is less than $100. Certain types of loss are excluded, such as loss from the spilling or upsetting of food or beverage, damage to a vehicle, or property in the custody of the insured for laundering or cleaning.

It should be pointed out that many of an innkeeper's liabilities may be covered under various forms of policies. A checkroom liability policy, for example, may be issued as an inland marine coverage to cover the liability for loss of hats and coats which may be checked in the hotel checkroom or the dining room checkroom. The inland marine policy may be of a bailees' customers type, or it may be issued as a liability coverage, covering only the liability of the insured and providing no coverage for the owner of the property. One of the troublesome questions in connection with innkeepers' liability is loss due to delivery of property to the wrong person. Many policies exclude such losses because they generally result from carelessness on the part of the insured's employees, and underwriters tend to regard such loss as uninsurable.

Office Burglary and Robbery Policy

This is another variation of a burglary and robbery policy that is designed to meet the needs of a particular market. Coverage applies to: (1) robbery inside the premises, including kidnapping for the purposes of robbery; (2) theft inside the premises, applying to loss of office equipment by theft; (3) safe burglary, with a possible expansion to cover loss of money for a limited amount; (4) robbery outside the premises; (5) theft from a night depository or residence of a messenger; and (6) damage to premises in the actual or attempted robbery, theft, safe burglary, or burglary. Coverage applies to property owned by the insured and property held by the insured for others.

The intent of this policy is to cover loss of property from burglary or robbery. The most likely objective of such burglary or robbery would be money and securities and office equipment. It does not cover loss of merchandise.

Theft coverage inside the premises ordinarily does not apply during a fire on the premises. Neither does the coverage from a night depository or residence apply during a fire within the night depository or to a loss within the living quarters of the messenger during a fire there.

The policy is divided into the six sections listed above, and a $250 basic limit ordinarily applies to the coverage under each of these insuring agreements. The $250 amount may be increased for an additional premium. Coverage may be purchased under one or more of the various sections.

The policy is written for office occupancies. This would include doctors and dentists and other professional people, as well as commercial offices. Coverage may be provided for loss of precious metals and other materials used by dentists.

This policy provides a flexible type of insurance coverage for a limited exposure. Most offices do not have large amounts of money or securities. However, loss of electrical or electronic office equipment can be substantial. The flexibility of the policy and the division into several sections lends itself to providing exactly the coverage which the insured wants for the particular situation.

Storekeepers' Burglary and Robbery Policy

This policy provides essentially burglary and robbery coverage for mercantile insureds. It is designed primarily for small stores whose needs are for a limited dollar coverage for the various types of loss that may occur from robbery and burglary. There are seven insuring agreements or divisions with a basic limit of liability of $250 for each of the seven sections. This limit may be increased for the payment of an extra premium to a maximum limit of $1,000 per insuring agreement. The sections covering robbery inside the premises and robbery outside the premises have definitions and limitations similar to those which have already been described for robbery coverage. The kidnapping section is essentially an expansion of the robbery coverage and also applies to loss of money, securities, merchandise, furniture, fixtures, and equipment from within the premises as a result of kidnapping of a messenger or custodian.

Other sections cover safe burglary and premises burglary, theft from a night depository or residence, burglary or robbery of a watchman, and damage to premises and equipment. There is a limited coverage for the taking of merchandise by burglary or by the robbery of a watchman, in contrast to the other burglary and robbery policies, most of which do not provide burglary coverage for stocks of merchandise. It is considered feasible to provide this limited coverage of burglary because the amount of insurance under each section is limited. The policy usually limits the amount applying to any one article of jewelry to $50, in addition to the limit of $250 per section (up to a maximum of $1,000 per section if the limit is amended).

Broad Form Storekeepers' Policy This policy is an expansion of the storekeepers' policy to include certain employee dishonesty coverages, and coverage for destruction of money and securities.

This broad form policy also has coverage for loss of merchandise, furniture, fixtures, and equipment by burglary or by robbery of a watchman. This is comparable to the previously described storekeepers' policy coverage. There is an additional coverage for loss due to the acceptance of money orders and counterfeit paper currency. This policy is in effect a somewhat limited form of a 3-D policy which will be described in the next chapter.

Coverage for Forgery and Counterfeit Money

The loss from forgery of checks and other orders for payment traditionally has been insured under bonds rather than under insurance policies. However, the loss from the forgery of such an instrument used in commerce is really a form of theft by deception. Forgery coverage may be secured under individual policies or it may be provided under the comprehensive dishonesty, disappearance and destruction policy (3-D policy). The separate forgery policies may be written either in the form of a bond or as an insurance policy.

Insurance against forgery may be provided to a business organization, an individual, a bank, or a security organization. Forgery insurance protects against loss resulting from the forging of checks, drafts, and other instruments which the insured has issued or is purported to have issued. Loss resulting from the acceptance of forged checks may be covered for an additional premium. A policy issued to a bank may protect against forgery losses resulting from withdrawals from accounts by means of forged instruments. Credit card coverage is essentially a form of forgery insurance. Another form of loss resulting from forgery might be from the lending of money on forged or counterfeit securities that are presented as security for the loan.

Counterfeit Coverage A business organization that handles large amounts of cash or money orders may find it advisable to purchase specific insurance against loss resulting from the acceptance of counterfeit money or documents.

Limited Policies for Special Purposes

Church Theft Policy An example of a limited policy to meet a special need is that of the church theft policy. This covers the loss of money, securities, and other property by theft or attempted theft and also covers damage to the interior of a structure to which the coverage applies. It should be noted that this does not cover damage to the exterior of the structure. Such coverage to the exterior would more properly be provided by means of vandalism and malicious mischief coverage under a fire insurance policy.

This church theft policy is broad in its coverage as far as the perils are concerned because it covers loss from theft or attempted theft. The policy as ordinarily issued does not require that the theft result from burglary or robbery, but merely that the act of theft and the resulting loss be provable.

Public Entrances Theft Coverage Many apartment buildings or other public buildings, such as offices and waiting rooms, have expensive furniture, carpets, and other equipment. There may be times during which the lobbies of such buildings are not under observation by employees or security personnel. Many such buildings find it advisable to buy insurance against theft or attempted theft of such furnishings, and damage due to attempted theft. Coverage may be limited to loss from burglary, or coverage may be provided against any theft of the property.

Many other special forms are available in order to meet the exposures of business organizations to the crimes of burglary, robbery, and theft. The policies described in this section are intended primarily for protection against loss of money, securities, and equipment. Policies covering loss of merchandise are discussed in the next section of this chapter.

INSURANCE AGAINST LOSS OF MERCHANDISE

Many stocks of merchandise have a high value to weight and volume ratio so that goods can be stolen and converted into cash with relative ease. There is some theft exposure in connection with the manufacture, storage and sale of all merchandise, but the probability of theft is higher with valuable types of merchandise. The principal exposure to loss is from burglary. The relative bulk of merchandise, as compared to money or securities, reduces the probability of robbery. Therefore, insurance underwriters have developed a type of insurance coverage to cover the merchant's exposure to burglary losses. Robbery loss to merchandise and other property is covered under the robbery policies already discussed.

Mercantile Open Stock Burglary Policy

The mercantile open stock burglary policy obligates the insurer to pay the insured for loss of merchandise, furniture, fixtures, and equipment, occasioned by burglary, or by robbery of a watchman, when the premises are not open for business. Burglary is defined in terms similar to those already described in connection with insurance for burglary losses of money and securities. That is, the definition requires forcible entry into or exit from the premises, with signs of force at the point of entry or exit.

Robbery of a watchman is defined as the taking of insured property by violence or the threat of violence inflicted upon a private watchman employed exclusively by the insured and while such watchman is on duty within the premises. The coverage very clearly is limited to times when the premises are closed for business. The insurance company also agrees to pay for damage to property within the premises which is caused by such burglary or robbery of a watchman or attempt thereat, and for damage to the premises if the insured is the owner or is liable for such damage.

The policy covers merchandise owned by the insured and also any other merchandise held by the insured. This coverage applies regardless of whether or not the insured is legally liable for it. Thus the coverage actually is effective for the benefit of customers of the insured and for suppliers who may have sent goods to the insured on consignment or for approval.

The mercantile open stock burglary policy is designed for ordinary merchandise such as food, clothing, and the general merchandise which might be handled by a retail store. There ordinarily is a limit of $50 applying to any one article of jewelry. This is intended to cover loss of costume jewelry, but the policy is not designed to cover gems and precious metals. It is possible to cover jewelry under the policy, but the premium ordinarily would be higher than for a jewelers' block policy providing comparable coverage.

There is a provision applying to property on which money has been loaned. A pawnbroker, for example, might find this a suitable policy to cover merchandise on which loans have been made, provided that the pawnbroker's principal property subject to pledges does not consist of valuable jewelry.

Limitations apply to certain types of property or certain types of loss. There is no coverage for manuscripts, books of account or records. Neither is there coverage for furs or articles of fur which are stolen by the breaking of a show window from outside the premises. There is no coverage for damage by vandalism or malicious mischief. Neither is there coverage of loss by fire. The objective is to provide coverage on ordinary merchandise which may be stolen from the insured.

Coinsurance The coinsurance principle which applies to the mercantile open stock burglary policy is the same as other coinsurance but the application is different. The percentage of coinsurance which is required for this policy varies by territory. This territorial variation is considered justifiable because large burglary losses are less likely in some areas than in others.

Another important feature of the coinsurance provisions is a maximum amount of insurance which always complies with the coinsurance requirement for that particular business even though the amount might not comply with the percentage requirement. The coinsurance percentage requirement varies from 40 percent to 80 percent in different territories. However, the coinsurance limit (the maximum amount of insurance which always meets the coinsurance requirement) varies according to the particular kind of merchandise.

The application of this coinsurance provision can best be illustrated by an example. Assume that the coinsurance percentage requirement in a particular territory is 80 percent. However, for a millinery store the coinsurance limit is $10,000, regardless of the coinsurance percentage. If the actual cash value of the merchandise is also $10,000, the amount of insurance required to meet the coinsurance requirement is $8,000. This is the same amount of insurance that would be required to comply with an 80 percent coinsurance clause in a fire policy. For a somewhat larger millinery store, with stock having an actual cash value of $20,000, the 80 percent coinsurance clause would require that the insured carry $16,000 of insurance. However, because of the coinsurance limit, $10,000 is the maximum that would be required to meet the coinsurance requirement no matter how high the value might be. The insured might wish to carry insurance to the full value of the covered property in order to be fully protected, but only $10,000 of insurance would be necessary in order to meet the coinsurance requirement. This idea of setting a maximum amount of insurance which will always meet the coinsurance requirement regardless of percentage is based upon the theory that a burglar is not likely to carry off more than the specified amount. In the example given, it is considered unlikely that more than $10,000 worth of millinery merchandise would be stolen in any one burglary. Thus, the amount would vary according to the type of merchandise and what the underwriters consider to be the maximum amount subject to loss in a single burglary occurrence.

Theft Coverage of Merchandise Theft insurance on merchandise may be added to a mercantile open stock burglary policy for a substantial additional premium. This coverage normally is subject to a deductible of $50 for retail stores. Theft coverage does not include theft by employees, nor mere disappearance nor shortage disclosed by inventory. There must be an actual incident which is clearly caused by theft. Shoplifting losses would be covered, subject to any deductible, provided the incident is identifiable.

Another interesting variation is coverage for loss involving forcible exit. The definition of burglary is such that there must be a breaking and entering in order for the loss to be considered as having resulted from burglary. Sometimes a thief will hide within the premises during business hours and then break out with the stolen merchandise. Such an occurrence would be covered only if the policy makes specific provision to cover that particular situation.

Use of the mercantile open stock burglary policy has been reduced to some extent by the increased use of "all-risks" types of insurance. The "all-risks" policies usually are written as combinations of property loss insurance. The burglary and theft aspects of such policies will be considered separately.

"ALL-RISKS" COVERAGE
OF BUSINESS PERSONAL PROPERTY

The coverage of property against all risks of loss and damage includes coverage against loss from crime. The expansion of the "all-risks" concept of insurance to mercantile property was a fairly late development among insurance policies. The concept of an "all-risks" type of insurance for personal property of individuals goes back to the early days of the personal property floater during the 1920s. The jewelers' block policy had been written as an "all-risks" coverage since its inception during the early part of this century. However, these were considered to be inland marine insurance. "All-risks" coverage for general mercantile property did not develop until much later.

There are several policies available to provide "all-risks" coverage for business personal property. These include the special multi-peril policy in its special personal property form, the businessowners policy, which is designed for small business operations, and several similar policies that have been developed by individual insurers. These policies all provide a degree of protection against losses from crime as a part of the broad coverage against loss or damage to business personal property. No attempt is made here to analyze the coverage of these individual policies. They are discussed in detail in Chapters 14 and 15.

Property Subject to Limitation or Exclusion

The coverage of the broad commercial insurance policies is "against all risks of direct physical loss" to business personal property such as may be described by the individual policy. Without modification, this would include every fortuitous loss. It is recognized in the drafting of insurance policies for general commercial property that certain types of property are especially susceptible to loss from crime. Therefore, limitations and exclusions apply to certain of these properties as far as losses from crime are concerned.

A typical "all-risks" policy limits loss of furs and fur garments to an aggregate of $1,000 in any one occurrence. The limitation applying to jewelry, watches, precious and semi-precious stones, and precious metals may also be $1,000 in any one occurrence. In addition, there may be a limitation applying to jewelry and watches of $25 per item. The objective of these limitations is to provide coverage for ordinary merchandise, such as costume jewelry of low value or garments that may have some fur parts, but to exclude garments that are entirely of fur or whose principal value consists of fur, and to exclude jewelry and watches of any considerable value. Coverage on patterns and dies, molds, models, and forms may be limited to $1,000 or some similar figure.

Some of the property for which the amount of insurance is limited as far as the "all-risks" coverage is concerned may be covered under the policy for specified perils, which usually do not include crime. The specified perils in one policy are fire, lightning, aircraft, explosion, riot, civil commotion, smoke, vehicles, windstorm or hail, vandalism and malicious mischief, and leakage from automatic fire protective systems. These, of course, are not usually related to crime, and are not affected by limitations applying to losses from crime.

Many of the policies also exclude entirely from coverage such articles as currency, money, stamps, bullion, notes, securities, deeds, accounts, bills, evidences of debt, letters of credit and tickets. Here again, the objective is to exclude from the crime coverage of the "all-risks" insurance those articles which by their nature are peculiarly subject to crime losses. These articles which are especially susceptible to crime losses should be covered by insurance that is designed to fit the exposure. The intent is to cover ordinary merchandise for which the exposure to a crime loss is relatively moderate.

Exclusions of Perils Certain perils are excluded in "all-risks" policies in order to avoid paying losses which may result from carelessness or where there is no clear indication that the loss resulted from an insurable occurrence. Usually excluded is "unexplained or mysterious disappearance of property, or shortage of property disclosed upon taking inventory." Such loss may result from carelessness in the handling of property, or from inaccurate records. Such losses are not considered to be insurable. They can be kept to a minimum in any mercantile operation by proper security measures and adequate records.

Also excluded is the "voluntary parting with title or possession of any property by the insured or others to whom the property may be entrusted if induced to do so by any fraudulent scheme, trick, device or false pretense." This is intended to avoid losses which result from the carelessness of the insured in the handling of property. Such losses, again, can be avoided by a careful insured through good procedures.

Loss due to the dishonesty of any insured, partner or joint adventurer, or of an officer, director or trustee is excluded. Also excluded under this type of coverage is any loss from a fraudulent, dishonest or criminal act of any employee or agent of any insured, or of any person to whom the covered property may be entrusted. Many of these policies provide fidelity coverage as an option; if so, this is written under a separate portion of the policy. Insurers prefer that fidelity exposures be treated separately.

The "all-risks" insurance policies on commercial personal property also exclude from the physical damage insurance any loss from delay, loss of market, interruption of business, or consequential loss of any nature. These losses usually can be covered under special provisions of the policy, but it is believed by insurers that such consequential losses should be covered under special provisions that are particularly applicable to those conditions.

Deductibles in "All-Risks" Coverage

Under "all-risks" policies, difficulty may arise in many cases in determining whether an insured loss has occurred. Even with the exclusion of unexplained or mysterious disappearance of property, there are circumstances where there may be some evidence of theft or other insured loss, but the evidence is not clear.

There is also the problem with any broad insurance coverage that numerous small losses occur which can be handled by the insured more economically as a normal business expense. Considerable expense is involved in the processing of numerous small insurance claims. It is customary in connection with these broad policies to have a deductible applying to each occurrence. This deductible enables the insurer to provide a broad form of insurance coverage for the important losses without incurring the considerable additional expense of processing numerous small claims.

The amounts of the deductibles vary according to the type of merchandise, the insured's willingness to accept responsibility for losses of a particular size, and other factors which affect the probability of numerous small losses. A deductible of $50 is the minimum that would apply to a commercial policy of the "all-risks" type, and the deductible may range upward to as much as $1,000 or more per occurrence. There may be a difference in the amount of the deductible applying to losses from different perils. For example, one policy contains a $100 deductible applicable to all perils except theft, and a $250 deductible applicable to each theft loss. It is also customary for the deductibles to apply separately to the personal property in separate buildings, and separately to personal property in the open or on vehicles.

Crime Losses Covered by "All-Risks" Policies

It may be helpful at this point to summarize the kinds of crime losses that are covered by an "all-risks" policy. Property losses from burglary and robbery are covered subject to any deductible or any exclusions or restrictions that might apply to a particular type of property. Property is also covered for loss from shoplifting and other theft by outsiders. The concept of "all-risks" insurance coverage still requires that there be an actual occurrence that can be identified—the mere fact that a particular piece of property is missing is not enough to generate a claim under the policy.

The crime insurance coverage of an "all-risks" insurance policy on business personal property is roughly comparable to that of a mercantile open stock burglary policy with the theft endorsement attached. However, limits of coverage and coinsurance are applied as in other property forms.

FEDERAL CRIME INSURANCE

Reasons for and Development of the Program

To provide crime insurance coverage, underwriters must consider whether or not the exposure is insurable at a price that is economically feasible. Some exposures are so great that it is not feasible for a private insurer to provide coverage.

The Federal Crime Insurance Program was initiated because

Congress decided that insurance against losses from crime was unavailable at affordable rates in many parts of the country. The program became effective in 1971, and by 1977 had been made available in twenty-one states and the District of Columbia. The program is administered by the Federal Insurance Administrator who determines the states in which a critical problem of securing crime insurance exists.

The program is intended to be operated through servicing insurance companies. These companies service the program through any licensed property insurance agent or broker in the eligible states. There are provisions for residential crime coverage and for commercial crime coverage—commercial crime coverage will be considered here.

Policy Coverage and General Provisions

Perils Covered The perils covered by the Federal Crime Insurance Program are essentially burglary and robbery, with some minor extensions to other crime perils. Definitions of the perils are similar to those in crime insurance policies issued by insurance companies. Burglary, and larceny incident to burglary, is the stealing of property from within premises which have been forcibly entered, with visible marks of such forcible entry at the place of entry.

Robbery is the stealing of business personal property from the insured in the insured's presence and with the insured's knowledge both inside and outside of the premises. The term robbery is defined to include a theft which is observed by the insured. Thus, a grab and run incident would be covered by the policy as a robbery.

There also is coverage for damage to the premises committed during the course of a burglary or robbery or attempted burglary or robbery. An extension covers loss by theft from a night depository or the burglary of a safe. Limitations apply as to the amount under these extensions and also with respect to the class of safe in which the property is kept.

Damage to the premises during the commission of a burglary or robbery might be considered to some degree a coverage against vandalism and malicious mischief in connection with such an occurrence but there is no intent to provide full vandalism and malicious mischief coverage such as might be provided under the usual insurance policy applying to those perils.

Property Covered and Limits of Liability The property covered by the commercial policy under this program includes merchandise, furniture, fixtures, and equipment; it also covers the loss of money and securities by robbery or safe burglary.

The amount of insurance that can be purchased under the program is limited. Commercial insurance may be purchased in amounts up to $15,000 per occurrence. This is a modest amount of insurance in view of the potential losses faced by large commercial operations. The possible losses in stores that carry valuable merchandise such as jewelry, furs, and other high value merchandise, could be many times the $15,000 limit under this program. However, the program is intended primarily to provide a degree of crime insurance coverage for smaller merchants who are unable or find it extremely difficult to secure crime insurance in any amount.

Deductibles All policies are subject to a deductible applicable to each loss. The deductibles under commercial policies vary according to the annual gross receipts of the insured, with a minimum of 5 percent of the gross amount of the loss. For example, the deductible is $50 for a business with gross receipts of less than $100,000 annually. It ranges upward to a $200 deductible for businesses with annual gross receipts of $500,000 or more. This provision for a variation in the deductible according to the gross receipts of the business is different from the usual crime insurance coverage offered by insurance companies. This principle has been followed to some extent in the writing of commercial insurance policies by insurance companies but it is on an informal basis according to the judgment of the underwriters. It is not a usual part of manual rules or formal rating procedures of insurance companies.

Exclusions The most important exclusion is that of mysterious disappearance. There must be an actual incident of breaking and entering or of robbery for the loss to be covered. This insurance is not intended to cover inventory shortages.

Locations Where Available Federal crime insurance is made available only after a state or other area is specifically designated. The Federal Insurance Administrator is obligated to conduct a continuing review of the market availability situation throughout the country. The program is not instituted in any location in which the Federal Insurance Administrator finds that insurance companies are providing crime insurance at reasonable cost.

It should be noted that a part of the requirement is that insurance be provided under the program at affordable rates. The rates vary according to the class of business, its location, and the gross receipts of the business from the previous year. However, the rates are not based upon an actuarial evaluation of the loss experience in the manner that commercial crime insurance rates of insurance companies are determined. This means, in effect, that the program is being subsidized by general tax revenue.

Commercial insurance may be purchased under the program for

burglary only, for robbery only, or for a combination of the two. The premium for the combined policy is somewhat less than the sum of the separate premiums.

Protection Requirement   One of the interesting provisions in the program is a requirement that certain protective devices be maintained by the insured firm before it is eligible for federal crime insurance. In general, a commercial property must have its doors, windows, and other accessible openings adequately protected against burglary during nonbusiness hours. This protection requirement may include certain types of locks on the doors, bars on windows and doors of glass, and other bars or protective devices that would impede entry by a burglar.

The usual procedure is for the servicing insurance company to make an inspection of the premises in order to determine whether the requirements for protective devices are met. Payment of losses is dependent upon the maintenance of the protective devices by the insured during the term of the policy.

No attempt has been made here to describe fully the details of the Federal Crime Insurance Program. The intent has been primarily to point out some of the more significant differences between this program and usual practices of insurance companies.

NONINSURANCE TECHNIQUES

In comparison with other property exposures, the crime exposure is somewhat more likely to be retained. This is so because, in most cases, the probable severity of a crime loss is less than that from other exposures. A fire may destroy the entire contents of a building, but a thief is likely to steal only a small percentage of the total contents. Likewise, theft of cash in any one occurrence is limited to the amount of cash on hand. However, despite the lower severity of crime exposures, the overall frequency of crime loss is greater than the frequency of fire losses.

Loss control techniques can effectively reduce the crime exposure. Protective procedures, in some cases, may be so effective that an exposure can be avoided so that there is no need for insurance. For example, if no money is kept in an office overnight, there is no longer an exposure to burglary of money while the premises are closed—the exposure has been avoided.

There is a close relation between crime loss control and crime insurance, perhaps more so than in any other line of insurance. First, underwriters may not be willing to provide insurance unless sound loss control measures are in force—an unprotected jewelry store, for example, is an open invitation to a burglar. Secondly, extensive credits are granted in burglary rates for various protective devices and systems. As the exposure is reduced through noninsurance techniques, the premium to insure the remaining exposure is reduced. In selecting a proper combination of insurance and noninsurance techniques, risk managers must weigh the cost of protective systems versus the cost of insurance with or without protective systems. Of course, the risk manager must consider collateral, and indirect and consequential loss exposures in evaluating an overall approach to handling the exposure. Finally, through the use of protective devices and systems, the potential loss frequency and severity may be so reduced that the exposure can be satisfactorily retained.

To further complicate matters, insurance may be combined with retention, either consciously or unconsciously. Deductible insurance may be used wisely to reduce the frequency of insurable claims, while keeping protection for severe losses. Retention may also be involved when crime limits are inadequate, either because the exposure was underestimated, or because it was not feasible to purchase higher limits. With the exception of the mercantile open stock policy, most crime policies have no insurance to value requirements.

Loss control techniques are used extensively in handling crime exposures. As mentioned, the existence of preventive measures has an effect on the availability and the pricing of commercial and federal crime insurance. For these reasons, the remainder of this chapter will concentrate on loss control techniques for handling the crime exposure.

Protective Devices

The principal methods of protection against loss from crime by outsiders are: (1) limitation of access by the criminal to the property; (2) the early detection of criminals who have gained access to the property; and (3) the identification of criminals to facilitate their arrest and conviction, thus preventing future crimes. There is no absolute protection. Every device and procedure that is developed for protection against crime loss can be circumvented by an experienced criminal if given the time. For example, alarm devices on doors and windows have been circumvented by entering through an unprotected wall, roof, or floor. In some cases, alarms have been defeated by criminals who were sufficiently familiar with them to do so without activating them. There is a continuing struggle between the criminals in their efforts to circumvent protective measures and property owners in their efforts to devise protective measures. Any measure that can delay access, detect, or identify the criminal helps to avoid a loss.

The protective measures that are taken against crime loss may be divided roughly into three groups. The first group is that of physical protection to premises in order to delay access by the criminal. The second is the installation of alarm systems and other surveillance devices which will indicate when access to the premises has been gained by an outsider. The third possibility is the use of automatic cameras or closed circuit television systems to help identify criminals in order to facilitate their arrest and conviction.

There also are various protective procedures that can be set up by a property owner. These may include procedures for the handling of money and securities that will reduce the likelihood of theft or reduce the amount of property accessible to a thief. All of these devices and procedures will be considered in their relationship to protection of the insured's property and the relation to insurance that may be carried.

Physical Protection There is much that a property owner can do in the way of installing passive restraints to entry. The type of lock that is used on doorways can make a difference of several minutes in the entry time needed by a thief. The ordinary snap lock can be manipulated in a matter of seconds. The so-called dead-bolt lock cannot be manipulated in the same way as a snap lock, and usually requires the picking of the tumblers or the use of force in order to enter. This picking of the tumblers requires tools and expertise that many ordinary burglars do not possess.

The rear doors to a store can be barred from the inside so that access is difficult. Bars, grills, and gates can be put across windows and doorways. An unbreakable glazing material can be used for doors or windows where the proprietor wishes to maintain a clear view for display purposes.

A frequent type of burglary is the breaking of a show window for the purpose of grabbing valuable items that are on display. Ordinary plate glass is easily broken. There are varieties of breakage resistant glass, and plastic materials particularly for smaller windows. There is also a device that is used, particularly in jewelry display windows, that effectively impedes the access of a burglar to a show window display. This is the installation of a sheet of breakage resistant glass behind the show window glass. This second sheet is hung on chains from the top of the show window so that it swings backward when it is struck by an object. The show window can be broken but this second sheet of glass is difficult to break because of its composition and also because of its mobility. It is difficult for a thief to reach around such a glass when it is properly installed.

The installation of good locks, gates, bars, breakage resistant glass, and similar devices may provide adequate protection for mercantile

Figure 11-1

Safe and Vault Classification—Money and Securities*

Broad Form Policy	Construction			Mercantile Safe Policy
Safe, Chest, Cabinet or Vault Classification	Doors	Walls		Safe, Chest, Cabinet or Vault Classification
		Safe, Chest or Cabinet	Vault	
B (Fire-resistive)	Steel less than 1" thick, or iron	Body of steel less than 1/2" thick, or iron	Brick, concrete, stone, tile, iron or steel	B (Fire-resistive)
	Any iron or steel safe or chest having a slot through which money can be deposited		Not Applicable	
C (Burglar-resistive)	Steel at least 1" thick	Body of steel at least 1/2" thick	Steel at least 1/2" thick; or reinforced concrete or stone at least 9" thick; or non-reinforced concrete or stone at least 12" thick	C (Burglar-resistive)
	Safe or chest bearing the following label: "Underwriters' Laboratories, Inc. Inspected Keylocked Safe KL Burglary"		Not Applicable	
E (Burglar-resistive)	Steel at least 1 1/2" thick	Body of steel at least 1" thick	Same as for C	E (Burglar-resistive)
ER (Burglar-resistive)	Safe or chest bearing the following label: "Underwriters' Laboratories, Inc. Inspected Tool Resisting Safe TL-15 Burglary"			ER (Burglar-resistive)
F (Burglar-resistive)	Safe or chest bearing one of the following labels: "Underwriters' Laboratories, Inc. Inspected Tool Resisting Safe TL-30 Burglary" "Underwriters' Laboratories, Inc. Inspected Torch Resisting Safe TR-30 Burglary" "Underwriters' Laboratories, Inc. Inspected Explosive Resisting Safe with Relocking Device X-60 Burglary"		Not Applicable	F (Burglar-resistive)
G (Burglar-resistive)	One or more steel doors (one in front of the other) each at least 1 1/2" thick and aggregating at least 3" thickness	Not Applicable	Steel at least 1/2" thick; or reinforced concrete or stone at least 12" thick; or non-reinforced concrete or stone at least 18" thick	G (Burglar-resistive)

Continued on next page

| G (Burglar-resistive) | Safe or chest bearing one of the following labels: "Underwriters' Laboratories, Inc. Inspected Torch and Explosive Resisting Safe TX-60 Burglary" "Underwriters' Laboratories, Inc. Inspected Torch Resisting Safe TR-60 Burglary" "Underwriters' Laboratories, Inc. Inspected Torch and Tool Resisting Safe TRTL-30 Burglary" | Not Applicable | H (Burglar-resistive) |
| G Burglar-resistive) | Safe or chest bearing one of the following labels: "Underwriters' Laboratories, Inc. Inspected Torch and Tool Resisting Safe TRTL-60 Burglary" "Underwriters' Laboratories, Inc. Inspected Torch, Explosive and Tool Resisting Safe TXTL-60 Burglary" | Not Applicable | I (Burglar-resistive) |

*Reprinted with permission from *Condensed Burglary Insurance Manual* (Hamilton, OH: The Mosler Safe Company, 1971), p. 7.

stocks of low value. This may be particularly true if the premises are under frequent surveillance by police, and in a low crime area. It must be kept in mind by the proprietor of such an establishment that such passive restraints merely delay the entrance of a burglar and are not a guarantee that a burglary will not occur. The adequacy of such measures also must be considered in the light of the values involved and whether small volume and weight plus high value would make the merchandise attractive to a burglar.

Safes Safes are another type of physical protective device. There is a great variation in the vulnerability of safes to burglary. Many safes are basically fire protection devices, referred to as "record safes," which offer little resistance to a burglar. They are designed to protect money and valuable records from fire damage. Fire resistive safes generally have square doors, and are mounted on wheels.

Money safes are designed to be burglar resistive. Money safes generally have round doors, and are not mounted on wheels. (Some of the latest money safes have been designed with square doors to facilitate their use with cash register trays, etc.)

Within each category, there are degrees of resistiveness the safes offer to fire and/or burglary. Figure 11-1, which lists the classifications used in rating some crime policies, will give some idea of the different degrees of protection afforded by the various types of safes.

Safes can be most readily identified by reference to the Underwriters Laboratories label found inside the door of most quality safes. (In older safes the label was located on the outside of the door, but it

Figure 11-2

Underwriters' Laboratories, Inc., Safe Label*

*Reprinted with permission from *Condensed Burglary Insurance Manual* (Hamilton, OH: The Mosler Safe Company, 1971), p. 9.

was deemed undesirable to tell burglars how much difficulty they might have in trying to break a safe.) One such label is shown in Figure 11-2.

Safes, like other physical protective devices, do not eliminate the possibility of a loss. However, they reduce the likelihood of loss in proportion to the quality of the safe and the skill of the thief.

Alarm Systems There are many kinds of alarm systems that indicate when an intruder has gained access to a building. It is axiomatic that alarm systems do not prevent the entry of a burglar. The sole effect of an alarm system is to indicate when an intruder has entered the premises. The existence of an alarm may also discourage burglars.

Some of the alarm systems make use of simple electrical circuits which give an alarm when an electrical connection is made or is broken, depending upon the nature of the system. Other systems make use of more sophisticated electronic devices and principles. These may give alarms when a foreign object, such as the body of a burglar, is present within the premises. Some of these use invisible light rays which, when broken, give an alarm signal. The principal varieties of these devices will be described here.

One of the simpler forms of alarm systems consists of electrical contacts or metal tapes on each door, window, or other opening into the building. Usually the system is so wired that an electrical current is passing through the system constantly. The opening of a door or window interrupts the electrical current, which activates an alarm system. This is a perimeter system in which the intent is to give an alarm whenever entry is made into the building through a door, a window, or other opening which is protected by the system.

Such a system on doors, windows, and other openings gives no protection if entry is made through a roof or a wall. A more complete system can be installed which will give an indication if entry is made through a roof or wall. This may require the installation of wires, or other devices which protect the areas of wall or roof that may be accessible from neighboring buildings. Various sensing devices are illustrated in Figure 11-3. These sensing devices are then connected to either local or central station alarms.

Alarm systems may also be used to reduce the robbery exposure. Holdup buttons or foot pedals may be situated so that they can be triggered by a bank teller or store clerk, and this sends a silent alarm to a central station company or to the police. If rapid response is possible, the police may arrive while a robber is still on the premises.

Local Alarms. Many of the simpler alarm systems are connected to an interior gong or alarm and also to a gong on the outside of the premises. Such an interior alarm system may be effective in a store where there are security personnel on duty at all times and where the alarm system would alert such security personnel to entry by a burglar. However, the outside alarm may be almost completely useless at a location in an industrial or mercantile area where few people are present during the night. It has been the experience that these local alarms may ring for hours before anyone pays any attention to them. Sometimes neighbors call the police after the bell has been ringing for hours. In the meantime, the burglars may have come and gone with their loot.

Central Station Alarms. A more effective type of alarm system is that which is connected directly to a central station of an alarm company or to a police department. The central station of an alarm company is monitored at all hours. Electrical or electronic monitoring of all circuits is performed from the central station. An alarm to the central station usually results in the sending of a guard by the alarm company to the premises, and also a notification to the police department that an alarm has been received from those premises.

Selection of Alarm Systems. Alarm systems vary as to their quality and extent of protection. Insurance rates generally give credits only for "approved" alarm systems. An "approved" system is one installed by an "approved burglar alarm company" named in the burglary manual. Underwriters Laboratories, Inc., issues alarm certificates which indicate the grade, type, and extent of the alarm system, which are considered in granting insurance rate credits. An Underwriters Laboratories certificate is shown in Figure 11-4. No matter how expensive, an alarm system not "approved" may receive no premium reduction, a fact discovered belatedly by many risk managers.

Burglary alarms should not be confused with fire alarms. Each type of alarm is designed to accomplish a different purpose. A fire hose is no more effective against a burglar than an armed policeman is against a fire.

Deficiencies of Alarm Systems. There are many problems in the handling of burglar alarm systems. One of the most difficult problems is

Figure 11-3

Burglar Alarm System Design*

Door switches (contacts) These devices are usually magnet-operated switches. They are affixed to a door or window in such a way that opening the door or window breaks the magnetic field which, in turn, activates the alarm. These devices may be surface-mounted or recessed, exposed or concealed. A variety of switches exist for every type of door or window.

Metallic foil (window tape) Metallic foil is widely used to detect glass breakage. Strips of thin lead/tin foil are affixed to a glass surface, so the foil will break as the glass cracks to the edge of the frame. Metallic foil is economical protection; however, it requires frequent maintenance, especially on glass doors.

Wooden Screens These devices are made of wooden dowels assembled in a cage-like fashion no more than four inches from each other. A very fine, brittle wire runs in the wood dowels and frame. An intruder must break the doweling to gain entry and thus break the electrical circuit, causing an alarm. Wooden screens require little maintenance; however, they are not aesthetically pleasing and are usually used where appearance is not important. Normally, screens are permanently mounted, but movable screens are available for removal when the alarm system is turned off.

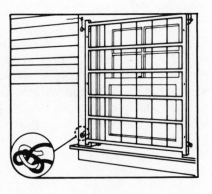

Continued on next page

Lace (paneling) The surfaces of walls, door panels, and safes are often protected against entry by lacing, i.e., weaving a close lace-like pattern of metallic foil or a fine brittle wire on the surface. Entry cannot be made without first breaking the foil or wire, thus activating the alarm. A panel of wood is usually placed over the lacing to protect it from being accidentally broken.

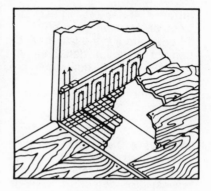

Photoelectric eyes (beams) Photoelectric devices transmit a beam across a protected area. When an intruder interrupts this beam, the photoelectric circuit is disrupted and the alarm is initiated. Modern photoelectric devices are much improved over their predecessors. Today's photoelectric eyes use light emitting diodes which makes the beam invisible to the naked eye. These devices are very effective and reliable. Some have ranges of over 1,000 feet for large buildings and hallways. Photoelectric devices provide excellent area protection in areas of relative low risk.

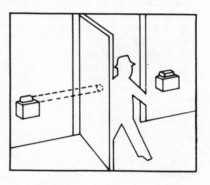

Ultrasonic Detectors These devices are part of the motion detector group. Movement of an intruder in a protected area disrupts a high pitched sound (ultrasonic) wave pattern which, in turn, activates the device. Ultrasonic devices can be mounted either on the ceiling or on the wall. Ultrasonic devices are the most economical type of motion detectors. They protect a three dimensional area with an invisible pattern. However, they can be prone to false alarms due to excessive air currents and certain ultrasonic noises from mechanical equipment. Again, proper application of this equipment is important.

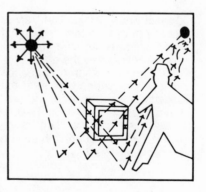

Continued on next page

Infrared Detectors These devices detect heat given off by an intruder and are the latest development in motion detectors. Although infrared detectors are relatively free of false alarms, their range is limited to a small pattern.

Microwave Detectors This type of motion detector uses high frequency radio waves (microwaves) to detect movement. Microwave has greater range than ultrasonic. Since it does not use sound (air), microwave is not prone to false alarms caused by air currents. However, they can penetrate such materials as glass and are reflected by metal objects and can cause false alarms if not properly installed.

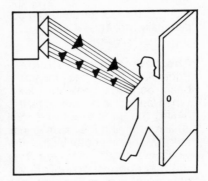

Object Protection

Object protection provides direct security for "things." It is often the final stage of an "in depth" protection system utilizing perimeter and area protection devices. The objects which are most frequently protected include: safes, filing cabinets, desks, models, and expensive equipment.

Capacitance (Proximity) Detectors With this system, the object itself becomes an antenna, electronically linked to the alarm control. When a person approaches or touches (depending upon the sensitivity level desired) the "antenna," an electrostatic field is unbalanced and the alarm is initiated. Only metal objects can be protected in this way.

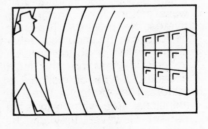

Continued on next page

Vibration Detectors These devices utilize a highly sensitive and specialized microphone called an electronic vibration detector (EVD). The EVD is attached directly to objects such as safes, filing cabinets, and art objects or to surfaces such as floors, walls, windows and ceilings. When an intruder causes vibration, it is instantly detected. These sensitive microphones can be adjusted to detect a sledge hammer attack on a concrete wall or a delicate penetration of a glass surface. Vibration detectors have an advantage over capacitance detectors since they can protect even non-metallic objects. They will alarm only when the object is moved, as compared to capacitance devices which will detect an intruder who is in close proximity to the protected object.

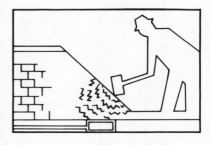

*Reprinted with permission from *Alarm Handbook for the Insurance Industry,* Honeywell, Inc., 1975, pp. 8, 10, and 11.

that of false alarms. One survey, for example, indicated that more than half of the major police emergency calls in a large city were actually false alarms. The result has been that police departments in some cities assign a low priority to calls that come in from burglar alarm systems.

There is the problem of time even when the alarm is valid and the alarm company guard and the police do respond. Response of the guard or police to an alarm within ten minutes is considered excellent service. This ten-minute delay may be sufficient for the burglars to get away with a substantial amount of merchandise. For example, there was one case in Chicago in which burglars entered through the front door of a men's clothing store and were able to get away with more than $20,000 worth of merchandise before the alarm company guard and the police arrived, although they responded within a few minutes.

Central station contracts with merchants ordinarily require that the central station guard remain on the premises for up to two hours after the alarm has been received in order to give the proprietor time to arrive and arrange for the securing of the premises. There have been cases where the proprietor failed to arrive within the specified two hours and the alarm company guard left the premises at the end of the two-hour

Figure 11-4
Underwriters' Laboratories, Inc., Certificate*

No 840419

——— OCCUPANT ———

EQUIPMENT

Type ——— Extent ———
Model ——— Key or no Key ———

Installing
Company ———

By ——————— No. ———
Issued ——— 19 ———
Expires ——— 19 ———

CENTRAL STATION GRADE AA ALARM CERTIFICATE

UNDERWRITERS' LABORATORIES, INC.

333 PFINGSTEN ROAD • NORTHBROOK, ILLINOIS 60062

an independent, not-for-profit organization testing for public safety

This Certifies *that the Installing Company Whose Name Appears Hereon is listed by Underwriters' Laboratories, Inc. as furnishing GRADE AA CENTRAL STATION BURGLAR ALARM SYSTEMS and is authorized to issue this certificate to the equipment described hereon as its representation that such equipment and all connected wiring and devices is in compliance with requirements established by Underwriters' Laboratories, Inc. for the class.*

UNDERWRITERS' LABORATORIES, INC.

Ben Whith PRES.

(Not to be issued for a term of more than 5 years)

Underwriters' Laboratories, Inc. conducts countercheck field inspections of representative installations of the installing company, but assumes no liability for any loss which may result from failure of equipment, incorrect certification, non-conformity with requirements, cancellation of the certificate, or withdrawal of the listing of the installing company prior to the expiration date appearing on this certificate. If an installation is found not in conformity with requirements, it shall be corrected or the certificate is subject to cancellation.

*Reprinted with permission from *Alarm Handbook for the Insurance Industry,* Honeywell, Inc., 1975, p. 19.

period, after which the burglars entered the premises at their leisure and made off with the property that they came to get.

One of the more recent alarm devices for use where a central station service is not available is an automatic device which will dial the police telephone number and transmit a recorded message to the police department when it is activated. Such a system can be arranged to send a robbery alarm when a button is pushed, or it can be arranged to indicate a burglary when the premises are entered. Unfortunately, there are ways to deactivate such a system by placing other telephone calls from nearby phones, or by disconnecting the telephone lines. One of the problems with all central station and lines to police departments is the fact that telephone circuits generally are used for the transmission of the signals from the premises to the central station or police department. A sophisticated burglar may be sufficiently familiar with these transmission lines and telephone lines in general so that the security can be breached at some point where the telephone lines are accessible to a burglar. This may be at some point in a multiple occupancy building, or even in the overhead lines or a telephone line on a pole or box outside of the building.

An alarm system may have what is called a shunt switch, which gives the store operator a few seconds to get out of the store when the premises are closed for the night, or get into the store upon entering in the morning, without giving an alarm. This is particularly likely in the case of a local alarm where the proprietor does not wish to activate the outside gong when leaving or entering the premises. It is a simple matter for the sophisticated burglar to determine in advance exactly what the proprietor does in using the shunt switch. The burglar then does the same thing and shuts off the alarm system so that the gong does not go off after the building has been entered.

The point that the business proprietor must remember in evaluating the effectiveness of an alarm system is that it merely indicates that an intruder has entered the premises. There is always a delay of from five minutes to fifteen minutes or more from the time an alarm is given until a guard or police officer can reach the premises. This time may be sufficient for the burglars to complete their work. The response time is a vital consideration in determining whether the expense of a sophisticated burglar alarm or robbery alarm system is worthwhile.

Watchman or Security Patrols Many organizations find it worthwhile to maintain watchman service on the premises. The watchman goes through the building at periodic intervals to see that everything is in good order. This, of course, is a protective feature against fire and other catastrophes as well as against burglary. It is considered necessary to use some device to make certain that the watchman does patrol at the required intervals. A standard arrangement is for the watchman to go through the building once every hour. One frequently used system is a special clock which records the visit of the watchman to stations throughout the building. A key is fastened to each location, and the inserting of the key into the special clock records the time that the watchman visited that particular station. By checking the records, the employer can be sure the watchman completed his rounds. The weakness of this system is that nobody would know if the watchman were overpowered during the night until the premises are opened in the morning. The presence of the watchman is a deterrent factor as far as burglars are concerned but it is by no means complete.

The central station alarm companies also maintain a supervised system under which the watchman signals to the central station as he visits each station throughout the premises. These systems are arranged so that a watchman is sent to the premises by the central station alarm company if the watchman at the premises fails to signal as required. Sometimes burglars or robbers will force a watchman to continue making his rounds while a theft is being carried out. Most of the signaling systems contain an arrangement whereby the watchman can secretly signal for help even while making the rounds under the eyes of the burglar. This consists of an unusual type of signal which would be difficult for the burglars to detect.

Larger organizations may maintain a complete security system with a central station on the premises for the supervision of one or more watchmen. The expense of such a system would only be justified if large values are involved.

Surveillance Cameras Banks and other firms with high robbery exposure frequently install automatic cameras to photograph criminals in the process of committing a crime. Such installations discourage robbery in two ways. This facilitates the identification and conviction of criminals after the offense has been committed, making the offenders unavailable for future offenses, at least for a short time. Also, the increased probability of identification and conviction discourages robbery.

Protective Procedures

There are many procedures that a property owner can institute in addition to the physical protection and the alarm protection that have just been described. One simple procedure that is followed by many merchants is to have the safe, or other particularly valuable property, located in such a place that it can be observed by police patrols from outside the building. A light is installed so as to keep the inside of the premises illuminated.

Procedures in the handling of money and securities may deter burglars or robbers. Organizations that handle large quantities of money or securities may arrange for frequent deposits at a bank in order to keep the amount of money or securities at a minimum. This results in a smaller value on the premises at any one time, and also means that messengers carrying property to the bank would be carrying smaller quantities. It is important in this respect to keep in mind that high values are an incentive to burglary or robbery.

Another procedure that is followed by many mercantile organizations is to place receipts in a safe that can only be opened by an armored car messenger service. The cash that is kept outside for operating purposes is thus kept at a small amount. The safe is opened by the guard from the armored car company and this is done under the protection of armed guards, which reduces the chances of armed robbery during business hours.

Evaluation of Protective Measures Versus Insurance

The owner of property finds it is more important with burglary and robbery insurance than with other forms of property insurance to evaluate the effect of protective measures and the purchase of insurance. This is affected by the exposure to loss. An important feature is the relationship between the value of the property and its weight and volume. Money, securities, and jewelry, all have a high value in relation to weight and volume. The values on a particular premises may be such that the owner must have insurance in order to prevent bankruptcy in case of a severe loss. Extreme protective measures may be advisable in order to reduce the probability of loss and also to reduce the cost of insurance.

The small merchant may face the same problem even though the loss from a burglary or robbery may be smaller. For example, a $10,000 burglary loss may result in bankruptcy for the small merchant if the loss is not covered by insurance. The proprietor, in any case, must determine whether it is possible to assume all or part of the losses, and determine what insurance is feasible in the particular circumstances.

There may be many cases where a deductible will help to reduce the cost of insurance. However, the deductible is effective principally upon frequency of insured loss and has little effect upon severity. The proprietor must use every feasible means of impeding the access of a criminal to the premises and of reducing the values that are accessible to the burglar or robber.

Chapter Notes

---

1. *Insurance Facts 1977*, Insurance Information Institute, p. 61.
2. Ronald A. Anderson and Walter A. Kumpf, *Business Law*, 9th ed. (Cincinnati: South-Western Publishing Co., 1973), p. 49.
3. *Crime in Retailing*, United States Department of Commerce, 1975 (available from Government Printing Office).
4. Encyclopedia Britannica 1977 *Book of the Year*.
5. *The Cost of Crimes Against Business*, United States Department of Commerce (November 1974), p. 3.
6. *Crime in Retailing*, p. 4.
7. *Crime in the United States*, published by the Federal Bureau of Investigation.
8. *Crime in Retailing*, United States Department of Commerce, 1974.

CHAPTER 12

Employee Dishonesty Exposures and Their Treatment

Employee dishonesty is a major cause of loss to business firms. Reliable statistics on the magnitude of such losses are not available because many of these losses are not reported to law enforcement authorities, and many business firms are not insured. According to one estimate, only 15 to 20 percent of mercantile establishments are insured against employee dishonesty losses.

EXPOSURE OF PROPERTY VALUES TO LOSS FROM EMPLOYEE DISHONESTY

When employee dishonesty losses are mentioned, one naturally thinks of thefts of money, jewelry, securities, or other property combining high value with low bulk. While such property is likely to be the prime target of any kind of crime, employee dishonesty losses may involve any kind of property. One business firm, a pickle manufacturer, was forced into bankruptcy through the theft of $600,000 worth of sugar over a period of several months by several employees acting in collusion.

Most employee dishonesty losses result from theft of property for the personal gain of the employee. However, some result from destruction of property by an employee in retaliation for some offense, real or imaginary, committed by the employer.

Employee dishonesty losses pose a particularly serious threat to employers because they are open-ended losses. That is, there is no reliable way to make an advance estimate of the maximum possible loss. There have been instances in which the total loss over a prolonged period of time exceeded the assets of the firm at any one point in time. While such instances are unusual, they do illustrate the potential danger of employee dishonesty.

The Crime of Embezzlement

Losses to a business organization from employee dishonesty can take several forms, but embezzlement is the principal cause of such losses. Embezzlement is a form of larceny in which a person takes for his or her own benefit property belonging to another. Therefore, embezzlement can be perpetrated against anyone whose property may be in the custody or control of the embezzler. Employees are in a particularly favorable position to commit such crimes because of their frequent and convenient access to their employer's property. Embezzlement can be perpetrated by a trustee of an estate, by public officials who have money or securities in their custody, or, in fact, by anyone who is in control of property belonging to someone else. However, this chapter will be concerned primarily with embezzlement and other forms of loss which may be caused by employees and involving the property of their employers.

Although no accurate estimates of the total loss from employee dishonesty are possible, employee dishonesty is considered by many people to be the largest cause of crime loss to business organizations in the United States. A high proportion of employee embezzlements are not reported to the police. Insurance loss figures are not a good indication because a high proportion of employers do not carry insurance that would cover employee thefts.

The crime of embezzlement must be distinguished from actions of an employee that are the result of poor judgment and not of intent to appropriate property for the employee's own use. This distinction was brought out in an Oklahoma case a few years ago. An organization that was interested in community development set up a special corporation to help increase local industry and the job market. The development corporation became indebted to the parent corporation and eventually defaulted on loans. All of this was arranged by an employee who was accused of dishonesty because of the loss. The court held that the employee had not been dishonest and was not guilty of embezzlement because no funds had been appropriated to his own use. All of the actions which were taken, while subsequently shown to be unwise, had been approved or subsequently ratified by the interested parties. The court pointed out that bad or unwise judgment without any intent by the person involved to profit personally does not constitute dishonesty. The court made the interesting comment that an attempt was made to prove the manager dishonest because of the losses, although he would have been a hero if the project had succeeded.

Who Embezzles   An attempt sometimes is made to describe the typical embezzler, but this has not been possible. An embezzler may be male or female, of almost any age, married or unmarried, of any income bracket from penniless to wealthy, and from any type of background.

The embezzler characteristically operates alone, although there have been cases where two or more employees were involved in a theft scheme. One study of thefts from savings and loan associations showed that only three out of seventy-five losses involved more than one person, and in no case were more than two acting in collusion.

Causes of Embezzlement   What are the causes of embezzlement as related to the embezzler? Fidelity underwriters of insurance companies often refer to the following as the four principal causes for embezzlement:

1. Compulsive gambling is often a cause of embezzlement. A typical case involved a man who borrowed $5,000 to bet on a "sure thing" at the race track. He lost, and continued to lose over a period of several years, during which he embezzled several hundred thousand dollars. He covered up the thefts by manipulating the accounts until an audit revealed his activities.
2. The desire to live far beyond their means has also led many to embezzle. The maintenance of an expensive apartment, car, or even another person has been the cause of embezzlement in many cases.
3. Alcoholism and other types of drug addiction are another major cause of embezzlement. The costs of the habit to be supported and the fear of losing a job which often accompany addiction both contribute to the decision to embezzle.
4. A fourth major cause of embezzlement is the result of the astronomical increase in health care costs. An employee may see embezzlement as the only way to meet extremely high medical expenses.

A large proportion of embezzlers contend that they intended only to borrow the money and expected to pay it back. The availability of the money, and the ever-increasing amount of defalcations, prevent the embezzler from making good.

The effect of ego must not be overlooked. There have been many cases where the embezzler used the funds for contributions to charities, church organizations, and other projects from which the embezzler did not get any actual personal financial benefit. The motive behind some of these embezzlements has been the enhancing of the embezzler's prestige and standing in the community.

Characteristics of Embezzlement Losses

The property taken by an embezzler may be money or any other type of property. Money may be pilfered from a cash register, particularly for sales which are not rung up, or which are rung up for an amount less than the actual sale.

The susceptibility of property to embezzlement is similar to that of property which is taken by an outside thief. Property that is embezzled is usually property with high value and low volume and weight. The higher the value in relation to volume and weight, the greater is the chance of its being pilfered.

The methods of accomplishing the theft will be covered later. The essential characteristic of the embezzlement loss is that money or property is taken physically, or is credited to the embezzler, by some method which transfers the value to the embezzler.

Conditions Conducive to Embezzlement

There are basically two elements that create a situation conducive to employee theft. The first is an employer's lack of control over money and property. One employee may have charge of receipts that come in from customers and may also have check writing authority and can easily adjust accounts, take money, or credit funds to a personal bank account.

One such actual case that reached the courts involved the secretary of a lawyer-real estate agent. The principal of the firm left the entire financial operation of the office to the secretary, who took checks out of the back of the checkbook, forged the employer's name, and deposited the checks to her own account in another bank. The employer eventually was startled to find that his bank balance was much less than he knew it should be, and an investigation revealed the defalcations, which ran to many thousands of dollars.

Lax inventory control is another practice that encourages theft of property by employees. One of the more modern developments in connection with computers is the maintaining of a computerized inventory which gives a constant record of additions to inventory and sales from inventory. Discrepancies between the computed inventory and the physical inventory indicate the degree of shrinkage from other than sales.

The second element that opens an employer to theft is the belief by the employer that a long-time, trusted employee could not be an embezzler. The fact is that most embezzlers are trusted employees.

Otherwise, they would not have access to the money or other property that is taken. Controls must be established in such a way that embezzlement will be revealed by routine checkups.

Types of Embezzlement Losses

Like other property exposures, employee dishonesty may cause both direct property losses and indirect losses resulting from the direct losses. However, the incidence of indirect loss is much lower for employee dishonesty than from the major property damage perils, such as fire.

Direct Property Losses It must be recognized that there are reasons for inventory shortage other than the theft of property. As pointed out in a previous chapter, there is a substantial likelihood of shrinkage from shoplifting in any mercantile operation. Shrinkage of inventory also can result from spoilage of the goods and from breakage, both of which may result in the disposal of property without a proper note being taken that the property is being deleted from inventory.

Another possibility is nondelivery of goods that have been ordered. An absence of control after the property has been ordered and before the actual delivery takes place may result in the showing of an inventory figure higher than that actually on hand. Inventory figures should be established from actual receipt of the property and not from the orders that have been placed.

The most common form of employee embezzlement is in the theft of merchandise. It has been estimated that the theft of merchandise is from seven to ten times greater than the theft of cash. Many employers recognize the susceptibility of cash to theft but do not realize how much of their property is being taken out day by day by their employees.

Another method of theft is the sale by an employee of the employer's property. This may consist of scrap metal or other scrap items that are sold for cash by the employee. It may also consist of the fraudulent delivery of property to an accomplice outside the premises. This may be accomplished by false delivery vouchers which are subsequently destroyed by the employee so that they do not go through the accounts of the employer.

Still another method of theft is the writing of false labor vouchers. This may consist of fictitious employees whose paychecks or cash pass through the hands of a supervisor who extracts them and deposits them to bank accounts that have been set up for this purpose. Occasionally, there may be collusion between the supervisor and the employees who are credited with fictitious overtime work, and the pay for overtime is then split between the supervisor and the employee.

The growth of drug addiction in the United States has increased the problem of inventory control in such operations as pharmacies and hospitals. The persons in control of drug inventories may be tempted to sell some of the drugs to addicts or drug suppliers and then falsify records to show proper use of the drugs. This possibility exists not only with such drugs as morphine but also for the barbiturates and amphetamines which are used in substantially larger quantities for legitimate medical purposes.

Indirect Losses The loss of property entails additional, indirect losses to the employer. The work necessary in replacing lost merchandise and in making the necessary accounting checks can be very expensive. Employee time must be taken to determine the items which have been lost, additional orders must be sent to suppliers, and auditors or accountants must adjust records to conform to the situation.

An important indirect cost is the effect upon employee morale when an embezzlement is discovered. Ordinarily, there is no way that the fact of a discovered embezzlement can be kept from other employees. There is the same kind of loss of effective working time on the part of employees that was described in the preceding chapter following a burglary or robbery in an establishment. There is the additional problem that discovery of an embezzlement by a top official of an organization may cause other employees to feel that theft is an acceptable occurrence because one of the bosses has been caught. The discovery of theft by one of the lower echelon employees may cause other employees to feel that they could have gotten away with it by being more careful.

Still another important indirect loss from employee theft is the cut-price competition from the sale of stolen merchandise in the market place. Police officials state that some of the so-called discount houses operate with a high proportion of stolen merchandise. The exceptionally low prices at which this stolen merchandise is sold decrease the sales of legitimate merchandise at regular prices by honest merchants. This loss of business because of competition from the sale of stolen merchandise causes a further loss to the legitimate merchant.

Damage to Property There are cases where employees damage the property of their employers for purposes of revenge or malice. This is not embezzlement because it does not involve conversion of the property to the personal use of the thief. However, it is a variety of employee dishonesty and can be extremely expensive. It is a threat in many industrial and mercantile operations, particularly where employee morale is low. One case involved an employee who immobilized the computer operation whenever he wanted to take time off. There may be cases where it is difficult or impossible to distinguish arson or vandalism by outsiders from that which is perpetrated by employees. Also, vandalism or arson may be an attempt to cover up a theft on the premises.

Frequency and Severity of Embezzlement Losses

It is extremely difficult to arrive at any adequate figures regarding the frequency or severity of embezzlement losses. It has been estimated that the theft of cash and merchandise from employers amounts to $10 million or more per day. Employee theft sometimes is more difficult to prove than theft by an outsider, and there are many cases where employee theft is evident but where the person(s) responsible cannot be discovered.

For example, in an industrial operation that used large quantities of silver, an internal audit of inventory indicated that $3 million worth of silver was missing. The manufacturer called in external auditors and proceeded with a detailed investigation to find out where the silver went, who was responsible, and whether any of the value could be recovered. The disappearance was so well engineered that the method of disposal was not immediately evident and it was doubtful that it could even be proved a theft.

Experts in this field have concluded that the incidence of embezzlement is much higher than the incidence of crime not involving employee dishonesty. Many of the embezzlements are small in nature and consist of pilferage from cash registers and from mercantile stock. These may not be detected at all, or may be considered inventory or cash shortages from the normal operations of business. It is only the incidents involving larger values that result in discovery. The potential loss is great in relation to a firm's assets in any operation where money or merchandise is subject to theft by employees. No business is immune, and the total loss from employee dishonesty is an important factor as a threat to profitable operation of a business.

Evaluating the Impact of Potential Embezzlement Losses

Several formulas have been devised to guide a business organization in estimating the potential loss. Unfortunately, these formulas do not give much help to the smaller business organization, and they are indicative only of the averages as far as the larger organizations are concerned. However, an analysis of the factors that are used in these formulas will indicate the weak spots where thefts are most likely to occur.

Estimating Loss Potentials   The various factors which are taken into account in estimating the exposure to embezzlement loss are generally the following: (1) the firm's assets, (2) current inventory of physical goods on hand, (3) the annual income or gross sales of the organization, (4) the nature of the business and the nature of the product or goods handled, (5) the size of the organization, and (6) the number of employees.

The current assets of the organization are perhaps the most important indication of exposure. These include cash, bank deposits, securities, accounts receivable, and inventory. The larger the current assets, the greater the exposure to theft.

Perhaps the best of the formulas is that developed by the Surety Association of America and published in the booklet *How Much Honesty Insurance?* The factors included in the formula were derived from a study of a large number of actual claims, and the use of the formula would have resulted in full coverage for the vast majority of the claims.

There are two steps in the application of the formula. First, an exposure index is calculated through the use of the formula; then the exposure index is used to enter a table of insurance amounts to find the suggested bond limit for the firm. The suggested insurance amounts are, of course, indicative of the potential loss, though larger losses are possible. The exposure index formula is:

$$\text{Exposure index} = 0.20A + 0.05B + 0.10C$$

where A = the firm's current assets minus the value of goods on hand, B = the value of goods on hand, and C = the firm's annual gross sales or income.

After the exposure index has been calculated, it is used to find the suggested bond limit as shown in Table 12-1.

As an illustration, assume that a firm has the following values:

1. current assets	$ 500,000
2. goods on hand	200,000
3. annual gross sales	2,000,000

Then, its exposure index would be:

$$\text{Exposure index} = 0.20(500{,}000 - 200{,}000) + 0.05(200{,}000) + 0.10(2{,}000{,}000)$$

$$= 60{,}000 + 10{,}000 + 200{,}000 = \$270{,}000$$

The suggested bond limit, from Table 12-1, would be between $75,000 and $100,000. Since the exposure index is near the lower end of the bracket into which it falls, the recommended bond limit probably

Table 12-1

Suggested Minimum Amounts of Honesty Insurance*

Exposure Index		Bracket Number	Amount of Bond	
Up to — $	25,000	1	$ 15,000 —	25,000
$ 25,000 —	125,000	2	25,000 —	50,000
125,000 —	250,000	3	50,000 —	75,000
250,000 —	500,000	4	75,000 —	100,000
500,000 —	750,000	5	100,000 —	125,000
750,000 —	1,000,000	6	125,000 —	150,000
1,000,000 —	1,375,000	7	150,000 —	175,000
1,375,000 —	1,750,000	8	175,000 —	200,000
1,750,000 —	2,125,000	9	200,000 —	225,000
2,125,000 —	2,500,000	10	225,000 —	250,000
2,500,000 —	3,325,000	11	250,000 —	300,000
3,325,000 —	4,175,000	12	300,000 —	350,000
4,175,000 —	5,000,000	13	350,000 —	400,000
5,000,000 —	6,075,000	14	400,000 —	450,000
6,075,000 —	7,150,000	15	450,000 —	500,000
7,150,000 —	9,275,000	16	500,000 —	600,000
9,275,000 —	11,425,000	17	600,000 —	700,000
11,425,000 —	15,000,000	18	700,000 —	800,000
15,000,000 —	20,000,000	19	800,000 —	900,000
20,000,000 —	25,000,000	20	900,000 — 1,000,000	
25,000,000 —	50,000,000	21	1,000,000 — 1,250,000	
50,000,000 —	87,500,000	22	1,250,000 — 1,500,000	
87,500,000 —	125,000,000	23	1,500,000 — 1,750,000	
125,000,000 —	187,500,000	24	1,750,000 — 2,000,000	
187,500,000 —	250,000,000	25	2,000,000 — 2,250,000	
250,000,000 —	333,325,000	26	2,250,000 — 2,500,000	
333,325,000 —	500,000,000	27	2,500,000 — 3,000,000	
500,000,000 —	750,000,000	28	3,000,000 — 3,500,000	
750,000,000 — 1,000,000,000		29	3,500,000 — 4,000,000	
1,000,000,000 — 1,250,000,000		30	4,000,000 — 4,500,000	
1,250,000,000 — 1,500,000,000		31	4,500,000 — 5,000,000	

*Reprinted with permission of The Surety Association of America.

would be nearer to $75,000 than to $100,000, though this is a matter of individual judgment.

It must be kept in mind that the formula is based on averages, and an individual firm's loss exposure may be more or less severe, depending on the kind of business, the safeguards established, and other factors.

Also, the suggested limits are not maximum possible losses. Larger losses can and do occur.

The business organization, therefore, faces a difficult task in determining what its potential embezzlement loss may be. This is particularly true for the small organization that may be subject to a single catastrophe loss or a repetitive series of embezzlements that would add up to a catastrophe loss over a period of time. Loss control techniques will be discussed later in this chapter. An important point to be considered in estimating the potential loss is the time period between audits or inventory controls. Ordinary bookkeeping audits have been notoriously weak in determining embezzlements and fraud. Many of the auditing firms require their clients to acknowledge that the audit is merely a check of bookkeeping procedures and of assets on hand.

The figure of 5 percent of goods on hand or inventory is low for a small organization, although it is probably a satisfactory figure for a large manufacturing or mercantile operation where averages would apply. The business organization would have to estimate how much of its inventory could be stolen by employees over a period between the times when physical inventory is reconciled with purchases and sales. This might well amount to 10 percent or 20 percent of the inventory at any one time in a small organization.

The net result of a careful estimate on the part of a business organization may reveal that the exposure over a period of time comes close to the organization's total assets. The seriousness of the exposure cannot be underestimated.

Estimating the Impact on the Financial Stability of the Firm Numerous insolvencies of business organizations due to employee theft, embezzlement, and fraud testify to the seriousness of the exposure. Fraud and embezzlement on the part of employees have resulted in the bankruptcy of even large organizations. It may be said in general that a cumulative theft amounting to more than the firm's surplus is likely to result in insolvency. Analyses that have been made of employee attitudes indicate that many employees feel that it is perfectly all right to steal from the employer if it can be accomplished without being caught. This may range from petty theft, such as that of the employee who walked out of the plant every day with two cans of beans under his arms, to the legal secretary who forged checks and stole $17,000 from the bank account of her employer. It has already been pointed out that there are no accurate estimates of the total loss to business from employee theft, embezzlement and fraud, but the total is estimated to be far in excess of the total loss from crime not involving employee dishonesty. Generally, the exposure to smaller organizations is greater in proportion to the assets than in the case of a large organization.

BASIC CHARACTERISTICS OF FIDELITY BONDS

Insurance companies offer a variety of contracts to indemnify employers against losses from employee dishonesty. These contracts may be referred to as honesty insurance but are known more commonly as fidelity bonds.

Principles of Suretyship and Fidelity Bonds

Fidelity bonds constitute one specialized segment of suretyship, a relationship in which one person (or firm) agrees to indemnify a second person (or firm) for loss caused by the failure of a third person (or firm) to perform some act in an agreed manner. In general suretyship there may be a wide variety of persons involved, and the nature of the act to be performed also may vary widely. However, fidelity bonds always deal with the employer-employee relationship. They usually indemnify the employer for loss resulting from the dishonest acts of employees in the course of their duties as such. However, in the case of public employees, the bond may cover loss resulting from lack of faithful performance of duties. The latter coverage is somewhat broader, as is shown later in this chapter.

Although surety bonds, including fidelity bonds, usually are written by insurance companies and bear a strong resemblance to insurance, there are some technical and theoretical differences between bonds and insurance.

Theoretical Relationships The theory under which an employer is guaranteed against loss because of employee dishonesty differs from insurance. An insurance contract is executed between two parties, the insurer and the insured. The insurer agrees to pay the insured any losses that result from occurrences covered by the insurance contract.

The fidelity bond theoretically is a guarantee to the employer that the employee will be honest. The bond provides further that the person or organization which guarantees the honesty will reimburse the employer if the employee proves to be dishonest. Historically, fidelity bonds were three-party contracts involving the employer, the employee, and the person or organization that makes the guarantee. However, with the spread of *blanket* fidelity bonds, employees may not even know that they are bonded in many cases.

The employer-employee relationship has been used here for simplicity. Actually, a fidelity bond could be used to cover other circumstances, but the employer-employee relationship is the one most frequently involved. The bond guarantees the honesty of a person who is in a position of trust. In a few cases, primarily for public officials and public employees, fidelity bonds may guarantee faithful performance of duties, which is much broader than a guarantee of honesty. The person or organization making the guarantee on the bond would indemnify the employer for loss of money or property which might be sustained because of dishonesty.

Fidelity bonds, in theory and practice, are similar in many ways to surety bonds which are discussed in CPCU 4. The practice of suretyship goes back thousands of years. There are references in the Bible and in ancient history to suretyship on the part of individuals who guaranteed the honesty or faithful performance of duties by other individuals. There still may be cases where an individual will guarantee the honesty of some other person, but most surety and fidelity bonding today is done by corporations such as insurance companies.

There are three persons or organizations in the relationship involved in fidelity bonding. These are:

1. The *principal*—the person whose honesty is guaranteed. This would be the employee in the case of an employer-employee relationship.
2. The *obligee*—the beneficiary creditor, the employer in the case of an employee-employer relationship. This is the person or organization to whom the guarantee is made.
3. The *surety*—the person or corporation which provides the guarantee. In modern practice, the surety usually is a corporation, and ordinarily would be an insurance company.

It is desirable to distinguish between suretyship in a fidelity bonding situation and a guarantee as it is usually understood in a business transaction. The fidelity bonding relationship guarantees to the obligee that the principal will carry out in an honest manner the duties which are covered by the bond. A business guarantee, in contrast, usually assures that a product is of a special quality or that a purchase price will be refunded if the product is unsatisfactory in some respect.

Practical Applications Personal suretyship has proved to be a burden upon the surety throughout the ages. A default by the principal and subsequent payment of the obligation by the surety many times results in a real hardship to the surety. There may be cases where the assets of the surety are insufficient to meet the obligation, with consequent loss not only to the surety but also to the obligee.

The corporate surety has an assured continuous existence, in contrast to the personal surety who may die, thus ending the obligation. The corporate surety is expected to have sufficient assets to meet any obligation that is accepted. The corporate surety also has an established practice or procedure for the handling of obligations if the principal defaults.

The theory of fidelity bonding is that the obligee (the employer) would try first to collect from the principal (the employee) in case of fraudulent or dishonest acts. However, the general practice is for the corporate surety to step in and pay the loss, and then the surety determines whether there is any possibility of recovering from the principal.

The theory of fidelity bonding also requires that the fraudulent or dishonest act be shown to have been committed by the principal under the bond. However, modern business is so complex that it is impossible under many circumstances to determine precisely which person or persons caused the loss. The result is that so-called fidelity bonds have tended more and more to take on the characteristics of insurance policies. They tend to provide for payment of any loss that can be proved to come within the coverage provisions of the policy or bond regardless of whether or not a particular employee can be identified as having caused the loss.

The various types of fidelity bonds are described herein according to the commonly used names. It should be kept in mind that many of them have become two-party contracts under which the surety, or insurance company, agrees to pay any losses which arise from dishonesty of employees or others who are in a position of trust. The employee is not a direct party to some form of fidelity bonds, and may not even know that a bond exists. The original theory of a three-party contract which guarantees honesty tends to be disappearing even though the terminology applicable to fidelity bonding is still maintained.

Common Features in Fidelity Bonds

Perils Covered The coverage of a typical fidelity bond applies to "the amount of any direct loss through larceny, theft, embezzlement, forgery, misappropriation, wrongful abstraction, willful misapplication, or any other act of fraud or dishonesty committed by," with appropriate notation as to whether the coverage applies to a named individual or is a blanket coverage applying to any employee. Dishonesty must be the cause of the loss. There is no coverage of a loss resulting from an error or omission or from bad judgment on the part of an employee.

The coverage of the fidelity bond must also be distinguished from that of an "all-risks" type of insurance. There is no coverage for inventory shortage or other unexplained disappearance where there is no indication nor evidence that employee dishonesty was the cause of the loss. A mercantile operation, for example, might have substantial losses from shoplifting which would have to be distinguished from losses caused by employee dishonesty.

There is a type of combination fidelity bond and insurance policy which does cover loss from dishonesty, disappearance, destruction, fraud, and forgery, but this is broader than the coverage of a pure fidelity bond. This 3-D, or dishonesty, disappearance, and destruction, insurance policy will be discussed in greater detail in Chapter 14.

Property Covered A typical fidelity bond covers loss of any type of property if the loss results from the dishonesty of an employee. This includes money, securities, and practically any other personal, or even real, property that is lost to the obligee because of employee dishonesty. Coverage usually applies also to property of others in the custody of the employer and for which the employer is legally responsible.

Persons Covered The fidelity bond applies only to the acts of employees. Coverage does not apply to brokers, agents, contractors, or other representatives of the insured, nor does it apply to acts of partners. The acts of corporate officers are covered because they are employees of the corporation. The bond may exclude directors or trustees, particularly if they are not employees in some other capacity.

The original form of fidelity bonds named the person who was covered by the bond. Such fidelity bonds which individually name the employee or employees who are covered are still issued, though less frequently than in the past.

The complexities of modern business make it difficult for a large organization to name individually the persons who are covered. One variation, which will be described later, applies to named positions within the organization rather than to named employees. This permits coverage of the employees who occupy the specified positions even though the persons holding those positions may change.

Various forms of blanket fidelity coverage have also been developed. Provisions differ as to whether identification of the dishonest employee is required before the amount of the loss can be collected. These various features will be discussed in connection with the different kinds of bonds that are issued. The requirements of modern business make it more and more common for coverage to apply on a blanket basis to all employees rather than to named individuals.

Time Period Covered A fidelity bond may be written for a specified term, but many bonds are written from a specified effective date until canceled. Such a continuous bond would provide for periodic payment of premium, with payment at least annually. There is a provision which limits recovery to the amounts named in the bond even though the coverage may be continuous over a period of several years.

There is an important feature of fidelity bond coverage which differs from insurance coverage. An employer may not discover a loss for a considerable period of time after the loss actually occurred. Fidelity bonds provide for a limit as to the time of discovery following the termination of the bond. All such bonds cover a loss which both occurs and is discovered during the time the bond is in effect. In addition, losses which occur while the bond is in effect but are discovered after the bond is terminated are covered, provided the loss is discovered before the expiration of the discovery period. Some bonds provide for discovery within one year after termination, while others allow two years for discovery.

Complications may arise in cases where an employer changes bonding companies for a fidelity bond. The bond that is canceled normally would cover losses that occurred while the bond was in effect and were discovered before the expiration of the discovery period. Thus, the bonding company whose bond was cancelled would provide no coverage for an act that is discovered after the expiration of the discovery period, and the new bond would not cover any losses which occurred prior to its effective date. This could leave the employer without coverage for some losses. It is common practice for a newly written bond to include a clause which extends the new bond to cover losses which would have been covered under a prior bond except for the expiration of the discovery period under the prior bond. Such coverage of losses that occurred during the term of a previous bond is limited to the smaller of: (1) the amount which would have been covered under the prior bond, or (2) the amount covered under the existing bond. This acceptance of losses which occurred during the period of a previous bond is called *superseded suretyship*, or, in some contracts, the clause is entitled *loss under prior bond or policy*. This superseding suretyship is effective only if the succeeding bond goes into effect immediately upon termination of the canceled bond.

Amounts Covered A fidelity bond has what would be called in an insurance policy a limit of liability. The amount of the coverage may be a total amount applying to the bond, or it may be separated so that specified amounts apply to named persons or to named positions within the organization.

Subrogation and Salvage The surety (the insurance company) is entitled to recover any loss payment from the dishonest employee. The function of the surety is to guarantee the honesty of the principal, and recovery is expected to be made from the principal if the principal has any assets that can be attached. The surety, therefore, can be expected to proceed against the principal if there is any possibility of recovery. Sometimes a relative of the dishonest employee may be persuaded to make restitution in order to avoid or alleviate criminal proceedings against the defaulting employee.

There are many cases where the amount of the bond is insufficient to cover the loss. The employer is first indemnified to the full extent of the loss before the bonding company secures any part of a recovery.

Automatic Cancellation It is a principle of fidelity bonding that coverage on a particular employee is immediately and automatically canceled upon discovery of a fraud or dishonest act on the part of that employee. This, of course, would not have any effect upon coverage for acts of the employee which were committed prior to that time but would apply to any further acts of the employee from the date of discovery.

There are many employers who hesitate to discharge a valuable employee even though the employee has been discovered to have acted dishonestly. Such an actual case involved a salesman for a corporation who was found to have stolen $100,000 worth of merchandise from the corporation. The manager of the corporation would not discharge the employee nor take legal action against him because the salesman was responsible for about $1 million of profit per year to the organization. The manager said that when the thefts of this employee exceeded the profit he made for the organization he would then discharge the employee and proceed against him. Many employers are willing to overlook employee dishonesty as long as the particular employee has other valuable assets for the organization. The bonding company cannot afford to continue coverage on an employee who has been discovered in a dishonest act. Therefore, the bond contains a provision which immediately excludes coverage as to any future acts of such an employee. Some of the blanket bonding forms which cover all employees without naming them also exclude an employee for whom the coverage has been canceled by a previous insurer of the employer.

Fraud on the Part of the Employer Fraud on the part of the employer in securing the fidelity bond would cause the bond to be voidable. A bond may contain a fraud provision similar to that appearing in most insurance policies, or the bonding company may depend upon the general legal principle that any contract that is procured through fraud is void.

Requirements in the Event of Loss Fidelity bonds have provisions, similar to those in insurance policies, requiring the filing of a notice of loss and of a claim. A written notice must be given to the bonding company setting forth the name and address of the employee or employees causing the loss. A proof of loss must be filed according to provisions which are similar to those in insurance policies. The employer is required to cooperate with the bonding company in connection with any investigation that may be made or in any recovery proceedings.

Fidelity bonds also have provisions similar to those of insurance policies regarding the filing of suit or taking other legal proceedings against the bonding company. A typical provision is that suit may not be brought until two months have elapsed after the proof of loss has been filed with the company, and cannot be brought later than twelve months after discovery of such loss. These provisions are subject to modification according to some state laws which lengthen the period during which suit may be filed.

TYPES OF FIDELITY BONDS

Fidelity bonds may be categorized according to the employees covered. Some bonds cover only those employees listed by name in the bond. Others cover only those employees who occupy certain positions (e.g., cashier or treasurer) listed in the bond. Finally, some bonds, called blanket bonds, cover all employees except those specifically excluded in the bond.

Individual Bond

The individual bond in its simplest form is an actual three-party contract naming the employer, the employee, and the bonding company (the insurance company). This is a direct descendent of the fidelity bonds in which the surety was an individual. Such a bond includes provisions stating the dishonest acts that are covered, plus the usual provisions setting out the obligations of the various parties. A limit of liability, or penalty, is also stated which limits the amount for which the surety would be liable in case of defalcation by the principal.

The individual bond is used only where there is one or a small number of employees to be covered, and particularly where it is anticipated that there would be a continuity of employment. This type of bond is not suitable where there is a large number of employees, a large number of positions to be covered within the company, or where there is a large turnover in personnel.

Name Schedule Bond

The name schedule bond is essentially an expansion of the

individual bond with a format that permits the listing of employees by name, with the amounts of coverage set opposite each individual name. The difference is primarily one of format which makes it easier to list several employees and, if desired, to indicate different amounts of coverage for the various employees. Changes in the employees can be accomplished by means of endorsements to delete the names of those who have left the employment and add new names.

Position Schedule Bond

The position schedule bond is a break from the traditional principle under which the bond was intended to guarantee the fidelity of named persons. The position schedule bond specifies positions within the employer's organization and does not name any individual persons. For example, the position schedule bond might list the positions of messenger, bookkeeper, receiving clerk, and shipping clerk. The amount of coverage for each of these positions may vary, depending upon the employer's estimate of the value that could be stolen by a person occupying that position.

It can be seen that the position schedule bond has advantages to the employer because no changes are necessary in the bond as individual employees leave and are replaced. The addition of a new position normally would require notification to the bonding company within a specified time. Automatic coverage may be provided for the new position for an interim period. The bond also may provide that the existing coverage will be prorated to include the new position if notification is not made within the required time. For example, the addition of another messenger position might result in the coverage for both messenger positions being reduced to one-half the amount which previously was in effect for the single messenger position. These variations are subject to individual underwriting on the part of the bonding company, depending upon circumstances.

The position schedule bond is advantageous to the employer whose organization is relatively stable and where the duties of the persons filling the different positions are clearly defined. It may not be suitable for a situation where employees tend to move from one position to another as the work load demands. The bonding underwriter must determine whether there is a clear-cut division between the positions before deciding to write a position schedule bond.

A disadvantage of the position schedule bond as compared to the name schedule bond as far as underwriting is concerned is the fact that the bonding company is not notified of the individual persons who are covered. The employer may be lax in pre-employment investigation of new employees. The persons filling the various positions may have histories of previous dishonest acts. The use of the name schedule bond, on the contrary, does give the bonding company an opportunity to make its own checks on the previous history of persons who are added to the coverage of the bond.

Underwriting of the position schedule bond must depend to a large extent on the employment practices of the employer. The coverage may be written for an employer who is known to make pre-employment investigations as to honesty and previous history, whereas a name schedule bond might be insisted upon for an employer whose hiring practices do not include such pre-employment checks.

Even though coverage is by position rather than by individual, these bonds also have a provision that coverage ceases for any employee who is discovered to have committed a dishonest or fraudulent act. This suspension of coverage applies to the individual employee and not to the position. The employer has no coverage under any position for an individual for whom the employer has discovered a dishonest act. Coverage cannot be reinstated for this person by moving the employee to a different position within the company. Coverage just does not apply for that person for that employer from that time on.

Blanket Bonds

Bonding companies have tended to be more and more liberal in their willingness to provide coverage against dishonesty of employees without naming the individual person. An important move in this direction, already described, was the coverage of specific positions within the employer's organization. A further important step is the issuing of blanket bonds.

A blanket bond covers all employees of the organization without any schedule or listing. The surety which issues the bond to the employer agrees to reimburse the employer for all losses resulting from dishonest acts of employees. This covers loss of money or other property, real or personal, belonging to the insured or in which the insured has a pecuniary interest. There is also coverage for loss of money and property of others for which the insured is legally liable, or which is held by the insured in any capacity, without regard to legal liability for loss of the property.

There are two blanket bonds which are generally available to cover businesses. One is the commercial blanket bond and the other is the blanket position bond. The details of these will be described later, but there is one important difference between the two that is worthy of note here. The difference in actual coverage as far as the employer is concerned relates to a loss which results from collusion by more than one employee. The commercial blanket bond limits the recovery in such a case to the penalty or limit of liability which is named in the bond. This is the limit no matter how many employees may participate in the dishonest act.

The blanket position bond, on the other hand, permits recovery for the named penalty or limit of liability for each employee who is identified as participating in a collusive loss. For example, assuming a $20,000 penalty named in the bond, the maximum that could be recovered under the commercial blanket bond for a single collusive act would be the $20,000. The blanket position bond, in contrast, would permit recovery of the $20,000 penalty for each of the employees who were acting in collusion in connection with the theft. Thus, collusion by two employees with a $20,000 penalty named in the bond would permit a $40,000 recovery under the blanket position bond.

There are other differences between the two principal blanket bonds, but this is one of the very important differences. Further details will be discussed in connection with the specific bonds.

The important feature of the blanket bond as contrasted to any kind of a schedule or individual bond is the fact that all officers and employees are covered without naming them. This, of course, further increases the difficulty of underwriting such a bond. Employees change from time to time, and new employees are covered. As pointed out in connection with the position schedule bond, the elimination of the names of individuals increases the difficulty on the part of the underwriter in detecting in advance potentially dishonest employees.

ANALYSIS OF SOME IMPORTANT FIDELITY BONDS

The foregoing paragraphs have outlined some of the principles of fidelity bonding. Those that follow will discuss the important provisions of some of the more important fidelity bond forms.

Commercial Blanket Bond

The declarations page of the commercial blanket bond names the bonding company, the employer (who in most current bonds is called the insured) specifies the bond period and the limit of liability, and includes a condition that acceptance of this bond terminates prior bonds. The bond normally states an inception date and then provides that the coverage shall be effective until cancellation or termination.

The limit of liability is stated in dollars, and is the amount applying to a single act. The terminology here also tends to follow that of insurance practices and usually is now called a limit of liability rather than the older term of penalty.

Insuring Agreement   The insuring agreement is the very heart of the coverage. The bonding company (in many bonds called the "underwriter") agrees to indemnify the insured against any loss of money or other property which the insured shall sustain through any fraudulent or dishonest act or acts committed by any of the employees, acting alone or in collusion with others, to an amount not exceeding the aggregate limit of liability stated in the declarations. This wording limits to the amount stated in the limit of liability the amount that can be recovered for an individual loss. It has already been pointed out that under the commercial blanket bond this limit of liability applies to any one act of dishonesty, even though it may involve more than one employee acting in collusion. It should also be noted that the insuring agreement applies to any loss of money or other property. There is no limitation nor other designation of the kind of property covered. Thus, a loss of real property as well as personal property would be covered.

General Agreements   There is provision for notice by the insured to the underwriter and for appropriate additional premium if the covered organization consolidates or merges with another organization, or purchases additional facilities. There is no additional premium charge for new employees acquired during the year except for those acquired by consolidation or merger.

There may be cases where more than one insured will be named in the bond. There is a provision so that payment of any loss can be made to a particular insured for any of the joint insureds. There is also a limitation that the coverage of more than one insured shall not extend the limit of liability. Discovery of dishonesty on the part of any employee by any insured covered by the bond is deemed to be knowledge by all of the insureds. This is necessary so that the entire coverage as to a dishonest employee would be canceled by discovery of a dishonest act by any of the joint insureds who may be covered under a single policy.

There is a specific provision in this bond relative to loss under a prior bond. This provides coverage for such a loss which is discovered during the currency of this bond even though the dishonest act may have occurred during the time of a previous bond, provided the discovery period under the prior bond has expired. Recovery under such a superseded suretyship situation is limited to the limit of liability in this bond, or to the limit of liability under the previous bond, whichever is less. The superseded suretyship does not increase the limit of liability under the current bond. Any loss is treated as if it were a loss under the current bond.

Conditions

Loss is covered under the bond only if it is discovered not later than one year from the end of the bond period. The dishonest act must occur during the bond period, but one year is allowed for discovery.

Many bonds limit coverage to the United States and Canada but may also extend coverage to employees who are outside those limits for a specified period. Territorial limits would be subject to negotiation depending upon the needs of the employer.

An exclusion applies to loss which in insurance terms might be considered mysterious disappearance. There is no coverage for a loss for which the proof of existence or amount is dependent upon an inventory computation or a profit and loss computation. However, this exclusion does not apply to a case where the fact of the loss can be proved from other evidence but the amount might be dependent upon some kind of an inventory or bookkeeping computation.

An employee is defined as a natural person while in the regular service of the insured in the ordinary course of the insured's business who is compensated by salary, wages, or commission. Excluded are brokers, factors, commissioned merchants, consignees, contractors or other agents. An employee must be a person who is acting in the generally understood capacity of an employee. The definition in the bond reinforces this intent.

It is not necessary that the dishonest employees be identified. There is coverage for a loss even if the insured is unable to designate the specific employee or employees causing such loss. It is necessary that the insured submit reasonable evidence which proves that the loss was in fact due to the fraud or dishonesty of one or more employees. The maximum amount payable to the insured under those circumstances is the limit of liability stated in the declarations.

Cancellation As to a Dishonest Employee There are two provisions which are related to each other and which provide for immediate cancellation of coverage as to an individual employee.

The first of these conditions provides that the coverage shall not apply to an employee from the time that the insured or any partner or officer thereof not in collusion with such employee shall learn that the employee has committed any fraudulent or dishonest act in the service of the insured or otherwise, whether such act was committed before or after the date of employment by the insured. This further provides that if coverage of any person has been canceled under a previous bond covering the insured, the coverage of this bond shall not apply to that employee unless the bonding company specifically agrees in writing to include such employee. The reasons for these provisions have already been discussed.

Provision is also made for cancellation by the bonding company as to any individual employee. The bonding company may discover evidence of previous or current dishonesty on the part of some employee, and it may be considered necessary to cancel coverage as to that employee. Fifteen days notice usually is required for exercise of this right on the part of the bonding company.

Notice and Proof of Loss The provisions for notice and proof of loss are similar to those which are used in insurance policies. The details can be determined by examination of a specific bond.

Recoveries The principles of subrogation have already been discussed in connection with bonds generally. The provisions in this bond follow the usual practices. It is customary for bonding companies to attempt recovery if the dishonest employee has assets which might be attached for this purpose. The bond provides that any recoveries which are made shall first apply to any loss of the insured which was not paid by the bond. After the insured has been made whole in regard to the loss, any additional recovery shall be applied to the reimbursement of the bonding company.

Limits of Liability The limit of liability under the bond is not reduced by the payment of a loss. Any separate and additional loss that may occur or be discovered would be paid, subject to the limit of liability for each such loss. There is also provision that continuity of the bond from year to year will not make the limit of liability cumulative. The limit of liability applies to each separate loss.

There may be a loss which occurs partly during the term of a preceding bond and also during the time of the present bond. The limit of liability under the present bond would apply to the aggregate of such a loss.

There is provision for the prorating of a loss if there happens to be other insurance or a bond that covers the loss. For example, there could be certain types of theft insurance that would cover a loss that is partly the result of employee dishonesty and partly the result of acts by outsiders. Also, forgery coverage may be written to cover employee forgery losses. There is also the possibility of there being more than one bond that would apply to a loss, although underwriters ordinarily would not arrange for more than one bond on the same employer.

Cancellation of Bond   There is provision for cancellation of the bond by the bonding company or by the insured. As has already been pointed out, the typical bond shows an effective date but provides for cancellation or termination whenever the insured or the bonding company wishes to terminate the coverage.

Blanket Position Bond

The blanket position bond is similar to the commercial blanket bond with one important exception, which has already been pointed out in the discussion of blanket bonds in general. The principal difference between these two bonds is the fact that the limit of liability under the commercial blanket bond for a single act of one or more employees is the limit of liability stated in the declarations. The blanket position bond, in contrast, applies the limit of liability to *each* employee. The effect is that when several employees act in collusion the limit of liability applies to each employee separately and not to the act of the entire group. This increases the recovery in the case of a collusive act to the number of employees involved times the limit of liability.

This effect relating to collusion is accomplished in the insuring agreement. The bonding company agrees to indemnify the insured against any loss of money or other property which the insured shall sustain through any fraudulent or dishonest act or acts committed by any one or more employees, acting alone or in collusion with others, the amount of indemnity on each of such employees being the limit of liability stated in the declarations.

The other provisions of the blanket position bond are closely similar to or identical with those of the commercial blanket bond. There may be a difference in the discovery period allowed under the different bonds (usually two years after termination for the blanket position bond) but this may be a matter of negotiation in the writing of the bond for a particular employer.

Common Endorsements and Variations

Fidelity bonds may be amended in several ways to meet the needs of a particular employee. A few of the more common endorsements are discussed below.

Excess Indemnity for Special Employees   An employer may decide that the blanket coverage of the commercial blanket bond or the blanket position bond is sufficient for most of the employees but that certain employees have access to funds or to other property which might enable them to cause losses greatly in excess of the bond limit. The blanket bond may be amended by an excess indemnity endorsement to provide higher limits of liability for certain named employees or named positions.

Excluded Employees   Sometimes an employer will wish to retain a particular employee even though previous history or some other circumstance makes the bonding company unwilling to provide coverage for that particular person. The bond may be amended by excluding coverage for any loss involving the person named in the exclusion.

Partnership Coverage   The usual bond covers dishonesty on the part of employees in the usual sense of the word. Acts of partners in a partnership are not covered because they are not employees. However, there are circumstances in which one partner may commit a dishonest or fraudulent act that will deplete the assets of the partnership. The chances of such an occurrence are increased when there is a large number of partners, as there may be in some operations. Partners generally are liable personally for obligations of the partnership. Therefore, a misappropriation of funds by one partner might obligate the remaining partners to make up the deficit from their personal assets. Some bonding companies will redefine the term employee to include partners in order to protect the remaining partners against a loss caused by one or more partners.

Other Variations   It should be remembered that the endorsements which have been described may not be available to a particular employer. The bonding company usually will adapt the coverage to the particular needs of an employer, but may be unwilling to provide some of the broader coverages in cases where the employer's exposure is high or where the employer is unable or unwilling to institute effective preventive measures. Bond underwriters try to keep in mind that fidelity bonds are intended to guarantee the honest performance of employees. The objective of such underwriting is to avoid loss. Therefore, the attempt is to avoid covering any employee whose potential for dishonesty is questionable. Variations and extensions of coverage may be provided by the bonding company only if the exposure is such that the underwriter feels that coverage can be safely extended.

Bankers Blanket Bond

Special insurance and infidelity coverages have been developed to cover the loss exposures of financial institutions. One of the most important of such special bonds or policies is the bankers blanket bond form no. 24, a commonly used form which is the basis of a wide variety of bonds for other financial institutions.

The bankers blanket bond is more than an employee infidelity coverage. It is called a bond but it is, to a large extent, an insurance coverage, as will be seen from the kinds of losses which are covered by it.

The form of the bankers blanket bond is similar to that of the bonds which we have discussed. The bank is called an insured, in common with insurance terminology. However, the form abandons to a large degree the traditional fidelity bond principle of a three-party contract. It is similar in this respect to the blanket bonds which have just been discussed.

The bond period starts with the date noted in the declarations and runs until termination or cancellation. The bankers blanket bond, in this respect, is similar to the other blanket bonds. It is not written for a specified term as is the case with most insurance policies.

The limit of liability provisions are different from the blanket bonds just discussed in that provision is made for limits of lesser amounts or deletion entirely of coverage for any insuring agreements that may be specified. In this respect, it resembles the comprehensive 3-D policy.

Much of the coverage applies to named premises of the insured. The declarations page includes provision for deletion of coverage for certain offices of the insured in cases if the insured for some reason does not wish to cover them, or if the underwriter considers such locations unacceptable for coverage.

There are several insuring agreements applying to various situations and types of loss. These are all subject to a descriptive statement to the effect that the insurance company will indemnify and hold harmless the insured with respect to loss which is sustained by the insured at any time but which is discovered during the bond period. It is important to note here that the act causing the loss may have occurred any time, even prior to the effective date of the bond, but that discovery must occur during the bond period.

The various insuring agreements are headed by titles which indicate in general the nature of the coverage under those titles. The effect of each insuring agreement is summarized here, with notations of any special features, but the full text should be consulted for details.

Fidelity This insuring agreement covers loss resulting from any dishonest or fraudulent act committed by any employee anywhere and whether committed alone or in collusion with others. This includes loss of property which is held by the insured for any purpose and in any capacity, whether it is held gratuitously and whether or not the insured is liable therefor. This is a very broad fidelity coverage applying to all employees and is limited only to the amount or amounts specified in the limit of liability provision. It is comparable to and in some respects even broader than the blanket bond coverages already described for commercial operations.

On Premises Property, as defined in the bond, is covered for loss due to robbery, burglary, theft, false pretenses, misplacement, mysterious unexplained disappearance, and damage to or destruction of such property. Also covered is loss from conversion, redemption, or deposit privileges because of such misplacement or loss of property, all while the property is within the offices or premises which are covered by the policy. This is an insurance coverage and applies whether or not there is negligence or violence in connection with the damage to or disappearance of the property.

An interesting extension in this paragraph applies to damage to property of customers on the premises of the bank, including outside parking lots or deposit facilities, which occurs to the customers' property from the perils listed.

In interpreting the foregoing paragraph and those that follow, it is important to take notice of the policy definition of property. Property includes money (that is, currency, coin, bank notes, and Federal Reserve Notes), postage, and revenue stamps, bullion, precious metals, jewelry, gems, and a number of similar items listed in the bond. Property, as used in the bond, does *not* include furniture, fixtures, office equipment, and similar items. Consequently, the broad coverage outlined in the preceding paragraph does not apply to such items.

Coverage does apply to furnishings, fixtures, stationery, supplies and equipment within the insured's offices for loss caused by larceny, burglary, robbery, or by vandalism or malicious mischief. This constitutes a very broad theft and vandalism coverage for equipment of the bank on the premises. Loss or damage by fire is excluded. It is expected that a bank would have fire insurance which would apply to any such loss even though it might have originated from theft or vandalism. There also is an exclusion applying to property in the mail or in the custody of a carrier for hire other than an armored motor vehicle company.

In Transit The coverage of loss of property in transit applies to acts of robbery, larceny, theft, misplacement, mysterious unexplainable disappearance, or property otherwise lost, damaged, or destroyed. This includes coverage of loss resulting from subscription, conversion, redemption, or deposit privileges through the misplacement or loss of property. This coverage applies while the property is in transit anywhere in the custody of any person or persons acting as messenger, except that there is no coverage for property in the mail or in the custody of a carrier for hire other than an armored motor vehicle company. This also is an insurance coverage and is not related to the dishonesty of employees.

Forgery or Alteration   A rather lengthy section provides coverage against loss from forgery or alteration of specified documents. This covers practically any loss that the bank might sustain because of a forgery or alteration in documents which pass through the custody of the bank. This, too, applies practically regardless of who is responsible for the forgery or alteration and is an insurance coverage rather than a fidelity coverage.

Securities   This, too, is a lengthy provision covering loss to the insured in connection with the handling of securities. This may occur because of counterfeit or forged securities, raised or otherwise altered securities, and a variety of other losses that can occur in the handling of securities for the bank itself or for others. This coverage is separate from the coverage from forgery or alteration and applies principally to the loss that might occur because of transactions involving the securities.

Redemption of United States Savings Bonds   This covers loss through the insured's paying or redeeming, guaranteeing, or witnessing any signature which has been forged, counterfeited, raised or otherwise altered, lost or stolen, or on which the signature to the request for payment shall have been forged. This protects the bank against loss that may occur from its handling the redemption of United States Savings Bonds on behalf of customers.

Counterfeit Currency   This covers loss through the receipt by the bank in good faith of any counterfeited or altered paper securities or coin of the United States or Canada.

Of the seven coverages which have just been reviewed, six are insurance coverages. Only the first is a fidelity coverage. The six insurance coverages apply regardless of whether the loss is perpetrated by an employee or by outsiders. There is no mention of what person shall have committed the various acts. Of course, if the loss does occur through a dishonest or fraudulent act of an employee, it would be considered as covered under the first paragraph applying to fidelity losses.

It should be remembered that such a bankers blanket bond can be written with one or more of the optional coverage paragraphs deleted from the contract. There may be situations where an underwriter would be unwilling to provide the extremely broad coverage under one or more of these coverage paragraphs. Underwriting considerations may also dictate that the limit of liability under one or more of these coverage paragraphs be less than the general limit of liability applying to the bond. As has been pointed out, limits of liability and other features are subject to negotiation between the insured bank and the insurance company. Therefore, the provisions of any particular bond as it is written are likely to differ from the provisions of other bonds written for similar insureds.

The general agreements and other conditions and limitations usually follow a standard language. The paragraphs below will review those and point out their effects upon the coverages provided by the bond.

General Agreements Several agreements apply to circumstances which may affect losses under the bond. These are in the nature of clarifications and, to a certain extent, are extensions of coverage.

Coverage is provided for any nominee which is organized by the insured for the purpose of handling certain of its business transactions and which is composed exclusively of the bank's officers, clerks or other employees. This recognizes the desirability or necessity for banks to operate certain facilities through organizations which are essentially a part of the bank's operations even though they are set up or incorporated separately.

Additional offices established by the insured bank during the term of the bond are covered automatically. Any additional premium that would be justified by the additional offices is not chargeable until the end of the premium period. However, it is intended that the premium be adjusted for the additional exposure which would accrue in the case of a merger of the insured organization with another institution.

A provision relating to warranties says that no statement made by or on behalf of the insured, whether contained in the application or otherwise, shall be deemed to be a warranty of anything except that it is true to the best of the knowledge and belief of the person making the statement. This is intended to clarify the intent of the parties regarding statements of fact or situations. There is no intent that the coverage would be voided by some technical misstatement that was made without intent to defraud or misrepresent.

There are provisions for the bonding company to pay certain court costs and attorneys' fees that may be incurred and paid by the insured in defending any suit or legal proceedings brought against the insured to enforce the insured's liability or alleged liability on account of any loss. This applies where the loss or damage would constitute a valid loss under the terms of the bond. These provisions spell out the relative obligations of the bonding company and the insured bank in cases where a deductible or other provision of the bond might result in a splitting of the legal expenses between the bonding company and the insured.

The insurance company is not required to pay any part of the defense costs if the amount of the claim is less than the deductible amount. If the claim is greater than the deductible, the insurer's liability for defense costs is found by multiplying the total defense costs by a fraction of which (1) the numerator is the portion of the claim in excess of the deductible amount, and (2) the denominator is the total amount claimed, including the deductible amount.

Conditions and Limitations   The definition of employee includes the insured's officers, clerks and other employees. These are natural persons while engaged in the services of the bank. Also included under certain conditions are attorneys and the employees of attorneys while performing services for the insured.

An employee also includes partnerships or corporations which are authorized by written agreement with the insured to perform services such as electronic data processing of checks or other accounting records of the insured. Thus, the coverage as to an employee applies to almost anyone and even to outside partnerships and corporations and attorneys and employees of such organizations, where those persons or organizations are performing services for the bank. However, it is further provided that each such processor and the partners, officers and employees of such processor shall, collectively, be deemed to be one employee for the purposes of the bond. This limits the amount that might be recovered to the limit of liability applying to a single employee.

The property covered is defined to include almost any kind of valuable personal property, documents, and "chattels which are not hereinbefore enumerated and for which the insured is legally liable." Specifically mentioned are such things as money, postage and revenue stamps, bullion, precious metals, jewelry, securities, checks, notes, bills of lading, abstracts of title, deeds, mortgages, and similar valuable papers. The intent obviously is to cover practically anything of value which the bank may hold for its own account or which it may hold for others either gratuitously or for pay, and whether or not the insured is liable therefore. This recognizes that banks have occasion in the conduct of their business to handle or to keep for their clients many different kinds of valuable properties. It also recognizes that the bank may have in its possession bills of lading in connection with business transactions for overseas or domestic commerce.

Exclusions   The exclusions are important in defining certain types of loss which are not intended to be covered in spite of the extreme breadth of coverage under the bond.

Loss resulting from forgery or alteration of any instrument is excluded if it is not covered by the insuring agreements applying to fidelity, the specific provisions applying to forgery or alteration, the provisions applying to securities, the provisions applying to redemption of United States Savings Bonds, or the provisions relating to counterfeit currency. It is the intent of the underwriters to cover forgery or alteration only under the specific provisions of the agreements listed.

Loss due to riot or civil commotion outside the United States and Canada is excluded. Also excluded are described acts of war or the effects of nuclear fission or fusion or radioactivity, excepting that loss resulting from industrial uses of nuclear energy are not excluded.

Acts of directors of the insured are excluded unless they are employed as salaried, pensioned, or elected officials.

Exclusions also apply to certain nonpayment losses or defaults of loans unless covered under the fidelity, forgery or alteration or securities provisions of the bond.

An important exclusion is that of loss of property contained in customers' safe deposit boxes unless such loss is sustained through any dishonest or fraudulent act of an employee in such circumstances as would make the insured legally liable. Thus, the bond would not cover loss resulting from a burglary or robbery of customers' property from a safe deposit box if there were no infidelity on the part of an employee in connection with the loss.

Loss through cashing or paying forged or altered traveler's checks and loss of traveler's checks entrusted to the insured for sale are excluded unless there is fraud or dishonesty on the part of an employee and the checks are paid or honored by the drawer.

Loss of property due to misplacement or mere loss is subject to an excess provision where the property is in the custody of an armored motor vehicle company. The bond covers only the amount which cannot be recovered from the armored motor vehicle company or insurance which the armored motor vehicle company may carry to cover such loss. An excess provision also applies to chattels which are specifically insured elsewhere. A shortage due to error in any teller's cash is excluded, regardless of the amount of such shortage.

An exclusion applies to any person who is a partner, officer or employee of any processor covered under the bond after the time that the insured or an officer of the insured not in collusion with such person learns that such a person has committed a fraudulent or dishonest act. This is comparable to the provision in fidelity bonds generally that the dishonest acts of an employee are not covered from the time that he or she has been discovered as having committed a dishonest act.

Other Provisions The bond does not provide any coverage to a processor or employee of a processor but merely protects the insured against infidelity of the processor or an employee. After payment of the loss by the bonding company, any rights which the insured may have

184—Commercial Property Risk Management and Insurance

against a processor must be assigned to the bonding company by the insured.

Provisions for reporting of loss and for providing a proof of loss are similar to those in other insurance policies.

Detailed provisions apply to methods of valuation of securities, books of account and other records, and of property other than securities or records. The insurer may replace lost or damaged securities in kind or, at its option, pay in cash the cost of replacing them. If foreign money is lost or destroyed, the insurer may replace the foreign money or pay its value in United States money. In the case of other property (as defined in the bond), damage to the insured's office, or loss or damage to furniture or fixtures, the insurer's liability is limited to the lesser of (1) actual cash value, or (2) the cost to repair or replace the items damaged or destroyed. These provisions for valuation are geared to the needs of the bank in connection with its handling of securities and other properties. Coverage of books of account and other records is limited to the cost of blank books plus the cost of labor for transcription or copying of data. There is provision for arbitration in the case where certain types of property cannot be valued by agreement between the bonding company and the insured.

Provisions for salvage are similar to those of other bonds and provide that in case of loss and recovery the insured shall first be made whole, and the bonding company can apply to its loss any amount beyond the insured's loss.

Payment of loss under the bond does not reduce the liability of the bonding company for other losses. Provisions relating to the limit of liability spell out the application of the limits to various situations. The limits of liability are not increased by a continuation of the bond over a period of several years.

Provisions similar to those in other fidelity bonds apply to a situation where there may be coverage under the current bond and a bond previously in effect. There also is an excess provision making this coverage excess over any other insurance which might apply to a loss.

Provisions also apply to the termination or cancellation of the bond. These generally provide that thirty days' notice shall be given by the bonding company to the insured. There is also the usual provision of fidelity bonds that the coverage is terminated or canceled as to any employee as soon as the insured shall learn of any dishonest or fraudulent act on the part of such an employee.

There are provisions for extension of coverage after termination or cancellation if required notice is given to the bonding company. There are also provisions relating to termination in case the insured is taken over by a receiver or liquidator or by state or federal officials.

Other Bankers Bonds

The bond which has just been described, bankers blanket bond no. 24, is one of the broadest that can be provided for banks. More limited forms are used in some cases. For example, one such form limits the premises to places which are designated in the policy, or any recognized place of safe deposit in another organization. The more limited bonds may exclude loss resulting from loans obtained from the insured even though procured through fraud or false pretenses, unless covered in specific manner by the policy.

It is beyond the scope of this chapter to detail the various differences which may apply in the various bonds that can be written for a bank or other financial institutions. The differences between the forms may have little effect on outright dishonesty of employees, burglary or robbery losses, but may affect drastically the coverage of peculiar kinds of loss involving forgery or alteration of documents. A detailed examination of different forms would reveal some of the more common differences between them.

Excess and Catastrophe Coverages for Banks

One of the most important questions facing the officers of a bank is how much coverage to buy. One case revealed that the loan officer of a medium-sized bank had transferred funds from an account to a fictitious organization which he had established subject to his withdrawal signature. This transfer of funds was made over a period of several years, with an aggregate loss to the bank of almost $2.5 million.

There have been other cases where bank officials have made loans which were in default, and then felt it necessary in order to preserve their reputations and positions in the bank to cover up the bad judgment in making the loan. Thus, what originated as a case of bad but honest judgment is converted to a dishonest act. There also have been cases where the success in covering up the bad judgment initially has led the bank official to appropriate funds to his or her own benefit. The potential loss to the bank in spite of the bank's own auditing procedures, periodic examinations by governmental officials, and other attempts at control, can be extremely high where fraudulent activity is perpetrated over a period of years. Therefore, the limits of liability must be set with this in mind.

One method of covering the large loss possibilities from employee dishonesty is by means of an excess bond. This usually is written for high amounts, such as $1 million or more and covers as excess over other applicable bonds and insurance. It is an acceptable method of covering the potentially large infidelity exposure, where the extremely large losses usually occur. Lesser amounts are subject to loss from burglary and robbery, for example, so that the usual limits in a bankers blanket bond may be sufficient for such exposures. Losses due to the forgery or alteration of securities are likely to include dishonest employees.

There also have been catastrophic losses from the burglary of safe deposit boxes. A bank that operates a safe deposit box facility needs to consider the purchase of a safe deposit box legal liability policy to cover any liability that the bank might incur as a result of a burglary of the facility.

Bonds for Other Financial Institutions

The bankers blanket bonds are designed to meet the extremely broad exposures to loss of the commercial bank. Other types of financial institutions have less exposure to loss in some respects, but they also have some greater exposures in other respects. Insurance companies have designed special kinds of blanket bonds to cover the exposures of other financial institutions. These are reviewed briefly here in order to distinguish them from the bankers blanket bond, which is designed for commercial banks.

The divisions of coverage in the blanket bonds which are issued to other financial institutions follow generally those which appear in the bankers blanket bond. These include fidelity coverage, on-premises coverage, transit coverage, forgery or alteration losses, loss of securities, and loss from accepting counterfeit currency. There are some differences in the details of the coverage, depending upon the exposures and needs of the particular type of financial institution.

Stockbrokers Blanket Bond   The exposure of the stockbroker to loss relates primarily to the handling of securities. There may be loss due to dishonest or fraudulent acts of employees, and there may also be theft of securities from the premises or while in transit. Forgery or alteration losses may occur where forged or altered documents are accepted in exchange for cash by the insured.

The increasing use of electronic data processing in connection with securities handling requires special provision relating to losses from this operation. There may be a loss due to diversion of funds or fraudulent debits and credits within the data processing operation. It is common practice for this exposure either to be included specifically or excluded specifically in the coverage of the stockbrokers blanket bond. One of the important exposures to loss is the counterfeiting of securities. This is done professionally by highly skilled criminals who then present the securities for purchase by the stockbroker or as security for loans. The exposures to loss to the stockbroker are such that high limits of liability are needed. The limit of liability must be related to the aggregate value of the securities which may be in the custody of the stockbroker at any one time.

The various stock exchanges, and particularly the New York Stock Exchange, have requirements that members carry fidelity coverage and other insurance to protect against losses from fraud and theft. Minimum requirements of the stock exchanges are related to the type and volume of business done by the stockbroker and the size of the accounts.

Stockbrokers Partnership Bond The fidelity coverage of the stockbrokers blanket bond and of similar bonds such as the bankers blanket bond covers loss from the infidelity of employees. As already pointed out, the coverage of some bonds can be extended to loss caused to other partners by the fraudulent acts of one or more partners. The stock-brokerage is particularly susceptible to partnership losses. There may be several active partners in a stockbrokerage. This potential loss from dishonesty of one or more of the general partners of a firm may be covered by the stockbrokers partnership bond. Stock exchanges sometimes require their member firms to carry this coverage. This generally is written only for organizations for which the insurance company carries the stockbrokers blanket bond.

The stockbrokers blanket bond excludes loss resulting from misrepresentation made by a partner regarding the value of securities.

Finance Companies Blanket Bond The finance companies for which this bond was designed are those which handle mortgages, commercial paper and notes, holding companies which act as managers of stocks and securities, real estate investment trusts, and similar organizations. This does not include personal finance companies or small loan companies.

Many of these organizations have electronic data processing operations, and this exposure to loss must be either included or excluded specifically. There is a variation of this coverage known as the small loan company blanket bond which is used for the coverage of personal finance companies and similar organizations.

Credit Union Blanket Bond The credit union blanket bond is similar to a small loan company blanket bond with provisions designed to cover the exposures of the credit union to loss from dishonesty of officers and employees, and from other crime losses. Exact coverage, including coverage for loss from electronic data processing, would be adapted to the needs of the insured.

Savings Bank and Savings and Loan Blanket Bonds The bonds for these institutions are similar in nature to the bankers blanket bond. Minimum requirements are set up for organizations that are under the insurance protection of the Federal Savings and Loan Insurance Corporation. Such bonds normally would cover the fraudulent acts of directors as well as officers, employees and agents. The coverage may be somewhat broader as to a director than the coverage of other blanket bonds because the directors of such organizations may take an active part in the operation of the organization. In contrast, the director of a bank who is not otherwise an employee of the bank is not likely to be involved in the active day-by-day operation of the bank.

A bond similar to a bankers blanket bond may be written for almost any organization of a financial nature with an exposure to loss from fraudulent activities of the officers or employees. This could include insurance companies whose operations necessarily include the handling of substantial amounts of securities. The fraudulent acceptance of forged or counterfeit securities may result in loss to the organization. Theft by employees is a hazard in any organization where money and securities are a necessary part of the organization. The basic provisions which have been described for the bankers blanket bond are followed for practically all of these other bonds, subject to the peculiar exposures of the financial institution that is to be covered. It is emphasized again that adaptations of the coverage are made to fit the needs of each insured.

Kidnap-Ransom-Extortion Coverage

A relatively new threat of loss to a bank or other financial institution is extortion under threat of kidnapping or other violence. A typical situation is where an officer of a bank receives a telephone call saying that a relative, an officer of the bank, or an employee of the bank, is being held and will be killed if a specified amount of money is not turned over to the kidnapper. The usual extortionist in such a case will instruct that arrangements must be carried out in great secrecy and that the police are not to be advised of the situation. Other types of threats against financial institutions include the threat of bombing or other catastrophe to the bank if money is not provided as instructed.

Several such cases that resulted in the payment of money for the release of a bank official or family member subsequently resulted in claims being made under bankers blanket bonds. In most cases, the money was delivered to the kidnapper away from the premises of the bank. In certain cases, the money was handed over on the bank's premises. There appears to be agreement that such payment is covered by the bankers blanket bond if the delivery of the money occurs on the bank's premises. This results from the exact wording of the bankers blanket bond relating to premises coverage. However, there was disagreement as to whether the bankers blanket bond covers the situation where the money is delivered to the kidnapper away from the bank's premises. Some insurance companies did pay such claims under the bankers blanket bond, while others denied liability. The result has been the development of an endorsement to the bankers blanket bond (or to comparable bonds for other financial institutions) that covers loss incurred by the insured as the result of surrender of property because of an extortion incident to the kidnapping or alleged kidnapping of a bank official or employee. Coverage usually is also extended to the members of the household of a threatened person.

Underwriters have recognized that kidnap and extortion threats are a real exposure to a financial institution. Money must be paid where such payment is a reasonable alternative to physical harm to the kidnap victim. Fortunately, most victims of bank extortion cases have been returned safely after payment of the money. This record is more favorable than has been the case with ordinary kidnappings where victims often are killed.

Underwriters have set up certain requirements which are considered essential in the providing of insurance against loss from kidnap-ransom-extortion attempts. One principle is that the financial institution should pay a certain proportion of any loss from a kidnap incident. This is considered necessary in order to influence the bank officials to consider seriously any situation which may or may not be an actual kidnap threat.

The second principle is that a reasonable effort must be made by the threatened official to determine that the threat is genuine. It is also required that the threat be reported to at least one other officer or employee of the institution and also to local law enforcement officials or the Federal Bureau of Investigation. Insurance companies do not feel justified in paying for a kidnap-ransom-extortion attempt unless the threatened official reports the incident to other officials and employees and to law enforcement officers before any money is paid. The threats of the kidnapper relating to law enforcement authorities must be ignored.

Coverage of any kidnap-ransom-extortion case usually is delayed for thirty days from application. A policy may also contain a warranty that no such threat has been made at the time the extortion endorsement is added. The receipt of a real or suspected threat might influence bank officials to buy the insurance. The thirty-day waiting period is intended to prevent such purchase of insurance after a threat is received or suspected.

The kidnap-ransom-extortion coverage is bought in a specified amount, subject to a deductible which is to be paid by the insured. The endorsement includes provisions relating to the requirements noted above. The threatened person or someone else on his behalf must attempt to verify that the alleged kidnapping has actually occurred. It is required that the threatened person communicate the circumstances to another official or employee and to law and enforcement officials.

It is also required as a part of the coverage that the board of directors of the institution within ninety days after the surrender of the property shall ratify such surrender as an official act of the institution. This is to avoid any payment for an uncertain or indefinite situation.

In order to be covered by the endorsement, a ransom payment must occur away from the premises of the bank. As pointed out above, payment on the premises of the bank is considered to be covered under the bankers blanket bond. There could be a difference in the limits of liability under the provisions of the bankers blanket bond and under the provisions of the kidnap-ransom-extortion endorsement. Payment of the money on the premises of the bank would make it subject to the limit of liability in the bankers blanket bond. Payment away from the premises would be subject to the limit of liability in the endorsement.

The coverage may also be subject to an aggregate limit of liability during the bond period or the limit of liability may be for each loss that occurs during the bond period. This provision would be subject to negotiation between the insured and the insurance company.

Bomb Threats   Another form of extortion that has occurred is a telephoned or written threat to a bank or other institution that a bomb will be placed or has been placed at the premises which will be detonated unless a specified amount of money is paid out. Here also such coverage, if written, would apply only if the payment is made away from the bank's premises. Payment on the premises may be considered as covered under the usual provisions of the bankers blanket bond. Loss due to payment under the threat of a bomb explosion ordinarily is not covered under the kidnap-ransom-extortion endorsement. This would have to be negotiated separately between the insured and the insurance company. Rates and exact provisions would depend upon the surrounding circumstances and whether this institution or others in the area had previously been subjected to such threats or incidents.

LOSS CONTROL TECHNIQUES

Losses due to the dishonesty of employees are largely subject to control. However, the control measures require detailed attention to many facets of an organization's operations. Many employers are reluctant to establish controls, particularly because they believe that employees will resent measures which seem to reflect upon their honesty. Many employers want to buy insurance to cover their losses with the almost certain knowledge that losses will occur. Such employers will install only the devices or procedures that are demanded by underwriters as a condition of providing coverage. It is impossible to divorce underwriting and loss control. Theoretically, fidelity bonding contemplates no losses. It is a guarantee of the honest performance of the employee's duties. Losses do occur, of course, and the objective of insurance company inspection is to reduce these losses to a minimum.

The reluctance of employers to establish control measures is true in all facets of business, including banking. One official has pointed out that convenience is the key in banking, and convenience for the customer is also convenience for the criminal. Bank security in many cases is poor with dependence on gimmicks which are sold to the bank and then forgotten. Bank guards and security officers in mercantile establishments are seldom given adequate training. A security officer who is provided with a gun without being trained in proper handling and the time and place for its use is more of a threat to customers than to robbers or burglars. This lax attitude on the part of business firms regarding internal security forms one of the most difficult parts of underwriting fidelity coverages.

The following paragraphs discuss the various ways to control exposure to loss from employee dishonesty. Loss from theft of money, for example, is controllable generally by different methods from those used to discourage theft of merchandise. The various principles of control, therefore, are segregated according to the type of property and the exposure that it presents.

Theft of Money

Cash Sales The pocketing of money from cash sales or from collections of customers' accounts is an exposure in a mercantile operation. Cash registers are the most commonly used control device. Accessibility of the cash register to several employees permits theft without any regular means of determining who is stealing the money. Each sales clerk who handles cash sales should be assigned a separate machine or locked drawer in the cash register. An official of the store should be the only one who has access to all of the drawers or cash registers and this official should clear the cash registers several times during a day's operations. Sales tickets should be checked with the amount of cash with a reconciliation at regular intervals. Continuing efforts should be made to detect sales that are made without being recorded on the cash registers, or the recording on the register of a lesser amount than the actual sale.

Cash Receipts Many organizations receive a substantial amount of their receipts by mail in the form of cash and checks. The actual receipts should be tabulated by a person other than the cashier or bookkeeper, and then the cashier or bookkeeper should be required to reconcile the actual amount of receipts which are recorded by the person handling that operation.

The preparation and handling of bank deposits is an important function that should be supervised by the proprietor in a small operation and by a responsible official in a larger operation. One method of control that can be worked out with the cooperation of many banks is to use deposit slips in triplicate. One of these remains with the bank for its records, a second copy is returned with the person making the deposit, and the third can be mailed by the bank to the auditor of the merchant.

Bank statements should be reconciled each month by the proprietor in a small operation or by a responsible official in a larger operation. This reconciliation of bank statements should be handled separately from any other accounting operations of the organization. One of the most frequent causes of cash theft is the placing of all financial operations in the hands of one person such as a bookkeeper or cashier. Division of responsibility is essential to control of theft.

A mercantile operation of any kind should establish some method of inventory control that ties in with cash receipts and disbursements. Many mercantile operations have a fixed percentage of mark-up over the cost of goods in order to establish the sales price. This should result in a comparable percentage differential between cost of merchandise and sales. Mark-downs and sale prices have to be taken into account in judging whether the differential is correct, but this and other inventory control procedures will indicate whether a substantial amount of money or property is being lost by employee theft.

Theft of Merchandise

One of the best methods of controlling theft of merchandise is to separate the duties of receiving, storekeeping, and delivery. Receipt of merchandise should be handled as a function to be coordinated with the placing of orders for merchandise. Controls should be established between the placing of orders and the receipt of merchandise to make certain that orders are filled as required. A system of numbered purchase orders is one part of such a procedure. The receiving department or individual should have the responsibility of making certain that the orders are filled and actually received. The orders should not be placed with suppliers by the receiving department. Here again, the principle of separation of duties is an important part of embezzlement control.

Storekeeping and inventory control should be in the hands of someone other than the receiving clerk or receiving department. It should be the responsibility of the storekeeper to see that merchandise is provided according to requisitions and that the merchandise that is provided to other departments for sale matches the totals that have been received. The shipping department should be separated so that all shipments are controlled at point of delivery.

It is an important part of employee theft control to observe employees entering and leaving the premises. Doors and windows should be controlled so that employees cannot pass merchandise through them to confederates outside the building.

Embezzlement of Funds in a Financial Institution

There are cases where losses result from collusion among employees, but the typical embezzler in a financial institution works alone. One method which has been used frequently by embezzling officials of financial institutions is to make loans to an organization in which the embezzler has a financial interest or maintains financial control. A loan officer in a bank may transfer such funds to a nonexistent organization. The loan may subsequently be written off as a bad loan without discovery of the fraud if other bank officials or the directors do not pay sufficient attention to bad loans that are written off. Careful attention must be paid by auditors, controlling officials of the bank, and the directors to all loans that are written off or compromised.

Another method of embezzlement is the transfer of funds from an account for which the bank has management control to another account which is controlled by the embezzler. All such accounts over which the bank has management control should be examined periodically, and should be transferred periodically from one official of the bank to another. The essential features of control are separation of operations as far as possible and periodic transfer of responsibilities from one official to another.

Employee Investigation It is essential that all employees in a financial institution be investigated thoroughly as to their previous record of honesty and personal habits which may lead to dishonest acts. In one case, a responsible official was hired by a bank after having been given clear references from three previous bank employers. This employee was detected as having embezzled funds from the current employer, and it was then revealed that he had previously embezzled from all three previous bank employers. The previous employers were reluctant to give a bad report on the former employee because of fear that they would be accused of some unfair employment practice or sued for defamation.

Embezzlement may be uncovered within a financial institution by careful observance of employee activities. Embezzlement through transfer of funds between accounts requires constant attention on the part of an embezzling employee. There have been several cases where an embezzlement was discovered because the employee was unavoidably away from the institution when outside accountants appeared to make an audit. Unusual scheduling of vacations, or the absence of any vacation time at all on the part of an employee, or any other out-of-pattern activities may call for a special audit.

Electronic Data Processing

The introduction of electronic data processing into an organization increases the potential for embezzlement. This may be accomplished by placing the computer orders for delivery of merchandise to a fictitious buyer which is under the control of the embezzler.

The embezzler also may transfer funds between accounts within the computer. The account to which the funds are transferred may be a fictitious entity which again is controlled by the embezzler. Funds may be transferred out of the organization's own accounts into outside accounts in a bank. The methods by which embezzlement can be accomplished with the aid of a computer are numerous. Management must understand the potential for embezzlement with the aid of a computer and must take appropriate safeguards. This is a highly specialized type of exposure which should be considered by management in connection with any financial operations. One of the safeguards which is recommended routinely is that programming of the computer and operation of the computer be rigidly separated. The same person should never function as both computer operator and computer programmer.

Collateral Programs

Expensive medical treatment for a member of the embezzler's family has been pointed out as one of the reasons for employee embezzlement. Many employers have relieved this temptation by offering good employee hospitalization plans. Such a plan is especially valuable for catastrophe medical expense. It appears that a high proportion of employees are subject to temptation under financial stress. The original intent of such employees may be merely to borrow the funds with the idea of putting them back when the financial stress ends. It is wise on the part of employers to keep in touch with employee situations as far as possible and to avoid situations that may result in financial stress to employees who are in a position to embezzle.

Retention   One of the most effective methods of encouraging control procedures is to require the insured to participate in every loss that occurs. This frequently is accomplished by means of a deductible on the fidelity bond coverage. The amount of the deductible may be established by reviewing the experience or the potential loss to determine the amount for which loss frequency is probable. The employer who is obligated to pay all of the smaller losses that occur is more likely to adopt preventive measures, which will affect the larger losses as well.

CHAPTER 13

Other Property Loss Exposures and Insurance

INTRODUCTION

Chapter 13 analyzes a variety of property policies—insurance coverages that do not quite fit under the headings of previous chapters. To be discussed are the nuclear exposures, boiler and machinery, glass, animal mortality, insurance against loss of crops, rain insurance, various types of credit insurance, and title insurance.

There is a great diversity in these exposures and the types of insurance approaches used to cover them. For example, insurance against nuclear loss provides coverage for a peril excluded by other policies. Boiler and machinery insurance and glass insurance cover property and perils excluded by many other forms. Rain insurance, animal mortality, and credit insurance cover losses which do not necessarily involve direct damage to property. Title insurance and crop insurance provide coverage on assets which are somewhat different from those covered by other property forms. Because of the variety of properties, losses, and perils to be discussed in this chapter, the approach will vary with the exposures and insurance forms under discussion.

NUCLEAR EXPOSURES AND THEIR TREATMENT

Almost all property insurance policies exclude coverage for losses caused by nuclear reaction. Such "nuclear exclusions" eliminate coverage for a peril which is generally deemed to be commercially uninsurable because losses are of very low frequency and potentially high severity.

This section will analyze the exposures to loss by nuclear hazards,

197

and the risk management alternatives available to treat those exposures, with emphasis on the types of insurance available. Nuclear energy liability insurance will be discussed along with property insurance, just as fire liability insurance was discussed in the sections of Chapters 3 and 4 on fire insurance. In both cases, the discussion applies to different types of losses caused by the same peril.

Nuclear Energy Loss Exposures

While radioactive materials have been known and used for many years within the scientific community, the potential for substantial economic loss or injury to the public is relatively new, and has accompanied the extensive use of radioactive material in commercial nuclear reactors.

Experimental uses aside, it was not until the mid-1950s that commercial development of the peaceful atom could begin. The Atomic Energy Act of 1954 and the Price-Anderson Act of 1957, together with the latter act's subsequent renewal legislation, have permitted and fostered the growth of the commercial nuclear reactor and its associated support industries.

Today the term "nuclear energy" has become associated by many with nuclear power plants, nuclear fuel fabricators, and nuclear waste burial sites, collectively referred to as the "nuclear fuel cycle." However, the largest number of users of radioactive material are not directly involved in this nuclear fuel cycle. Instead, the most frequent uses of radioactive substances and products are in the fields of medicine, industry, and research. Generally these sectors utilize "by-product material" in broad ranging applications. "By-product materials" are in effect radioactive isotopes which are produced in an operating nuclear reactor.

The types of hazards presented by radioactive materials are similar regardless of application (i.e., whether the material is used in nuclear power plants or in industry). The difference is a matter of potential loss severity. Thus, there has been great emphasis that safety guarantees be incorporated into the design, construction, and operation of nuclear power plants, where exposures are much more severe than in most industrial or research applications.

A nuclear reactor is not an atomic bomb and therefore cannot possibly explode like one. However, the absence of explosive capabilities does not mean that the operation of a nuclear power facility is free of any chance of loss. Exceedingly large amounts of radioactive material contained in the core of a reactor and the remote possibility of release of this material imply a chance of loss. There is a potential for loss involving the release of radioactivity which could result in catastrophic bodily injury and property damage.

Exposure Severity The magnitude of potential exposure to loss resulting from the use of radioactive material extends over a wide spectrum, depending in part on the quantities of radioactive material in use. Minimal exposure would be associated with small quantities of radioactive material (e.g., a radioisotopic source used in a flow meter or in a residential smoke detector). More substantial exposure can be associated with larger quantities of radioactive material (e.g., nuclear reactors or other installations handling large quantities of certain radioactive isotopes or special nuclear material). There are numerous intermediate levels of potential exposure between these extremes depending largely upon the types, quantities, and physical forms of the radioactive material involved.

Hazards of Radioactive Material Radioactive material can be said to present two main types of hazard to people and property: radiation and contamination.

Radiation. The nuclei of all radioactive substances are unstable. Unstable nuclei disintegrate spontaneously. In the disintegration process the unstable nucleus ejects or "radiates" subatomic particles and energy. The final result of this process, which may take place over a period of seconds, days, years, or millennia, is a nonradioactive substance. The nuclei of nonradioactive substances are stable and therefore retain their form indefinitely. The biological effect of the energy transmitted to living cells by such radiation is similar to that produced by an X-ray machine. However, unlike an X-ray machine, radioactive material cannot be turned off or on at will.

Persons or property in proximity to radioactive material may be irradiated. For human beings and animals the effect of radiation can be beneficial, harmful, or even deadly, depending in part upon the type of radioactive material, the portion of the body being irradiated, the physical separation between the two, and the period of irradiation. Thus the potential for radiation injury or damages can be reduced by shielding the radioactive material, providing sufficient physical separation between it and persons or property, or reducing the exposure time to the source of radiation.

Contamination. The hazard of radioactive contamination is in reality an extension of the radiation hazard, which becomes critical when the radioactive material is brought into direct contact with a person or property. In fact, the damage potential to most inanimate property (excluding certain substances such as unexposed photographic film) from radioactive contamination would be barely perceptible but for the fact that such contamination increases the potential that a person or animal coming into contact with that property could in turn experience transfer contamination.

The most serious aspect of personnel contamination (more particularly inhalation or ingestion or skin contamination) is that while the radioactive strength of the material internalized or topicalized may be low, that substance may easily be retained within or on the body, thereby permitting the source of radiation to remain in close and possibly prolonged contact with the surrounding tissue. Radioactive material left in contact with living tissue is especially harmful because the mitigating effects of separation, distance, existence of barriers and possibly of limiting the period of exposure are lost.

Hazards of Nuclear Reactors The normal use of most radioactive isotopes in medicine, industry, or research does not represent the potential for catastrophic exposure that may be associated with nuclear reactors. Again, for reactors, this exposure potential is directly related to the substantial quantities of nuclear material present as fuel. This highly radioactive material is directly produced as the nuclear fuel fissions. The fission process yields enormous quantities of usable energy (heat) and in turn produces numerous types of unstable nuclei. The environment into which nuclear fuel is placed (water or steam at high pressures and temperatures) is carefully engineered to provide maximum safety as well as maximum energy utilization characteristics.

A specific example of an accident which might produce severe losses would involve a primary coolant pipe rupture. This type of failure would interfere with the normal flow of coolant to the reactor core, and possibly lead to serious overheating of the core. If the large number of redundant safety systems built into the plant to anticipate such a mishap were then to simultaneously fail, the release of radioactivity beyond the power plant's environs could be substantial. The extent and severity of the contamination and exposure would depend heavily upon the prevailing weather conditions and the location of the reactor with respect to population centers.

The loss potential due to the operation of a large nuclear reactor is a classic illustration of a severe chance of loss with extremely low frequency. The consequences of an accident at a nuclear power plant could result in losses exceeding several billions of dollars—not including the value of the plant itself. However, since the operation of commercial nuclear reactors began in 1958, there has not been a release of radioactive material from any nuclear reactor that has caused injury to a member of the public outside the installation.

Risk Management Alternatives

The responsibility for the safe utilization of nuclear material, and the possible severe effects should a nuclear accident occur, rests with those entities desiring to employ this material for beneficial purposes. In addition to extreme, highly redundant loss control measures that attempt to remove any chance of loss, such entities have the other standard risk management alternatives with respect to nuclear energy exposures: (1) they can avoid the exposure by not becoming involved with nuclear material, (2) the inherent exposures could be retained by the organization itself, or (3) some way could be found to transfer the exposure to some other interested group.

Assuming the other factors weigh in favor of using nuclear reactors for generation of electricity, the first alternative, avoidance, becomes inappropriate. Total retention, in view of the substantial capital investment in the plant itself and the remote, but not impossible, potential for severe loss would be an unacceptable exposure of assets for many. (As will be described later in this section, the nuclear reactor owner now retains a portion of the exposure.) This leaves transfer as the only viable alternative.

Insurance Against the Nuclear Exposure

Treatment Under Other Insurance Policies The liability exposures inherent in the use or transportation of radioactive isotopes for medical, industrial, or research purposes have usually been assumed by insurers under their general liability policies. Such exposures are not excluded by the policy's nuclear energy liability exclusion.

Most, if not all, first-party property insurance policies not issued by the nuclear insurance pools specifically exclude loss by "nuclear reaction, nuclear radiation or radioactive contamination. . . ." However, for users of radioactive isotopes, these policies can be amended by attaching the radioactive contamination assumption endorsement discussed in Chapter 4. That endorsement extends coverage to direct loss by sudden and accidental radioactive contamination, including resultant radiation damage to the property covered, resulting directly from any perils insured against by the policy, but only if the loss arises out of radioactive material on the insured's premises at the time of loss.

Development of Pools The types and extent of exposures presented by the nuclear fuel cycle required capacity beyond that available from any single insurer or group of insurers. In order to assemble the greatest capacity possible, insurers in the United States formed four "pools":

1. *MAELU*—Mutual Atomic Energy Liability Underwriters—an underwriting syndicate comprised of six mutual insurance companies provides nuclear energy liability insurance.
2. *MAERP*—Mutual Atomic Energy Reinsurance Pool—having in excess of one hundred mutual insurance company members, provides reinsurance of MAELU and certain mutual "fronting companies" that write "all-risks" first-party property insurance for nuclear facilities.
3. *NELIA*—Nuclear Energy Liability Insurance Association—comprised of over one hundred stock insurance companies, writes nuclear energy liability insurance.
4. *NEPIA*—Nuclear Energy Property Insurance Association with a membership comparable to NELIA's—writes "all-risks" first-party property nuclear insurance under a syndicate form.

In 1974, NELPIA—Nuclear Energy Liability-Property Insurance Association—was formed through the merger of NELIA and NEPIA. For ease of identification, this discussion will utilize the earlier acronyms NELIA and NEPIA when referring to the liability and property segments of NELPIA.

In 1956, these four pools, utilizing the capacity of their member companies and worldwide reinsurance, assembled $120 million in capacity (divided equally between nuclear liability and first-party property coverages). Although this represented one of the largest accumulations of capacity to date, it was acknowledged that a severe accident involving large quantities of nuclear material could result in losses substantially in excess of this figure.

Effect of Price-Anderson Act of 1957 The commercial development of nuclear power could have been substantially retarded if the owners of such facilities could not obtain sufficient protection.

In order to fulfill its commitments to promote the safe commercial development of nuclear reactors, Congress passed the Price-Anderson Act of 1957. Among this act's provisions were:

1. The requirement that operators of commercial nuclear reactors must maintain adequate *financial protection* to compensate the public in the event of a nuclear accident. (For operators of the larger nuclear power reactors, this is defined as an amount equal to the amount of liability insurance made available by the nuclear insurance pools.)
2. The requirement that the Atomic Energy Commission, the agency responsible for the licensing of nuclear reactors, would,

for a fee, indemnify the operators of nuclear reactors for that portion of their nuclear liability losses which exceeded the required financial protection limit of liability. (This indemnity, which originally had a $500 million limit of liability, is reduced by an amount equal to any increase in the financial protection available from the private insurance pools.)

3. The termination of legal liability should the combined limits of financial protection and indemnity be exhausted, and the commitment of Congress to take appropriate compensatory action should that ever happen.

The Price-Anderson Act was originally to have ten years' duration, permitting Congressional review at the end of that period. With each of the act's extensions, important modifications have been introduced.

In the earliest extension (1966) provisions were incorporated which (1) established that a single federal court will handle all claims arising from a serious nuclear incident, and (2) required reactor owners and their insurers to waive almost all defenses should the consequences of a nuclear incident exceed certain criteria (an extraordinary nuclear occurrence).

Under the latest amendment of the act, utilities operating power reactors are required to participate in a secondary financial protection program. This program, managed by NELIA and MAELU, requires a reactor operator to pay retrospective premiums to the pools should liability losses due to a nuclear accident involving any such reactor exceed the pool's primary financial protection limit (originally $60 million but increased in several stages until today it is $140 million). Should one or more reactor owners be unable to pay its retrospective premium obligations, NELIA and MAELU would respond up to a maximum of $30 million per accident ($60 million all-time aggregate), but repayment would be sought by the pools. Thus the total financial protection available at this writing is $450 million—$140 million primary financial protection plus $310 million secondary financial protection ($5 million multiplied by sixty-two operating power reactors).

Until such time as the two financial protection layers equal $560 million, government indemnity (today $110 million) will comprise a third layer. As the pools increase the limit of liability under their primary financial protection policies and as the number of operating reactors grows, the combined total of the two financial protection layers will exceed the $560 million figure.

Nuclear Energy Liability Insurance The liability policies provided by NELIA and MAELU cover bodily injury and property damage caused only by the radioactive, toxic, explosive, or other hazardous properties of nuclear material. Liability for injuries or damages not resulting from this "nuclear energy hazard" (e.g., someone at a reactor site being hit by a falling object) would not fall within the protection afforded by the pools. Rather, it would be handled in the same manner as a similar accident at a nonnuclear location.

Two basic types of nuclear energy liability policies are available: the facility form and the supplier's and transporter's policy (S&T). The former is for operators of nuclear facilities (e.g., nuclear reactors, nuclear fuel fabricators, and nuclear waste burial sites) and the latter for entities which provide services, material, parts, or equipment in connection with such nuclear facilities or who transport materials to or from a facility.

Facility Form The facility form is unusual in several respects:

1. The policy's definition of insured includes not only the named insured but any other person or organization (except the United States of America or any of its agencies) liable for damages caused by the nuclear energy hazard at the specified nuclear facility.
2. Property of the named insured located away from the nuclear facility is deemed to be "property of another," making the named insured eligible for compensation should its offsite property be damaged.
3. In a similar manner this policy will reimburse an insured's workers' compensation insurer for sums paid for injuries to employees of the insured not employed at or in connection with the nuclear facility.
4. In addition to providing "premises" nuclear energy liability coverage the facility form also covers its insureds for liability due to nuclear accidents during certain specified shipments of nuclear material to or from the insured location.
5. The policy is continuous until canceled or terminated, with a single all-time aggregate limit (subject to possible reinstatement at the pool's discretion) which includes all claims expenses.

Supplier's and Transporter's Policy. The S&T policy, basically a single interest policy, will respond to protect its insured on an excess basis if that policy's named insured is also insured under someone else's facility form. The policy can also respond on a primary basis in the absence of other insurance. The S&T policy, however, specifically excludes coverage with respect to a nuclear facility for which the owner is required to maintain financial protection (most reactors, fuel fabricators processing plutonium in excess of specified quantities, and spent fuel reprocessors).

Both the facility form and the S&T policy are liability policies and exclude damages at any nuclear facility caused by nuclear material at that facility. Thus, although a supplier would be an insured under the facility form covering a fuel fabricator and may even have its own S&T policy as "excess" protection, it would have no coverage under either policy with respect to its liability for damage to the nuclear facility itself.

Regardless of the types or how many policies apply to a nuclear accident, both nuclear liability policy forms provide that the pool's maximum liability under all applicable policies is the lesser of the sum of the policies' limits or the pools' maximum limit (i.e., NELIA $108.5 million, MAELU $31.5 million as of mid-1977).

Nuclear Property Insurance Coverage The pools' liability policies cover only the perils associated with nuclear energy. General liability insurance is also needed. In contrast, their property policies are "all-risks" forms, including coverage of losses caused by nuclear contamination. The pools' policies provide up to $220 million of protection and cover (1) nuclear facilities both under construction—whether or not nuclear material is onsite—and operating; and (2) nuclear material, including its shipping container, in transportation. Depending upon the type of property insured there are mandatory deductibles with higher optional deductibles available. For certain nuclear facilities (nuclear reactors, fuel reprocessors, and plutonium fuel fabricators) business interruption coverage is unavailable. Gradual radioactive contamination of property is excluded, as is contamination of land unless specifically granted by endorsement.

The policy provides an automatic waiver of subrogation by the insurers with respect to nuclear damage to the insured property caused by a third-party supplier. The insured may waive the right of subrogation with respect to loss from other perils before the loss occurs. Although the property pool policy does "protect" the supplier, it does not cover all exposures in full. It should be noted that the policy (1) has deductibles, (2) may not cover all property (e.g., land) at the nuclear facility, (3) may have a maximum limit lower than the actual property value, and (4) may not cover business interruption or loss of use. If the loss happens to be in one of these areas where the property policy is not applicable, the automatic waiver of subrogation is useless. Since the liability policies issued by NELIA and MAELU and the conventional policies issued by individual insurers exclude coverage for a supplier's liability for damage to the nuclear facility itself, insurance for this liability exposure of the supplier is unavailable. One remedy frequently utilized by the supplier is to obtain a hold-harmless agreement from the facility owner.

As an alternative to purchasing nuclear property insurance from NEPIA or a member of MAERP, several electric utilities operating nuclear reactors have formed Nuclear Mutual Limited, a Bermuda-based company. This company's policy coverages closely approximate those offered by NEPIA and MAERP. In the event of an accident causing property damage to a Nuclear Mutual Limited member's facility, each member may be assessed in an amount up to fourteen times its annual premium. Currently, the maximum limit offered by Nuclear Mutual Limited is $175 million.

Extraterritorial Nuclear Insurance Coverage   The preceding analysis has placed its emphasis upon domestic nuclear exposures. Generally, outside the United States, a country having commercial nuclear power plants also has a nuclear insurance pool comprised of its domestic insurers and utilizing the reinsurance capacities of its worldwide counterparts. Under various international agreements (the Vienna and Brussels conventions), many such countries have agreed to channel liability for a nuclear incident to the operator of the nuclear facility. Except in cases of intentional acts by suppliers, such suppliers cannot be held liable under these countries' "domestic" laws. However, since the completeness of this absolution is unknown (e.g., if an accident in Country A injures a resident of Country B who brings suit against a supplier in the United States), NELIA and MAELU have available foreign supplier's and transporter's form policies. These policies are similar but not identical to the forms used for domestic United States exposures. The maximum limit is substantially lower (currently $20 million versus $140 million) and may be subject to further limitation due to the United States pool's reinsuring the liability policies of certain foreign nuclear pools.

While the United States nuclear pools do not provide direct first-party property protection for property outside the United States, they do participate as reinsurers of the foreign "domestic" pool writing the coverage on such property.

BOILER AND MACHINERY EXPOSURES
AND THEIR TREATMENT

Boiler and machinery insurance developed to fill a need for coverage against certain types of loss exposures. The development of the exposures and the development of insurance to treat the exposures occurred almost simultaneously.

History of Boiler and Machinery Exposures and Insurance

With the development of steam power came losses caused by steam boiler explosions. By the middle of the nineteenth century, pressures in boilers had increased to a maximum of 100 pounds per square inch. Many boiler explosions caused heavy loss of life and extensive property damage. One such explosion at the Fales and Gray Car Works in Hartford, Connecticut, in 1854 killed nineteen and injured twenty-three.

The first boiler inspection and insurance company in the United States issued its first policy in 1867. Before the turn of the century, the company was involved with the inspection and insuring of not only boilers but also of many other kinds of pressure vessels. Insurers involved with other lines also became involved with inspections and insurance on boilers and pressure vessels.

Accident prevention and loss reduction became important as the business developed, and the principles established with inspection and insurance of boilers started to be applied to other equipment associated with boilers. In 1909 "flywheel insurance" was developed, to cover loss caused by bursting or explosion of flywheels. This was the beginning of modern machinery insurance.

When steam turbines came into use, a few serious accidents indicated the need for insurance applying to such items. It was decided that the existing forms of boiler insurance and flywheel insurance could be combined and made to apply to turbines. As a result, there was coverage against explosion of the parts of the turbine subject to steam pressure and against disruption of certain rotating parts of the unit.

The next development was to provide more complete protection for engines on which flywheels were mounted. Whereas available insurance covered only bursting of flywheels, insurance was necessary for the entire machine. In 1919, engine breakdown insurance was made available applying to steam engines, internal combustion engines, reciprocating pumps, and compressors. Electrical machinery insurance began in 1922, followed by breakdown insurance for turbine generators. In 1928, flywheel insurance, engine breakdown insurance, turbine insurance, and electrical machinery insurance were combined under the general classification of machinery insurance.

From the beginning, boiler and machinery insurance differed from most other lines of insurance in its emphasis on loss prevention. Today more than $.40 of each premium dollar is spent by the insurer for engineering and inspection services aimed at loss prevention.[1]

Most states and some municipalities require owners or users of certain boilers and pressure vessels to have this equipment inspected in order to operate it. Insurance inspectors are licensed to inspect equipment on behalf of the states and municipalities and to report their findings to the state or municipality in which insurance company inspections are acceptable in lieu of inspections made by a state inspector.

Boiler and Machinery Hazards

Boilers and other pressure vessels have an obvious hazard in the pressure contained within the vessels. The contents of boilers are steam or water; other pressure vessels may contain other liquids or gases. In addition to the hazard of pressure, the expansive force of the contents in most cases will lead to additional destruction after the initial rupture of the boiler or pressure vessel. Because of this expansive force, many boiler and pressure vessel explosions are very violent.

Machinery objects contain a different type of energy. A flywheel, like a boiler, contains a great amount of energy. However, the destructive effect of this energy is due to centrifugal force rather than to pressure and expansive force. Flywheels have a tendency to want to fly apart when rotating, and when this happens energy is released with an explosive effect. Any piece of rotating equipment has such stored energy. Some types of machinery, such as steam turbines, also have the hazard of steam pressure.

Electrical machines also are exposed to the hazards of energy. Electrical discharges may cause failure of insulation and burning of electrical conductors. Electrical energy may also place a mechanical strain on parts of a machine and cause a tendency for the machine to fly apart.

Types of Losses

Many boiler and machinery losses are severe, running into the hundreds of thousands of dollars. Losses of over $1 million occasionally occur. In some cases the direct damage loss is minor when compared with the indirect loss. Several examples illustrate the types of losses which can occur to boilers and machinery.

- Automatic controls failed to shut off the oil burner in a hot water boiler used to provide heat in a public school. The pressure relief valve was defective, and pressure increased until the strength of the boiler was exceeded. The resulting explosion destroyed the boiler room and seriously damaged other parts of the school building. The loss amounted to $79,000.[2]

- A hot water heater tank in a motel blew up, apparently as the result of over-heating or uncontrolled firing. The tank split in two, propelling the upper half like a missile through the roof. The explosion shattered a snack bar at the motel, demolished three guest rooms, and damaged a utility and laundry room, with total damages over $30,000.[3]
- Two hundred boiler tubes were destroyed by overheating when automatic controls on a boiler used in a chemical plant failed. Replacement of these tubes cost $14,000.[4]
- A boiler in a dry cleaner blew up with such force that it damaged almost all stores in the downtown area of a small town. Glass breakage was so widespread that the National Guard and Civil Defense units had to be called out. The building housing the boiler was condemned.[5]
- A thrust bearing of a 10,000 kw steam turbine allowed the turbine shaft to shift out of position. Blading on the shaft rubbed against stationary blading in the machine, resulting in repairs costing $135,000.[6]
- The concrete base under a 2,500 horsepower gas-diesel engine was installed in subzero weather. Later the base shrank, leaving the engine improperly supported. This caused misalignment and eventual failure of a crankshaft. Damage to the machine of $66,000 was substantial enough, but the resulting business interruption loss was $160,000.[7]
- A short circuit in the main switchboard of a paper mill shut down all production in the plant. Temporary repairs restored operation within twenty-four hours, but a second short circuit caused another twenty-four hour shutdown. Permanent repairs to the board cost $35,000, but the indirect loss of $28,000 resulted in a total loss of $63,000.[8]

Kinds of Firms Exposed to Boiler and Machinery Losses

Any business operating pressure vessels or machinery is exposed to loss arising out of rupture or explosion of pressure vessels, or machinery breakdown. Failure to recognize the exposure may result in unintentional retention of potentially severe losses.

Many large firms obviously have boiler and machinery exposures, including firms such as large paper mills, electric utilities, chemical plants, and steel mills. Medium-sized firms also frequently incur exposures. Firms in this category would include medium-sized food processing firms, textile firms, electronics manufacturers, drug manufacturers, high-rise offices and stores, newspapers, cold storage firms, breweries, dairies, and hotels.

Less obvious are the exposures of small firms, including dry cleaning plants (which always have boilers), stores (with boilers and air conditioning systems), garages (which may use boilers for heating and unfired pressure vessels for compressed air), churches, theaters, small offices, schools, small manufacturers, bowling alleys, and so forth.

In short, a majority of business firms have some exposure to boiler and machinery loss. Once the exposure has been recognized, one way of treating it is with the purchase of boiler and machinery insurance.

Boiler and Machinery Insurance

In general, boiler and machinery insurance provides coverage for those losses and loss exposures discussed in the preceding pages. High pressure boilers and low pressure boilers, steam boilers and hot water boilers, and everything from piping to air conditioning compressors, deep well pumps, refrigeration and air conditioning systems, air compressors, turbines, and various types of electrical apparatus can be insured with a boiler and machinery policy.

Scope of Coverage The boiler and machinery insurance policy, in its insuring agreement, covers loss involving "accidents" to "objects." Before any further analysis of coverage can be made, it is necessary to carefully define these two terms.

Object. The "object" is the boiler or machinery which is insured. Objects to be insured are listed specifically in the policy declarations unless the blanket group plan is used, in which case groups of objects are described. An endorsement attached to the policy provides a detailed definition of the term "object." Because there is a great variety in the type of boilers and machinery that may be insured, there are numerous definitions and special provisions available for use in specific cases where they might apply.

Accident. The following definition of accident is found in one broad form boiler and machinery policy:

"Accident" shall mean a sudden and accidental breakdown of the Object or a part thereof, which manifests itself at the time of its occurrence by physical damage to the Object that necessitates repair or replacement of the Object or part thereof; but Accident shall *not* mean (a) depletion, deterioration, corrosion, or erosion of material; (b) wear and tear; (c) leakage at any valve, fitting, shaft seal, gland packing, joint or connection; (d) the breakdown of any vacuum tube, gas tube or brush; (e) the breakdown of any electronic computer or electronic data processing equipment; (f) the breakdown of any structure or foundation supporting the Object or any part thereof; (g) an explosion of gas or unconsumed fuel within the furnace of any Object or within the passages from the furnace of said Object to the atmosphere; nor (h) the functioning of any safety device or protective device.

This definition would include situations such as a sudden and accidental tearing asunder of the entire object or any part of it, but would not include cracking or damage to safety devices or leakage at any valve or connection. In addition, with respect to boilers, the broad form quoted above includes cracking of any cast metal part of the object, crushing inward, and a sudden and accidental bulging or burning of the object caused by pressure or a deficiency of water or steam.

Insuring Agreement The insuring agreement in the typical boiler and machinery policy contains six "coverages"—property of the insured; expediting expenses; property damage liability; bodily injury liability; defense, settlement, and supplementary payments; and automatic coverage.[9]

Property of the Insured. Payment will be made for loss to the insured's property directly damaged by an accident to an insured piece of equipment (object). Coverage is provided not only for the object itself, but also any other property belonging to the insured.

Expediting Expenses. Coverage is provided for the reasonable extra cost of temporary repair and for expediting the repair of the damaged property of the insured. Included are items such as overtime and the extra cost of express transportation of materials. There is a basic limit of $1,000 automatically provided for expediting expenses, which is a part of the policy limit. This amount can be increased by endorsement if additional coverage is desired.

Property Damage Liability. Payment is made for property of others directly damaged by an "accident," for which the insured is legally obligated to pay. Liability for loss of use of damaged property is also covered, as is property of others in the care, custody, and control of the insured. This coverage is excess over the insured's other liability coverages.

Bodily Injury Liability. Optional coverage is available to provide for the loss of services, bodily injury or death of a person as the result of an "accident," if the insured is legally obligated to pay by reason of liability. Payment will not be made for losses which come under workers' compensation, unemployment compensation, or other disability benefits laws. This coverage is also excess insurance, over the insured's other liability coverages.

The last two "coverages"—defense, settlement, and supplementary payments; and automatic coverage—will be discussed later.

Application of Limits of Liability. Boiler and machinery insurance policies are written with a single limit per location which applies per "accident." When a loss falls under more than one section of the policy, losses are paid on a priority basis, according to a sequence of payments outlined in the policy. Since this is a unique arrangement, it bears explanation.

When a loss occurs, payment is first made to cover loss to property of the insured. Any remaining portion of the limit of liability can be used in payment of insured expediting expenses. If property damage liability loss is involved, any remaining portion of the limit of liability may be used to pay for such loss. Then, if the optional bodily injury liability coverage is carried, any remaining portion of the limit of liability may be used to pay bodily injury losses.

Figure 13-1 illustrates how this sequencing of loss adjustments might apply to a claim.

Defense, Settlement, and Supplementary Payments. The insurer will defend the insured against any suits alleging property damage liability as the result of an "accident." The same costs will be paid for suits alleging bodily injury, if the optional bodily injury coverage is carried. These provisions are typical of those found in other general liability policies, and are paid regardless of the limit per "accident."

Automatic Coverage. This "coverage," which is really more of an extension of coverage, allows the insured ninety days of automatic coverage on equipment at newly acquired locations provided the objects are of the same general character as the ones already insured in the policy. The insured agrees to notify the insurer in writing within ninety days after property is acquired, and also agrees to pay the additional premium for insurance on the newly acquired property.

Policy Exclusions Like any insurance policy, the boiler and machinery policy has exclusions. The insurer will not indemnify the insured for losses arising from war or nuclear hazards. As might be expected, the policy (in the insuring agreement) also excludes coverage for any increase in loss which results from an ordinance or law regulating or restricting repair, alteration, use, operation, construction, or installation of property involved in the loss.

Less common exlusions state that the policy does not apply to losses under the sections of the insuring agreement dealing with property of the insured and expediting expenses:

- from fire concomitant with or following an "accident," or from the use of water or other means to extinguish fire;
- from an "accident" caused directly or indirectly by fire, or from the use of water or other means to extinguish fire;

Figure 13-1

Example of the Sequence of Payments Under a Boiler and Machinery Policy

This is an example of how payments would be made under a policy with a per accident limit of $1,000,000. The boiler and machinery policy provides a single per accident limit for each location. Losses are paid in sequence under sections 1, 2, and 3 until the limit is exhausted or the claim is paid in full.

Amount of Insurance (Limit of Liability) $1 million

Loss as shown below:

- Loss under damage to property of the insured is $225,000. This is paid in full since it is less than the limit of liability.

- Loss under expediting expenses. Actual loss is $2,500, but payment by the insurer is limited to $1,000 under the usual policy provision limiting payment for such loss to $1,000.

- Loss under liability for damage to property of others. Actual liability of the insured in this example is $850,000, but $226,000 has already been paid out of the $1 million limit of liability. Therefore, the insurer is liable for only $774,000 of the insured's liability.

Note as to bodily injury liability:

Bodily injury liability insurance can be written under a boiler and machinery policy. There would still be a single limit under the policy, and bodily injury liability payments would be subject to any payments that have been made or are payable under the first three coverages. In this example, there would not have been anything left to pay a bodily injury claim.

- from a combustion explosion outside the object concomitant with or following an "accident";
- from an "accident" caused directly or indirectly by a combustion explosion outside the object;
- from flood, unless an "accident" ensues and then only for loss from the "accident";
- from delay or interruption of business;
- from lack of power, light, heat, steam or refrigeration;
- from any other indirect result of an "accident."

Fire losses and explosions outside the object can be insured with fire and extended coverage forms. Indirect loss coverage can be purchased in boiler and machinery forms discussed later.

Other Provisions

Repair or Replacement Coverage. Boiler and machinery losses are adjusted on an actual cash value basis unless repair or replacement coverage is included. Repair or replacement coverage eliminates the deductions for depreciation in the settlement of claims and can be added to the policy for an additional premium. Because this coverage is so important, most boiler and machinery policies are purchased with repair or replacement coverage.

Blanket Group Plan. Equipment may be insured under a boiler and machinery policy by classifications known as blanket groups. These object group descriptions provide the insured with coverage on all equipment meeting the description of equipment in that group. In addition, all equipment added to the location at a later date that falls within the group description is covered from the time it is connected and ready for use. The use of blanket groups has removed the necessity of individually listing each object insured under the policy and continually reviewing the list to be sure that each piece is specifically insured on the policy. Equipment that is not insurable according to inspection standards is listed as uninsured until such time as it meets insurable standards.

Inspection. Since the engineering service is most important, the company is permitted, but not obligated, to inspect the insured's equipment at any reasonable time.

Suspension. The purpose of insurance company inspections is to uncover defects that may cause an accident so that the defects can be corrected. The suspension condition gives the insurer some leverage to enforce correction of a dangerous situation. This reduces the morale hazard that might be involved when an insured refuses to correct an unsafe condition because insurance would respond to any loss.

The suspension condition permits any representative of the insurance company to *suspend* coverage on any insured object immediately upon discovery of a dangerous condition. Written notice of suspension must be mailed or delivered to the insured at the mailing address indicated in the policy. Although coverage for one object is suspended, coverage will remain in force on other objects insured under the policy.

The suspension privilege is normally used only when all other efforts have been exhausted to rectify a condition in the equipment potentially dangerous to the property of the insured and to the public.

Cancellation. Suspension should not be confused with cancellation. Cancellation provisions of the policy are similar to those of most other insurance policies. The insured may cancel at any time by mailing a letter to the insurer. The insurer may also cancel by mailing written notice to the insured indicating the. effective date of cancellation. The insurer must, of course, conform to the state laws regulating the cancellation of insurance.

Notice of Accident, Adjustment, and Subrogation. The insured is required to give prompt written notice of a boiler and machinery accident, to allow the insurance company to examine the damaged property and to ask any questions about the loss necessary. The insured must not voluntarily assume any liability or incur any expense other than at its own cost. In the event of a loss payment, the insured agrees to assign its subrogation rights of recovery from a third party (i.e., under a manufacturer's warranty) to the insurance company.

Other Insurance. A "joint loss" occurs when the same property loss is covered under both the boiler and machinery policy and some other policy carried by the insured. For example, if an air tank exploded, the loss incurred would be shared by the boiler and machinery insurer and the fire insurer (provided that extended coverage is included). In this instance, the total amount of loss, if sufficient limits have been purchased, is proportioned between the fire insurer and the boiler insurer.

The optional liability coverage of the boiler and machinery policy is excess over all other valid and collectible insurance, including deductibles and "self-insured retention provisions." Because most liability losses arising out of boiler and machinery accidents are also covered under general liability policies, it may seem unnecessary to carry liability insurance in a boiler policy. Where broad general liability coverage is carried, with high limits of liability (under a CGL policy or an excess or umbrella policy) this may be true. Yet several points should be considered. A boiler accident often produces a severe loss. Firms which cannot obtain high general liability limits elsewhere can often obtain coverage on a boiler and machinery policy for this severe loss exposure. Also, because of the potential severity of boiler losses some risk managers prefer extra liability insurance for this exposure. Likewise, many property damage liability policies exclude coverage for property of others in the insured's care, custody, and control. There is no such exclusion in the boiler and machinery policy.

Indirect Damage Coverage   There are several forms of indirect damage coverage available under boiler and machinery policies. All forms are optional and may be added to the basic policy by endorsement.

Direct damage coverage is required before the insured can purchase indirect coverage. Some indirect damage coverages available on boiler and machinery policies are:

1. *Business Interruption Coverage*—previously known as use and occupancy coverage—is intended to reimburse the insured for loss

of income as a result of boiler and machinery "accident." A manufacturing plant, apartment building, hotel or motel, theater, or dry cleaner might be a purchaser of this type of coverage. Other than the difference in perils covered, business interruption coverages on boiler and machinery policies are similar to the fire business interruption coverages.

2. *Extra Expense Coverage*—Extra expense coverage can be provided to offset the additional cost of conducting business during the period of restoration over and above the cost that normally would have been incurred to conduct business during the same period, had no accident occurred. Such businesses as newspapers, hospitals, schools, colleges and nursing homes may have need for this coverage.

3. *Consequential Damage Coverage*—Consequential damage coverage provides indemnity for loss on specified property of the insured when such loss is due to spoilage from lack of power, light, heat, steam or refrigeration caused by an accident to an insured object. Dairies and other operations with cold storage facilities frequently purchase this coverage. A breakdown in the refrigeration system could cause substantial consequential losses in spoiled milk or other perishable commodities.

Comprehensive Coverage   Comprehensive coverage, a relatively recent development in boiler and machinery insurance, can provide a firm with company-wide catastrophe coverage with a single definition of "object," substantial deductibles and coverage tailored to meet an individual firm's needs.

One of the first comprehensive policies was written for a large chemical company which was rapidly diversifying its operations into several completely unrelated fields. Its management had bought a boiler and machinery insurance program carefully tailored to the exposures of its chemicals production. With each new acquisition arose a new set of requirements, often quite different from the preceding ones. Types of equipment multiplied and their importance to production varied from location to location. Eventually, the unwieldy size of the policy, combined with the need for constant review of its coverages, stimulated the insured to ask for some means of simplifying the decision-making. From these circumstances developed the first single definition of "object" in a boiler and machinery policy.

The basic intent of that first comprehensive policy, like that of each succeeding one, was to provide a broad program of catastrophe coverage, corporate-wide, simple in form and in operation, yet realistic in cost. Such a program enables the insured to make maximum use of the insurer's engineering, inspection, and loss prevention facilities, while protecting the company's assets against loss resulting from the breakdown of virtually any piece of pressure equipment or any mechanical or electrical machine. It is not the intent to overlap other traditionally separate lines of insurance by covering such equipment as automobiles, other vehicles, elevators, data processing machines, cranes, or other well established inland marine exposures, but rather to include any and all equipment which properly comes within the province of boiler and machinery insurance. More specifically, all kinds of fired vessels, unfired vessels, and piping as well as motors, generators, turbines, engines, compressors, transformers, switchboards, and cables are insured; and in addition, many kinds of machinery used directly in production, such as packaging machines, rolling mills, molding, forming, laminating, and shaping presses.

Deductible. Besides the distinguishing single definition of "object" mentioned earlier, the other distinguishing feature of the comprehensive policy is an appropriate amount of retention, often substantial, in the form of deductibles for both property damage and business interruption (or other indirect coverages). The policy language is so broad and the exclusions so few that the deductible requirement acts like an exclusion by eliminating effective coverage for maintenance items, especially expendable parts on which no coverage is intended or desired.

Once it is understood that coverage is provided for the breakdown of the clock on the wall, electric typewriters, telephones, coffee machines, and similar relatively unimportant items, the need to exclude failures to such property in terms of dollars rather than in words becomes more apparent. As a result of the substantial deductibles, minor losses would never be submitted as claims. Broad coverage with high deductibles preserves the intent of providing catastrophe coverage, but reduces the need to precisely define all objects and accidents covered and excluded.

Another important purpose of the deductible is to keep the cost within acceptable limits. Quite obviously the premium varies inversely with the size of the deductibles applied. The minimum acceptable deductible is determined by the size and type of equipment operated and the ability of the buyer to retain smaller losses. It is clearly more economical to retain the smaller, more frequent type of failure than to pay a premium charge large enough to cover the insurance company's overhead expenses which include the cost of inspections and of loss investigation for noncritical items.

Individual "Tailoring." The previously mentioned features of this policy, its simple, broad description of insured equipment, and the predetermined amount of retention are the only uniform aspects of this coverage. Manuscript policies are usually used, so there is considerable variation in format among insurers and types of businesses insured. Specific exclusions may be used in certain industries in order to clarify intent. This type of exclusion obviously may be required for items which, although relatively expensive, may by their inherent nature be subject to rapid deterioration. The number and type of specially tailored exclusions vary significantly among policies and are determined primarily by the size of the deductible, nature of the exposures and the need to clarify intent.

Advantages and Disadvantages. Some of the clear advantages of "comprehensive" over the conventional boiler and machinery policy are:

1. its comparatively brief, simplified form;
2. the elimination of the need for the insured to preselect exposures and equipment for coverage;
3. its great flexibility in adapting to the needs of individual industries;
4. the reduction in paper work for in-term policy changes; and
5. a great reduction of the chance that the insured may suffer an uninsured loss.

Some of the possible disadvantages to a particular buyer are:

1. the relatively large retention required;
2. the lack of standardization in language which may result in misinterpretation or misunderstanding; and
3. the probability of a higher insurance cost than under conventional policies.

MISCELLANEOUS GLASS EXPOSURES AND THEIR TREATMENT

Glass is normally a part of the building to which it is attached. In some cases, glass is a part of the contents of a building, for example, glass in movable showcases. In still other cases, glass may be a part of improvements and betterments, as in glass office partitions. Exposures to buildings, personal property, and improvements and betterments have already been discussed in previous chapters. As noted, glass coverage is often limited, or entirely excluded, by general property insurance policies because separate glass insurance is available. Likewise, named peril policies do not provide for glass breakage unless it is caused by a specified peril. Because of a few unique loss exposures and because of the availability of separate glass insurance, glass exposures and their treatment will be examined here as a miscellaneous property item.

Exposures of Glass to Loss or Damage

The following analysis of glass loss exposures will examine first the types of glass under discussion. Following this is a discussion of perils and types of glass losses, and glass loss frequency and severity.

Types of Glass Property Different kinds of glass have varying degrees of transparency. The brittle nature of glass makes it subject to a wide range of damageability. Plate glass is formed in a large sheet which may be ground and polished. This type of glass is used especially for store show windows and similar display application. There are literally dozens of varieties of glass which are used for different purposes. Some are tempered in such a way that they absorb heat, or so that they are resistant to breakage. Glass may be laminated with a plastic material to produce "bullet proof" glass which is highly resistant to breakage. Glass may be colored, or molded into various shapes, depending upon the particular use in construction of buildings or equipment.

The settings which are required to hold plate glass windows and other structural applications of glass may be expensive. In addition, signs and decorations commonly are placed upon the glass, particularly in show windows and similar applications. Loss of the glass will also entail loss of lettering, ornamentation, or settings and these collateral materials may be expensive. The lettering and decorations usually would be less expensive than the glass itself, but the additional cost of the lettering and decorations may substantially increase the total cost to the owner.

Perils and Types of Glass Losses Many perils may result in damage to glass. The three general types of damage are breakage, abrasion, and chemical damage. The brittle nature of glass results in obvious loss due to breakage. A high proportion of glass losses involves cracking or breaking without an identifiable blow from an outside source. Over time, window settings tend to loosen and this may permit vibration of the window to a point where breakage occurs. Glass is also subject to abrasion. Windblown sand or dust such as may occur in a dust storm or sand storm may damage the glass to an extent where transparency is decreased. A plate glass show window that is damaged in this manner may no longer be suitable for its purpose. Certain acids also damage glass. The following list identifies nineteen common causes of glass breakage:

1. Wind
2. Contraction or expansion of glass

3. Poor store front construction
4. Large crowds
5. Slamming of doors
6. Falling of goods on display
7. Window dressing and cleaning
8. Settling of building
9. Burglars
10. Riots and civil commotion
11. Explosions
12. Stones or other missiles thrown by children
13. Heat from radiators placed too near the glass
14. Window frames warped
15. Persons leaning or falling against windows or show cases
16. Articles dropped on show cases
17. Racketeers and malicious breaking of glass
18. Tripping or falling against inside glass
19. Use of stepladders, tools, etc., inside of store[10]

Frequency and Severity of Glass Losses There are several factors that influence the severity and frequency of glass losses—size, type of glass, its location in the building, and the location of the building itself. Large panes of glass are more susceptible to loss than small panes, and of course will sustain more severe losses. Different types of glass vary in their susceptibility to breakage. Glass inside a building, or in the upper levels is not exposed to many of the perils affecting exterior glass or glass at the street level. Logically, glass exposed to heavy traffic or in areas with heavy crime or vandalism rates also faces increased loss exposures.

The potential loss from glass breakage or other damage usually is not catastrophic to the same extent that a fire loss or windstorm loss may be. The cost of replacing a large plate glass window may amount to several hundred or even a few thousand dollars, as contrasted to the many thousands of dollars that could be lost when a building is destroyed by fire or as the result of a tornado. However, any building with many plate glass windows may face a severe loss potential if many windows are broken as a result of a storm or a riot.

A comparatively new exposure to additional loss results from laws and ordinances in some geographical areas which require "safety glazing material" in some parts of structures. A merchant whose windows are of ordinary glass may find it necessary to install the more expensive safety glazing materials in case the windows are broken. This is a consequential loss exposure which may be substantial in some cases.

Glass in windows or other applications may be installed in such a way that removal of other fixtures would be necessary in order to make a replacement of the glass. This, too, is a consequential loss exposure which could be substantial for the owner of the glass. Lettering and ornamentation painted on or affixed to glass ordinarily would be destroyed if the glass is broken or damaged, so that the entire amount of the damage would be substantially increased if there is expensive lettering or ornamentation that must be replaced.

Immediate replacement of damaged glass is essential for show windows and similar situations. Many stores depend upon show window displays to generate sales. The proprietor of a mercantile establishment is especially eager to have show windows replaced just as soon as possible after a breakage. Broken glass also affects a building's security. A tornado, riot, or other occurrence that results in many breakages in a particular neighborhood may make it difficult for a store proprietor to get immediate replacement, or even to get a store front protected by boarding up. Substantial additional damage or business interruption may result if the property owner does not have some arrangement for prompt replacement. The need for immediate replacement of broken glass is a factor which the property owner must consider in connection with potential glass losses.

The Comprehensive Glass Insurance Policy

Much of the insurance on glass is written under package policies such as the SMP, but the coverages of these policies follow rather closely those of the comprehensive glass policy. Its provisions and the practices in connection with glass insurance generally are discussed here.

Property Covered   The property covered is the glass described in the declarations in the policy, plus any lettering or ornamentation which is also scheduled in the declarations. It is customary for each specific piece of glass to be scheduled with a description of its size and position in the building. Any glass that is set in doors, in transoms, or in showcases, or which is otherwise in some special location, or glass which has a special use, must be so described. Lettering and ornamentation must be described specifically and there may be specific amounts of insurance on lettering or glass.

The glass is described as to location and size, and there may be an additional item listing a dollar amount of insurance on lettering decoration that is on the glass. The description of the lettering or decoration may be specific as to type of lettering, whether it is gold leaf or other, and may even give the wording of the lettering. In a situation involving a store with large numbers of windows or other pieces of glass to be insured, the listing of each piece on the policy would result in an extremely bulky policy. Such situations may be handled by the preparation of a list, copies of which are kept by the insured with copies also kept by the insurance company. There are occasions where glass is covered on a blanket basis without specific description of each piece, but the premium to be paid in such cases would be dependent upon the number of pieces, their size and use, and any other factors that would affect the probabilities of loss.

It is interesting to note that glass that is already cracked may still be insured under some circumstances. The break or crack would be described in the policy in such a case. The coverage does not apply to any loss resulting from the named break or crack or to any extension of the break or crack that already exists. An insurer might be willing to cover a plate glass window, for example, if there is a crack across a corner of the window which does not appear to affect the stability of the window in other respects.

Losses Covered The comprehensive glass policy (or the glass coverage endorsement of a package policy) covers damage to the glass and to the lettering and ornamentation described in the schedule, caused by breakage of the glass or by chemicals accidentally or maliciously applied. The policy does not include the word "accidental" as applying to the breakage of the glass. This means that any breakage of the glass, except as otherwise excluded, would be covered. There would be coverage, for example, if the insured were locked out and had to break the glass in the door to regain entry.

Coverage applies for loss from chemicals accidentally or maliciously applied. Acids or other chemicals have been thrown on glass during riots and labor disturbances.

It should be noted that the damage covered is only that from breakage or the application of chemicals. While broad, the comprehensive glass policy does not provide "all-risks" coverage. There is no coverage for accidentally or maliciously scratching glass as long as there is no break in the glass. There is no coverage for the sandblasting effect if glass is injured by blowing sand or dust during a dust storm. This exclusion probably results from a feeling that abrasion damage to glass is a type of wear and tear. Small abrasions are almost certain to occur with the passage of time.

It is possible for an insurance company to issue an "all-risks" type of coverage for certain kinds of glass. For example, art glass windows, which are in the nature of fine arts, may be covered by a very broad type of insurance under a glass policy or under an inland marine policy.

Extensions of Coverage. There are three extensions of coverage which usually appear in the policy or the glass coverage endorsement. The company agrees to pay for:

1. Repairing or replacing frames immediately encasing and contiguous to insured glass when necessary because of such damage.
2. Installing temporary plates in, or boarding up, openings containing insured glass when necessary because of unavoidable delay in repairing or replacing such damaged glass.
3. Removing or replacing any obstructions, other than window displays, when necessary in replacing such damaged glass, lettering or ornamentation.

Payment under these three extensions is customarily limited to $75 per occurrence, unless there is specific provision for a larger amount, which would require payment of an extra premium. It should be noted that these are really consequential losses, but they are normally covered by the policy.

Safety Glazing Material Endorsement Since glass breakage may result in bodily injury, many governmental bodies have ordinances which require breakage-resistant glass in locations such as doors, windows adjacent to doors, glass shower enclosures, and so forth. When a pane of ordinary glass is broken in a location affected by such ordinances, it will be necessary to replace it with more expensive breakage-resistant glass. This consequential loss exposure resulting from such ordinances may be insured with the safety glazing material endorsement. This endorsement provides coverage for the minimum cost to replace the damaged glass with safety glazing material which meets applicable codes.

Exclusions Three exclusions customarily appear in the glass insurance policy or endorsement. These are (1) loss by fire, (2) loss due to war, whether declared, civil war, insurrection, rebellion, or revolution, or to any act or condition incident to any of the foregoing, and (3) loss from nuclear damage. The exclusion of loss by fire is reasonable because buildings (including their glass) are expected to be covered by fire insurance. It is interesting to note that the exclusion of fire loss goes back many years, actually prior to the time when insurance against loss from windstorm was not commonly written together with fire insurance. Thus, a windstorm loss may result in coverage under both a glass policy and under an extended coverage endorsement to a fire policy.

Limits of Liability Unlike most property insurance policies, glass insurance contains no dollar limit of liability applying to the glass. The limit of the company's liability for damage does not exceed either (1) the actual cash value of the property at the time of loss or (2) the cost to repair or replace the damaged property with other property of the "nearest obtainable kind and quality." When glass is replaced, no deduction is made for depreciation. A dollar limit usually is placed on the liability for lettering and ornamentation. It is customary to specify an amount of insurance for the lettering on each piece of insured glass.

There may be situations where a dollar limit of liability would be stated in the policy. This would be the case with glass signs, neon signs, fluorescent signs and lamps, motion picture screens, memorial windows, stained glass windows or other art glass, and special types of tempered or expensive glass, which may be subject to varying values.

Other Policy Provisions Glass insurance customarily is written on a one-year basis. Because there may be a considerable fluctuation in the price of glass, the premiums that are charged usually are based upon the kind and size of each particular piece of glass. Annual renewal of glass coverage gives the insurance company an opportunity to keep the premium charges in line with the current prices for glass.

The policy has requirements similar to other property insurance policies relating to proof of loss, notice of loss, action against the company, and subrogation. It is customary to require a proof of loss *only* upon a specific request of the company. The only document needed when a replacement is made is a receipt to the effect that the glass was replaced.

The provision relating to other insurance requires that any loss be apportioned according to the limit of liability under the glass policy in relation to the total limit of all valid and collectible insurance. The total limit of liability for apportionment purposes usually is the amount of insurance that applies to the glass in the structure and not the amount of other insurance on an entire building. Apportionment procedures have been worked out that apply to cases where a loss might be occasioned by windstorm, and where there would be duplicate coverage under a windstorm or extended coverage policy and a glass policy.

Replacement Service The glass policy gives the insurer the option of paying for a loss in money or of replacing the property. In many glass losses, the replacement is arranged directly by the insurance company. This practice is so well established that one of the important reasons for the purchase of glass insurance is to secure the replacement service of the insurer.

The replacement service of an insurance company may be especially important where there is a storm that results in heavy breakage in a neighborhood. An individual storekeeper might find it difficult to secure replacement under those circumstances, whereas the volume of business which an insurance company gives to a glass dealer will secure preferred service for the insurance company replacement.

ANIMAL MORTALITY INSURANCE

Animals are a unique type of personal property. They are exposed to loss by damage or destruction caused by fire, windstorm, and so forth. In this context, animals are like other personal property. Coverage for these exposures is available under various inland marine floaters, and under fire and allied forms covering farm property. Limited coverage is also provided under general property forms such as form FGP-1, which covers animals and pets held for sale.

In another sense, animals are unlike other personal property. Like human beings, they are exposed to the chance of premature death caused by injury, illness, or other natural causes. Standard property insurance forms do not protect an animal owner against loss occasioned by premature death. To provide protection against this exposure to loss, life insurance for animals was developed. The term applied, however, is not life insurance but "mortality insurance."

Livestock Mortality Insurance

Livestock mortality insurance is term life insurance. This policy covers against loss by death from all natural causes, including death from illness or disease, accident, fire, or lightning. There are some conditions and restrictions applying to coverage. Since the livestock mortality policy covers death only, it does not cover minor injuries, depreciation in value, or failure of an animal to perform certain duties or functions.

Consent of the insurance company must be secured for destruction of an injured animal except where certain bone fractures have occurred which require immediate destruction and for which a licensed veterinarian certifies that immediate destruction is necessary.

As mentioned, there normally is no coverage for loss resulting from depreciation in value due to an animal becoming unfit for, or incapable of, fulfilling the functions or duties for which it is kept. However, there are rare occasions where fertility of a breeding animal may be covered, with a premium commensurate with the chance of loss.

Insurable values under livestock mortality policies are carefully determined. The insured value ordinarily does not exceed the cost of the animal to the insured. However, increased values may be acceptable to the insurance company in cases where the animal has been proved to be worth more because of performance or prize winnings.

Livestock mortality insurance is generally written to cover horses, registered cattle, calves being grown and exhibited under sponsorship of clubs such as 4-H and Future Farmers of America clubs, feeder cattle, and registered dogs. This coverage is not designed for the average cow or bull, but it is a desirable coverage where the animal has a special and demonstrable value.

The insuring of purebred livestock and other valuable livestock has very interesting connotations. Bulls that are used for breeding purposes may be insured for amounts in the hundreds of thousands of dollars. A famous race horse which was retired to breeding was reported to have been insured for more than $6 million, the insurance including not only mortality but loss of fertility. An average champion show dog may be worth up to $5,000, and one show dog was sold for $25,000.

Livestock mortality insurance is a highly specialized market and is written by only a few insurance companies. The extremely high values usually are insured by Lloyd's of London, or may be reinsured by a Lloyd's policy. Insurers are extremely careful in their underwriting and may require certification by a licensed veterinarian that the animal is in good health at the time insurance takes effect.

Pet Insurance

A variety of animal livestock mortality insurance may be written to cover pets, especially dogs. Ordinarily the coverage is written only on pedigreed dogs. A variation of the coverage might be written by some companies to cover only medical treatment in case of injury or illness. Coverages and availability of such insurance vary from time to time as companies find it feasible or desirable to offer such specialty coverage. There is little stability in such a specialty market.

INSURANCE AGAINST LOSS OF CROPS

There .are many perils which threaten loss to a farmer's crops. Drought, flooding, or other weather conditions may severely damage or completely destroy the crops in a particular area. Fire occasionally has caused widespread loss in the prairies when grain is ripe and dry. Many of these perils tend to be widespread and catastrophic in nature and thus cannot be insured against under the normal considerations of spread of risk. Hail damage, on the contrary, is usually local but may be severe in a particular area. The path of a hailstorm usually is narrow and erratic. A hailstorm, for example, would not affect an entire state or region. It is the limited area and the erratic nature of hail damage that makes this loss exposure insurable.

Hail is a severe threat to a farmer's crop. A hailstorm can severely damage the crop, and varying degrees of damage may result from lesser falls of hail. Hail occurs in practically every crop-growing area of the United States but is most severe in the plains states of the Midwest. Leaf crops such as tobacco are particularly susceptible to hail damage, but grain crops such as corn, wheat, and soybeans can also be severely damaged.

Efforts have been made to find methods of controlling or reducing damage by hail. These have included the seeding of clouds with chemicals from airplanes or from the ground, the attempt to develop hail resistant plants, and the planting of crops in ways that might lessen hail damage. None of these attempts has resulted in any significant reduction in hail damage. Since satisfactory loss control techniques have not been developed, the only way to treat the exposure is to retain losses, or to purchase crop hail insurance.

Crop Hail Insurance

A crop hail insurance policy is usually written for the term of one growing season. Coverage of the policy is against all direct loss or damage by hail to the crops described in the policy. The word "hail" is not defined in the policy but is generally accepted to mean the roughly circular pieces of ice precipitated from thunderstorms. Insurance against loss by hail does not include loss resulting from a beating rain nor loss by wind. An actual fall of hail must occur if the loss is to be covered as hail damage.

The procedures involved with applications and binders for crop hail insurance take into account the possibility that a farmer might be tempted to ask for insurance when weather conditions appear to threaten a severe storm. The application must be in writing, and standard procedure requires that payment for the insurance accompany the application. Insurance does not take effect until a specified time after the application has been made, usually at least twenty-four hours after actual signing. The application is not only dated but includes the hour of signing.

Insurance may become effective twenty-four hours after the applicant signs the application but the insurance company has ten days in which to reject the application if for any reason it does not desire to issue the policy. If canceled by the company, coverage can cease no less than five days after notice is given.

Expiration dates vary according to the time that a particular crop normally is harvested. This may range from August 1st to November 1st, depending upon the type of crop and the section of the country. The insurance also expires if the crop is harvested even though the expiration date on the policy has not yet arrived.

Limits of Liability Limits of liability usually apply per acre. The limit may vary from $5 per acre to $200 per acre, depending upon the crop and the amount of hail insurance that the insurer is willing to write in that locality. The amount that a farmer would want to secure would depend upon the type of crop and the expected return per acre. The farmer ordinarily can secure coverage from as many companies as are willing to write coverage in that area. The farmer may thus be able to secure the necessary amounts of coverage by buying insurance from several different companies, all with a limitation per acre.

Identification of Crop and Location The policy specifies the particular crop that is covered and its location. The location designation is carefully specified by county, township, range number, and/or section or quarter-section, depending upon the designation that is necessary to identify the exact location of the crop.

There is another plan used by some companies called a "farm unit plan." Insurance under this plan covers the entire farm unit. This ordinarily is an excess type of coverage with various percentages of participation by the farmer, ordinarily from 5 percent to 20 percent. An excess of over 50 percent might be written in some cases.

Loss Reporting The insured ordinarily is required to report losses directly to the insurer. Notice to a local agent is not ordinarily accepted. Hail losses must be handled quickly. Notice must be given within forty-eight hours after loss or damage has occurred. Careful examination of the damaged areas usually would be made by an adjuster together with the farmer. Samples are taken to indicate the percentage of loss. These samples may include actual count of stalks and the proportion of stalks damaged by the hail in representative sections of the area where hail damage occurred. Hail storms may cover a narrow swath, so that one portion of a field typically would be more heavily damaged than another. The damage to an entire field or farm can be averaged and adjusted on a percentage basis for the entire farm or the entire growing area.

Crop Coverage for Perils Other Than Hail

Fire insurance on growing crops is written along with hail coverage in some areas. This covers fire damage to the crop while standing in the field. It may also cover fire damage during harvesting and while the crop is being transported to the first place of storage. It does not cover during storage because such coverage is available under ordinary farm fire insurance policies.

Insurance companies have also broadened their coverage in some areas to include damage by windstorm if accompanied by hail, fire, lightning, livestock, and aircraft, and perhaps loss by explosion, riot, and damage by vehicles, until the crop reaches a place of storage. These expanded coverages have been developed in order to provide the farmer with a broadened coverage that ties in more closely with the actual exposure to loss.

Government Crop Insurance Programs

The federal government has instituted a program of crop insurance through the Federal Crop Insurance Corporation. Because the actual conditions affecting this program vary from one session of Congress to another, the program cannot accurately be summarized in this text.

"All-Risks" Crop Coverage

Insurance companies have experimented with an "all-risks" type of crop coverage. This has been developed to a certain extent in order to insure against crop failure. Such programs are still in a developmental stage, at the time this is written.

RAIN INSURANCE

The promoters of any event that may be adversely affected by rain may have a need for rain insurance. The exposure is most severe for limited-time events, such as festivals or concerts sponsored by a church or civic organization, or for a sports event. Events operating over a longer period of time, or series of events (such as a season's baseball games) are less exposed to severe losses by rain. The operators of long-time events can anticipate some loss due to rain, but that loss is somewhat predictable, and will be offset by the number of days with no precipitation. Nonrepeatable events scheduled for only one or two days may be totally canceled due to rain. The operators of concessions near an event, and transportation companies providing transportation to and from an event, may also face an exposure to loss if it rains.

Most property policies require that there be direct damage to tangible property by an insured peril before insurance coverage applies. Rain insurance is an exception to this rule. Losses are covered even if no property is damaged by the rain.

The need for rain insurance varies according to the type of event to be covered. Coverage for an indoor event is needed for the hours immediately preceding the scheduled time of the event. Rain would not affect attendance after the audience has arrived, but might keep people from taking the trouble to transport themselves to an event in a downpour. On the other hand, fairs or other open-air events would need coverage for the hours immediately preceding the event, and also for the early hours of the event itself.

Rain insurance is written to indemnify the insured against loss of income or profit, or extra expense, which results from rain, hail, snow, or sleet. To qualify for coverage, the insured must be in a position to suffer a financial loss if bad weather reduces the attendance.

Rain insurance policies differ in their details. They are designed to fit the needs of persons or organizations having an interest in events that would be affected by the weather. A commonly written policy is designed for events for which admission is charged. This policy may be written to cover for a length of time that is appropriate for the event, such as three consecutive hours on each day that coverage applies. Or, it may be written for a single day with a minimum number of hours. Ordinarily the policy specifies that a certain amount of rainfall must occur if a loss is to be paid. The minimum rainfall specified may be one-twentieth of an inch, one-tenth of an inch, two-thirds of an inch, or some other amount which is appropriate to the event and the anticipated attendance. Snow, sleet, and hail are considered the equivalent of rainfall when melted down according to standards of the National Weather Service.

Coverage may be written to cover events from which no income is expected if abandonment of the event would result in loss of the expenses which have been incurred.

A policy that is designed for fairs and horse races may have the amount of coverage adjusted based on three consecutive years of prior experience. A valued policy may be written in some cases with a stated amount to be paid if rain falls within the period specified in the policy. There may also be provisions for covering refunds where reserved tickets have been sold subject to such a refund if the event is canceled because of weather.

Publishers and merchants may have losses as a result of a cancellation of advertising space, or where there is an agreement on the part of the publisher that the advertising charge will be refunded or that the advertisement will be reprinted at a later date if rain falls during the period specified in the policy.

The measurement of rainfall in order to determine whether there is a covered loss would be taken at the nearest National Weather Service station if there is one sufficiently close to provide a good estimate of the rainfall. Otherwise, a rain gauge may be set up at the location of the event.

The amount payable in case of covered loss is the difference between actual receipts and the amount of insurance specified in the policy. Or, a valued policy may be used, in which case a specified amount would be paid if certain conditions are met. The amount of insurance is developed in conference with the insured according to the receipts in previous years, if there is previous experience. Coverage may also be related to the expenses in setting up the event, or, in the case of an event that runs for several days, the basis may be the receipts for days in which no rainfall occurs.

Application for rain insurance policies ordinarily must be made at least seven days before the effective date of the policy, and coverage is not subject to cancellation by either the insured or the insurer. These provisions are necessary because an insured might be able to anticipate the weather if some shorter period were allowed.

Rates for rain insurance are calculated according to the average amount of rainfall reported for the location and time of year in which the event is held. The insurer also takes into account the probability of thunderstorms if the event is scheduled during the summer months when isolated afternoon thunderstorms are probable.

It should be emphasized that mere threatening weather does not result in any valid claim under a rain insurance policy. Actual precipitation must occur.

CREDIT AND MORTGAGE EXPOSURES AND INSURANCE

Businesses face loss if for any reason they are unable to collect from their debtors payments that fall due. Such exposures to loss caused by damage or destruction of accounts receivable records can be treated with noninsurance techniques (such as duplicate records) or with accounts receivable insurance. The chance of loss due to inability of debtors to meet payments is generally a "business peril," as discussed in Chapter 1, and most such exposures are uninsurable. Noninsurance techniques to prevent such losses would include such practices normally involved with conservative lending practices, such as credit checks on would-be debtors. Some such losses, however, may be fortuitous pure loss exposures, and may be considered as a proper subject for private insurance. Some of the insurance policies designed to treat such fortuitous losses involved with the granting of credit will be discussed in this section, including commercial credit insurance, credit insurance for exports, and mortgage guarantee insurance. A subject somewhat related to mortgages—title insurance—will be treated in the next major section of this chapter.

Commercial Credit Exposures and Insurance

Commercial credit insurance is a nonstandard type of consequential loss coverage which may be purchased by businesses. It is intended to indemnify a business firm for loss which has been caused by "insolvency" of its customers. Because this is a specialty coverage, policies may vary among the insurers offering a market.

Credit insurance ordinarily is not written for retail merchants. The retailer sells in relatively small amounts with a large spread of obligations over many customers. Careful selection of customers and close attention to accounts receivable can provide a low average credit loss which the merchant retains as a business expense. The manufacturer or wholesaler, in contrast, may have large amounts tied up in one or a few accounts. The inability of one or more of these important accounts to pay its obligations may result in a substantial credit loss.

Insurance coverage recognizes that businesses normally sustain some losses from inability of customers to pay their obligations. Credit insurance covers the loss above the normal credit losses of the insured. Coverage applies only to what is defined as "insolvency" in the policy. Insolvency, for purposes of this policy, may occur due to events such as:

1. death of the debtor,
2. insanity of the debtor,
3. appointment of a receiver,
4. absconding of the debtor,
5. attachment of the debtor's stock in trade,
6. an offer by the debtor to compromise with his creditors,
7. foreclosure under a chattel mortgage applying to the debtor's stock in trade, or
8. an actual voluntary or involuntary bankruptcy proceedings.

There may be other situations which are covered by the policy depending upon the circumstances and the types of business conducted by the insured and customers.

Coverage may apply to all customers of the insured so that the insolvency of one or more customers which results in an excessive loss would be covered, or the policy may apply to specified accounts only. Coverage applying to specified accounts generally would be used where a few debtors are responsible for a large proportion of the insured's accounts receivable.

Policies may provide for two limits of liability. There ordinarily would be a limit on the loss that is to be paid for any one account, and there would also be a limit on the total amount that would be paid as a result of losses during the policy term.

There may be occasions where the insurance company could more effectively collect past due accounts than could the insured. Therefore, policies may provide for collection of the past due accounts by the insurance company. This may be a mandatory provision under which the insurance company would take over the collection of such accounts or it may be optional in which case the insured could submit overdue accounts to the insurer for collection. Another common provision is that the insured may be required to report overdue accounts to the insurer within some specified length of time, such as sixty or ninety days after the account becomes overdue.

The policy defines what is the normal credit loss of the insured, above which the insurance applies. The coverage usually is subject to what is called "coinsurance" but this provision operates as a deductible. Depending on the percentage of coinsurance, the insured may retain from 10 percent to 35 percent of losses above the normal credit loss, depending upon the past experience of the firm and the willingness of the insurer to cover the losses. The limit of liability under such a policy might be $100,000, for example. The insurance company might be obligated under the policy terms to pay from 65 percent to 90 percent of a credit loss above the normal credit loss of the insured. The percentage to be paid by the insurer would be specified in the policy. The normal credit loss would probably be stated in the policy in the form of a deductible. For example, the policy may provide that the insured would pay the first $20,000 of credit losses during the policy term, with the insurer to pay the specified percentage above the $20,000 deductible, subject to the policy limit of $100,000.

Policies may cover losses resulting from sales made during the policy term, or they may cover losses from insolvency that occurs during the policy term. The insured is not permitted to make any compromise with a debtor without the consent of the insurer, once an insolvency has occurred within the definition of the policy. Policies usually are drafted individually to meet the requirements of the insured. There may be a provision permitting recovery for a loss that was not discovered until after the policy had expired. Losses in such a case may be limited to those from sales made during the policy period, but coverage could extend to losses that are not discovered until after the policy had expired. This would be similar to the discovery period which is allowed under some bond contracts.

Related Coverages   The term "credit insurance" is often used to refer to a form of insurance written in connection with installment sales contracts and revolving credit facilities of retail merchants. This type of coverage is discussed briefly here only to separate it from the credit and guarantee insurance programs that have just been described.

The "credit insurance" policies that are written for retail merchants ordinarily cover the installments that are due from purchasers. The policies are a form of group life and/or accident and health insurance. Provisions ordinarily are made to cover death, specified accidents, hospitalization of the debtor-purchaser, or other disability. Some of these contracts even cover loss of employment. A typical policy obligates the insurance company to pay the installments that are due from the debtor during a period of disability, usually subject to a waiting period of perhaps thirty days.

A related form of "credit insurance" is the installment sales floater coverage which is written as an inland marine policy. The installment sales floater, discussed in Chapter 10, covers loss of property from perils which are specified in the policy, usually perils such as fire, the extended coverage perils, and perhaps burglary.

The inland marine coverage should be distinguished from the credit life and credit accident and health insurance which normally covers installment payments following death, or during the period of disability. The installment sales floater, in contrast, usually covers the value of the property which may be destroyed while it is subject to an installment sales contract.

Credit Insurance for Exports

Business firms that export goods to foreign countries have special credit problems. The methods of collecting accounts receivable that would be effective in domestic commerce ordinarily cannot be used to make collections from businesses located in foreign countries. A group of insurance companies have formed what is known as the "Foreign Credit Insurance Association" in order to write a form of credit insurance on exports. The Foreign Credit Insurance Association operates in conjunction with the Export-Import Bank of Washington.

The Export-Import Bank of Washington is an independent United States agency which was established in 1934. The functions of the bank are the financing, guaranteeing, and insuring payment for goods and services that originate in the United States. The Foreign Credit Insurance Association is a group of insurers that provide credit insurance in connection with foreign obligations. The facilities of the Export-Import Bank are available for financing through regular banking channels, and the credit insurance may be arranged through regular banking channels or through insurers that are representing the participating insurers.

The insurance is arranged to reimburse an exporter for a portion of the loss when the purchaser of goods in a foreign country fails to make payment because of insolvency, and other commercial reasons.

The insurers in the Foreign Credit Insurance Association are not expected to provide coverage where the foreign country prohibits conversion of foreign currency to dollars, or where political situations may result in the confiscation of property, or where war or civil commotion hazard exists. These are considered political exposures, and the Export-Import Bank can cover up to as much as 85 percent or more of the political exposure in a particular transaction.

Coverage for insolvency and commercial risks usually applies up to 85 percent of the exporter's loss. Political risks, when insured, may also cover up to 85 percent or more of the loss from these risks. The political risks coverage is eventually sustained by the Export-Import Bank rather than by the insurance companies in the group.

There are various terms for which the insurance may be written. Coverage may apply to specific items of export, or on a more or less continuous basis where the exporter is operating continuously in the foreign market. This type of coverage has been viewed briefly here in order to alert the student to the fact that a version of credit insurance is available to the exporter of goods.

Mortgage Guarantee Insurance

A mortgagee faces a loss if the mortgagor should default on payments. The two conventional methods of reducing this loss exposure have been (1) limiting the amount of the loan to a reasonable percentage of the value, usually 75 percent to 80 percent of the value of the property; and (2) making the loan for only a relatively few years so that economic and social conditions and the status of the borrower can be determined to a reasonable degree. These limitations of a low percentage of loan to value and a short period of years are undesirable for a large proportion of people who wish to finance their homes. The federal government has recognized this problem by making available to qualified buyers loans which represent a high proportion of loan to property value and which extend for long periods of time. A similar facility is made available through mortgage guarantee insurance to lenders who wish to provide mortgages for persons who do not make use of the government financing programs.

The mortgage guarantee insurance contract agrees to protect the lender from loss if the borrower fails to meet payment requirements. A typical mortgage insurance policy requires that the mortgagee report to the insurer when the mortgagor is two months in default. Foreclosure may be required when the mortgagor is six months in default. The insurance contract provides coverage for the amount of the loan, plus interest, plus any taxes and insurance costs that may have been advanced by the mortgagee in connection with the loan transaction plus certain other expenses. It is intended that the mortgagee-lender acquire title to the property in case of default by the mortgagor.

Mortgage guarantee insurance is written for banks, savings and loan associations, and other persons or organizations whose business is lending money on mortgages. A high proportion of the business involves residential property. This type of insurance facilitates the providing of mortgages for amounts up to 95 percent of the property value. The essential occurrence which precipitates a loss is default on the mortgage payment by the borrower. Details of coverage and settlement arrangements vary somewhat from company to company. This is a specialized business which is written by a limited number of insurers which specialize in this type of coverage.

TITLE INSURANCE

A title in connection with real property is a right to ownership of the land. It normally is evidenced by a document which may be called a "title." The title to or ownership of land may be complete, in which case the title holder is said to have a "clear title." This indicates that the ownership is free of encumbrances of any kind. The ownership may also be subject to certain restrictions or defects. The original ownership of land in the United States goes back several hundreds of years to the time when a sovereign power from overseas claimed the land from its aboriginal state. It was customary in those years for the sovereign to grant title to individuals. The ownership of a particular piece of land in the meantime may have passed through many hands by purchase, inheritance, or other transfer of title. It may be difficult in a particular case to establish a clear title through all of the intervening transfers.

A defect in a title may be costly to the titleholder. Some other person who has a claim to the property may demand payment in order to eliminate the defect. There may be extreme cases where a titleholder would actually lose the property because some other person had a superior claim to the property. It is extremely important that the purchaser of real property make every effort to have search made for defects in the title.

Defective titles may arise in a variety of ways. Some of the typical situations are as follows:

1. A deed which records the transfer of title in the history of a particular piece of property may be a forgery.
2. Sometimes it occurs that a reported transfer never actually took place and the owner who is reported to have transferred the title did not do so. It may be that the owner, or his or her descendants, would have a claim on the property because the transfer did not actually occur.
3. Transfer of title by inheritance normally requires the signature of all heirs to the transfer. Sometimes an unknown heir will appear at a later date and claim a portion of the property because his or her signature was not secured.
4. False statements may have been made in connection with a transfer of title in order to get the transaction closed.
5. Errors may have been made by recorders of deeds, or errors may have been made in the recording of court transactions in connection with transfer of title.
6. Mechanics or architects may have placed liens upon the property which have not been discharged. These may cloud the title or cause other expense to the titleholder.

There are a great many ways in which the current title to real property may be defective. Any such defective title may cause expense to the titleholder if a claim is made because of some alleged defect in the title.

Insurance Against Loss from Defective Title

It is extremely difficult to be absolutely sure that a title is clear even with the most careful search. Therefore, insurance against loss of the title or against expense because of a defective title is a reasonable additional precaution against loss.

Title insurance policies that are issued to the owners of property usually have no termination date. The protection against loss from a defective title may extend to heirs in the event of death or to corporate successors of a corporate owner of property. However, sale of the property to a new owner probably would require a new search to make certain that the title passed properly, and a new policy would undoubtedly be issued to the new owner.

Policies that are issued to mortgagees to guarantee that the borrower has proper title for the property which is pledged as security normally end with the payment of the mortgage debt. Another difference between the owner's policy and the mortgage policy is that the limit of liability in the mortgage policy normally would decrease as the mortgage payments are made.

Title insurance companies have extensive and accurate methods of checking titles. A thorough search is made in order to locate any possible defects in the title. The title company will then guarantee the title to the owner or to the mortgagee and agree to indemnify them for loss which might result from some defect which had not been discovered or is not discoverable by a careful search.

Title insurance companies are often local companies because of the need for careful search of titles. There are many areas of the country where the title records to real property are held by title companies. This is true to a large extent in the Chicago area, for example, because the Chicago fire of 1871 destroyed many of the governmental and other records relating to real property up to that time.

A title insurance contract may be written to indemnify a former owner who has sold property under a warranty deed. Such a deed provides that the former owner warrants the validity of the title which he or she has passed on. A quitclaim deed, in contrast, merely passes whatever title and right the former owner has in the property. The new owner has no recourse against the former owner in case the title should prove defective under a quitclaim deed.

The title insurance policy does not cover defects in the title which are set forth in the policy. It is customary to describe in the policy any known defects in the title. Any results of such known defects are excluded from the coverage. Also excluded are any defects which may develop as a result of the insured's action subsequent to the time the title insurance policy was effective. Title insurance is different from other property insurance coverages in that it relates to past situations and not to future occurrences.

The title insurance company agrees to pay the insured for loss which may be sustained as a result of four different situations: (1) the insured may be evicted from the premises because of title defect, (2) he or she may lose title to the property, (3) a sale or mortgage may be rejected because of defective title, or (4) a purchaser may be relieved from an obligation to complete the purchase contract. In addition, marketability is a factor which may or may not be covered by the title insurance contract, depending upon the circumstances. The title insurance company agrees to defend the insured in case of court action as well as to make payment for the loss. The amount of insurance under a title insurance policy normally would be the purchase price of the property if it is an owner's policy, or the remaining amount of the mortgage under a mortgagee policy. Title insurance does not cover the amount of any increase in value after the policy is written. It is also characteristic of title insurance that the policy is purchased only once and is effective for that insured as long as he or she has an insurable interest in the property.

The Torrens System

A few states have a system of title recording and indemnification known as the Torrens System. The procedure is for the property owner to prove his or her title by abstract and any other available evidence and to have his or her title registered in a court.[11] He or she receives a certficate of clear title. The fees collected for these titles then go into a fund which is used to pay off any claimant who subsequently may appear against the titles so registered. Under these laws a claimant is prevented from acquiring title to the disputed property, but may be reimbursed by the Torrens System fund for whatever claim the courts may decide he or she has against the property in question.

This system is in effect in limited areas. It is voluntary in the few states in which the system has been set up. It has the disadvantage that legal proceedings must be used to secure a certificate of title. Some authorities on title to real property have questioned the finality of the guarantee of title under the Torrens System.

SURPLUS LINES INSURANCE CONTRACTS

The term "surplus lines" has come to mean specialized types of insurance coverage—particularly those needed by unusual businesses or industrial operations. Surplus lines may be written by only a few insurers because they tend to specialize in particular kinds of coverage. An important reason why authorized insurers in many states do not write insurance on the surplus lines exposures is that these exposures generally are extra hazardous. Many liability insurers, for example, do not write insurance on automobile or boat races, amusement parks, swimming or other athletic clubs, fireworks displays, and golf driving ranges. Some forms of property loss insurance are extra hazardous, including such exposures as crop dusting from airplanes, and burglary or robbery coverage on check cashing exchanges or all-night mercantile operations.

It has proved feasible for insurance companies to specialize in certain of these extra hazardous coverages, especially where the coverage and rates can be adapted to the actual exposure. Lloyd's of London, of course, is famous for its willingness to insure against almost any kind of loss if an acceptable premium can be secured. There are also many American insurers that make a specialty of writing insurance for particular kinds of unusual loss exposures.

All states have procedures for the licensing of insurers that meet certain financial and other qualifications. An insurance company that has not met the qualification requirements for a state and has not secured a license or a certificate of authority to operate in that state is referred to as an "unlicensed" company. State laws generally prohibit producers from the selling of insurance in unlicensed companies. This has had the effect of prohibiting a business owner from insuring against unusual exposures to loss where a particular kind of insurance is not written by authorized companies. Such a business owner with an unusual exposure might be tempted to go without insurance, or could buy insurance by mail from a foreign or alien insurer. Some state legislatures eventually realized that facilities should be made available for the purchase of insurance from unlicensed insurers when the coverage desired could not be secured from a licensed company. Therefore, many states have what are called surplus lines laws. These laws make it possible for an insurance agent or broker to secure insurance in an unlicensed company if a search has been made for a licensed insurer to write the coverage. Special requirements exist and in some states the agent or broker must be specially licensed to place surplus lines business. The agent or broker may be held responsible for checking the financial standing of such an unlicensed insurer. Some states publish lists of acceptable unlicensed insurers for surplus lines and they may also publish a list of the lines of insurance that may be written by such companies.

An important reason for the development of the surplus lines problem is the requirement for the filing of rates in many states. It is difficult and in many cases impossible to develop a rate schedule that will fit all circumstances and all of the specially hazardous situations that arise. The long and sometimes impossible process of getting approval for special rates may influence an insurance company to avoid writing a coverage for which there is a limited demand. The unlicensed insurer, in contrast, is free to quote whatever rate appears proper for the risk, and the policyholder may be perfectly willing to pay the price in order to secure the coverage. Some of the surplus lines laws are so arranged that licensed companies can be exempted from the rate filing requirements where a coverage cannot be sold under normal conditions and where the coverage is properly a subject for surplus lines treatment.

The surplus lines approach to unusual and specially hazardous situations is an important part of the insurance market for miscellaneous coverages.

Chapter Notes

1. Robert Riegel, Jerome S. Miller, and C. Arthur Williams, Jr., *Insurance Principles and Practices: Property and Liability*, 6th ed. (Englewood Cliffs, NJ: Prentice-Hall, Inc., 1976).
2. Example supplied by the Hartford Steam Boiler Inspection and Insurance Company.
3. *FC&S Bulletins*, Sales Section, p. Bm-2.
4. Hartford Steam Boiler.
5. *FC&S*, p. Bm-3.
6. Hartford Steam Boiler.
7. *FC&S*, p. Bm-3.
8. Hartford Steam Boiler.
9. As this text goes to press, bodily injury liability coverage is being made completely optional in many states. The coverage is excess to other forms of insurance, and has become much less important than in the past, since most firms today have general liability coverage. Since the coverage generally is not purchased, many companies are deleting bodily injury coverage from the form itself, but will provide coverage by endorsement for a small additional premium.
10. Aetna Life and Casualty Commercial Lines Casualty & Surety Division Educational Course Group II, Lesson 6, December 1967.
11. An "abstract of title" is defined in Black's Law Dictionary as:

   A condensed history of the title to land, consisting of a synopsis or summary of the material or operative portion of all the conveyances, of whatever kind or nature, which in any manner affect said land, or any estate or interest therein, together with a statement of all liens, charges, or liabilities to which the same may be subject, and of which it is in any way material for purchasers to be apprised.

CHAPTER 14

Combination Policies—SMP

In this chapter and the one that follows, combination policies, often called package policies, are analyzed. These policies have evolved from the single-line policies and endorsements reviewed in the previous twelve chapters of the text. This analysis is divided into two parts. The first section discusses the evolution and development of package policies, the reasons for their development, the purposes they serve, and their proper use. The second section reviews the actual content of one such combination policy: the special multi-peril policy (SMP). In this review, eligibility rules are analyzed as well as the contents of the various forms used with the SMP program. In Chapter 15, several other multiple-peril forms, such as the industrial property program, the manufacturers output policy, the farmowners-ranchowners program, and the business-owners program are investigated.

In order to be consistent with the rest of the text, all discussion is limited to property insurance. Although the package programs often contain liability coverages, analysis of these policies and forms is deferred until CPCU 4.

GENERAL NATURE AND USE OF "COMBINATION" OR "PACKAGE" POLICIES

Any treatment of combination or package policies must involve several new terms, some of which are poorly defined and frequently used incorrectly. For example, the terms *multi-peril* and *multiple-line* are sometimes used synonymously, though they have different meanings. A multi-peril policy, as the name implies, is a policy which covers more than one peril. The familiar fire and extended coverage policy is an example of a multi-peril policy.

The term multiple-line is more difficult to define because the definition requires an understanding of the history of American insurance practices. In the fairly recent past, up to the middle of the present century, property and liability insurers in the United States were limited as to the coverages they could write both by their corporate charters and by the statutes of many states. Companies which were chartered as fire insurers could write only fire, allied lines, and marine coverages. Automobile physical damage coverage was written by fire insurers. Companies which were chartered as casualty insurers could write only casualty insurance and fidelity and surety bonds. Casualty lines included automobile liability, general liability, workers' compensation, burglary, theft, robbery, glass, and boiler coverages. A multiple-line policy is a policy which includes one or more coverages previously written by fire insurers along with one or more coverages previously written by casualty insurers. It is apparent, therefore, that a multi-peril policy is not necessarily a multiple-line policy, but a multiple-line policy is necessarily a multi-peril policy. One of the first multiple-line policies was the combination automobile policy, which included both physical damage coverages (previously written by fire insurers) and liability coverages (previously written by casualty insurers). However, most people now think of the automobile policy as a single-line policy.

Some people would define the terms *combination policy* and *package policy* to include either multi-peril or multiple-line policies. Others would restrict those terms to multiple-line policies. The first, and more inclusive, definition will be used in this chapter.

Influence of Past Conditions

Package policies have evolved as a result of the interaction of several forces: tradition, needs of business people, regulatory officials, and underwriting and pricing practices of insurers.

Tradition   Insurers in the United States were first established on a single-line basis, writing only one line of insurance. Later, regulatory officials adopted this established tradition as the correct one, and single-line regulation was developed. These historical facts established a tradition which worked against the development of package policies. This approach was the opposite of that taken in Europe where multiple-line regulation and policies have existed for many years.

It has been said that this development occurred in the United States because the original companies were quite small and had little capital to spare.[1] Therefore, they concentrated on what they knew best. Whatever the reason, it set a precedent that lasted nearly two centuries.

Company Practices While a company might have sold more than one type of property insurance, it did so in separate policies. In time, firms began to combine coverages from separate policies into one policy. An early example of such a movement was "supplemental coverage"— known today as extended coverage (EC), one of the basic fire and allied lines forms. It is multi-peril but still single-line. Another early example of the combination technique is the jewelers' block policy which combines crime and physical damage protection on the premises and while property is in transit.

The jewelers' block policy was and is underwritten as a single-line inland marine coverage under a special provision of the Nation-Wide Definition designed to permit admitted insurers to offer the coverage in competition with nonadmitted insurers, which were not limited by mono-line regulation. However, it is actually a multiple-line coverage because it combines fire and allied lines coverages with crime coverages, which were traditionally written by casualty insurers. Although the fire and extended coverage policy and the jewelers' block are combination or package policies within the definition we are using, they are not generally recognized as such because they are not multiple-line policies, at least in the legal sense.

However, the single-line packages were important to the evolution of multiple-line packages because the existence of some policies providing broad coverage brought demand from producers and insureds for still broader policies. This demand led ultimately to the development of multiple-line contracts.

By 1960, multiple line policies became a reality in many areas of the United States, and today they are a major factor in providing coverage to insureds. The most common example of a multiple-line policy in the commercial area is the special multi-peril (SMP) policy. The most common personal lines example is the homeowners policy.

Government Influence Regulatory officials accepted the fact that insurers were organized along fire or casualty lines and acted in ways which perpetuated this organization, hindering the development of package policies—especially multiple-line packages.

State laws requiring single-line operation of insurers were major deterrents to the development of multiple-line packages. This was especially true of the New York law because of the effect of the Appleton rule and because the New York law was one of the last to be amended to permit multiple-line operations. The Appleton rule, named after the Superintendent of Insurance who first promulgated it, prohibited insurers which were admitted to do business in New York from doing anything (in New York or in any other state) which would be prohibited by New York law. The rule applied to all insurers licensed in

New York, even though they were domiciled in other states. Consequently, an insurer licensed in New York could not operate on a multiple-line basis even in those states where such operations were legal. Since most large insurers were licensed in New York, they were effectively prevented from issuing multiple-line policies.

Of course, there were ways of circumventing the problem, but they were cumbersome, expensive, and not widely used. Companies operated in groups or fleets, usually including at least one fire insurer and one casualty insurer under the same ownership and management. Automobile liability and automobile physical damage coverages were provided in a single policy under single-line regulation by having the liability coverages underwritten by a casualty insurer and the physical damage underwritten by an affiliated fire insurer. But this method was seldom extended to other lines.

To acquire the coverages which can be provided by the SMP required one or more fire contracts, a liability contract, one or more crime policies, a boiler contract, a glass policy, and possibly others. A minimum of two policies were necessary and as many as six or seven were common. In fact, if one does not choose a multiple-line policy, the same situation exists today. Property is insured in one policy, liability in another, and boiler and machinery in a third, and so on. The multiple-line approach allows one to write all these coverages on one policy. The combination approach offers obvious cost savings and service benefits.

Needs of Business Persons Business firms buy insurance to protect themselves against fortuitous loss. From their standpoint, the best insurance policy would be one which would cover all significant fortuitous losses, with no gaps and no overlaps of coverage. Both gaps and overlaps were and are common in an insurance program involving numerous single-line policies.

While it is doubtful that many buyers of commercial lines insurance knew exactly what kind of policy they wanted, they knew that they were not satisfied with the single-line policies they were getting. Their dissatisfaction was made known to producers and insurers on many occasions, and was a motivating force in the development of combination or package policies.

Influence of Producers In most cases, producers have the responsibility for designing and providing suitable insurance programs for their clients, programs with a minimum of gaps and overlaps. In fulfilling this responsibility, producers found it necessary to request many amendatory endorsements to avoid gaps and overlaps, particularly gaps, in coverage provided by the several single-line policies needed to complete an adequate insurance program. As the list of amendatory endorsements grew, it became apparent that a restructuring of the coverages was needed in order to simplify the task of providing an adequate insurance program for business firms. Package policies were conceived as one answer to this problem.

As a sales person, each producer is engaged in a constant search for ways to differentiate his or her product from the products of competing producers, to provide some advantage to the insured which is not provided by competitors. One method of differentiation adopted by some producers was to deliver an entire insurance program bound in a loose-leaf binder. The binder included all of the necessary policies, frequently a detailed summary of the coverage and rating of each policy, and sometimes a detailed index to the contents of the binder.

It should be noted that these binders were *not* combination or package policies. They were bundles of single-line policies assembled in a manner designed to facilitate storage and reference by the insured. However, the practice was an early, but tentative, step in the direction of packaging.

The producers' desire for product differentiation also accounts for the rapid growth of the package policy market and for the wide variety of commercial package policies now available. Producer pressure also was a major factor in the introduction of the businessowners policy program by the Insurance Services Office. In that case, producers were less interested in differentiating their own product from other's products than in countering the product differentiation of an independent insurer which had introduced a similar product.

Types of Combination Policies

Since the definition of combination policies is quite broad, a little time should be spent explaining the various types. In this discussion both single-line and multiple-line combination policies are examined.

Simple Collections In their most basic form, combination policies are only rearrangements of format. The packaging process is only window dressing. The contents of two or more contracts are placed in one. An example of such a combination is a direct damage fire policy packaged with an indirect loss business interruption contract. Another example is the comprehensive dishonesty, disappearance and destruction (3-D) policy in which over a dozen possible coverages are available. The insured picks and chooses the coverages desired, and no package discount is given. This approach provides a convenience to the insured, but little else.

Minimum Requirement Combination In this combination approach, coverages are combined and the insured must purchase a certain minimum amount of protection. The SMP property coverage is a good example of this minimum requirement type. The insured must purchase fire and extended coverage as a minimum in the SMP for property coverage, and must purchase some liability coverage. However, these minimum requirements also allow the addition of other coverages, such as vandalism and malicious mischief (V&MM), sprinkler leakage, and numerous other coverages.

Advantages. This approach has two basic advantages: cost and breadth of coverage. By requiring certain specified coverages, the insurer reduces adverse selection. The practice also results in a higher average premium than would be likely under single-line policies. Since the cost of policy writing, billing, and accounting does not increase significantly with premium size, and since it costs an insurer less to issue one multiple-line contract than three, four, or more single-line policies, the insurer realizes some expense reduction. The lower cost due to reduced expenses and reduced adverse selection is passed on to the insured in the form of package discounts.

Broader coverage is not an inherent advantage of combination policies, but insurers have, in fact, offered broader coverages as options under such policies. There are two reasons for the willingness to offer broader policies under combination policies. First, combination policies have been offered primarily to the more desirable insureds, for whom broader coverage is more likely to be profitable to the insurer. Second, the average premium for a combination policy is larger than the average premium for single-line policies, and the increased losses resulting from broader coverage can be absorbed more readily without producing an unfavorable loss ratio for the line.

Disadvantages. A possible disadvantage of a package policy, from the insured's point of view, is the possible requirement that the insured purchase coverage which would not be purchased otherwise. For example, under the blanket crime policy, a single-line package policy, the insured must purchase coverage for loss resulting from the acceptance of counterfeit paper currency and from forgery of checks on the insured's bank account. Many business firms would not purchase these coverages if they were offered on an optional basis.

Indivisible Combination Policies An indivisible combination policy provides a broad range of coverages on an all-or-nothing basis for a single, indivisible premium. It also may offer some additional coverages on an optional basis for an additional premium. The businessowners policy (BOP), as prepared by the Insurance Services Office, is a member of this category.

The indivisible package policy differs from the minimum requirement in several respects. First, the indivisible policy generally requires the insured to purchase more coverages than are required under the minimum requirement contract. Second, the premium for each coverage usually is calculated and shown separately under the minimum requirement contract, while the premium for an indivisible policy usually is shown only in total, and cannot be separated by coverage. Finally, the indivisible package policies generally were designed initially as packages and are self-contained contracts. The minimum requirement packages, on the other hand, are built up by combining coverage parts originally designed for single-line policies.

Minimum requirement policies are more flexible, permitting greater discretion on the insured's part in the selection of coverages to be provided. The indivisible packages are simpler and less expensive to handle for both the producer and the insurance company. Also, by permitting less coverage selection by the insured, they are more effective in reducing adverse selection. Consequently, they result in greater reductions in insurance costs for the coverages provided.

Nonstandard Combinations Up to this point, all combinations examined have been those provided on standard policies and forms. The ultimate combination policy is the manuscript contract written to the insured's specifications. In such a policy, all the advantages of the combination approach are obtained and most of the disadvantages eliminated. The manuscript policy is as flexible as the insured and insurer want it to be, and no minimums exist. Since these policies normally are purchased by large corporations, lower premiums are often available and the range of coverage is unlimited. Because of the great range of flexibility, one problem does arise. How shall the contract actually be written?

In preparing the manuscript policy, the insured should be represented by a well-trained and experienced risk manager who has a great deal of expertise in such endeavors. Therefore, while the manuscript policy is the ultimate package policy, it is not feasible for most insureds. Such policies cost too much (a large premium is necessary before an insurer will agree to a manuscript policy), and unusual expertise is required in its design. Because of these two items and the results they produce, the discussion on packages is restricted to standard combinations.

Use of Combination Policies

Having discussed the types of combination policies, it is appropriate to examine how each type of combination policy is used. The same classifications—collection, minimum requirement, indivisible combination, and nonstandard—are used in this analysis.

Use of "Collection" Variety of Combination Policies When an insured or producer chooses to use a "collection" type of combination policy, it is for a matter of convenience and efficiency. From the company viewpoint, fewer forms and policies need to be printed and stored. This reduces costs and improves handling efficiency. From the insured's perspective, problems concerning gaps in coverages between policies and insurers are reduced. If all perils are insured in one policy with the same insurer, there will be no arguments as to which policy will pay and how it will pay. Intercompany disputes are eliminated. Likewise, overlaps in coverage are eliminated. The insured does not have duplicate coverage and the corresponding higher cost associated with such overlaps.

However, the use of these "collection" type package forms is not always satisfying. These forms (such as the 3-D policy) often include provisions that are not applicable to the insured's protection. A firm may decide not to purchase fidelity coverage in the 3-D policy. Yet the terms and conditions of that coverage are contained in the policy even if the insured does not pay for it. Of course, there is no coverage since the appropriate premium was not paid. However, an insured, in reading the contract, could draw a different conclusion, especially if that person was not familiar with how the 3-D policy is written. Consequently, confusion can arise out of these "collection" policies. Their readability can be difficult because of the many coverages provided and the fact that each coverage can have separate conditions and requirements. The inside and outside premises money and securities coverage excludes employee theft, but the fidelity coverage provides it. Unless the insured knows and understands this arrangement, confusion may result. The fact that each section can have a different limit makes the problem even more complicated.

Careful explanation of policy coverage by the producer will reduce this potential confusion greatly. Also, it will show the insured where voids in coverage still exist, and will demonstrate the need for additional insurance if the situation warrants it.

Use of "Minimum Requirement" Combination Forms These forms have all the advantages of the "collection" variety without some of their difficulties. The policy normally will contain only those specific items that the insured desires to purchase. If business interruption coverage is not desired, it is not included in the SMP. The "minimum requirement" combination forms reduce the amount of irrelevant information in the contract. However, they do introduce a different type of confusion. The possibility of a large number of endorsements can arise. In the SMP, one could add V&MM and sprinkler leakage to the basic property coverages; the indirect loss can be insured under an attached business interruption form with a premium adjustment clause added. Extra expense could be included in the business interruption coverage or added as a separate item. The cancellation notice provision may be modified as well as the vacancy and unoccupancy clause in the V&MM endorsement. As a consequence, some of the simplification obtained by using the package approach can disappear. The actual policy can become quite cumbersome, and ease in handling is lost. Also, in attempting to determine the exact coverage of the insured, one must be very careful to see which modification affects which endorsement or policy. By allowing a large number of endorsements (which is desirable to provide flexible coverage), some of the reduction in the cost of printing and handling is lost.

Use of Indivisible Combination Policies As mentioned, the businessowners policy (BOP) is a member of this category of package policies. Its use will be discussed in detail in Chapter 15.

Use of "Nonstandard" Combination Forms In these policies and forms, most of the problems associated with the collection and minimum requirement forms are eliminated. One does not have to add an endorsement changing the vacancy and unoccupancy clause in the V&MM endorsement if the policy does not have a vacancy and unoccupancy restriction in the first place. Likewise, if the policy provides that all direct physical losses (except those excluded) and indirect losses resulting from the direct losses are insured, the need for various policies and forms is greatly reduced. However, there is one major problem with this alternative. Most insureds do not have a large enough premium volume to persuade the insurer to issue a manuscript policy. So smaller firms must be content with the standard policies and forms that are available.

A Note Concerning Property-Liability Combinations Although standard combination policies such as the SMP combine both property and liability coverages, this discussion will be restricted to property coverages. Liability coverages are discussed in CPCU 4. Also, all automobile and aircraft coverages are discussed in CPCU 4. The following discussion is restricted to fire and allied lines, marine, crime, and boiler and machinery property insurance.

SPECIAL MULTI-PERIL PROGRAM

The best known commercial combination policy is the special multi-peril policy. It is of the "minimum requirement" variety discussed in the preceding section and is both multi-peril and multiple-line. An insured must purchase both property and liability coverages in order to be eligible for the SMP program. Life, health, surety, automobile, and workers' compensation exposures, however, may not be insured in the SMP.

General Nature

The SMP program consists of eight different classification groups with each group having its own package discount. Consequently, the group in which a business is placed affects its rates. For the most part, the same contract is employed for all eight groups. In the original program, each group had its own set of policies. The approach used today is much simpler, since only one set of policies is needed. This simplification also reduces company costs.

Prior to 1977, only seven carefully defined classes of business firms were eligible for the SMP program. However, the 1977 revision of the SMP program revised the eligibility rules so that most insureds, other than personal lines insureds, can qualify for the program. The exceptions are:

1. boarding and rooming houses and other residential premises containing fewer than three apartment units;
2. farms and farming operations;
3. automobile filling or service stations; automobile repairing or rebuilding operations; automobile, motor home, motorcycle dealers; parking lots or garages unless incidental to an otherwise eligible class;
4. grain elevators, grain tanks, and grain warehouses; and
5. properties to be rated under (a) Rating Plan for Highly Protected Risks, (b) Schedule for Petroleum Properties, (c) Schedule for Rating Petrochemical Plants, (d) Schedule for Rating Electric Generating Stations, or (e) Schedule for Natural Gas.

Eligible insureds are grouped into eight groups with the magnitude of the package discount varying by group. The groups are: (1) apartment houses (Apt), (2) contractors (C), (3) motel-hotel (M/H), (4) industrial and processing (Ind), (5) institutions (Inst), (6) mercantile (Merc), (7) offices (Off), and (8) service firms (S). The abbreviation following each of the foregoing groups is the abbreviation used in the Risk Classification Table in the SMP manual. The table, which is eighteen pages in length, lists many classes of business, institutional, and governmental operations, showing a package modification assign-

Table 14-1

Selected Occupancies and Operations from the SMP Risk
Classification Table

Occupancy/Operation	Package Modification Assignment	Trade Group
Carpentry	C	4
Dam or reservoir construction	C	1
Hotels	H/M	7
Condominiums	Apt	*
Archery ranges	S	7
Billiard halls	S	7
Golf driving ranges	S	10
Swimming pools	S	2
Fire houses	Inst	4
Paint or varnish manufacturing	Ind	2
Jewelry stores	Merc	7
Restaurants	Merc	7

*A flat rate of $1 applies to personal property.

ment and a trade group for each. The package modification assignment, which uses the group abbreviations listed above, determines the size of the applicable package discount. The trade group, which ranges from one to ten, determines the rate for personal property for all perils other than fire and the extended coverage perils. Table 14-1 shows a few selected occupancy or operations classes from the Risk Classification Table. Table 14-2 shows representative package discounts for the various groups. The discounts vary by jurisdiction and change frequently, so those shown in Table 14-2 should be considered illustrative only.

Minimum Premium Requirements Another condition of eligibility for the SMP program is the minimum premium provision. The minimum premium for property coverage is $100. However, the minimum is increased to $200 if a reporting form is used and to $2,500 if the multiple location premium and dispersion rating plan is used. The $100 minimum premium for basic property coverage would not seem to affect any but the very smallest firms. Separate minimum premiums apply to the liability section of the SMP policy.

Table 14-2

Illustrative Package Discount for the SMP Program

Category	Discount for Parts I, II, III
Motel/hotel	0.05
Apartment house	0.15
Office	0.30
Mercantile	0.15
Institutional	0.30
Processing or service	0.20
Industrial	0.20
Contractor	0.05

15% discount for boiler and machinery applies to all eight groups.

Part I is property coverages.
Part II is liability coverages.
Part III is crime coverages.

STRUCTURE OF THE SMP POLICY

Thus far the discussion of the SMP has been limited to eligibility requirements. The paragraphs that follow will explore the actual structure of the policy and its relationship to other policies. An analysis of the contract forms will follow.

Contract Arrangement

The SMP policy is divided into four parts:

Section I—Property Coverage

Section II—Liability Coverage

Section III—Crime Coverage

Section IV—Boiler and Machinery Coverage

Only the first two parts, property and liability, are mandatory. An insured can choose to accept or reject crime or boiler and machinery coverages. Numerous endorsements are available within each of these parts. The basic minimum property coverage is for fire and extended coverage, but numerous endorsements are available. The optional coverages include V&MM, sprinkler leakage, and so on, up to "all-risks" protection. Besides these direct property loss coverages, indirect loss coverages may be added.

The coverages elected by the insured are indicated by inserting a limit of liability and a form number in the appropriate spaces in the declaration section of the policy. No coverage is provided for any section for which a limit of liability is not shown. The declaration page also provides space to list the covered premises, but if the space provided there is inadequate, a supplemental list can be added by endorsement.

Structurally, the SMP consists of a policy jacket, a declaration page, a form entitled "Special Multi-Peril Policy Conditions and Definitions" (Form MP-4), and such other forms as are required to provide the coverages elected by the insured.

Form MP-4 includes the general conditions usual to property and liability policies. They are shown under four headings: (1) General Conditions, (2) Conditions Applicable to Section I, (3) Conditions Applicable to Section II, and (4) Definitions Applicable to Section II. This chapter will deal only with items (1) and (2) above, since the remaining items apply only to liability coverages.

General Conditions The provisions in the General Conditions section of Form MP-4 apply to all coverages provided under the SMP policy except to the extent that they are modified or voided by other endorsements or forms attached to the policy. The 1977 edition of the SMP was designed to be issued without the 165-line standard fire insurance policy. Consequently, the General Conditions section and the section entitled Conditions Applicable to Section I include all of the provisions of the standard fire policy, though some of the provisions are slightly more favorable to the insured than the comparable provisions of the standard fire policy. For example, the SMP provides for ten days notice to the insured if the policy is canceled on the initiative of the company, whereas the standard fire policy requires only five days notice.

The SMP provisions regarding time of inception of the policy, assignment, concealment or fraud, and waiver of policy conditions are essentially the same as the comparable provisions under the standard fire policy, though the wording differs in some cases. The SMP provision regarding assignment spells out specifically the coverage provided for the insured's legal representatives if the insured dies during the policy term. However, the added provisions merely clarify the coverage and do not provide any protection that is not provided under the fire policy. The SMP liberalization clause is essentially the same as the one included in fire insurance forms, though the wording is somewhat different.

Subrogation. The subrogation provision of the SMP Form MP-4 is a combination of the comparable provision of the standard fire policy and a limited subrogation waiver clause. It first states that the company, after payment of loss, is subrogated to the insured's right to recover such loss from other persons or organizations, and that the company is not bound to pay any loss if the insured, after the occurrence of loss, has impaired the right to recover such loss; then it sets forth two exceptions, cases in which the insured may waive the right of recovery without impairing the coverage under the policy. The two exceptions permit the insured to waive the right of recovery in writing prior to loss for (1) property of others on the premises of the insured, and (2) goods in transit by accepting bills of lading or contracts of transportation ordinarily issued by carriers of such goods. It is doubtful that these two exceptions really add any coverage. Both require that the waiver be given in writing prior to loss, and the subrogation clause specifically provides that, "The insured shall do nothing *after loss* to prejudice such loss." (Emphasis added.)

Premium. This condition provides that the premium for the policy will be calculated in accordance with the company's rules, rates, rating plans, and minimum premiums. If the policy is issued for a definite period, longer than one year with a premium payable at each anniversary date, the premium payable at each anniversary date will be calculated on the basis of the rates and rules in effect on that anniversary date.

The final section of this condition includes a provision which has been uncommon in policies issued by independent agency companies in the past. It provides that if the policy is issued without a definite expiration date it can be extended by payment of the premium *before* each anniversary date. However, the policy will expire automatically in any year in which the premium is not paid *before the anniversary date.* This apparently is an attempt to (1) avoid giving the free insurance that often results from delayed termination of policies for nonpayment, and (2) speed up the cash flow so additional investment income can be earned.

Inspection and Audit. This provision gives the insurer the right, but not the duty, to make loss control inspections of the insured's property and operations. It specifies that such inspections do not constitute a warranty that the insured's premises are safe, healthful, or in compliance with laws or regulations. This disclaimer is an effort to avoid liability to the insured, employees of the insured, or other persons as a result of failure to detect unsafe conditions or violations of laws or regulations such as the Occupational Safety and Health Act.

The provision also authorizes the insurance company to audit the insured's books insofar as they are related to the insurance contract. Only a few property coverages, such as reporting form fire policies and transit floaters, are written in such a way as to make audits necessary or desirable. This part of the provision is important primarily for the liability coverages.

Conditions Applicable to Section I This section of Form MP-4 consists primarily of conditions usually found in the standard fire policy or fire insurance forms, but which would not be applicable to coverages other than those found in Section I of the SMP. The provisions regarding the duties of the insured at the time of loss, appraisal, company options for loss settlement, increase of hazard, abandonment of property, and suit are essentially the same as the comparable provisions in the standard fire policy. However, an added provision in the condition regarding the duties of the insured at the time of loss requires the insured to give prompt notice to the police if the loss resulted from a violation of law. This is similar to clauses found in most crime policies. The provisions regarding coinsurance, war risk, permits and use, nuclear radiation, protective safeguards and mortgagees, and the loss clause are those usually found in fire insurance forms. The other conditions in this section require brief discussion.

Territory. The policy covers insured property within or between the fifty states of the United States, the District of Columbia, and Puerto Rico. However, coverage off the designated premises will be limited by conditions in the forms attached to the policy, so it should not be assumed that all insured property is covered away from the insured premises in all circumstances.

Deductibles. The SMP declarations page provides space for entering two deductible amounts: one labeled "each occurrence" and one labeled "aggregate each occurrence." If amounts are entered in those spaces, those deductible amounts apply. If no amounts have been entered in the declarations, the applicable deductibles are (1) $100 applicable separately to loss to (a) each building, (b) the contents of each building, if buildings are not insured, and (c) personal property in the open and within vehicles; and (2) $1,000 to all losses arising from one occurrence. Thus, the effective deductible for any one occurrence may vary from $100 to $1,000, depending on the number of buildings damaged, the number of buildings in which damaged contents were located, and the presence or absence of damage to personal property in the open.

Other Insurance. This clause divides other insurance covering a loss into two classes: (1) other insurance written in the name of the insured and upon the same plan, terms, and conditions as the SMP; and (2) all other insurance covering the loss except as described in (1). The

SMP contributes pro rata on the limits of liability with other insurance described in item (1). It is excess as to insurance in item (2). For all practical purposes, an SMP contributes pro rata with another SMP providing identical coverage for the damaged property and is excess over all other property insurance covering the loss.

Payment of Loss. The intent of this provision is the same as the comparable provision under the standard fire policy. However, loss under the SMP must be paid within thirty days of acceptance of the proof of loss as opposed to sixty days for the standard fire policy.

Privilege to Adjust with Owner. This condition relates primarily to the adjustment of losses to property of others in the care, custody, or control of the insured. The insurance company reserves the right to adjust such losses directly with and make payment for them directly to the owners of the damaged property. The company also reserves the right to defend any suit against the insured arising from such loss, and agrees to pay the cost of such defense on behalf of the insured. All other losses are to be adjusted with and paid to the insured.

Vacancy and Unoccupancy. The insurer is not liable for loss while an insured building is vacant for more than sixty consecutive days. A building under construction is not considered to be vacant. Vacancy means that the building does not contain any personal property usual to its occupancy.

Permission is granted for the building to be unoccupied. Unoccupancy is not defined in the policy. It usually means that the building does contain personal property usual to its occupancy, but no people are present.

No Control. This condition provides that the rights of the insured under the policy will not be prejudiced by (1) any act or neglect of the building owner, if the insured is not the owner, or any act of any other tenant of the building, or by (2) any failure of the insured to comply with any warranty or condition of the policy in any portion of the building over which the insured has no control, provided any such act, neglect, or failure in either (1) or (2), is beyond the control of the insured. These are exceptions to the provision which suspends coverage during any increase in hazard.

Relation to Nonpackage Forms

Almost all of the coverages available in the SMP program are available in single-line policies. A firm can purchase a separate fire and extended coverage policy and a liability policy and receive basically the same coverage as provided in the SMP. Even the wording of the nonpackage forms will be quite similar to the SMP forms. In fact, most firms will need some single-line policies, since workers' compensation and automobile insurance are not provided under the SMP. The main advantages to the SMP program are ease in handling and package discounts.

Individuality of Forms

Each insurer has the right to modify the Insurance Services Office (ISO) forms as that firm sees fit or to file and use totally independent forms. In many cases the insurer will call its commercial multi-peril package something other than SMP—names like portfolio policy, the business special, or cornerstone. These policies may differ in content, but most are arranged in much the same manner: Section I is property; Section II is liability; and so forth. Because it would be inappropriate here to examine the many independent forms used by multiple-line companies, the discussion in this text is limited to the ISO forms. These policies serve as the basis for most commercial multi-peril forms, and they have the widest acceptance and use. However, many companies do deviate from ISO forms, sometimes quite substantially.

Content of Property Forms

In the SMP program there are four major property forms. The content of these forms will be discussed in the sections that follow.

SMP General Building Form (MP-100) In the basic general building form, property is divided into two categories: property covered and property not covered. If the account is so large that a single company does not have capacity to write all the property, then more than one company may be used. When this is done, a contributing insurance endorsement is attached and the insurers pay losses on a pro rata basis. Besides the basic coverage, the general building form provides debris removal. The debris removal coverage does not increase the policy limits.

Property Covered. The definition of building is basically the same as that in single-line fire insurance forms. The building includes all additions and extensions that are attached to the building, service equipment that is a permanent part of the building, yard fixtures, and supplies and materials used in repair or alteration; personal property of the insured used for the service of the building, such as stoves, air conditioners, washers, and similar property are considered part of the building, but only while on the insured's premises. This last portion is important in the case of apartment houses because it permits the insured to cover these items at the building rate rather than the contents rate. Since the building rate is generally lower than the contents rate, this classification is desirable from the insured's viewpoint.

Property Not Covered. This section of the policy excludes from coverage some kinds of property which might otherwise be considered a part of the building. Among them are (1) outdoor signs, whether attached to the building or not; (2) outdoor swimming pools; fences; piers, wharves, and docks; beach or diving platforms or appurtenances; retaining walls not constituting a part of a building; walks, roadways, and other paved surfaces; (3) the cost of excavations, grading, or filling; foundations of buildings, machinery, boilers, or engines if such foundations are below the undersurface of the lowest basement floor, or where there is no basement below the surface of the ground; pilings, piers, pipes, flues, and drains which are underground; pilings which are below the low water mark; and (4) lawns; outdoor trees, shrubs, and plants except as provided in the extensions of coverage.

Most of the foregoing kinds of property are excluded because most insureds would not want to pay the necessary premium for coverage. For example, foundations and excavations are seldom damaged by fire or the extended coverage perils, so most insureds would prefer to exclude them from coverage and reduce the insured value and the premium accordingly. Others, such as outdoor signs, are excluded because there are other, better ways of insuring them.

Extensions of Coverage. The SMP general building form provides extensions of coverage for (1) newly acquired property; (2) property off premises; (3) outdoor trees, shrubs, and plants; and (4) replacement cost. The first three are quite similar to the extensions provided under the building item in single-line fire forms, but the limits may differ.

The replacement cost extension applies only if both (1) the full cost of repairing the damaged property is less than $1,000, and (2) the insured has fully complied with the coinsurance clause. If both of these conditions have been met, the company will pay the full cost of repairs, without deduction for depreciation. However, the replacement cost coverage does not apply to outdoor furniture, outdoor equipment, floor coverings, awnings, or appliances for refrigerating, ventilating, cooking, dishwashing, or laundering, whether such property is permanently attached to the building or not.

All of the extensions except the replacement cost extension provide additional amounts of insurance. The coinsurance clause does not apply

Table 14-3

Extensions of Coverage—SMP General Building Form

Extension	Limits
Builders' risk on property	25% of the building coverage, up to $100,000 for 30 days
Building at new location	Same as above
Trees, shrubs, and plants; no wind coverage	$250 per plant, $1,000 aggregate
Replacement cost coverage	$1,000
Off-premises coverage for building items while away from premises for cleaning or repairing	2% of building coverage, up to $5,000

to loss under any of the extensions except replacement cost. The limits applicable to the extensions are shown in Table 14-3.

Perils Insured Against. Fire, extended coverage (EC), and V&MM are the perils insured against in the general building form. The exclusions under the SMP general building form are the same as those under mono-line fire, EC, and V&MM forms and endorsements.

Interests Covered. The interests insured are the interests of the named insured and, in the event of the death of the named insured, the legal representatives of the named insured. The interest of one or more mortgagees can be covered by inserting their names in the appropriate space on the declarations page.

Valuation. All building items are valued for loss adjustment at actual cash value. However, that value cannot exceed the smaller of (1) the actual cost to repair or replace the property, or (2) the interest of the insured in the damaged or destroyed property. The replacement cost extension discussed above is an exception to this valuation rule, and an endorsement is available to change to replacement cost coverage.

SMP General Personal Property Form (MP-100A) If both buildings and contents are insured under an SMP, it is necessary to use two forms, one for buildings and one for personal property. This is contrary to the practice in single-line fire policies, which generally cover buildings and contents under a single form. Earlier versions of the SMP also used a combined form for buildings and contents.

The basic form for covering contents under the SMP is the general personal property form, Form MP-100A. The perils insured and the exclusions under the SMP general personal property form are the same as those under the SMP general building form. As in the building form, personal property is divided between property covered and property not covered.

Property Covered. The SMP general personal property form provides coverage for:

1. business personal property owned by the insured and usual to the insured's occupancy and the insured's interest in the property of others to the extent of the value of labor, materials, and charges furnished or incurred by the insured; however, coverage for all of the foregoing property applies only while it is in the buildings on the designated premises or in the open or in vehicles within 100 feet of the designated premises;

2. if the insured does not own the building, the insured's use interest in improvements or betterments to the building; and

3. if a limit of liability for personal property of others is shown on the declaration page, personal property of others in the care, custody, or control of the insured while it is in the buildings on the designated premises or in the open or in vehicles within 100 feet of the designated premises; such coverage is for the account of the owners of such property, and the insurer reserves the right to adjust any loss with the owners.

The coverage above for property of others does not apply unless a limit of liability for such property is shown in the declarations. However, the extension of coverage for property of others, discussed later, applies if no limit is stated in the declarations for such property.

Property Not Covered. The SMP general personal property form does not provide any coverage for the following kinds of property:

1. unless held for sale or sold but not yet delivered: animals and pets; motorcycles, motor scooters and snowmobiles; trailers designed for use with private passenger vehicles for general utility purposes or carrying boats; watercraft, including motors, equipment, and accessories (these are not covered in any case while afloat); outdoor trees, shrubs, or plants except as provided under extensions of coverage;

2. unless manufactured, processed, or warehoused by the insured: watercraft, including motors, accessories, and equipment, but these are not covered in any case while afloat; aircraft, automobiles, trailers, semitrailers, or any self-propelled vehicle or machine;

3. personal property while waterborne;

4. household and personal effects in living quarters occupied by the insured or any officer, director, or partner of the insured or any

relative of any of them, except as provided in extensions of coverage;

5. accounts, bills, deeds, currency, evidences of debt, money, and securities;
6. outdoor signs;
7. growing crops or lawns; and
8. property more specifically insured under the SMP or any other policy.

Several of the classes of property excluded above can be insured under other forms or endorsements available for use with the SMP.

Extensions of Coverage. The SMP general personal property form includes extensions of coverage for (1) nonowned personal property in the care of the insured; (2) property at newly acquired locations; (3) personal property off premises; (4) personal effects belonging to the insured or officers, directors, or employees thereof; (5) valuable papers and records; (6) outdoor trees, shrubs, and plants; and (7) extra expense. The first five of these extensions of coverage are essentially the same as those provided under the General Property Form FGP-1 though the limits may differ. The limits for all of these extensions are shown in Table 14-4. The extra expense extension provides up to $1,000 of coverage to pay the necessary extra expenses incurred by the insured to maintain operations at the normal level following damage to the designated premises by an insured peril. The coverage is essentially the same as that provided under an extra expense policy, except that only the insured perils of fire, lightning, EC and V&MM will cause the contract to pay, except that the contract will only respond for loss caused by fire, EC, and V&MM. All of the extensions provide additional amounts of insurance, and none of them is subject to the coinsurance clause.

Valuation. With the exceptions noted below, personal property is valued for loss adjustment at actual cash value at the time of loss, but not more than the smaller of (1) the cost to repair or replace it, or (2) the interest of the insured therein. Stock sold but not yet delivered is valued at the price at which it was sold, less all discounts and expenses not incurred because of the loss (such as delivery expenses).

The valuation of improvements and betterments depends on who, if anyone, repairs or replaces them. If repaired or replaced by the insured, they are valued at actual cash value. If they are repaired or replaced at the expense of others but for the use and benefit of the insured, there is no liability under the policy because the insured has not sustained a financial loss. If the improvements and betterments are not replaced for the use and benefit of the insured, the amount payable under the policy is calculated by multiplying the original cost of the improvements and

Table 14-4

Extensions of Coverage—SMP General Personal Property Form

Extension	Limits
Property at newly acquired locations	10% of the limit for personal property of the insured, up to $10,000
Off-premises coverage	2% of the limit for personal property of the insured, up to $5,000
Personal effects of officers, directors, and employees	Up to $100 for one person, subject to a limit of $500 for all persons
Valuable papers and records	$500
Outdoor trees, shrubs, and plants	$1,000, but not more than $250 for one tree, shrub, or plant
Extra expense	$1,000
Nonowned personal property in care, custody, and control	2% of the limit at each location for personal property of the insured, up to $2,000

betterments by a fraction. The numerator of the fraction is the time remaining under the insured's lease at the time of the loss, and the denominator is the time remaining in the insured's lease at the time the improvements and betterments were installed.

Books of account, manuscripts, abstracts, drawings, card index systems, and similar records are valued at the cost of new blank books, cards, or records plus the cost of transcription. Electronic storage media, such as tapes, discs, and drums, are valued at the cost of new blank media. Note, however, that the extension of coverage for valuable papers and records in the general personal property form does provide up to $500 for the cost of research or other expenses necessary to reconstruct the content of valuable papers and records. This extension is a limited exception to the immediately foregoing valuation rule.

SMP Endorsements Available Involving Fire and Allied Lines Perils There are numerous endorsements that can be used to modify the basic property contract. In this section they will be grouped by function and analyzed accordingly. Also, form numbers will be given since they are standardized. The basic notation is MP-XXX. The MP stands for multiple-peril and the XXX is the number of the form. A letter is sometimes appended to the form number. The general building form is MP-100, and the general personal property form is MP-100A.

Changing Property Insured. In the SMP program there are several endorsements that expand coverage to include additional types of property. Also, there are forms that give broader coverage to specific types of property, such as cameras. Both of these types of endorsements will be analyzed in the paragraphs that follow.

THE OUTDOOR SIGN ENDORSEMENT (MP-128). This endorsement is needed because all the SMP building and personal property forms exclude outdoor signs whether or not such signs are attached to a building. The endorsement merely extends the policy to cover signs scheduled thereon. Limits of liability and premiums are shown for the scheduled signs. The perils covered are the same as those for the basic property form. The $100 deductible shown in Form MP-4 applies separately to each sign.

THE HOUSEHOLD AND PERSONAL PROPERTY ENDORSEMENT (MP-127). This form is only used with the general building form (MP-100) and extends coverage to household and personal property of the insured, members of the insured's family, or a servant. A specific apartment must be designated in the endorsement. The insured also can apply 10 percent of the amount of insurance indicated on the endorsement to cover similar property anywhere in the continental United States, Hawaii, or Canada.

THE LIABILITY FOR GUEST'S PROPERTY ENDORSEMENT (MP-160). Insureds use this modification to provide innkeepers' liability coverage on the insured premises. The insured premises is limited to the portion of the building occupied by the insured as an innkeeper, and the endorsement covers the insured's liability for loss or damage to property of hotel or motel guests while such property is in the care of the insured. The endorsement has an aggregate limit of $25,000 and a per person limit of $1,000; a $25 deductible is applied to each loss.

THE ACCOUNTS RECEIVABLE ENDORSEMENT (MP-175). Using this endorsement, the policy is extended to cover not only the cost of reestablishing the records of accounts receivable but also the loss from inability to collect amounts due because of the destruction of records. The reason for the noncollection must be the destruction of records and the resulting inability to determine who owes what. In addition, all collection expense is covered as well as any interest on loans the insured must obtain because receivables cannot be collected. The endorsement provides a specific amount of insurance for these coverages on an "all-risks" basis. Typical exclusions are officer theft, accounting errors, erasure of electronic recordings (except by lightning), war, and nuclear. This insurance can be written on a specific (MP-174) or reporting form

(MP-175) basis. The specific form is used in connection with MP-175 and is restricted to amounts of less than $100,000.

THE GLASS COVERAGE ENDORSEMENT (MP-179). This endorsement serves the same purpose as the comprehensive glass policy. It provides coverage for the breakage of glass or loss due to chemicals accidentally or maliciously applied. The only exclusions are for loss due to fire and war. The basic policy covers glass breakage by fire. The endorsement specifies which SMP policy provisions apply. Coverage is on a scheduled basis, and besides paying for breakage, it will pay up to $75 at any one location for repairing or replacing frames, installing temporary plates, or boarding up openings and removing any obstructions when replacing the damaged glass. Insureds with large amounts of plate glass may desire this coverage. One of the reasons this endorsement is desirable is because the V&MM coverage excludes loss to glass.

Changing Measure of Loss. In this category of endorsements we are concerned with those forms that modify the amount recovered. For instance, all indirect loss coverages fall into this category. As in the preceding material, only forms that change the basic property forms will be reviewed here.

THE GROSS EARNINGS ENDORSEMENT (MP-140). The gross earnings form in the SMP is like the gross earnings form examined in Chapter 5. The forms pay on an actual loss sustained basis for loss of earnings less noncontinuing charges and expenses. The coverage is only activated if an insured peril causes damage to real or personal property. The insured must take reasonable steps to minimize the loss, and costs so incurred will be reimbursed by the insurer if they reduce the loss. This last provision is often called extra expense insurance in business interruption. However, that terminology is misleading, in a way, since there is no reimbursement unless the loss is reduced by the insured's expenditure of extra funds. While the form will pay for loss sustained throughout the period of interruption of business, the insured must use due diligence and dispatch in making repairs. The time of insured interruption is measured from the date of loss to the time it would take to repair the property with due diligence and dispatch. If the interruption is caused by an insured peril to electronic data processing equipment, then the insured has only thirty days to restore operation. Because of this provision, insureds often purchase the EDP policy that is analyzed in Chapter 15. Since the gross earnings endorsement includes ordinary payroll in the definition of earnings, it must be specifically excluded if the insured does not want it covered.

THE ORDINARY PAYROLL EXCLUSION ENDORSEMENT (MP-141). This form excludes coverage under MP-140 for ordinary payroll. Ordinary payroll is defined in the form as all payroll except that for officers, executives, department managers, employees under contract, and other important employees. When this form is attached to the gross earnings form, the insured must accept an 80 percent coinsurance clause in the business interruption contract. If the insured only desires a partial exclusion of ordinary payroll, the following endorsement should be used.

THE ORDINARY PAYROLL LIMITED COVERAGE ENDORSEMENT (MP-142). This form can be used to limit ordinary payroll coverage to ninety days or some other specified number of days. The same definition of ordinary payroll is used as in form MP-141, and a minimum coinsurance clause of 80 percent also is required. In the SMP program, the premium adjustment and agreed amount clauses are not generally available. However, if the underwriter is willing, they can sometimes be added.

THE LOSS OF EARNINGS ENDORSEMENT (MP-143). One way to avoid the coinsurance problems in the gross earnings forms is to use the loss of earnings endorsement. It also is a useful tool when the insured does not want to divulge sales, profits, or other such information. This form is not as complicated as the gross earnings form and has no coinsurance clause. The form has a per month limit and an aggregate limit. The higher the per month limit, the higher the rate. In no event will the policy pay more than the aggregate limit for a single loss. As in the gross earnings form, recovery is on an actual loss sustained basis, and the insured must take reasonable steps to reduce the loss and restore normal operations. Usually this form is used by smaller insureds and nonmanufacturing concerns. However, the SMP program does not restrict coverage to such businesses. One disadvantage of the form is the rates charged. Rates range from 110 percent to 85 percent of the 80 percent coinsurance building rate. The gross earnings form rates vary from 80 to 60 percent for mercantile establishments and 90 to 70 percent for manufacturing establishments. The higher the insured's thirty-day limit, the closer the rate is to 100 percent of the 80 percent coinsurance building rate. Generally, the thirty-day amount is set as some percentage of the aggregate such as 16⅔ percent, 25 percent, or 33⅓ percent. The provisions in this form are similar to those found in other earnings forms. Also, the earnings form excludes loss arising out of theft of property that is not permanently attached to the building unless theft occurs during a riot or civil commotion. This exclusion pertains to a situation where the theft of property would cause a business interruption loss and theft is an insured peril.

THE EXTRA EXPENSE ENDORSEMENT (MP-144). Often an insured cannot afford to cease operations after a loss because customers will go to other firms and may not return when operations are restored. Common examples are newspapers and dairies. Other insureds may need extra expense insurance because they want to resume operations as quickly as possible, and the extra expense provision under business interruption coverage is not adequate to cover the resulting expenses. Under business interruption, extra expenses are covered only to the extent that they reduce the business interruption loss.

If the insured is a large concern with several geographically dispersed warehouses, much of the business interruption loss can be eliminated. Goods can be shipped in from other locations and business conducted as usual from rented facilities. This situation is more true for wholesalers than it is for retailers, since location in a community is more important to a retailer.

As is common for extra expense forms, there is a per month limit that is a function of the policy limit. The normal limitations are 40-80-100. This means only 40 percent of the policy limit may be used in the first month, and 80 percent the first two months. After two months there is no internal limit. When an insured believes $5,000 of extra expense insurance is needed the first month, $12,500 must be purchased to give adequate coverage (0.4 × $12,500 = $5,000).

THE LOSS OF RENTS ENDORSEMENT (MP-146). This coverage serves the same purpose to a landlord as a loss of earnings or a gross earning form does to other business persons. It pays on an actual loss sustained basis for losses resulting directly from necessary untenantability of the insured premises because of damage by an insured peril. Typically, the insured premises are rented to others, and the landlord receives revenue in the form of rents from the buildings. However, the form also covers the fair rental value of any part of the premises occupied by the insured.

As in other types of consequential loss insurance, expenses which cease when a loss occurs reduce the amount paid by the insurer, and the insured is required to take action to reduce the loss. In this form the insured must accept a 60, 80, or 100 percent coinsurance clause. This provision requires the insured to purchase coverage equal to 60 percent or more of the rents that would have been earned by the insured during the twelve months immediately following the loss. Just like business interruption insurance, it is concerned with future revenues, not the past. While no actual form exists in the SMP manual for coverage on a noncontributing basis, such coverage can be provided by using a form with a monthly limitation clause as used in the earnings form. For smaller insureds this approach may be more desirable.

THE COMBINED BUSINESS INTERRUPTION AND EXTRA EXPENSE ENDORSEMENT (MP-147). For those who have a need for both business interruption and extra expense coverages, a combination form is available. This form was designed for such persons and the rate was modified so that it is less than when the two coverages are purchased separately. An example of such insureds is the case of the multiple location business where accounting, warehousing, and record keeping are done at the main store. If loss occurs at the main store, business interruption coverage is needed to offset the loss of income, but the satellite stores need only extra expense insurance to cover their increased cost of operating. Those stores will use other services to replace those formerly performed at the central location. Coverage in this form is like the individual forms. The business interruption portion has an insurance to value clause and an EDP limitation provision, and the extra expense coverage has monthly limitations stated as a percent of the total extra expense insurance purchased.

TUITION FEES ENDORSEMENT (MP-145). The tuition fees endorsement is to schools and colleges as the gross earnings business interruption form is to businesses. It pays on an actual loss sustained basis for loss of tuition and fees resulting from damage by an insured peril to real or personal property. An insured can purchase gross earnings business interruption coverage if it is desired, but the tuition fees form is especially designed for schools and has unique features that make it more attractive. Of course, these added features increase the cost, but they seem worth the difference.

The gross earnings form only provides funds during the restoration period; the tuition fees form goes beyond that period. The endorsement states that it will pay for, "the actual loss of tuition fees sustained by the insured less charges and expenses which do not necessarily continue during the period of time, not limited by the date of expiration of this endorsement, commencing with the date of such damage or destruction and ending on the day preceding the beginning of the first school year following the date that the damaged or destroyed real or personal property described could, with the exercise of due diligence and dispatch, be rebuilt, repaired, or replaced." The term *tuition fees* is defined in the policy to include tuition fees and other income from students, less the cost of merchandise sold and materials and supplies consumed in services sold to students. The phrase *beginning of the school year* means the opening date in the fall as shown in the school catalog.

An example will illustrate how the foregoing clause operates. Assume a fire damages the property on November 1, and it is restored on February 28. Under the gross earnings form there is a four month restoration period. Under the tuition fees form, the restoration period extends to September or for a period of ten months. While the property may be repaired in February, it is quite unlikely that the school could begin anywhere near normal operation or collect adequate funds in February. Since many private schools and colleges receive their main source of revenue from tuitions and fees, this settlement procedure is quite attractive to them.

While the foregoing clause is liberal, the second half of the clause makes it even more so. The form states, "if the period of time as provided above shall end on a date within 30 days immediately preceding the beginning of the first school year specified above, the period of liability for loss is hereby extended to end on the day preceding the beginning of the second school year." For example, if school was scheduled to open on September 15, 1977, and repairs could not be completed until September 1, 1977, the restoration period would be extended until September 14, 1978. This adjustment process is true even if the accident occurred in November 1976. If repairs had been completed on August 1, 1977, then the restoration period would have ended on September 14, 1977.

Besides the preceding situations, the insurer will also pay for a period up to two weeks for loss caused when the school is closed by action of civil authority as a result of damage by an insured peril to adjacent property. Like the standard gross earnings form, there is a thirty-day limitation on losses due to damage to electronic data processing equipment or media, and the insured must attempt to reduce the loss and use due diligence and dispatch in making restoration.

LIMITATIONS. Loss caused by enforcement of building ordinances is excluded as is loss due to on-premises strikes during the period of restoration; that is, a strike which causes the restoration period to be extended. In addition, loss due to suspension, lapse, or cancellation of any lease or license is excluded. However, if the lapse is a direct result of the interruption of the business, then this exclusion does not apply. That is, if a school loses its license because of the interruption from an insured peril, the exclusion is not effective. However, if the license is lost for other reasons, the resulting loss is not insured.

Changing Perils Insured Against. There are by far more forms available for the purpose of changing perils insured against than for any other purpose. This discussion will begin with the named peril forms and terminate with the "all-risks" forms.

THE VANDALISM AND MALICIOUS MISCHIEF EXCLUSION ENDORSEMENT (MP-124). Most of the endorsements discussed in this section will be used to add coverage, but this one is used to delete V&MM coverage which otherwise would be covered under the basic property forms.

THE SPRINKLER LEAKAGE ENDORSEMENT (MP-122). Loss from accidental discharge from an automatic sprinkler system is insured against in this form. It is attached to the SMP policy, and Section I provisions apply unless the sprinkler leakage form states otherwise. The sprinkler leakage form insures either personal property or real property or both. Also, the endorsement has its own coinsurance percentage which can be different from that used for the rest of the SMP policy. As a consequence of this different coinsurance clause, the amount of coverage under sprinkler leakage may be less than that of the rest of the perils insured against in Section I. When personal property of others is insured under the form, at least a 25 percent coinsurance clause is required and a higher one may be chosen. Besides this form, sprinkler leakage also is available under reporting forms in the SMP program. A person can choose between a reporting form on a specific rate basis (MP-129) or an average rate basis (MP-130).

THE OPTIONAL PERILS ENDORSEMENT (MP-123). This endorsement is a package endorsement that can be attached to an SMP policy. It is a combination of five perils: breakage of glass, falling objects, weight of ice and snow, water damage, and collapse. This optional perils endorsement is not the same as the one contained in the fire manual. This endorsement can be used only with forms MP-100 and MP-100A.

The optional perils form can apply to buildings or personal property or both. All of the conditions of the applicable property form apply to coverage under this endorsement. Because some of the perils insured against in this form have not been discussed in detail in this book, and other perils are defined differently, a detailed discussion follows.

The *breakage of glass* peril only covers glass that is a portion of the building and only breakage is insured. Coverage is restricted to $50 per plate, pane, multiple plate insulating unit, radiant heating panel, jalousie, louver, or shutter. There is also an aggregate limit of $250 per occurrence. Because of these constraints, this coverage is sometimes referred to as limited glass breakage. If the insured has a large exposure in this area, the glass coverage endorsement should be used.

The *falling objects* peril is not defined in the form. However, it is stated that personal property in the open is not insured and that a falling object must first damage the exterior of the building before any losses for interior damage will be compensated. This latter provision is necessary to avoid paying for paint and caustic chemicals dropped on the insured's floor, carpets, or personal property. Given the preceding qualifications, possible examples of falling objects include trees, utility poles, other buildings, and cranes.

The *weight of snow, ice, or sleet* peril covers direct loss to real or personal property resulting from the weight of ice, snow, or sleet. There is a long list of excluded property of which the following items are just a sample: metal smokestacks, outdoor antennas, gutters, downspouts, yard fixtures, fences, outdoor swimming pools, and paved surfaces.

The final two perils insured against in the form are *water damage* and *collapse*, which have been discussed elsewhere in this book.

However, the SMP version of water damage is a little different. Water damage coverage is restricted to loss resulting from the breaking or cracking of pipes, fittings, parts, or fixtures forming a part of any heating, plumbing, or air conditioning system, or domestic appliance. The water form in the fire manual also includes industrial appliances. Thus, the SMP version is slightly more restrictive. The collapse peril is virtually the same as in the fire manual. The important thing to remember about collapse is that insurers mean total collapse and not partial collapse.

THE SPECIAL BUILDING FORM (MP-101). This form can be used instead of the general building form (MP-100) to provide "all-risks" coverage on buildings. The term *"all-risks"* means all direct losses except those excluded. The definitions of property covered and property not covered are the same as in the general building form. However, because the insuring agreement provides "all-risks" coverage, there are additional restrictions on certain categories of property and perils.

Damage to plumbing, heating, air conditioning, and other equipment (except fire protective systems) caused by freezing is not insured if the building is vacant or unoccupied unless due diligence has been taken to maintain heat or unless the equipment was drained. The exception is made for fire protective systems since sprinkler leakage insurance provides freezing protection and one would expect "all-risks" coverage to be as broad as the named peril coverage.

Loss to steam boilers, pipes, turbines, and engines is not covered except for loss by furnace explosion. The special building form does not replace boiler and machinery insurance.

Hot water boilers and other water heating equipment are not covered for damage by any internal cause except explosion. Glass coverage is limited to $50 per plate and $250 per occurrence unless caused by fire, the EC perils except smoke, or discharge from fire protective or building service equipment.

Fences, pavements, outdoor swimming pools, and similar property are not covered for loss caused by freezing or thawing even if they are covered for other perils. They are excluded entirely in most cases.

Metal smokestacks, outside television and radio antennas, and cloth awnings are not insured for windstorm, ice, snow, or sleet unless the policy is specifically endorsed to provide such coverage.

No coverage is provided for rain, snow, sand, or dust damage to the interior of the building unless the exterior of the building is first damaged by one of the perils specified in the form. The specified perils are wind, hail, fire, lightning, aircraft, vehicles, explosion, riot or civil commotion, and V&MM.

Buildings or structures under construction are not protected except for fire, EC, and V&MM. Builders' risks would normally be insured under a builder's risk SMP form, discussed later. However, the special building form provides up to thirty days automatic coverage on new buildings being constructed on the premises. Such property is insured for only 25 percent of the policy building limit, subject to a maximum of $100,000. It is this extension of coverage which is affected by the limitation.

Property undergoing alterations or repairs is not covered for damage directly attributable to such alterations or repairs unless damage by an insured peril ensues, and then only the damage ensuing from the peril is covered.

All of the exclusions of the general building form also appear in the special building form. The special building form also contains some additional exclusions which are required because of the "all-risks" coverage. The following paragraphs will discuss only those exclusions which are peculiar to the special building form.

No coverage is provided for loss caused by wear and tear; deterioration; rust or corrosion; mold; wet or dry rot; inherent or latent defect; smog; smoke, vapor, or gas from agricultural or industrial operations; mechanical breakdown; settling, cracking, shrinkage, bulging, or expansion of pavements, foundations, walls, floors, roofs, or ceilings; animals, birds, vermin, termites, or other insects; unless loss by a peril not otherwise excluded ensues and then only the ensuing loss is insured. From this rather long exclusion, an individual can see that many perils are still not insured, but these items represent almost uninsurable losses and it is very difficult, if not impossible, to buy insurance for them.

The form does not cover loss resulting from explosion of steam boilers, pipes, turbines, and engines if owned by, leased to, or operated by the insured. Loss caused by explosion of accumulated gases or unconsumed fuel within the firebox or combustion chamber of any fired vessel or within the flues or passages which conduct the gases of combustion therefrom is still covered. Loss resulting from sonic boom, electric arcing, water hammer, and bursting of water pipes is not excluded as it is in the extended coverage endorsement.

When the building is vacant or unoccupied thirty days, V&MM and theft coverage is suspended. Vacancy or unoccupancy also causes loss due to leakage or overflow of plumbing, heating, air conditioning, or other appliances because of freezing to be excluded unless due diligence is taken to maintain heat or drain equipment. This section excludes loss to these items resulting from freezing; the property limitations section excludes other damage to this equipment.

The theft peril is qualified by stating that mysterious disappearance, fidelity losses, and inventory shortages are not insured. Also any property stolen must be an integral part of the building. This last condition seems reasonable since this form is supposed to cover the building and not personal property.

The extensions of coverage and the valuation provision of the special building form are the same as the comparable provisions of the general building form. The only significant differences between the two forms are the "all-risks" coverage.

SPECIAL PERSONAL PROPERTY FORM (MP-101A). The definitions of property covered and property not covered are the same in the special personal property form as in the general personal property form. The valuation clause and the extensions of coverage also are the same. However, because the special personal property form provides "all-risks" coverage, it includes several additional exclusions and limitations designed to define and clarify the property and perils insured.

Coverage for some classes of property is limited to approximately the coverage that would be provided under the general personal property form. This is done by restricting coverage to *specified perils*, with that term being defined to include direct loss by fire, lightning, the extended coverage perils, V&MM, and sprinkler leakage. The windstorm peril applies only to property located in a building.

There is a limitation of $1,000 aggregate in any one occurrence for damage to furs and fur garments, but the limitation does not apply to loss by specified perils.

Coverage is limited to $1,000 per occurrence for loss to jewelry, watches, precious metals, and similar property, but the limitation does not apply if (1) the loss is caused by specified perils, or (2) to jewelry or watches valued at less than $25 per item.

Coverage for patterns, dies, molds, models, and forms is limited to $1,000 per occurrence unless the loss is caused by specified perils.

There is a limitation of $250 per occurrence for damage to stamps, tickets, and letters of credit unless the loss is caused by specified perils.

Valuable papers and records are covered only against loss by specified perils.

Animals, pets, and outdoor trees, shrubs, and plants are not covered unless they are held for sale or sold but not delivered, and then coverage is only for specified perils.

Glassware, statuary, and other fragile items are covered for breakage only if such breakage results from specified perils. However, this limitation does not apply to bottles or similar containers of property held for sale.

Steam boilers, steam pipes, and other steam equipment are not covered for explosion originating within them except for explosion of fuel or accumulated gases in the firebox or flues.

Machinery is not covered for loss caused by bursting or rupture of rotating parts.

The SMP special personal property form contains all of the exclusions in the general building form and general personal property form plus several additional exclusions required because of the "all-risks" insuring agreement. The additional exclusions are:

1. loss caused by actual work being performed on covered property unless fire or explosion ensues, and then only the fire or explosion damage is covered;
2. delay, loss of market, interruption of business, or consequential loss of any kind;
3. unless resulting from fire, smoke, explosion, collapse of a building, glass breakage, or water not otherwise excluded, there is no coverage for wear and tear, deterioration, inherent vice, rust, mold, rot, dampness, dryness, change in temperature, smog, smoke from agricultural or industrial operations, birds, rodents, insects, and other similar causes;
4. loss caused by voluntarily parting with possession of the property due to a fraudulent scheme or false representation;
5. loss caused by fraudulent or dishonest acts of the insured or any partner, officer, director, or employee of the insured; and
6. loss caused by rain, snow or sleet to property in the open.

Changing Special Limits. The extensions of coverage in the various forms provide limited amounts of coverage for losses which would not otherwise be covered under the forms. Examples are the replacement cost coverage extension, the valuable papers and records extension, and others. A firm which has a significant exposure to such losses may find it desirable to purchase a larger amount of coverage under one of the SMP forms provided for that purpose. The paragraphs that follow will discuss several such forms.

REPLACEMENT COST COVERAGE ENDORSEMENT (MP-126). The replacement cost extension in the SMP building forms provides replacement cost coverage only on losses of less than $1,000, and the personal property forms do not provide any replacement cost coverage on fixtures, machinery, or similar personal property. The replacement cost coverage endorsement can be used to provide full replacement cost coverage for buildings, personal property, or both. The insured must specify the property to be insured for replacement cost, and such property must be scheduled on the endorsement.

The following kinds of personal property are not covered for replacement cost: stock, merchandise; property of others; household furniture or residential contents; books of accounts, abstracts, manuscripts, drawings, card indexes, or similar papers or records; paintings, etchings, tapestries, statuary, or similar art objects; carpeting, cloth awnings, air conditioners, domestic appliances, or outdoor equipment.

The insurer is liable for replacement cost only if the property actually is repaired or replaced with due diligence and dispatch. Otherwise, liability is limited to actual cash value. The insured can elect to make claim initially for the actual cash value of the property and make claim later for the difference between actual cash value and replacement cost. If this option is elected, notice must be given to the insurer within 180 days of the loss that a claim for replacement cost will be made. In any case, the insurer's liability will not exceed the smallest of (1) the amount of insurance applicable to the damaged property; (2) the cost to replace or repair the property on the same presmises, for the same occupancy and in identical form; or (3) the amount actually expended to repair or replace the property. Note that the endorsement does not require the insured to rebuild at the same location or to rebuild a building identical to the old one. The building can be rebuilt at another location, and by a different design, if the insured prefers to do so. However, the insurer's liability cannot be increased by the insured's election to rebuild elsewhere.

The coinsurance clause in the replacement cost endorsement is quite similar to the comparable clause in actual cash value forms, but there is one major difference. The coinsurance percentage is applied to the replacement cost of property insured on a replacement cost basis and to the actual cash value of property insured on an actual cash value basis. Note that the coinsurance percentage is applied to the replacement cost on items so insured even if the insured elects to make claim on the basis of actual cash value. Consequently, the insured could sustain a coinsurance penalty on an actual cash value claim even though the amount of insurance exceeds the amount that would be required for the same coinsurance percentage under an actual cash value policy.

VALUABLE PAPERS AND RECORDS ENDORSEMENT (MP-176). A limited amount of coverage for valuable papers and records is provided under extensions of coverage in the general personal property form and the special personal property form. However, the $500 limit of the extension will not be adequate for many business firms and, in the case of the general personal property form, broader coverage may be desired. The valuable papers and records endorsement provides "all-risks" coverage for such property.

The endorsement divides valuable papers and records into two categories: category (a) consists of valuable papers and records which can be replaced or reconstructed after a loss, and category (b) consists of papers, such as valuable literary manuscripts or historical documents, which cannot be replaced. Category (a) is insured on a blanket basis with a single limit of liability applying to all such papers and records. Items included in category (b) must be specifically scheduled on the endorsement with an agreed value stated for each item. Each category has its own separate limit.

Coverage is restricted to the premises, and the insured must specify the type of storage receptacle used for the insured property. While the valuable papers are temporarily outside the premises, there is an extension of coverage equal to 10 percent of the combined amounts (a and b) on the property at other locations. However, the maximum recoverable under the extension is $5,000.

The valuable papers endorsement has several exclusions. They are:

1. loss due to dishonest acts of officers;
2. processing errors;
3. loss due to wear and tear, gradual deterioration, vermin, or inherent vice;
4. loss due to electrical or magnetic injury (except by lightning);
5. loss due to war, nuclear reaction, or radioactive contamination; and
6. loss to property not included in category (b) if it cannot be replaced with like kind and quality.

ENDORSEMENTS EMPLOYED TO MEASURE CHANGING VALUES. Many insureds do not maintain stable inventory values. In such situations, the insured may have difficulty obtaining proper amounts of insurance. If coverage equal to the maximum exposure is purchased, the insured is often overinsured. If the insured reduces coverage as values decline, refunds are made on a short-rate basis. This problem was discussed in Chapter 3 where reporting form policies were analyzed. The SMP offers the same solution. A firm can use a reporting form for personal property on either a specfic rate basis (MP-119) or on an average rate basis (MP-120). In either case, a $200 minimum premium is required for Section I exposures.

Another solution to the fluctuating value problem is the peak season endorsement (MP-125). This endorsement can be used if a reporting form is not desired because the insured cannot meet the minimum premium requirement or does not want to or cannot meet the reporting requirements demanded by a reporting form.

This endorsement is quite useful for those insureds, such as a clothing store, that have well defined seasonal patterns of sales. High sales volumes occur in the spring and at Christmas for clothing stores. During these time periods, the insured can have the policy modified to provide higher limits by attaching the peak season endorsement. The endorsement can provide for more than one peak season, and premiums are calculated on a pro rata basis. If the peak season is for two months and the increase is for $100,000, the premium would be one-sixth of the annual premium for $100,000 of coverage.

SELLING PRICE ENDORSEMENTS. There are two SMP endorsements used to modify the insured value of stock. One is the selling price clause (MP-191), which changes the recovery basis of goods sold but not delivered to selling price less all discounts and unincurred expenses. Such expenses might be for delivery and special handling. Usually it is used for mercantile establishments.

The second endorsement utilized in this area of selling price clauses is the manufacturers' selling price endorsement (MP-197). It is used for manufacturing establishments and states, "the actual cash value of finished stock manufactured by the insured shall be that price, less all discounts and unincurred expenses, for which said stock would have sold had no loss occurred." Through the use of this clause, the insured is able to insure the gross profit in the firm's inventory. Business interruption insurance for manufacturers does not cover loss resulting from damage to finished goods.

ADJUSTMENTS FOR INFLATION. When property contracts are written for a three-year term, the chances that inflation will increase the value of the firm's property is quite high. Unless the policy limit is adjusted periodically, a coinsurance penalty is very likely at the time of loss. In case of total loss, the insured could be severely underinsured. To help solve the problem, the automatic increase in insurance endorsement (MP-198) was developed.

When this endorsement is attached to the insured's policy, its limits are increased automatically each quarter by a predetermined percentage. The insured chooses the percentage to be used. If an insured chose a 2 percent adjustment and had $1,000,000 of property insured at inception, the limit of the policy would be increased to $1,020,000 at the end of March, $1,040,000 at the end of June, and so on for each of the nine remaining quarters of the policy, assuming an effective date of January 1. The increase is always a percentage of the original insurance amount. If this figure ($1,000,000) were inadequate to begin with, then the automatic adjustment would not compensate for that inadequacy. It would only try to keep up with inflation. Insureds need to review their property values for insurance purposes at least once a year with or without this endorsement.

INSURING CONDOMINIUMS

Before discussing insurance for condominiums, it is worthwhile to examine a little of the legal background of such properties. This examination should be made at the state level, since each state has its own laws concerning condominiums. Because of this diversity, this text will analyze the situation generally and will not attempt to deal with specifics. Only general definitions and doctrines will be given, along with insurance solutions to these general situations. Individuals should become familiar with applicable state laws and a given condominium's bylaws before any specific insurance recommendations are made.

Definitions[2]

It seems logical to begin this analysis with an explanation of some standard concepts associated with condominiums. By doing this all readers will be on common ground, and the succeeding discussion will be more relevant and informative. Once again, these are general definitions, and the laws of a specific state may differ.

Condominium In a condominium the owner has a fee simple title to the individual unit and an undivided interest in common with the other owners of the condominium with respect to the land, buildings, and other property that is not considered a part of the unit.

Consequently, what is considered to be included in the unit determines what the unit owner should insure and what the condominium association should insure. Therefore, a definition of the unit is needed.

Unit In defining the unit certain problems arise because there are two doctrines as to what constitutes the unit. These two doctrines are called the barewall and single entity concepts.

Barewall Concept. Under this doctrine, the association has no ownership interest inside the barewalls of the building. All paint and wall coverings, carpet and floor coverings, drapes, cabinets, appliances, nonload-bearing interior walls, doors, plumbing, and electrical fixtures are considered to be owned by the individual owner. As a result, the owner is responsible for insuring these items. This doctrine was a minority one until 1973, when the Florida insurance commissioner issued Bulletin 596 questioning the single entity doctrine. Since that time, insurance forms have been modified to provide coverage under either doctrine.

Single Entity Concept. In this doctrine, the condominium association is considered as the owner of all values contained in the unit as it was sold to the original purchaser. Normally, at the time of sale, carpets, cabinets, electrical fixtures, and appliances have been installed. Consequently, the association would be responsible for insuring these items under the single entity doctrine.

Because of these two doctrines and the fact that not all states accept one or the other, insurers have had to develop forms that meet the requirements of either.

Common Elements This term is often defined as all other property except the unit. Examples of properties usually included in this term are land, basic building structures, lobbies, tennis courts, swimming pools, game rooms, general parking and storage facilities, and club houses.

Association This organization is the unit owners association. Each unit owner is a member. The association is often incorporated, but it does not have to be. It is this entity that purchases insurance on nonunit property, and the following material on condominium insurance pertains to the coverage bought by the association. The owners can purchase coverage for their units under homeowners form HO-6.

Property Forms for Condominiums

There are two property forms designed to be used for condominiums. These forms permit the insuring of condominiums on a barewall or single entity basis as well as on a named peril or an "all-risks" basis. Besides these primary forms, some of the endorsements mentioned in the preceding discussion of the SMP property forms can be attached to the condominium forms.

Condominium General Property Form (MP-29) Basic property protection is provided for nonunit property on a named peril basis (fire, EC, and V&MM) in this form. It covers both buildings and personal property. Of course, additional perils may be added by endorsement. Coverage in the form is according to the barewall doctrine of condominium ownership. Buildings and attached additions and extensions are covered as are fixtures, machinery and equipment constituting a part of the building. Also personal property in which the unit owners have an undivided interest is protected while on the described premises or within 100 feet thereof. The form has the same extensions of coverage as the basic SMP general property form and general personal property form. The typical exclusions of cost of excavations, outdoor signs, growing crops, foundations, swimming pools, animals, aircraft, watercraft, and automobiles also appear.

The condominium form does differ in some ways from the other SMP property forms. These changes have been made in order to meet the needs of condominium owners.

Waiver of Subrogation. The insurer waives its right of subrogation against any unit owner of the described condominium.

Loss Payable Clause. All losses are adjusted with the named insured, which usually is the association, but are payable to the insurance trustee designated by the association. The trustee can be the association's board or someone else. The second portion of this clause states that payment to the insurance trustee completely discharges the insurer's liability under the contract. This provision is specifically made subject to the mortgagee clause, if any, attached to the policy.

Excluded Building Property. It is this portion of the condominium form that really distinguishes it from the basic property form. For in this clause the question of who insures the property inside the individual unit is decided. In Form MP-29, "property of any kind or description contained within the unfinished interior surfaces of the perimeter walls, floors, and ceilings of the condominium units, except (1) common building elements and (2) pipes, wires, conduits, and other utilities contained within easements appurtenant to the common building elements and within such condominium units" is excluded. This clause follows the barewall doctrine. However, the laws of a state may not follow the barewall doctrine. Consequently, an alternative is needed. The alternative is provided in the SMP condominium endorsement (MP-29B). In this form, additional property coverage can be obtained. There are three categories of additional property, and the insured can choose one or more of the three.

The first option gives coverage for fixtures, installations or additions comprising a part of the building within the unfinished interior surfaces of the perimeter walls, floors, and ceilings of individual condominium units initially installed or replacements thereof, in accordance with the original condominium plans and specifications. Under this option, the single entity doctrine is recognized and original furnishings and their replacements may be insured. However, improvements and betterments are not covered.

Option two is the same as option one except that improvements and betterments made by the unit owner are covered. The clause is the same as option one except the words, "or at the expense of the unit owners" are added. This additional phrase allows improvements and betterments to be insured by the association. Since it is probably cheaper to have the association insure the property under the building coverage, this second option is highly desirable. The last statement assumes the single entity doctrine is legal in a given state and the Condominium Declarations allow such an arrangement.

The third option allows the insured to protect whatever is desired.

The clause is entitled "other." It is left to the insured to decide what additional property should be insured.

Through the use of forms MP-29 and MP-29B, insureds can design their named peril condominium coverage as they desire. Through the use of MP-29 by itself or in conjunction with MP-29B, the legal demands of either the barewall or single entity doctrine can be met.

Special Condominium Form (MP-29A) If the insured desires "all-risks" protection, then a specific form exists to provide such coverage. That form is the SMP special condominium form. It is quite similar to the SMP special building form and the SMP special personal property form. In fact, it includes the exclusions, extensions of coverage, and the definitions of property covered, property not covered, and property subject to limitation included in those forms.

Otherwise, the form is generally the same as the basic form (MP-29) except coverage is on an "all-risks" basis. The barewall doctrine is followed but may be modified by MP-29B.

INSURING BUILDINGS UNDER CONSTRUCTION

Both the general building form and the special building form provide a limited amount of builders' risk coverage under the extensions of coverage provision. However, the limits of the extension, in both time and money, are inadequate for all but the smallest buildings. The builders' risk forms were designed especially to provide coverage for buildings under construction.

SMP Builders' Risk Forms

Chapter 3 discusses several ways to insure buildings under construction: completed value form, reporting form, or a nonreporting form. The SMP program includes only the completed value form. Two forms are available: the SMP builders' risk completed value form (MP-102) and the SMP special builders' risk completed value form (MP-103). Like the other SMP forms, the basic form is on a named peril basis and the special form is "all-risks."

SMP Builders' Risk Form (MP-102) When this form is used, it replaces any other coverage on the structures insured. There is only one type of property covered and that is buildings. However, the definition of buildings includes personal property of the insured associated with erecting the structure. Specifically, the form covers "the building or structure at the described location while in the course of construction, including all additions directly attached thereto and all fixtures, machinery and equipment constituting a permanent part of said building." The policy also covers "temporary structures, materials, and supplies of all kinds owned by the named insured and incident to the construction of said building or structure; all while in or on the described buildings, structures or temporary structures or in the open (including within vehicles) on the described premises or within 100 feet thereof." In addition, similar property of others in the insured's care, custody, or control is insured up to limits equal to 2 percent of the coverage on buildings or $2,000, whichever is less.

Usually the insured under the SMP builders' risk form is the owner, but a contractor may be added as an additional insured. When the contractor is added, only Section I coverage applies to the contractor.

Property Excluded. Very little property is excluded. Property that is more specifically covered in another insurance contract is the only type of excluded property.

Perils Insured Against. Coverage is for fire, the extended coverage perils, and V&MM. However, other perils may be added if desired. Actually, if one desires broad peril coverage, the special form is normally chosen. That form will be analyzed in the following material.

Losses Excluded. The builders' risk form has the standard loss exclusions found throughout the SMP program. Loss due to the following are excluded:

1. enforcement of building ordinances;
2. electrical currents artificially generated (except for fire and explosion that ensues);
3. spoilage; and
4. earth movement, flood, water which backs up from sewers or drains, and water below the surface of the ground unless fire or explosion ensues.

Other Clauses. Like most other builders' risk forms, the SMP version has an occupancy clause. This provision states the structure may not be occupied without consent of the insurer except for the purpose of testing machinery. If occupancy takes place, coverage is void.

The standard deductible ($100 per item, $1,000 per occurrence) applies to all perils except V&MM for which the per item deductible is $500. As is true with other completed value forms, one must purchase coverage equal to the completed value of the structure in order to meet insurance-to-value requirements. This requirement is spelled out in the provisional limit of liability clause.

SMP Special Builders' Risk Form (MP-103) Like the basic builders' risk form, the special builders' risk form uses the completed value approach. The special form uses the same definition of building as the basic form and contains the same provisions with respect to occupancy, insurance to value, and other more specific insurance. The forms only differ in perils insured against and limitations on property covered. This difference is the typical difference between basic and special forms throughout the SMP program.

Perils Insured Against. The form insures against all risks of direct physical loss to the covered property subject to policy provisions and stipulations. These provisions take the form of exclusions which are the standard special form exclusions. All the loss exclusions of the form MP-102 are included as well as loss due to:

1. error, omissions, or deficiency in design;
2. wear and tear, inherent vice, animals, etc.;
3. explosion of steam boilers, pipes, or turbines;
4. leakage or overflow from plumbing, heating, or air conditioning equipment due to freezing when proper steps have not been taken to prevent freezing;
5. theft of any property which is not an integral part of the building; and
6. unexplained or mysterious disappearance and fidelity losses.

Limitations on Property. As with other special coverage forms, the special form has special limitations on certain properties. These restrictions are necessary because of the broad perils insured against under the form. Coverage is restricted on plumbing, heating, and air conditioning equipment from loss due to freezing. Steam boilers, pipes, and turbines are almost entirely excluded from coverage, and hot water boilers are not covered from loss from within them except for explosion. Glass is only insured on a named peril basis, and when fences, pavements, outdoor swimming pools are insured at all, they are not covered for loss due to freezing or weight of ice and snow. Finally, no loss to the interior of the structure due to rain, snow, or dust is covered unless exterior damage occurs first, and the exterior damages lead to the interior damage.

MARINE INSURANCE OPTIONS
CONTAINED IN THE SMP PROGRAM

Although marine insurance is not a major section of the SMP policy, there are several endorsements in the SMP program that are of a marine nature. These forms are used to insure personal property. Normally the property insured under the marine forms is of high value, such as cameras, fine art objects, or fragile items like neon signs. In total, there are six marine forms in the SMP program: radium, fine arts, cameras, musical instruments, neon signs, and physicians' and surgeons' equipment. If the underwriter is willing, other inland marine forms also may be added to the SMP policy. Five of the floaters are considered separate policies from the SMP to which they are attached. However, they are still subject to the package discount. The one form that is not considered a separate policy (physicians' and surgeons') replaces all personal property coverage in the SMP when it is attached.

Radium Floater

The radium floater endorsement (MP-166) provides coverage on an "all-risks" basis, except for loss due to gradual deterioration, war, shipment by mail (except registered first class mail), and nuclear reaction. The insured must give immediate notice of loss by telephone or telegraph and agrees to use due diligence and special care on each patient under radium treatment. The insured purchases a specific amount of insurance for this coverage, and the floater has a 100 percent coinsurance clause. Coverage is limited to the continental United States and Canada. All items of radium to be insured under the floater must be scheduled on the endorsement, with a description and a stated amount of insurance for each.

Fine Arts Floater

The fine arts floater endorsement (MP-167) provides "all-risks" coverage on a valued policy basis for all items scheduled in the policy and new acquisitions for ninety days. Coverage is limited to the continental United States and Canada. However, fairgrounds and expositions are excluded wherever located. The exclusions to the "all-risks" coverage include war, nuclear reaction, or radioactive contamination, wear and tear, and gradual deterioration. Breakage of glass and similar fragile articles is also excluded unless caused by certain named perils. Unlike most inland marine floaters, it does not have the standard pairs and sets clause, and loss of one of a pair is considered a total loss.

Camera Floater

The camera floater endorsement (MP-168) insures cameras, projection machines, films, and articles of equipment pertaining thereto on a worldwide, "all-risks" basis, subject to the exclusions of loss due to war, nuclear reaction, and radioactive contamination, wear and tear, insects, and inherent vice. Items are scheduled and insured on an actual cash value basis. Newly acquired property is covered for thirty days for up to $10,000 or 25 percent of the insurance in force, whichever is less. The standard pairs and sets clause applies.

Musical Instrument Floater

The musical instrument floater endorsement (MP-169) insures musical instruments and articles of equipment pertaining thereto on an "all-risks" basis except for the perils of war, nuclear reaction, radioactive contamination, wear and tear, and gradual deterioration. Property is scheduled on the policy and is insured on an actual cash value basis. The newly acquired property clause is the same as that of the camera floater, as is the pairs and sets clause. One interesting clause in this floater states that the instrument is not to be played for remuneration during the term unless an additional premium is paid and the floater endorsed. If this clause is strictly interpreted, and the insured plays for hire one time during the policy period and does not pay the additional premium, the floater is void. In the SMP program, this floater would most normally be purchased by schools which have large investments in musical instruments.

Neon Sign Floater

The neon sign endorsement (MP-170) is used to insure neon, automatic, or mechanical electrical signs on an "all-risks" basis, except for loss due to:

1. war;
2. nuclear reaction or radioactive contamination;
3. dampness of atmosphere or extremes of temperature;
4. neglect of insured to save and preserve property after a loss;
5. mechanical breakdown and electrical damage except that done by lightning;
6. breakage during installation or repair;
7. breakage during transportation except for the perils of fire, lightning, and collision;
8. faulty manufacture, wear and tear, and deterioration; and
9. shipment via the Panama Canal, to or from Alaska, Hawaii, or Puerto Rico.

This last exclusion is necessary because coverage applies within the United States, Canada, Puerto Rico and while in transit between them. The floater is intended to cover inland but not ocean marine exposures. Coverage is written on a schedule arrangement subject to a 100 percent coinsurance clause. Settlement of losses is made on an actual cash value basis. All losses are subject to a 5 percent deductible of not less than $10 or more than $100 on any one item. Protection under this endorsement is less broad than under the other four inland marine floaters. This probably is due to the fact that the insured items are fragile and are kept outdoors.

Physicians' and Surgeons' Equipment Floater (MP-111)

This endorsement is the most detailed by far of all the inland marine floaters in the SMP program. When an insured purchases the floater, all other personal property coverage under Section I is cancelled and the floater replaces it. Only the cancellation provision of the SMP applies to the physicians' and surgeons' floater. With respect to all other provisions, it is self-contained.

Property Insured The physicians' and surgeons' floater coverage is divided into two sections: (A) medical, surgical and dental equipment and instruments (including tools, materials, supplies, and scientific books) used by the insured in the medical or dental professions; and (B) office equipment, including furniture and fixtures, tenants' improvements and betterments while within the premises. Property included under coverage (A) is not restricted to location while that in (B) is covered only on the premises. The form defines premises as "that portion of the building at the address stated in this form which is occupied by the insured in the practice of his profession."

Extensions of Coverage. The physicians' and surgeons' floater has its own set of extensions of coverage. They are:

1. Theft Damage to Buildings. The insured must be the owner of the building or liable for such damage.
2. Off-Premises. Applies to furniture and fixtures while temporarily away from the premises (not more than thirty days). Coverage is for $1,000.
3. Extra Expense. Protection for $1,000 is included.
4. Currency, Money, and Stamps. Coverage is for $250 and all fidelity losses are excluded.
5. Personal Effects. Protects the property of the insured and others for 5 percent of policy limit up to $500. It pays only on a named peril basis (fire, EC, V&MM, and sprinkler leakage).

6. Valuable Papers and Records. Coverage is limited to $500 but is on an "all-risks" basis like the valuable papers and records policy.

Property Excluded. Radium is excluded. However, this coverage is available under the previously described radium floater. Loss to property that is being worked upon is also excluded if the loss results from the work being performed. An example of this exclusion is bridge work being repaired by a dentist. While not completely excluded, breakage of glass and articles of a brittle nature is restricted as to perils insured against.

Perils Insured Against Coverage is on an "all-risks" basis. It has very few exclusions with respect to perils insured against. Only losses caused by artificially generated currents, wear and tear, insects, inherent vice, war, and nuclear reaction and contamination are excluded. This list is among the shortest of any other such list in the fire or SMP manuals.

Other Provisions The physicians' and surgeons' floater has a pairs and sets clause, an 80 percent coinsurance clause, and coverage is limited to the United States and Canada unless otherwise endorsed.

The insured may choose whether to purchase coverage on an actual cash value or replacement cost basis. When protection is obtained on a replacement cost basis, the form represents one of the most liberal standard property contracts in existence: "all-risks" protection with few exclusions and recovery on a replacement cost basis.

INSURING AGAINST THE CRIME PERIL
IN THE SMP

In the SMP program there are numerous endorsements that can be used to insure against loss from theft, robbery, and burglary. It is the purpose of this section to analyze these options. Since they represent many of the same coverages examined in the chapters on crime insurance, the analysis will be brief.

Losses from theft, robbery, and burglary are insured in two different sections in the SMP policy. Section I, property insurance, contains several endorsements that pertain primarily to theft, robbery, and burglary of merchandise, furniture, and equipment. Section III, crime, consists mainly of the comprehensive crime and blanket crime forms and endorsements to them. The succeeding analysis will first examine the crime coverages in Section I, the property section, and then those in Section III, the crime section.

Crime Coverages in the Property Section of the SMP

In the property section there are eight endorsements pertaining to crime. The following material examines the content of those forms and how they provide protection for losses due to theft, robbery, and burglary.

Mercantile Open Stock Burglary Endorsement (MP-156) This endorsement is used as the primary means of insuring a firm's stock against loss by burglary. It pays "for loss by burglary or by robbery of a watchman, while the premises *are not open for business*, of merchandise, furniture, fixtures, and equipment within the premises or within a showcase or show window used by the insured and located outside the premises but inside the building line of the building containing the premises or attached to said building." It also pays for damage to the premises from burglary, robbery of a watchman, or attempts at either. Like the mercantile open stock policy analyzed in Chapter 11, this endorsement requires the insured to keep accurate records so the amount of loss can be determined. In fact, the SMP version is basically the same as that found in the burglary manual. Consequently, it states that SMP provisions for coinsurance, loss deductibles, valuation, and replacement cost coverage do not apply. The open stock burglary endorsement has its own versions of these provisions. Recovery is on an actual cash value basis even if a replacement cost endorsement applies to other property coverages. A loss reduces the policy limit until the integrity of the firm's safety devices is restored, and the endorsement has its own coinsurance requirements. As is true of the open stock burglary policy, there is coinsurance amount as well as coinsurance percentage. As a result, the open stock burglary limits will almost always be less than that of the personal property coverage in the SMP.

In order to make clear that other specific insurance should pay for certain types of losses, the open stock burglary endorsement excludes them. Among these excluded items are losses due to vandalism and malicious mischief, employee dishonesty (fidelity) losses, and loss to manuscripts, books of account, or records. All these losses can be insured with policies designed for those specific exposures.

Mercantile Open Stock Burglary and Theft Endorsement (MP-157) For those who want more than just burglary and robbery of watchman protection, another form is available. In this form, protection is expanded to cover "loss by theft or attempt thereat, *whether or not the premises are open for business*, of merchandise, furniture, fixtures and equipment within the premises or within a showcase or show window used by the insured and located outside the premises but inside the building line of the building containing the premises or attached to said building." Damage to the premises is also insured, and a mandatory deductible of $50 applies just to the theft protection.

The actual arrangement of the form is a little unusual. Burglary is insured under what is called coverage 1 and theft under coverage 2. Each peril has a separate limit, but the theft limit is not in addition to the burglary limit. The burglary limit is the maximum amount that will be paid for any loss, and the theft limit indicates how much of that maximum can be used to pay for theft losses.

The burglary and theft form has the same burglary provisions and exclusions and then adds some exclusions just for the theft portion. Loss by fraudulent scheme, trick device, mere disappearance, or mere inventory shrinkage is excluded. If an inventory shortage occurs and the insured can prove theft, then coverage applies.

Storekeeper's Burglary and Robbery Endorsement (MP-158)

The SMP version of this form is just like the same policy in the burglary manual. It is designed to meet the needs of small commercial concerns and offers a wide variety of coverages. Included among them are:

1. robbery inside the premises;
2. robbery outside the premises;
3. loss of property due to kidnapping;
4. burglary and safe burglary;
5. theft from night depository or residence;
6. burglary and robbery of watchman; and
7. damage to premises.

All of these items were explained in the chapters on crime insurance and all that needs explanation here is that item 4 pertains primarily to money, securities, and merchandise from within a safe, and that item 6 pertains primarily to other types of personal property. Also, loss due to employee theft is excluded.

The storekeeper's form has valuation, deductible, and replacement cost provisions separate from the SMP provisions. It has no coinsurance clause because the limits of liability are so low. Usually no more than $1,000 of protection can be obtained under this endorsement.

Broad Form Storekeeper's Endorsement (MP-161)

A small business which desires a package crime policy broader than that discussed above may buy this endorsement. To be eligible, the concern must not customarily employ more than four employees and must have only one location. This endorsement provides nine different coverages up to a maximum of $1,000 per item. The coverages provided are as follows:

1. employee dishonesty;
2. loss inside premises, "all-risks" on money and securities, and safe burglary or robbery for other property;
3. loss outside premises, "all-risks" on money and securities, and robbery on other property;
4. merchandise burglary and robbery of a watchman;
5. money orders and counterfeit paper currency;
6. theft from residence of a messenger;
7. depositors forgery;
8. vandalism and malicious mischief resulting from burglarious entry; and
9. other damage caused by persons committing a covered act.

These items and their exclusions have all been analyzed elsewhere in this text and will not be reexamined here. However, it should be remembered that the V&MM coverage in the broad form storekeeper's gives protection for glass breakage by burglars while the basic V&MM endorsement does not. Also, the broad form storekeeper's endorsement includes fidelity coverage which the other crime forms in the SMP thus far discussed did not.

The broad form storekeeper's endorsement is actually a policy inside a policy, much like the inland marine endorsements to the SMP. Except for a few specified provisions, such as subrogation, cancellation, war and nuclear exclusions, and some declarations information, the endorsement stands alone from the rest of the SMP policy. However, the insured still receives the SMP package discount.

Mercantile Robbery and Safe Burglary Endorsement (MP-162) This form, like the broad form storekeeper's, stands as a separate policy from the SMP except for the same provisions relative to the named insured, policy period, nuclear and war exclusions, cancellation, subrogation, and no benefit to bailee. The insured must specify in the declarations information concerning number of custodians, messengers, and guards. Type of armored car service used, a detailed description of all safes and vaults, and loss experience for the last five years also must be shown.

However, coverage is much more restricted and maximum limits are much higher than in the storekeeper's forms. Coverage is for (1) robbery within the premises, (2) robbery outside the premises, and (3) safe burglary, as well as damage to the premises resulting from one of these crimes or attempts thereat. Each of these coverages has its own separate limit, and the insureds can choose the combination of coverages desired. One, two, or all three may be purchased. Employee robbery is covered (it is not excluded), but robbery by the insured or a partner is not covered.

Church Theft Endorsement (MP-159) Basically, this endorsement provides the same coverage as the church coverage form in the burglary manual. Protection is on a theft basis, so robbery and burglary are insured. However, fidelity losses are excluded.

All clauses of Section I of the SMP policy apply except the loss deductible, coinsurance, and the valuation clauses.

Property Covered. Money, securities, and other property are insured while on the premises, within the night depository of a bank, or while in the care or custody of an authorized person. In the endorsement, property can be insured on a scheduled or a blanket basis. When scheduled, the amount appearing on the schedule represents the maximum liability of the insurer for that item.

Exclusions. The endorsement has six exclusions. They are:

1. loss due to employee theft;
2. loss occurring during a fire;
3. loss of the contents of an alms or poor box;
4. loss to nonowned property from within the premises if the property is not intended for the use of the insured;
5. loss due to fire except for loss to a safe or vault; and
6. loss to valuable papers.

When these exclusions are considered, it is evident that the church theft form does not provide comprehensive coverage. Fidelity losses are not covered, nor are fire losses to money and securities. Also, a church might still need valuable papers coverage.

Protection Systems Endorsements In the property section of the SMP there are two endorsements used to give rate credits for loss protection systems. One is for crime prevention and the other for fire and allied lines. Both are mentioned here, since they pertain to loss prevention.

Burglary and Robbery Protection Systems Endorsement (MP-163). This endorsement is used to give rate credits for alarms and protective devices installed on the insured premises. It is mentioned at this point of the SMP analysis because the analysis of the burglary and robbery section of the SMP has just been completed, and this endorsement is used with the robbery and burglary forms. Under this form, a rate reduction is given for devices such as premises protection, safes, holdup alarms, and guard services. When a rate credit is given for such items and they become nonfunctional and the failure is within the insured's control, insurance coverage is suspended until repairs are completed or services restored. If the failure is beyond the control of the insured and an additional inside guard is employed, coverage is reduced to the amount of protection which the premium would have bought if no alarm device were employed. Because of this provision, the insured must be very careful to maintain all alarm systems in working order.

Protective Safeguards Endorsement (MP-196). This form performs the same function for fire and allied lines coverages as the burglary and robbery protection systems form does for that line. Consequently, the fire alarms and automatic sprinklers often are involved. This form provides for coverage suspension or reduction when protective devices or services are not functional and a rate credit has been given for them.

Crime Coverages in Section III of the SMP

The crime coverages in Section III are built around two basic forms: the comprehensive crime (MP-300) and the blanket crime (MP-301) forms. A third, the public employees blanket coverage endorsement (MP-302), is used only for public officials. All the other endorsements in this section of the SMP are used to amend these three forms. However, the list of endorsements is not restricted to those in the SMP program. Any standard 3-D or blanket crime endorsement can be attached as long as it does not overlap any of the coverages in Section I and II of the SMP policy.

Eligible Insureds for SMP Crime Coverages This section of the discussion will examine eligibility requirements for the three basic forms used in Section III of the SMP. The eligibility rules given are from the SMP manual.

Eligible Insureds Under the Comprehensive Crime Form. Any person or organization that qualifies for the SMP program is eligible to use this form except certain financial organizations and public officials. The following organizations and their personnel are ineligible; banks, stockbrokers, savings and loan associations, credit unions, investment banks and trusts, safe deposit companies, stock exchanges, trust companies, dealers in mortgages and commercial paper and finance companies. These firms usually can qualify for bankers or brokers blanket bonds.

While the preceding list is lengthy, it still leaves certain financial organizations eligible. Insurance companies, personal finance companies, small loan companies, foundations, and endowment funds may use this form. A single state university, state college, state teachers' college, or state normal school also is eligible. However, eligibility of such educational organizations is limited. If faithful performance of duty is required, the insured is a state department or board, and the law requires officials to be bonded, the comprehensive crime policy cannot be used and the public employees blanket form must be written.

Eligible Insureds Under the Blanket Crime Form. The same insureds may be covered under this form as the comprehensive form except for insurance companies, personal finance companies, small loan companies, foundations, endowment funds, and armored motor vehicle companies. As a consequence of these restrictions, one can see that the list of eligible insureds for the comprehensive crime policy is greater than that of the blanket crime form.

Eligible Insureds Under the Public Employee's Blanket Form. This form is reserved for use by only the following insureds:

1. a state, county, city, town, township, village, or borough;
2. school, water, irrigation, power, bridge, fire, and similar districts or authorities; and
3. state universities, state colleges, state teachers' colleges, or state normal schools if they are not eligible for the comprehensive form.

Coverage of Major Crime Forms In this section, the coverage of the three major crime forms is examined as well as the SMP crime endorsements that may be used with them. The major forms are discussed in detail, but the endorsements will be treated in a less detailed manner.

The Comprehensive Crime Form. This form stands alone from all other coverages in the SMP policy. No provisions, stipulations, or other terms of the SMP policy apply to the form. In the comprehensive crime form there are five primary coverages with each one having its own separate limit. An insured can have the same limit on each one, separate limits, or may even choose not to purchase any protection for some of the coverages. The insurer or the insured may cancel one or more of the five coverages and the others can remain in effect. Each coverage stands alone. These exposures are covered by the comprehensive crime form:

1. employee dishonesty;
2. loss inside the premises;
3. loss outside the premises;
4. money and counterfeit paper currency; and
5. depositors forgery.

EMPLOYEE DISHONESTY. This insuring agreement covers fraudulent or dishonest acts committed by employees. There are two insuring clauses for employee dishonesty, and the insured can choose the one desired.

Clause IA (commercial blanket) covers loss of property resulting from dishonest acts of employees. This clause applies the coverage limit on a per loss basis. If the coverage limit is $100,000 and five employees, acting in concert, steal a total of $125,000, it only pays $100,000, not $125,000.

Clause IB (blanket position) pays on an employee basis. In the case just mentioned, it would pay $125,000. In fact, it would pay up to $100,000 for each employee involved if the loss equals or exceeds that amount.

The endorsement includes a definition of dishonest act, making it clear that the employee must intend to cause loss to the employer. It reads:

> Dishonest or fraudulent acts as used in this Insuring Agreement shall mean only dishonest or fraudulent acts committed by such Employee with the manifest intent: (a) to cause the insured to sustain such loss; and (b) to obtain financial benefit for the Employee, or for any other person or organization intended by the Employee to receive such benefit, other than salaries, commissions, fees, bonuses, promotions, awards, profit sharing, pensions or other employee benefits earned in the normal course of employment.

This clause was first introduced in the 1977 revisions of the SMP forms and may represent a significant reduction in coverage. Note that the employee must intend to both (1) cause loss to the employer, and (2) cause gain for the employee or some other person or group of persons. Consequently, it would not cover wanton destruction of the employer's property by a disgruntled employee merely seeking revenge. Also, there is some question that it would cover an incident in which the employee's intent was to defraud some other person or firm, such as a customer or supplier of the employer, but which resulted in a loss to the employer. Such a loss to the employer might result from the employer being held liable for the losses of others caused by the employee in the performance of duties apparently related to the employment.

Only two exclusions apply to the employee dishonesty coverage. The first excludes coverage for any loss caused by dishonest acts of the insured or a partner therein. The second excludes any loss, or any part of a loss, for which the proof of its existence or the proof of the amount of loss depends upon an inventory computation or a profit and loss statement.

With respect to these two clauses IA and IB, the manual has minimum limits requirements, and in the case of clause IB, a maximum limit. The commercial blanket coverage (IA) has a minimum limit of $10,000 and no maximum. The blanket position coverage (IB) has a minimum limit of $2,500 and a maximum of $100,000.

LOSS INSIDE THE PREMISES.   This insuring agreement covers money and securities while on the premises against loss due to destruction, disappearance, or wrongful abstraction. Other property on the premises is insured against loss due to robbery or safe burglary. The form defines *premises* as the interior portion of any building occupied by the insured in the conduct of its business. The money and securities coverage amounts to "all-risks" protection with few exclusions. Only employee theft (which can be insured under Coverage I), war, accounting errors, nuclear radiation, and loss from a vending machine are excluded with regard to money and securities. The coverage on other property is not as broad. Under this section, damage arising from safe burglary, robbery, or felonious abstraction to the building is covered if the building is owned by the insured or the insured is liable for the damage.

Loss Outside the Premises. Money and securities are covered for loss due to destruction, disappearance or wrongful abstraction outside the premises while conveyed by a messenger or any armored motor vehicle company, or by theft while within the living quarters in the home of any messenger. Other property is insured against loss by robbery or attempt thereat in the same circumstances as the money and securities coverage. *Messenger* is defined as the insured or a partner of the insured or any employee authorized by the insured to have care and custody of the insured property away from the premises.

The same exclusions of war, nuclear, and accounting errors apply to this coverage as applied to coverage inside premises. In addition, loss while property is in the care of an armored vehicle company is insured on an excess basis only. Also, as in Coverage II, fidelity losses are excluded.

Money Orders and Counterfeit Paper Currency Coverage. This insuring agreement covers loss resulting from the acceptance in good faith, in exchange for merchandise, money, or services of any post office or express money order, issued or purporting to have been issued by any post office or express company, if such money order is not paid upon presentation. Coverage pertains only to money orders and not to checks. The second part of this coverage insures against loss due to the acceptance in good faith in the regular course of business of counterfeit United States or Canadian paper currency. The only exclusion is for loss due to a dishonest act by any insured or a partner therein, whether acting alone or in collusion with others. This same exclusion applies to all five coverages in the comprehensive crime policy.

Depositors Forgery. This insuring agreement covers loss sustained by the insured by reason of forgery or alteration of checks, drafts, promissory notes, bills of exchange, or similar written instruments drawn upon the insured's bank account. Unlike most other crime coverages, the depositors forgery coverage does not exclude loss caused by employees. To this extent, it duplicates coverage provided under the fidelity insuring agreement. Of course, the insured cannot recover more than the amount lost. Examples of covered losses include the following:

1. A check drawn on the insured's account, payable to and endorsed by a fictitious payee. In one such case, criminals broke into an office and obtained possession of the firm's business checkbook and check writing machine. Over $10,000 was in the checking account when they started and, as would be expected, nothing was left when they stopped.
2. A check obtained from the insured or an agent of the insured by an imposter "in a face to face transaction" and endorsed by anyone other than the legitimate payee.
3. A payroll check endorsed by a third party without the authority of the payee.

Besides paying for these losses, the coverage will also pay for legal expenses arising out of refusal to pay checks that fit the examples just given. This last coverage is dependent upon the insurer giving its written consent. The insured may extend the coverage to the bank against which the forged instrument was drawn by including the bank in the proof of loss.

CONDITIONS OF THE FORM.   The form has numerous conditions. One states that any new employees acquired through merger or consolidation are insured as long as the insured notifies the insurer within thirty days and pays any additional premium that may be due. As is true of most crime policies, the form has a discovery period clause. It states that under IA (commercial blanket), the discovery period is one year and under IB it is two years. The one-year discovery period also applies to the other coverages except depositors forgery.

Covered losses under the contract also include losses in prior time periods but discovered during the policy period or discovery period, where applicable. In order for losses from prior periods to be covered, prior coverage must have existed up to the inception of the present policy. Besides this unbroken coverage requirement, the loss must be of such a nature that both the prior policy and the present policy would have covered them. If the new coverage is broader and would have covered the loss, but the old policy would not, no coverage exists. Also, if the prior policy would have covered the loss but the present policy does not, there is no coverage. Finally, the inability to collect such losses under the prior policy must be due solely to the expiration of the discovery period provided by that policy. If all of these conditions are met, the present policy will pay the lesser of (1) the amount that would have been paid under the prior policy if the discovery period had not expired, or (2) the amount which would have been payable under the existing policy if it had been in force at the time the loss occurred.

Blanket Crime Form.   Coverages under this form are the same as the primary coverages in the comprehensive crime form. The major difference between the forms is that in the blanket crime form the insured must purchase protection for all five coverages, and a single limit applies. The insured may purchase only those coverages desired under the comprehensive crime form. However, the limit applies on a per occurrence basis. If a messenger is robbed of $10,000 on the same day the insured has a check forged for $5,000, the $10,000 policy will pay both in full because they are separate occurrences.

The fidelity coverage in the blanket crime form is commercial blanket coverage. There is no optimal blanket position coverage available as there is in the comprehensive crime form. Another difference is a two-year discovery period.

Public Employees Blanket Crime Coverage. This form is designed for public employees and their fidelity exposures. This form does not include the other coverages provided under the comprehensive crime form and the blanket crime form. In the public employees form, two types of protection are provided on either a blanket or blanket position basis: honesty and faithful performance. The honesty coverage is like fidelity coverage provided for private businesses. It protects against loss from the dishonest acts of employees. The faithful performance coverage insures loss that arises through the failure of any of the employees to perform faithfully their duties or to account properly for all monies and property received by virtue of their positions or employment. This standard is greater than mere honesty. Persons may be held liable for funds entrusted to them and loss even though they have been completely honest. For example, a city treasurer might be held for lack of faithful performance for depositing city funds in an unsound bank which later fails, even though no dishonesty was involved. One somewhat celebrated claim under a faithful performance bond involved two drawbridge tenders who became intoxicated while on the job and raised the drawbridge while cars were on it, resulting in injury to occupants of the vehicles. The city did not have liability insurance, so it made claim under its faithful performance bond for the amounts it was required to pay for the injuries.

The insuring agreements are:

1. honesty blanket coverage;
2. honesty blanket position coverage;
3. faithful performance blanket coverage; and
4. faithful performance blanket position coverage.

Coverages 1 and 2 provide coverage comparable to the commercial blanket coverage and blanket position coverage, respectively, under the comprehensive crime form. Coverages 3 and 4 are the same as coverages 1 and 2, respectively, except that the coverage applies to lack of faithful performance of duties, which is much broader than coverage for dishonest acts.

The key word used in the insuring agreements for either coverage is *employee*, and the definition of that word changes from one coverage to another. Under coverages 1 and 2, employee means "a person while in the employ of the insured during the effective period of this endorsement who is not required by law to give bond conditional for the faithful performance of his duties and who is a member of the staff or personnel of the insured but does not mean any Treasurer or Tax Collector by whatever title known." Under coverages 3 and 4, the definition changes to "a person while the employee of the insured during the effective period of this endorsement who is not required by law to furnish an individual bond to qualify for office and who is a member of the staff or personnel of the insured but does not mean any Treasurer or Tax Collector by whatever title known."

BOILER AND MACHINERY COVERAGES IN THE SMP

Boiler and machinery protection in the SMP program is similar to that in boiler and machinery insurance policies. The SMP package discounts apply to boiler and machinery.

Boiler and Machinery Forms in the SMP

When boiler and machinery is written in the SMP, two forms must be used: (1) the basic boiler and machinery coverage form (MP-400), and (2) the boiler and machinery declarations form (MP-401). These two forms must be used to provide coverage. Other endorsements may be added to give broader coverage.

SMP Boiler and Machinery Coverage Endorsement (MP-400) In this form the basic coverage is presented. As opposed to the six coverages in the standard boiler and machinery policy, the SMP version has four. The four areas of protection are:

1. Loss to the property of the insured. This category includes the insured object as well as other real and personal property of the insured. The other property needs protecting, since the explosion of steam boilers is excluded from almost all property contracts.
2. Expediting expenses. This coverage is the same in the SMP program as it is in the standard boiler and machinery policies. Only $1,000 of coverage is provided.

3. Property damage liability. This item covers damage to property of others caused by an accident to an insured object. It is of significance because it covers property in the insured's care, custody, and control. The SMP Section II (liability) coverage excludes such property.
4. Defense, settlement, supplementary payments. This coverage is in addition to the policy limits and is the standard supplementary coverage found in liability policies. These benefits would be needed in case a lawsuit arose out of a loss to property for which the insured might be liable.

The two omitted items are bodily injury and automatic coverage. They are omitted because Section II of the SMP provides liability protection, and the premium adjustment clause in the SMP boiler and machinery forms allows for coverage of newly acquired property.

Definitions and Conditions of Boiler and Machinery Coverage. Most of the definitions in the SMP boiler and machinery policy are like the standard ones. An exception is the definition of accident which only gives protection on the broad coverage basis. The limited coverage definition of accident is not an option in the SMP programs.

With respect to an insured object, the SMP version has three basic groups: boilers, unfired vessels, and piping. If coverage is provided for one item in a given group, then all items in the group and on the premises must be insured. The insured cannot pick and choose. However, there is one exception to the rule in that coverage on additional unfired vessels is optional. Examples of such vessels include metal unfired pressure vessels subject to vacuum or internal pressure—other than static pressure of contents.

The SMP version contains the standard inspection and suspension clauses for boiler and machinery coverages, as well as exclusions for war and nuclear radiation and contamination. The other insurance clause makes property damage liability coverage excess over any other valid and collectible insurance. The phrase *other valid and collectible* insurance includes self-insured retention programs. Also, there is an increased cost exclusion which eliminates loss due to increases in cost of construction and from the enforcement of building codes. Besides these provisions, furnace explosion is excluded. However, furnace explosion is covered under extended coverage which is mandatory under the SMP program.

Machinery Coverage Declarations (MP-401) This form indicates policy limits, premiums due, which groups of objects are insured, as well as standard information found on insurance policies' declaration page. Besides the basic three groups (boilers, unfired vessels, and piping) there are eleven other groups of objects that may be insured. These groups are listed on the declarations page, and coverage is provided by inserting the word *included* by the group name.

In addition to the listed groups, there is a special space at the bottom of the form to list other objects to be insured. An additional form (MP-422) must be used if objects are listed in this space. This provision introduces a bit of flexibility into the form.

SMP Boiler and Machinery Endorsements For the most part, these endorsements involve indirect loss endorsements like use and occupancy and extra expense.

Use and Occupancy Endorsements. There are two use and occupancy forms in the SMP boiler and machinery manual. Both are on a valued basis. One is on a daily indemnity basis (MP-407), and the other (MP-408) is on a weekly basis. Otherwise, the two forms are basically the same.

The fact that only valued forms are available in the SMP program adds some rigidity to the program. Losses involving a total shutdown are easy to adjust. However, some losses occur where only a partial suspension of business results. When this happens, adjustment problems can arise and insureds need to consider this possibility before purchasing coverage on a valued basis. Also, if a firm's business is seasonal and a constant amount of indemnity per day is used, it may be inadequate if a loss occurs during the peak season. This last statement assumes the indemnity value reflects average earnings.

Prevention of Occupancy Endorsement (MP-410). This endorsement covers use and occupancy losses that result from an accident which prevents the insured from occupying the building. The limits for the coverage are stated in terms of dollars per month. Compensation also is paid for partial losses, which may result in the prevention of occupancy for less than a month or a partial prevention for all or a part of a month.

Consequential Damage Endorsement (MP-411). This endorsement covers loss due to spoilage from lack of power, light, heat, steam or refrigeration, resulting solely from an accident to an insured object.

Extra Expense Endorsement (MP-409). This endorsement provides coverage similar to the extra expense insurance found in other lines, but in this case, the event that triggers the coverage is an accident occurring to an insured object. Protection is on a period of restoration basis, and the insured can collect a certain percentage of the policy limit each month. Space is provided on the form for restoration periods up to and including twelve months.

INSURANCE TO VALUE AND DEDUCTIBLE PROVISIONS IN THE SMP PROPERTY PROGRAM

In this portion of the chapter, all insurance-to-value requirements and deductible provisions in the SMP property section are analyzed. Insurance-to-value requirements will be examined first, and then deductible options.

Insurance to Value

In the SMP program, at least 80 percent coinsurance is mandatory. A higher percentage may be chosen by the insured, or a rating bureau can require a higher percentage, but 80 percent is the minimum with respect to fire insurance on real and personal property. Protection provided by business interruption forms may be written with lower coinsurance limits, as may sprinkler leakage, burglary, earthquake, and certain other endorsements.

When the insured chooses blanket coverage, the standard 90 percent requirement applies but the 80 percent rate is charged.

An agreed amount clause can be used to replace the coinsurance percentage in some cases. When this approach is taken, a dollar amount replaces the coinsurance percentage. The major advantage of this approach is that the insured has certainty with regard to insurance-to-value requirements. If the agreed amount is purchased, there will be no coinsurance penalty at the time of loss regardless of what happens to property values between the date of the policy's inception and the date of the loss. It should be noted, however, that the insured may still not have adequate insurance to value and may, therefore, not collect the full value of the property in the event of a total loss.

The disadvantage to this clause is that the insurer often requires the agreed amount to equal 90 percent of the value of the property. The insured receives the 80 percent rate but still has to buy 12.5 percent more insurance than when the 80 percent coinsurance clause is used.

A similar device is used in burglary insurance. The insurance company uses a figure called the coinsurance limit. It serves the same purpose as the agreed amount clause. If the insured purchases an amount equal to the coinsurance limit, then no coinsurance penalty is incurred.

Deductible Provisions in the SMP

There are several deductible endorsements in the SMP. Some are used with just one form, and others may be attached to many forms and used in several programs. This discussion will examine the more important ones. However, the standard deductibles will be reviewed first and then those deductibles that are added.

Deductibles in the SMP Property Forms The deductible clause in the Conditions Applicable to Section I in form MP-4 applies to all coverages under Section I of the SMP, except as provided in individual forms. That clause provides for a deductible of $100 applicable separately to (1) each building, (2) the contents of each building, if the buildings are not insured, and (3) personal property in the open. However, an aggregate deductible of $1,000 applies to all losses arising from one occurrence. Both of the foregoing deductible amounts can be changed simply by entering higher amounts in the appropriate spaces on the declarations page.

Several forms provide for other deductibles. For example, the builders' risk forms include a $500 deductible applicable only to vandalism and malicious mischief perils, with the standard deductible applying to other perils. The neon sign endorsement provides for a percentage deductible, and some other forms, such as the physicians' and surgeons' equipment floater, are not subject to any deductible at all.

Chapter Notes

1. John C. Long and Davis W. Gregg, *Property and Liability Insurance Handbook* (Homewood, IL: Richard D. Irwin, 1965), pp. 731-737.
2. Santa Clara Valley Chapter, Society of CPCU, *The Insuring of Condominiums and Cooperatives* (Indianapolis: The Rough Notes Company, 1976), pp. 6-8.

CHAPTER 15

Other Combination Policies

In the preceding chapter, a description of combination policies and an analysis of the SMP program were given. This chapter also will deal with combination policies, but the emphasis is on programs other than the SMP. Coverages under consideration include the special office policy, the special commercial property policy, the industrial property policy, the manufacturers output policy, the farmowners-ranchowners policy, the businessowners policy, and the electronic data processing policy. From this list, it can be seen that the subjects analyzed include both single-line and multi-line combination policies. The final section of the chapter is a review of the entire text in the form of cases. Two cases are given on two different types of organizations: a hospital and a wholesaler. While each of these concerns has liability exposures, this chapter deals only with property exposures and coverages.

COMBINATION POLICIES—SINGLE-LINE

In this section several single-line combination policies are examined: the commercial property, the office property, the industrial property, and the manufacturers output policies.

The first two policies to be discussed, the office property and commercial property policies originated in the late 1960s.

Commercial Property Form

In the commercial property form, personal property of principally mercantile firms is insured on an "all-risks" basis. As is usual in such forms, debris removal is insured, but it does not increase the policy limits and it is not considered in insurance-to-value calculations.

The definition of personal property states that:

> . . . [the] policy covers business personal property of the insured usual to the occupancy of the insured, including manuscripts, furniture, fixtures, equipment and supplies not otherwise covered under this policy and shall also cover the insured's interest in personal property owned by others to the extent of the value of labor and materials expended thereon by the insured; all while in or on the described building or in the open (including within vehicles) on the described premises or within 100 feet thereon.

Tenants' improvements and betterments also are included in the definition of personal property. Personal property of others is covered for an additional amount of insurance for 2 percent of the insured's policy limit up to $2,000. This coverage for property of others does not affect the insurance-to-value calculations. The tenant's improvements and betterments protection does.

The territorial limits of the policy are the fifty states and the District of Columbia. Goods in transit are covered while in the U. S. and Canada and in transit between them, but this coverage is limited to that provided in the transportation extension of coverage.

Limitations on Property In the commercial property form there are eight restrictions on covered property. These restrictions range from complete exclusion to a dollar limitation.

Fur and fur garments coverage is restricted to a limit of $1,000 per occurrence. This limitation applies on an aggregate basis. If fifteen $100 items were damaged, the insured would receive $1,000. Actually, the limitation is not as strict as it seems because it does not apply if loss results from one of the list of "specified perils." These perils are defined to be fire, lightning, and the extended coverage perils when property is inside any building. V&MM and sprinkler leakage also are included in the list, but the requirement of being inside a building does not apply to them.

Jewelry, watches, precious and semi-precious stones, gold, silver, platinum, and other precious alloys or metals are covered for only $1,000 in the aggregate. Again, full coverage applies if loss is from a specified peril. Jewelry and watches with a value of $25 or less are covered on an "all-risks" basis, not subject to the $1,000 limitation. Consequently, 1,500 watches worth $15 each would be covered in full for loss from any insured peril, not just specified perils.

Because the underwriting manual allows for some manufacturing on the premises, patterns, dies, molds, models, and forms may be present at the insured location. Coverage is granted for these items but only for $1,000 in the aggregate. There are no exceptions with respect to perils insured against with these assets as was the case with jewelry and watches.

Live animals, birds, and fish are not covered except when held for sale or sold but not delivered. When they are insured, it is only for the specified perils which directly cause death or destruction.

Trees, shrubs, and plants are insured on the same basis as animals, fish, and birds, but partial losses are compensated. Death or destruction does not have to result directly from a specified peril.

Glass, glassware, statuary, marbles, bric-a-brac, porcelains, and other fragile articles of a similar nature are insured for breakage only if breakage occurs from one of the specified perils. However, bottles or similar containers of property held for sale or sold but not delivered are covered for "all-risks." Bottled perfume and liquor in a store would be covered if, for example, a shelf collapsed. Destruction of these bottles could be quite expensive. Lenses of photographic or scientific instruments are also covered for "all-risks" whether or not they are held for sale.

Damage to boiler and machinery is excluded. Insureds still need to purchase boiler and machinery insurance. As is fairly standard in "all-risks" contracts, furnace explosion is covered.

Property Excluded In addition to the preceding limitations, seven different groups of property are completely excluded. However, most of these groups can be covered either by endorsements to the commercial property form or by separate insurance policies.

Growing crops and lawns are excluded, as well as currency, money, stamps, bullion, notes, securities, deeds, accounts, bills, evidences of debt, letters of credit, and tickets. This latter group can be insured under a money and securities form. Also totally excluded is property sold under a conditional sale, trust agreement, installment or other deferred payment plan, after delivery is made to the customer. This protection is available under inland marine forms.

All the following types of property are excluded by the basic commercial property form:

1. watercraft, including motors, equipment and accessories (can be covered only while not afloat)
2. motorcycles and motorscooters
3. trailers designed for use with private passenger vehicles for general utility purposes or carrying boats (semitrailers are excluded and cannot be covered by endorsement)
4. outdoor signs, whether or not they are attached to the building
5. household and personal effects contained in living quarters occupied by the insured, or by any officer, director, stockholder, or partner of the insured or any of their relatives

Table 15-1

Extensions of Coverage for the
Commercial Property Form

Property	Limit
Newly acquired	10% of limits up to $10,000
Personal effects of employees	$100 per employee— $500 total
Valuable papers	$500
Extra expense	$1,000
Damage to building from theft, burglary, or robbery	Policy limit
Transportation	$1,000

Aircraft, automobiles, semitrailers, or any other self-propelled vehicles are excluded. However, motorized equipment not licensed for use on public thoroughfares and operated principally on the premises is insured. Lift trucks would be included in this category as well as mobile cranes that do not leave the premises.

Extensions of Coverage The commercial property form provides several extensions of coverage which do not represent additional amounts of insurance. They give the insured protection for *incidental* exposures. If *substantial* exposures exist, additional insurance should be purchased. These items are summarized in Table 15-1.

Most of these extensions are quite common and need no further explanation. The loss to building from an act of theft, burglary, or robbery deserves explanation in that it covers real property. All other coverage in the form is for personal property. Also, it is unusual in that there is no dollar limit in the extension, so the policy limits apply. There is no coverage for glass under this extension. The building coverage is effective only if the insured owns the building or is legally responsible for damage to it.

The transportation extension also needs further explanation. Insured personal property is covered for losses up to $1,000 during transportation by motor vehicles owned, leased, or operated by the insured. If the goods are transported by a common carrier, no coverage exists since the insured does not own, lease, or operate the vehicle. Property in the care, custody, or control of salespersons is excluded. The coverage includes the perils of fire, lightning, windstorm, hail, explosion, smoke, riot, V&MM, and collision or upset. It is not "all-risks" like much of the contract and all of the other extensions. In addition to the preceding there is coverage for theft of an entire shipping bale, case, or package from inside a locked vehicle, provided there are signs of forcible entry.

Perils Excluded As was true of "all-risks" contracts discussed earlier, the commercial property form excludes numerous perils. These include loss from the enforcement of building codes, inventory shortage, mysterious disappearance, electrical currents artificially generated, inherent vice, wear and tear, insects, vermin, change in temperature or humidity, fraudulent scheme or trick, dishonest act of employee, and rain, snow, or sleet damage to property left in the open.

The inventory shrinkage and mysterious disappearance exclusions do not exclude all shoplifting. Only those losses for which there is no external evidence of theft are excluded. For instance, in one case the lower court did not allow the external evidence to be entered as evidence to support a claim for a shortage which was discovered on taking inventory. Part of the evidence was testimony of a man who had been convicted of stealing some of the merchandise.[1] The appeals court said it should be admitted. The insurer argued that the loss should not be paid because it was originally discovered through the taking of the quarterly inventory.

Further exclusions apply to loss by leakage or overflow from plumbing, heating, air conditioning, or other equipment or appliances caused by freezing when the insured does not use due diligence to maintain heat in the building or drain the equipment when the building is vacant or unoccupied. Consequential losses and losses resulting from actual work upon or installation of covered property also are excluded, as is loss due to faulty materials or workmanship. Losses due to latent defect, breakdown, or failure of machines also are excluded—boiler and machinery insurance is needed to cover such losses. However, loss caused by a boiler explosion (except damage to the boiler) is not excluded. Loss from legal proceedings is excluded. It is not the intent of the form to provide liability insurance.

In addition to the exclusions that are usual for "all-risks" contracts, there are several standard exclusions which are found in most property forms. Spoilage is not covered unless on-premises equipment is damaged by an insured peril. For the purposes of this latter exclusion, loss by riot, civil commotion, riot attending a strike, and V&MM is excluded in any case.

Earth movement, mudslide, earthquake, flood, water which backs up through sewer drains, below the surface water, war, and nuclear reaction or contamination also are excluded.

Clauses Limiting Recovery   Usually, the commercial property form has an 80 percent coinsurance clause, but a higher one can be inserted if the insured so desires. Unless endorsed for replacement cost coverage, claims are paid on an actual cash value basis. Property specifically insured under another policy is not covered under the commercial property form. Books of record, manuscripts, drawings, and other records and card index systems are only covered up to the cost of blank materials and the cost of labor in transcribing or copying them. Computer tapes and similar items are insured only for the value of the blank materials. Valuable papers insurance is still needed to cover the cost of research and the cost of reconstructing the information on computer records.

A flat $100 deductible is applied to all losses except fire, lightning, and the EC perils. When in conflict with state rules that require $100 deductibles on all perils, the commercial property form must be endorsed to conform with those rules.

Office Personal Property Form

In many respects the office property form is similar to the commercial property form; consequently, frequent cross references will be made between the two forms.

The office property form is designed to cover personal property found in a typical business office. Normally, if property would fit the categories eligible for coverage under the inland marine forms, such as a physician's office, it would be insured under those policies rather than the office property form.

Like the commercial property form, debris removal is covered, and in most versions 2 percent of the policy limits up to $2,000 can be used to protect property of others in the insured's care, custody, or control.

Property Subject to Limitation   The number of limitations in the office property form is not as great as in the commercial property form. Breakage of fragile articles is excluded, with the exception of bottles and similar containers. Explosion of steam boilers and other steam vessels is excluded. Machines and machinery are not covered against loss caused by rupture, bursting, or disintegration of their rotating or moving parts resulting from centrifugal or reciprocating force.

The definition of specified perils contained in the office property form is the same as the definition in the commercial property form. However, there are no limitations on dies and patterns, since there is very little possibility of them being on the premises. Actually, many of the limitations of the commercial property form are not contained in the office property form. These items are listed in the excluded property section of the forms and are not covered except in the extensions of coverage.

Property Not Covered   This section of the form contains a rather lengthy list of excluded property. Live animals, fish, and birds, aircraft, watercraft, furs, jewelry, trees, shrubs, currency, household and personal effects of employees and guests are excluded except for coverage, if any, in the extensions of coverage. Several of these categories are insured in the commercial property form if held for sale or sold but not delivered.

In fact, the office property form excludes all personal property held for sale and any samples in the care, custody, or control of salespersons when they are off the premises. In addition, growing crops, lawns, property shipped by mail once it passes into the custody of the Postal Service, and all outdoor signs are excluded.

Extensions of Coverage   The extensions of coverage in the office property form are the same as in the commercial property form except for two items: off-premises coverage and currency, money and stamps.

Newly Acquired Property Coverage.   For covered personal property, a limit of 10 percent of coverage up to $10,000 is available at newly acquired locations within the United States. Coverage ceases after thirty days unless the new location has been reported to the company.

Off-Premises Coverage.   Property away from the premises is covered for up to thirty days anywhere within the United States, and while in transit within the states or between the states and Canada. Off-premises coverage is limited to 10 percent of the policy limit, with a maximum off-premises coverage of $10,000.

Currency, Money, and Stamps.   There is $250 of coverage for these items. Protection is for the perils insured against while the property is on the premises, and while conveyed outside the premises by the insured or by an employee of the insured.

Perils Excluded   All the perils excluded by the commercial property form are excluded in the office property form. In addition, theft from any vehicle occurring while such vehicle is unattended is excluded, unless the vehicle was locked and there are signs of forceful entry, or unless the property was in the custody of a carrier for hire.

Clauses Limiting Recovery   Basically the same limiting clauses apply to the office property form as to the commercial property form. There is an 80 percent coinsurance clause, a $100 deductible, recovery on an ACV basis, and payment for accounting records only for the cost of blank material and labor to transcribe such data. Computer tapes are only covered for the cost of blank tapes. Insureds may still need valuable papers and accounts receivable insurance.

Other Clauses Many standard clauses are contained in the office property form. The other insurance clause of the office property form is rather complex. Coverage under the form is excess with regard to any other coverage for burglary, robbery, or theft. With regard to other perils, it is contributing with other policies written under the same form and conditions, and excess over policies not written under the same form and conditions.

Industrial Property Form

The industrial property form was one of the first forms, along with the manufacturers output policy, that could be used to give industrial insureds "all-risks" coverage. Actually, there are three different insuring agreements, differing with regard to the perils insured against. It was developed in the mid-1950s and is not used much today because very similar coverage can be provided under the SMP program. Given the discounts and liability coverage available in the SMP, the use of the industrial property form is limited and may shortly disappear.

Eligible Insureds An industrial concern is defined in the industrial property manual as "any insured whose principal activity is manufacturing or processing." Given this broad rule, the manual then restricts eligibility by excluding certain occupancies. Among those properties declared not eligible are: buildings and personal property rated under dwelling or apartment house schedules, cotton risks, dry cleaners, grain risks, laundries, petrochemical risks, public utilities, shoe repair shops, and mining properties.

Locations Covered The industrial property form is a multiple-location form. It is designed to insure firms with at least two locations. Property values at the second location must at least equal the lesser of $50,000 or 10 percent of the total average values at all locations. Both personal property (including tenants' improvements and betterments) and buildings are eligible to be insured under the industrial property form.

Besides minimum property requirements, the industrial property form has fairly high minimum premium requirements. Table 15-2 shows these requirements for various plans in the program. The minimum premiums are on an account basis.

Besides showing the minimum premium requirement in the program, Table 15-2 also shows the various plans under the industrial

Table 15-2

Minimum Premium Requirements—
Industrial Property Program

Plan	Premium
Named peril coverage only on personal property	$ 2,500
All-risks coverage only on personal property	5,000
Named peril coverage on personal property and buildings	7,500
Named peril coverage on building, "all-risks" on personal property	10,000

property program. The named perils coverage referred to in Table 15-2 includes fire, lightning, the extended coverage perils, V&MM, burglary, sprinkler leakage, falling objects, and collapse from weight of ice, snow, or sleet. Other named perils can be added by endorsement.

The "all-risks" coverage is on finished stock at any of the insured's locations. All other personal property is covered at all locations and in transit, except that there is no coverage for property other than finished stock while at manufacturing or processing locations. Property other than finished stock is insured only for named perils while at a manufacturing or processing location.

Property Excluded As is true with almost all insurance contracts, the industrial property form excludes several types of property. Aircraft, animals, growing crops, motor vehicles, trailers, and semi-trailers (designed for and licensed for highway use) and property while waterborne are excluded, as is property at a fair or exhibition. Coverage on furs is limited to $1,000, as is coverage on jewelry.

Clauses Limiting Recovery Coverage must be written with a 90 percent or 100 percent coinsurance clause, or a reporting form may be used. It is the intent that other insurance (unless it is specific, like a marine floater) not be used to protect the property. Consequently, if other insurance covers the property in a general nature, the industrial property policy is void. Often, there is a $100 deductible on the policy, and, for large accounts, the exposure is experience rated.

MANUFACTURERS OUTPUT POLICY

This policy was one of the first contracts to provide "all-risks" coverage on personal property for a manufacturer. When it was first developed, the manufacturers output policy (MOP) was classified as inland marine. At one time, the MOP was the most complete form of protection available for a manufacturer, covering all personal property while in transit and stationary away from the insured's manufacturing premises.

Policy Conditions

The MOP provides "all-risks" protection on the insured's personal property, including property of others, and the interest of the insured in improvements and betterments. Property in transit is covered, as are automobiles. However, autos are not covered for collision unless the policy is endorsed and a $500 deductible is used. The collision exclusion applies only to the vehicle and not its contents, and only while the vehicle is being towed or operating under its own power. If it is on a railroad car, or other conveyance, it is protected.

Interestingly, the basic policy is designed to insure property away from the insured's manufacturing premises. It may be endorsed to cover property on such premises. In addition to this coverage, protection is provided for personal property of others under the following three conditions:

1. property sold by the insured and which the insured agreed prior to the loss to insure for the account of the buyer until delivered;
2. property in the care, custody, and control of the insured if the insured is liable for the damage or if the insured had agreed to insure it; and
3. property sold by the insured under an installation contract where the manufacturer's liability continues until installation is accepted by the buyer.

Territory Coverage is provided within the continental U.S., or in transit between points therein, whether on land, air, or sea, and coverage applies while in transit in Canada. Several exclusions to this broad definition should be noted:

1. Property on the insured's manufacturing premises is excluded unless specifically included by endorsement.
2. Waterborne or air shipments to Alaska are not covered.

3. Waterborne shipments via the Panama Canal are excluded.
4. If not covered by ocean marine policies, imports or exports are only covered on land in the covered territory.

Limits on Coverage The MOP is a reporting form with the standard reporting form requirements. Consequently, one must insure 100 percent to value. Open limits exist at each location, subject to the stated maximum. However, special limits apply while property is in transit, on a per conveyance and a per occurrence basis. In addition, there are restrictions on flood and earthquake losses and property on exhibition at any convention. Earthquake and flood losses are restricted to salesperson's samples, patterns, dies, cameras and equipment, scientific instruments, and other mobile property of a like nature not intended for sale, property in transit, in custody of processors and automobiles.

Property Excluded The basic MOP does not cover money and securities, growing crops and timber, property insured under import or export ocean marine policies, animals, aircraft, or watercraft nor property sold under a conditional sales or other deferred payment plan. Indirect losses also are excluded.

Perils Excluded Like most "all-risks" contracts, the MOP excludes a number of perils: war, employee theft, inventory shortage, mysterious disappearance, flood and earthquake (except for the earlier mentioned exception), boiler explosion and machinery breakdown, artificially generated electrical currents, faulty workmanship, collision damage to vehicles, wear and tear, and inherent vice. Loss due to change in temperature is insured only if directly caused by a fire or EC peril. Property while being worked upon also is not protected.

Summary The MOP is designed to give "all-risks" coverage on a reporting basis to a manufacturer's products while being delivered and installed.

MULTIPLE-LINE POLICIES

This section of the chapter will discuss some additional multiple-line combination policies. The primary policies examined are the business-owners and the farmowners-ranchowners policies. Also, the electronic data processing policy is reviewed. The data processing policy is purchased separately and in addition to any of the other multiple-line policies.

Each of these policies meets the special needs of certain groups. The businessowners policy meets the needs of small businesses; the farmowners-ranchowners meets the needs of those in commercial farming; and the data processing policy meets the needs of those that have substantial EDP equipment and media exposure.

Businessowners Policy

The businessowners policy is designed to meet the insurance requirements of small businesses in the office, mercantile, or apartment house categories. On a national basis, it has been estimated that one-half million such accounts exist, indicating a large total market ($250 to $400 million) composed of small individual units.[2] These firms' insurance needs are generally quite simple. While many different types of businesses are eligible for businessowners policies, they are in many ways similar. Because of this similarity, it was possible to develop an indivisible package policy under which the insured purchases a rather broad group of coverages on an all-or-nothing basis. A few optional coverages can be added by endorsement or by entering a limit of liability in the appropriate space in the declarations.

The first policies of this type were developed by independent insurers. As a response to pressure from member companies that wanted a competitive product, Insurance Services Office (ISO) introduced their businessowners policies in 1976. The ISO forms will be discussed here. It should be noted, however, that forms with varying degrees of similarity are also available through insurers who have made independent filings.

General Characteristics There are two basic businessowners forms available, the named peril form and the special form. Both forms provide protection to buildings, business personal property, or both, on a replacement cost basis without a coinsurance clause. This no-coinsurance feature is unusual in modern property insurance. In theory, the insured is supposed to insure 100 percent to value, but since there is no coinsurance clause in the contract, there is no penalty if this is not done. Reliance is placed on the producer and underwriter to write full insurance to value.

The replacement cost coverage applies to all insured property: buildings, stock, contents, and improvements and betterments. The policy even provides an additional 25 percent increase in coverage for personal property to cover seasonal variations. Besides the preceding categories of personal property, similar personal property of others in the insured's care, custody, and control also is insured. Building coverage is increased automatically by a selected percentage per quarter to reflect inflationary increases in construction costs.

In addition to direct property losses, indirect losses are also covered for the perils insured against. Loss of income and extra expense exposures are automatically provided in the policy. This item includes business interruption and loss of rents insurance. Again, no coinsurance clause applies, and there is no specific limit of liability, but loss is limited to actual loss sustained and to a twelve-month period.

Optional property coverages include employee dishonesty, exterior signs, exterior grade floor glass, earthquake, boiler, pressure vessel, air conditioning equipment, and burglary and robbery coverage. Broad liability protection is provided, but that coverage is not discussed in this chapter.

From this overview, the reader can see that the businessowners policy gives the insured a wide range of mandatory coverages and, as compared to the SMP, the number of options available to the insured are greatly reduced. Besides this reduction in options, the rating process under the businessowners policy is much easier. All these factors combine to make the price of the policy attractive to its intended target market.

Eligibility   Whether a concern is eligible for the businessowners policy is determined by the physical size of the premises. The key variable is square foot area. If the premises exceeds the eligibility limitations, then another policy must be used.

Building and Building Owner's Personal Property.   The same eligibility criteria apply whether or not a building owner also occupies the property. There are three different rules applying to three different occupancies. In all these definitions of eligible occupants, the floor space variable does not include floor space in a basement not open to the public. Also, if the building and its contents are under one ownership, then both the building and personal property must be insured in the policy. However, coverage cannot be written on a blanket basis. All insurance must be specific.

APARTMENT BUILDINGS.   Apartment buildings which do not exceed six stories in height and contain no more than sixty dwelling units are eligible. No apartment building, to be eligible, can contain mercantile space over 7,500 square feet.

OFFICE BUILDINGS.   Office buildings principally occupied for office purposes, not exceeding three stories, and containing less than 100,000 square feet of total floor space are eligible. Office buildings that have more than 7,500 square feet of mercantile spaces are ineligible. The limitation on the size of office buildings is more restrictive than that of apartment houses. The apartment house can be twice as tall as the office building (in terms of floors), and there is no floor space limitation.

MERCANTILE. Buildings occupied principally for mercantile purposes, in which the mercantile area does not exceed 7,500 square feet, are eligible. Mercantile occupancy is defined as one where the principal business is the buying and selling of merchandise. The mercantile occupancy has the most stringent eligibility requirements. Many department stores would not be eligible, but most specialty shops would be.

Tenant's Personal Property. In this category, the insured leases the premises from another. Only personal property and the tenants' use interest in improvements and betterments would be insured in this situation. Since apartment houses would not fit this category, there is no need to set guidelines for them.

OFFICE. For a tenant in an office building to be eligible, the insured's offices must not occupy more than 10,000 square feet in any one building.

MERCANTILE. Again, the mercantile constraint is the stricter. No more than 7,500 square feet can be occupied in one building. However, if more than one building is involved, the total space could be greater than 7,500 square feet.

Ineligible Classes. While the preceding information provided general guidelines, eleven occupancies are specifically excluded:

1. Automobile repair or service stations, automobile, motor home, mobile home, and motorcycle dealers are not eligible. Parking lot and garages are only eligible when incidental to an otherwise eligible class. Although not specifically excluded, dealers in watercraft, snowmobiles, or other recreational motor vehicles would not use the businessowners policy because the policy does not respond to many types of claims pertaining to the operation of or injury to owned boats or vehicles.
2. Bars, grills, or restaurants.
3. Condominiums. The condominium forms in the SMP should be used.
4. Contractors. Not all types of contracting work are excluded. A hardware store that installs fences might be eligible, but the underwriter would have the final say in such a situation.
5. Buildings occupied in whole or part for manufacturing or processing.
6. Insureds whose business operation involves one or more locations which are used for manufacturing, processing, or servicing. A manufacturer could make items at one location and sell them through retail outlets at other locations. This kind of operation is excluded.
7. Household personal property of the owner of the business.

8. One- or two-family dwellings unless of garden apartment variety where multiple units are grouped within a single area and are under common ownership, management, and control. No private dwellings are supposed to be eligible.

9. Places of Amusement. Fairs, carnivals, theaters, bowling alleys, slot-car tracks, or skating rinks are ineligible. They are not in the business of buying or selling merchandise.

10. Wholesalers.

11. Banks, building and loan associations, savings and loan associations, credit unions, stockbrokers and similar financial institutions. The money and securities exposure is too great for these occupancies to be included in this program.

Eligible Classes. All of the following are examples of eligible businesses: antique stores, army and navy surplus stores, hobby shops, book and magazine stores, carpet, floor and wall covering dealers, delicatessens, florists, gift shops, hardware stores, jewelry and candy stores, and many others too numerous to list here.

Content of Forms In the following discussion, the actual content of the two primary forms will be examined. For the most part, these forms are identical, differing only in the area of covered perils and the declarations page. However, since the major interest here is property insurance, it will be necessary to examine these differences in detail.

Standard Form—Property Insured. The standard form provides named peril coverage for fire, lightning, extended coverage, V&MM, and sprinkler leakage. Property is divided into the two usual categories: buildings and business personal property.

BUILDINGS. The building coverage is separated into six categories, and coverage is on a replacement cost basis. The following are insured under the building item:

1. all garages, storage buildings, and appurtenant structures usual to the occupancy of the insured

2. fixtures, machinery, and equipment constituting a permanent part of and pertaining to the service of the building

3. personal property of the insured used for the maintenance and service of the building including fire extinguishing apparatus, floor coverings, and appliances for refrigerating, ventilating, cooking, dishwashing, and laundering

4. outdoor furniture and fixtures

5. personal property owned by the insured in apartments or rooms furnished by the insured as landlord

6. trees, shrubs, and plants at the described premises limited to not more than $250 per item or $1,000 in total

Besides these six groups, debris removal is insured as an additional amount of insurance and without dollar limit. Also, there is an automatic increase in protection clause that increases the original policy limits applicable to the building item by 2 percent per quarter. If a greater increase is desired, it may be provided by endorsement.

BUSINESS PERSONAL PROPERTY. This item also is covered on a replacement cost basis with debris removal insured as an additional amount of insurance. This coverage is much broader than most other contracts available. The description of business personal property insured is divided into three categories.

1. Property usual to the occupancy which is owned by the insured and while located at the premises designated on the declarations page and for the amount indicated on that page. Improvements and betterments and property of others for which the insured is legally liable are included. All such property is protected while in or on the building, in the open (including within vehicles) on or within 100 feet of the described premises.
2. Personal property (except money and securities) is insured for up to $1,000 while in transit or otherwise temporarily away from the premises.
3. Personal property at newly acquired locations is covered for up to $10,000. Coverage ceases after thirty days unless the new location is reported to the insurance company.

Automatic coverage is provided for seasonal variations for an amount up to 25 percent of the stated coverage for personal property. This percentage is an additional amount of insurance. It is effective if the insured at the time of loss carries an amount of insurance equal to or greater than the average value of business personal property during the twelve months preceding the loss. For example, assume that from January through October, values were $100,000 each month, and $150,000 of values was on hand in November, and $200,000 in December. The average of these figures is $112,500. If the insured carried this amount or more, a loss up to 25 percent greater than the policy limit ($140,625) would be paid. If less than $112,500 is carried, the policy limit applies.

PROPERTY NOT COVERED. The following types of property are not covered: exterior signs, growing crops and lawns, money and securities, aircraft, automobiles, motor trucks, and other vehicles subject to motor vehicle registration, and watercraft while afloat. It is this last item that makes the businessowners policy unsuitable for boat dealers, even though they are not specifically precluded from eligibility.

LIMITATIONS ON PROPERTY. Valuable papers, records, manuscripts, and similar property are insured only for the value of the blank material and the cost of labor incurred to copy or transcribe the data. Computer tapes, discs, and storage media are insured only for the cost of blank material. The insured needs valuable papers insurance if a substantial exposure exists.

Loss of Income. Coverage C in the businessowners policy covers loss of income. Payment is made on an actual loss sustained basis and the recovery period is limited to twelve months. There is no coinsurance clause or dollar limit. The only restriction is the twelve-month maximum recovery period. The loss of income "shall not exceed the reduction in gross earnings, less charges and expenses which do not necessarily continue during the interruption of business; and the reduction in rents, less charges and expenses which do not necessarily continue during the period of untenantability."

As is standard in business interruption insurance the insured must resume normal operations as soon as reasonably possible. In addition, it is required that all available means be used to avoid unnecessary delay. If the insured could reduce the loss by resuming partial operations and did not do so, this action or lack of action is taken into consideration in determining the actual loss sustained.

Under the coverage, the insurer is not liable for any increase in loss caused by strikes at the insured premises while repair or rebuilding is in progress. If an insured loses a contract because of the loss, only the loss of income during the restoration period is covered. After that time no further payment is made even though the insured cannot regain the lost contract.

Perils Not Covered. Several perils are excluded in this form. There is the broad water damage exclusion, which excludes, among other things, flood, water beneath the ground, and tidal waves. Earthquake and earth movement are not covered, nor is loss due to delay or loss of market. Spoilage caused by damage to off-premises power supply or equipment is excluded, as is loss due to enforcement of building laws. Finally, there is the normal electrical apparatus clause which excludes loss from artificially generated currents unless fire ensues.

Other Provisions. The businessowners policy does not contain the provisions of the standard 165-line fire insurance policy. However, provisions similar to most of the provisions of that contract are included in one place or another.

There are the standard war, nuclear reaction, and radioactive contamination exclusions. The usual provisions regarding subrogation, inspection and audit, liberalization, assignment, concealment or fraud, appraisal, duties of the insured, mortgagee, waiver, and abandonment are found in the policy. These are similar to such clauses found in most property contracts. Besides these clauses, the usual loss, no-benefit to bailee, no control, and suit clauses are included.

However, the businessowners policy does have other clauses which, while normally contained in property contracts, are worth special attention.

CANCELLATION CLAUSE. The cancellation clause requires thirty day's notice, as opposed to five days in the fire contract and ten days in the SMP. Cancellation for nonpayment is an exception to the thirty-day requirement. In that case, only ten day's notice is required. When the insured cancels, a refund equal to 90 percent of the pro rata refund is given, a provision somewhat different from the usual short-rate cancellation rule.

POLICY TERRITORY. The policy territory with respect to property consists of the states of the United States, the District of Columbia, and Puerto Rico. Normally, Puerto Rico is not included in the territory of property contracts. The time of inception is 12:00 noon; however, if the businessowners policy replaces a policy that terminated at 12:01 A.M., then it begins at 12:01 A.M.

OTHER INSURANCE. The other insurance clause states that the businessowners policy is excess over other valid and collectible insurance that would apply if it did not exist.

REPLACEMENT OF FORMS OR ENDORSEMENTS. When the policy is written without a termination date (on a continuous basis), the insurance company may add or substitute forms and endorsements which are authorized for its use upon any anniversary date in accordance with the rules of its manual. This provision gives the insurance company the right to modify continuous policies if experience indicates such modifications are needed. When a policy has a termination date, the changes can be made because a new contract is offered, so this clause is not needed in insurance contracts with a known termination date.

REPLACEMENT COST. Except for money and securities, all property is insured on a replacement cost basis which pays the lesser of:

1. the full cost of replacement of such property at the same site with new material of like kind and quality without deduction for depreciation;
2. the cost of repairing the insured property within a reasonable time;
3. the limit of liability applicable to such property shown on the declarations page; or
4. the amount actually and necessarily expended in repairing or replacing the property.

The insured is not required to build at the old location, and the contract will not pay for increases in construction costs due to quality improvements.

In order to collect under the replacement cost coverage, the insured must actually expend the money for repair. However, the insured can collect on an ACV basis immediately and then within 180 days of the date of loss indicate an intention to file on a replacement cost basis at a later date. It is usually wise to exercise this option, since it makes funds equal to the actual cash value available to the insured immediately to finance most of the cost of repair or reconstruction. However, the insured must remember to file the notice of intent to make a replacement cost claim within 180 days of the loss, not within 180 days of the ACV claim.

COMPANY OPTIONS. After receiving a signed statement of proof of loss, the insurer has thirty days in which to declare whether it will exercise its option to take part or all of any damaged property at an agreed value or to repair, rebuild, or replace it with equivalent property.

PAYMENT OF LOSS. The insurer has thirty days to pay the loss after presentation and acceptance of the proof of loss. The fire policy gives the insurer sixty days.

PRIVILEGE TO ADJUST WITH OWNER. Normally, the payee is the insured. However, in the case of personal property of others, the insurer reserves the right to make direct settlement with the property owner, and the insurer can, at its option, control any legal proceedings that arise out of such claims.

VACANCY AND UNOCCUPANCY. Coverage is suspended if the building is vacant for more than sixty days. A building under construction, however, is not considered vacant. Permission is granted for unoccupancy. Thus, coverage under the businessowners policy is broader than many other property contracts in that there is no occupancy requirement.

Deductible Clause. This policy has no deductible clause applicable to loss of income, but it does have a $100 flat deductible applying to buildings and personal property. The deductible applies separately to: (1) each building, including the personal property there; (2) personal property in each building if the policy does not cover the building; and (3) personal property in the open. The aggregate deductible applicable to any one occurrence cannot exceed $1,000.

Besides the flat deductible, a special $250 deductible applies to crime losses if those options are chosen. This deductible is a replacement for and not in addition to the $100 deductible.

Optional Coverages There are few optional coverages available. All of the options are self-contained in the policy form except the earthquake coverage. It is on a separate form that must be added to the policy by endorsement.

Employee Dishonesty. Fidelity insurance is provided in this option. The basic limit is $5,000 per occurrence and it cannot be raised. Covered property under this provision includes money and other personal property lost through dishonest acts of the insured's employees subject to several conditions.

No dishonest act of a partner, officer, or director is covered. Replacement cost at the time of loss is the basis for recovery for all property except securities, which may be valued at their market value at the time of such settlement. Upon discovery by any executive of a dishonest act by an employee, coverage on that employee is deemed cancelled. A series of dishonest acts by an employee or a group of employees acting together is considered one occurrence. If more than one insured is covered, the limit of liability is no greater than if only one insured was covered. Losses are subject to a twelve-month discovery period after the policy is terminated, and the limit of liability is not cumulative from year to year.

Exterior Signs. Coverage for this item is for direct physical loss except for wear and tear, latent defect, corrosion or rust, or mechanical breakdown. Owned signs as well as those in the insured's care, custody, and control are covered for the amount of protection indicated on the declarations page. The exterior sign coverage is broad "all-risks" protection.

Exterior Grade Floor Glass. The same perils insured against in the exterior sign option also are covered in this option. Protection under this item is slightly broader than normal plate glass insurance. Exterior grade floor and basement glass, plus encasing frames and all lettering or ornamentation thereon are covered, as is the cost of boarding up, removing, and replacing obstructions, and installing temporary plates. No separate limit applies to the glass coverage as the insured is supposed to include its cost in the building value if the building is owned or in the personal property coverage if the insured is a tenant.

Burglary and Robbery. This option is not needed in the special policy because it is already provided. However, it is available for the standard form. Coverage under the option is divided into three sections: (1) personal property other than money and securities; (2) money and securities on premises; and (3) money and securities off premises.

Personal property other than money and securities is covered for an amount equal to 25 percent of the personal property coverage. Inside the premises protection for money and securities is $5,000 and outside coverage is $2,000. The standard definitions for burglary and robbery apply as do seven exclusions and two limitations.

Specifically excluded are losses from employee dishonesty, fraudulent scheme or tricks, fire, consequential loss, and mysterious disappearance or disclosure of shortage by inventory. Property excluded consists of accounts, deeds, manuscripts, and household and personal effects in the living quarters of the insured or executive of the insured. This provision is inserted because coverage is provided away from the premises.

As is common with crime insurance, there are limits on recovery for furs and jewelry. Furs and fur garments are restricted to coverage of $1,000 per occurrence as are jewelry and watches. However, no such restriction applies to jewelry and watches valued at less than $25 per item. This limitation is like the one in the commercial property form.

Boiler Pressure Vessels and Air Conditioning Equipment. This option provides the insured with boiler and machinery insurance. Coverage is for loss from an accident to an insured object owned by, leased to, or operated under the control of the insured. An accident is defined as sudden or accidental breakdown, but does not include depletion, corrosion, wear and tear, leakage of any valve, furnace explosion, functioning of any safety device, or breakdown of any vacuum tube, gas tube, or EDP equipment.

Under boiler and pressure vessels coverage, "object" means any steam heating or hot water heating boiler, any condensate-return tank or expansion tank used with a steam heating boiler, any hot water heater, any other fired or unfired vessel used for maintenance or service of premises, piping used in connection with steam boilers which contain steam or condensate, and any feedwater piping between any steam heating boiler.

With respect to air conditioning, "object" means any air conditioning unit with a capacity between 60,000 and 600,000 BTU/hour. In addition, most of the parts associated with such a unit are included as part of the object definition.

As is usual in boiler and machinery insurance, the insurer has the right but not the obligation to inspect any insured object, and if a dangerous condition is found, coverage can be immediately suspended.

Earthquake Assumption. The term *earthquake* is not defined in this endorsement but loss from fire, explosion, flood, tidal wave, and nuclear radiation and contamination are excluded. Fire and explosion are covered under the basic coverage. Also, all exterior grade floor and basement glass is excluded.

A sizable deductible applies in the earthquake endorsement. As a minimum, a deductible equal to 2 percent of the limit of liability applies to the earthquake coverage. If $100,000 of personal property is insured, then for earthquake, a $2,000 deductible applies. In most western states the minimum deductible is 5 percent and can be as high as 15 percent. The deductible applies separately to buildings, personal property, and, if insured, outdoor signs. It does not apply to coverage for loss of income.

Special Form—Property Covered The special form provides coverage on all "all-risks" basis for direct physical losses to the same types of property covered by the standard form. Both buildings and personal property are insured on a replacement cost basis. Debris removal, automatic increase in insurance for buildings, and seasonal adjustments for personal property are automatically included in the contract. Also, the loss of income coverage is identical to the standard form except that it is "all-risks" coverage.

Unlike the standard form, money and securities are insured in the special form. Limits are $10,000 on the premises and while inside a bank or savings institution and $2,000 off the premises.

Property Not Covered. Since money and securities are covered, only three groups of items are excluded as compared to four in the standard form. Exterior signs, growing crops and lawns, aircraft, automobiles, motortrucks, other vehicles subject to motor vehicle registration, and watercraft while afloat are not insured.

Limitations on Property. The special form has the same limitation on valuable papers as the standard form. In addition, it restricts coverage on the following items except when the standard form perils occur:

1. Glass. Glass which is a part of the building is insured for only $50 per pane and $250 per occurrence. Glass breakage caused by vandalism is not covered, so one may still wish to purchase the glass option.
2. Glassware. Fragile articles (except for bottles or similar containers of property held for sale and photographic and scientific instruments) are not insured against breakage.
3. Furs and Jewelry. Furs are insured for only $1,000 per any one occurrence. The same is true for jewelry, watches, precious stones, and metals. This latter limitation does not apply to jewelry and watches valued at $25 or less per item.

Perils Not Covered. Because the special form is an "all-risks" contract, it contains numerous exclusions of perils. This pattern has been seen throughout this text, and the businessowners special form is no exception. The form lists sixteen categories of excluded perils, and several categories have multiple parts.

Some excluded perils are: enforcement of building codes, and spoilage due to either damage to off-site power equipment or riot or V&MM anywhere. This is the same wording as in other "all-risks" property contracts. Damage done by artificially generated electrical currents and dishonest acts of employees also are not insured. Unless due diligence has been exercised, leakage or overflow of plumbing, heating, or air conditioning systems caused by freezing is excluded while the premises are vacant or unoccupied. The standard "all-risks" exclusions of wear and tear, inherent vice, latent defect, mechanical breakdown of machines, faulty design or workmanship, rust, dry rot, dampness or dryness, smog, birds, vermin, insects, and animals also are found in the special form.

The boiler explosion peril is not insured. Damage done both by and to boilers is excluded. Explosion of hot water boilers is covered, but other losses to hot water boilers originating within the boilers is not covered. Property left in the open is not covered for loss due to rain, snow, or sleet. However, exterior damage to the building does not have to occur before loss to the interior is covered. This loss can come from rain, snow, dust, or falling objects. The coverage of the policy is, in this respect, like the homeowners and not the other commercial "all-risks" contracts. Any loss due to settling, shrinking, cracking of driveways, sidewalks, swimming pools, pavements, foundations, walls, floors, roofs, or ceilings is not covered. Only collapse of these items is insured.

The usual earth movement and broad water exclusions are contained in the form, as are the exclusions of mysterious disappearance, inventory shortage, and loss due to voluntary parting with title or possession of property by the insured because of fraudulent schemes.

Finally, the last two exclusions are for loss due to delay or loss of market and to property sold under a conditional sale, trust agreement, installment payment, or other deferred payment plan after delivery of the property to customers.

Farmowners-Ranchowners (FR) Program

Farm and ranchowners may purchase a package policy that is flexible enough to meet the unique needs of this class. The following discussion is based on the farmowners-ranchowners program of the Insurance Services Office. This program is widely used and most independently filed programs are very similar. The designation "FR" will be used to stand for this program and the forms used in it.

The manual defines farm property to consist of dwellings, barns, granaries, outbuildings, and other structures used in connection therewith, and their contents, livestock, hay and grain in stacks, farm machinery and equipment; situated on land used for poultry, truck, fruit, livestock, dairy, or other farming purposes, whether located inside or outside the corporate limits of cities, towns, or villages. The FR policy is a multiple-line combination policy designed to meet the personal and commercial needs of ranchowners and farmowners. In this program, the insured can choose from one of several forms to cover the farm dwelling and then add various other forms to cover farm equipment and buildings. As was the case with the analysis of the businessowners policy, liability coverage is not discussed in this book. Similarly, the portion of the policies pertaining to the dwelling is only briefly examined, since it is very similar to the homeowners policies discussed in CPCU 2.

Basic Coverages and Minimum Limits of Liability Before any discussion is given on eligibility and content of the various forms, an overview of the FR program is desirable. Such an outline is provided in Table 15-3 and the explanation that follows.

The three categories of dwellings are usually defined in the rating jurisdiction's rate book. The numbers denote quality, with 1 the highest quality and 3 the poorest. Often type 1 has thermostatically controlled central heating and indoor plumbing. Type 3 is a residual category. Actually there are three forms available to insure the dwelling, and these are shown in Table 15-4. These three forms are very similar to the HO-1, 2, and 4.

Coverages D, E, and F in Table 15-3 are the main subjects of this analysis and represent buildings and personal property used in the operation of the farm. In terms of forms, Coverage D is FR-6, Coverage E is FR-7, Coverage F is FR-8, Coverages G and H are FR-9. Note 3 of Table 15-3 indicates that FR-8 can be used for improvements and betterments. The FR program has no FR-3 in most states, and there is no FR-5.

Eligibility In the FR program, eligibility requirements are determined for each form. Consequently, our examination will follow that format.

FR-1 and FR-2 Requirements. These two forms can be written on an owner-occupied farm or ranch. In addition, if the premises is owned by the insured but not occupied by the insured, it may qualify under certain conditions. First, it must be tenant operated under the owner's direct or contract management. Secondly, the dwelling must be exclusively used for residential purposes (office, professional, private school, or studio occupancy excepted). For both these cases, no more than two families with not more than two roomers or boarders per family can occupy the main dwelling. A third eligible insured under these two forms is a ranch or farm owned by a corporation financially controlled by the named insured or by the named insured together with other individuals included within the policy definition of insured.

Table 15-3

Basic Limits of Liability*

The basic limits of liability required under the FR Policy are as follows:

Section I Coverages	Owner Occupant	Owner Nonoccupant Minimum Limits	Tenant Minimum Limits
A. Dwelling			
Type 1	$12,000	$12,000	—
Type 2	10,000	10,000	—
Type 3	8,000	8,000	—
B. Unscheduled Personal Property (Household)	50% of Limit on Dwelling (Coverage A)	—	Minimum Limit Type 1 $6,000 Type 2 5,000 Type 3 4,000
C. Additional Living Expense	10% of Limit on Dwelling (Coverage A)	10% of Coverage A	10% of Coverage B
D. Farm Personal Property (Scheduled)	—	$10,000 [1]	$10,000 [2]
E. Farm Personal Property (Blanket) 80% Coinsurance	$15,000	$15,000 [1]	$15,000 [2]
F. Barns, Buildings, Structures, and Additional Dwellings (Scheduled)	—	$10,000 [1]	— [3]
Section II Coverages		**Minimum Limits**	
G. Personal Liability		$25,000 Each Occurrence	
H. Medical Payments to Others		$ 500 Each Person $25,000 Each Accident	

1. If Coverage E is written for the minimum limit of $15,000, Coverage D or Coverage F may be written for less than the minimum limit of $10,000. If Coverage E is not written, either Coverage D or Coverage F must be written for the minimum limit of $10,000 and the other may be written for less than the $10,000 minimum limit.

2. If Coverage E is written for the minimum limit of $15,000, Coverage D may be written for less than the minimum limit of $10,000. If Coverage E is not written, Coverage D must be written for a minimum limit of $10,000.

3. Insurance under Form FR-8 covers on improvements and betterments as defined, and on such structures as may be legally removed by the Named Insured—Tenant.

*Reprinted from *Farmowners-Ranchowners Manual*, Insurance Services Office.

Table 15-4

Dwelling Forms

Form	Property Insured	Perils Insured Against
FR-1 Basic	Dwelling and contents	Fire, lightning, EC, V&MM, theft
FR-2 Broad Form	Dwelling and contents	FR-1 perils plus broad form perils
FR-4 Contents Broad Form	Contents	Same as FR-2

FR-4 Requirements. Tenants use this form. The manual states that a "tenant (non-owner) of a farm or ranch dwelling who farms on a full-time basis can use this form." However, the dwelling premises occupied by the tenant must be used exclusively for residential purposes (with the same exception as FR-1 and FR-2). Also, there can be only one additional family in the dwelling and no more than two boarders or roomers.

Additional Eligible Interests. In this category there are six different interests. Among these six categories, the interests of co-owners, executors, administrators, trustees, and beneficiaries can be included.

A co-owner either occupying or not occupying a dwelling on the premises and not engaged in the farm's operation, as well as one who is engaged in its operation but not occupying a dwelling, are eligible. Co-owners occupying separate dwellings on the premises and engaged in the operation of the farm also are eligible. In addition, a partnership operation of the farm (other than co-owner situation) with one partner not occupying a dwelling on the farm premises or both partners operating and occupying separate dwelling premises on the farm premises is eligible.

Ineligible Interests. There are three different categories of farms or ranches that are not eligible for the FR policy. These categories include farms or ranches: (1) that are vacant, (2) whose principal business is raising and using horses for racing or show purposes, or (3) whose purpose is to supply commodities for manufacturing or processing by the insured for sale to others. The last category includes creameries, dairies, farms operating freezing or dehydrating plants and poultry factories. The word *processing* is not defined in the manual, but it does state that processing, "does not apply to the slaughtering and dressing of livestock or to such operations as bunching of vegetables or crating of berries." Finally, mobile homes, trailer homes, house trailers, or their contents cannot be insured under Coverage A or B of forms FR-1, FR-2, or FR-4. However, they may be written under Coverage D (FR-6) or F (FR-8).

Content of Forms Used to Insure Farm Personal Property There are two basic forms used to insure farm personal property. These forms are analyzed in the following discussion.

In the FR policy, it is only mandatory to insure farm personal property if the insured is a tenant of the farm. An owner, whether occupying the farm or not, must purchase one or more of the farm property forms—FR-6, FR-7, or FR-8. Thus, if the FR-8 is purchased by a farmowner, farm personal property coverage would be optional.

As a general rule when coverage is required, a minimum of $10,000 of insurance must be bought if the scheduled form is used, and $15,000 if the unscheduled (blanket) form is used. Coverage D is the scheduled form and Coverage E the unscheduled form.

In Figure 15-1, a comparison is made between FR-6 and FR-7. Explanation is given concerning the scheduled form (FR-6) and only the differences for FR-7 are noted.

Personal Property Classes. The classes given are from the unscheduled farm personal property form. Under the scheduled form, one can insure any farm personal property that the underwriter is willing to accept, since the form has blank spaces available to schedule unusual property.

LIVESTOCK. The information on livestock and the other categories in Figure 15-1 is largely self-explanatory. With respect to livestock, an exception is the limit in FR-6 of the lesser of: (1) $1,000 per animal, or (2) 120 percent of the average limit per animal applicable to the class. If an insured has twenty hogs with a total limit of $2,000, not more than $120 ($2,000/20 = $100 × 1.20 = $120) could be collected on the loss of any one hog.

FARM MACHINERY, VEHICLES, AND EQUIPMENT. One potential problem in this coverage arises in the unscheduled form. Newly acquired, replacement, and borrowed machinery all are automatically insured on a blanket basis. However, their inclusion could affect the farmer's insurance-to-value requirements. A coinsurance penalty could apply to both farm machinery and other farm personal property damaged in the same accident. The form includes an 80 percent coinsurance clause.

GRAIN AND HAY. Off-premises coverage for form FR-6 is limited to 100 miles, while there is no such limitation in FR-7. This difference is not in the livestock and machinery coverage as both forms provide similar protection in those cases. However, neither form provides

Figure 15-1

Comparison Chart—Coverage D (Scheduled) and Coverage E (Unscheduled) Farm Personal Property*

This chart highlights differences between the two Farmowners forms as they relate to various aspects of farm personal property coverage. It is important to remember that under Coverage D property may be scheduled individually or as a class: $1,000 on a golden palomino described as . . ., or $1,000 on horses and mules—(or both)—for example. There is frequently a difference in coverage for scheduled items and scheduled classes.

LIVESTOCK:

	FORM FR-6	FORM FR-7
	Not defined. Scheduled as to class—horses and mules, dairy cattle, feeder cattle, swine, etc.	Defined as cattle, sheep, swine, goats, horses, mules and donkeys.
	Any animal acceptable to the underwriter may be scheduled individually.	Does not cover race horses, show horses, show ponies or any other animal not listed in "livestock" definition.
Limit:	Actual cash value, but not more than:	Actual cash value, but not more than Coverage E limit, or: $1,000 each animal ($500 if under one year old).
	Limit scheduled for individual animals —or	
	Limit scheduled for class, but not more than: the lesser of $1,000 each animal, or up to 120% of the average of limit applicable to class ÷ number of animals in the class. (Each animal under one year old is counted as one half.)	

Off Premises: — Coverage applies off premises or on. But insurance does not apply to animals in transit by common carrier, in slaughter houses, in packing plants, in public stock-yards, sales barns or sales yards. — Same. Same.

FARM MACHINERY, VEHICLES & EQUIPMENT:

Includes: — If scheduled as a class: "machinery, vehicles, tools and equipment of all kinds ...usual and incidental to the operation of a farm." — Blanket coverage of all property "usual and incidental," etc.

Excludes: — Fences, windmills, wind chargers and their towers; — Same.

Automobiles, trucks, motorcycles, snow-mobiles, mobile homes, house trailers. vehicles primarily designed for and used on roads (except wagons and trailers designed for and used on the farm), water-craft, aircraft; — Same.

Equipment, tires and parts of any of the foregoing; — Same.

Bulk milk tanks, bulk feed tanks, barn cleaners, pasteurizers, boilers or any permanent fixtures attached to or within buildings; — Same.

Portable buildings or other structures; — Same.

Continued on next page

	FORM FR-6	FORM FR-7
	"Property which is separately described and specifically insured by this or any other insurance";	Same
	Brooders;	All contents of poultry buildings.
	Tractors, combines, threshing machines, corn pickers, hay balers, harvesters, peanut diggers, potato diggers and pickers, cotton pickers, crop dusters and sawmill equipment. (The foregoing items may be individually scheduled and covered in that manner.)	No similar exclusion.
	Manufactured gas, liquified petroleum gas, gasoline and their containers.	No similar exclusion.
Limits:	If scheduled individually, individual limit applies.	Limit applicable to blanket Coverage E.
	If scheduled as a class, class limit applies, but not more than $1,000 on any one piece of machinery or equipment.	No internal, per article limit.
Off Premises:	Coverage applies up to 100 miles.	Same.
	* If scheduled as a class, cover limited to 25% of on premises amount.	Limits are same on or off premises.
	If scheduled as a class, no coverage off premises in manufacturing plants, in transit by common carrier, in public sales barns or yards or in warehouses.	No similar exclusion.

Newly Acquired Machinery, Vehicles & Equipment:	If similar items (tractors, combines, etc.) are scheduled, there is automatic coverage up to $5,000 for 30 days (unless policy expires first). If scheduled as a class, automatic coverage without increase in class limit.	Automatic coverage under blanket Coverage E. Could jeopardize compliance with coinsurance clause.
Replacement Machinery, Vehicles & Equipment:	Automatic coverage for replacement of scheduled *unit*. Subject to same limit as for old unit *plus* $5,000. Extra $5,000 ceases after 30 days (unless policy expires first). If scheduled as a class, automatic coverage, but no increase in limit.	Automatic coverage but watch coinsurance clause if values increase.
Borrowed Machinery, etc.:	May be scheduled as a class or as individual items. Or, if owned property is scheduled as a class, borrowed property is included as "usual and incidental to the operation of a farm."	Covered as unscheduled farm personal property. But watch coinsurance clause.
GRAIN AND HAY: "Grain" includes:	Threshed seeds, threshed beans, silage, ground feed, manufactured and compounded stock foods.	Same, plus herbicides, pesticides and fertilizers.
Limit:	As scheduled.	Blanket Coverage E.
Condition:	Covers property in buildings or in sacks, wagons or trucks. (See "Crops in Open.")	Excludes crops in the open. (See "Crops in Open" and "Unharvested Grain.")
Excludes:	Grain under government loan.	No similar exclusion.

Continued on next page

	FORM FR-6	FORM FR-7
Off Premises:	Coverage extends to 100 miles of insured premises. Limited to 10% of on premises amount. Excludes grain, etc., in manufacturing plants, public elevators, warehouses, seed houses and drying plants. Excludes grain, etc., in transit by common carrier or in public sales barns or yards.	No mileage limitation. No similar limitation. Same: No similar exclusion.
Unharvested Grain:	No coverage.	Fire insurance only on unharvested grain crops, flax and soy beans. Limited to 10% of Coverage E amount. Not applicable in all states.
Crops in Open:	Fire coverage only for grain in stacks, shocks, swaths or piles.	Same, but limited to 10% of Coverage E.
"Hay" Includes:	Hay, straw and fodder. Hay in barns and hay in stacks must be scheduled as separate items.	Same. Blanket coverage with other unscheduled farm personal property.
Limits:	Hay, etc., in barns, as scheduled. Hay, etc., in stacks, windrows and bales: $1,000 per stack of hay, $500 per stack of straw or fodder. All covered perils except windstorm and hail apply. Scheduled limit applies.	Limit applicable to Blanket Coverage E. Same limits per stack. Fire cover only.
Off Premises:	Extends to property within 100 miles. Covers up to 10% of scheduled limit.	10% of Coverage E. No mileage limitation. No special limitation.

	Excludes property in manufacturing plants, public elevators, warehouses, seed houses and drying plants.	Same.
	Excludes property in transit by common carrier or in public sales barns or yards.	No similar exclusion.
OTHER PROPERTY:		
Household Goods:	May be scheduled.	Not covered.
Poultry:	May be scheduled.	Not covered.
Portable Buildings:	May be scheduled.	Not covered. May be scheduled in Form FR-8 (farm buildings).
Animals other than Livestock:	Only if scheduled.†	Not covered.
Tobacco, Cotton, Vegetables. Root Crops, Bulbs & Fruit:	Only if scheduled.†	Not covered.
Race Horses:	Only if scheduled.†	Not covered.
Nursery Stock:	Only if scheduled.†	Not covered.
Farm Records:	Covers cost of blank books, etc., plus the cost of transcription.	Same.
	Covers cost of blank film, tape, etc., used in electronic data processing operations.	Same.

†Scheduling, of course, depends on the willingness of the underwriter.

*Reprinted with permission from *FC&S Bulletins,* Fire and Marine Section, The National Underwriter Company.

coverage while the grain is off-premises in manufacturing plants, warehouses, public elevators, seed houses, and drying plants.

FARM RECORDS. This category includes books of account, manuscripts, abstracts, drawings, card index systems, and other records. Also included are film, tape, drum, cell, and other magnetic recording or storage media for electronic data processing. As Figure 15-1 indicates, the standard coverage of cost of material and labor to transcribe data is available. There is no valuable papers insurance in the farmowners policy.

Perils Insured Against. While the dwelling coverage offers two different series of perils insured against (limited and broad), the farm personal property section has one set only of perils. These perils include fire, lightning, the extended coverage perils, V&MM, theft, and electrocution of livestock.

The standard definitions of fire, lightning, and extended coverage perils apply. The windstorm and hail coverage excludes losses to: (1) livestock or poultry caused in whole or in part by running into streams or ditches or against fences or other objects, or from smothering; also loss as the direct or indirect result of fright; (2) poultry, horses, mules, cattle, swine, and sheep caused by freezing or smothering in blizzards or snowstorms; and (3) hay, straw, and fodder while outside of buildings.

The usual V&MM definition applies except coverage is suspended only when the described dwelling is vacant for over thirty days. Permission is granted for the dwelling to be unoccupied.

The theft peril is defined as meaning any act of stealing or attempt thereat, but four exclusions apply. Losses that result from theft by the insured, mysterious disappearance, wrongful conversion and embezzlement, and loss discovered by taking inventory are all excluded.

Loss of insured livestock by electrocution is covered. No qualifications are given as to the meaning of the peril.

Perils Excluded. The FR farm personal property forms have several of the standard excluded perils provisions. Losses caused by the enforcement of building codes and ordinances, earth movement, volcanic eruption, flood, runoff of surface waters, and tidal wave are excluded. Spoilage due to damage to off-premises power equipment is not covered, but if the equipment damage occurs on the premises, protection is provided.

Besides these excluded perils, the fire peril is qualified in the FR-6 to exclude fire damage which results from a brooder or other heating device in a poultry house unless the heater or brooder is scheduled. Also, there is no coverage on the contents of tobacco barns while "tobacco firing" is in progress or for five days thereafter. Finally, outdoor television and radio equipment is excluded in both forms.

Policy Conditions. Form FR-6 has no coinsurance clause, but FR-7 has an 80 percent clause. The deductible provision in the dwelling coverage (FR-1, 2, or 4) applies to farm personal property. The usual deductible is $100 but may be raised to $250 to $500. Contributing insurance is allowed and an endorsement is used to show each insurer's liability. Other insurance (use of other forms, such as from the farm manual) is severely restricted. Only when written permission is obtained can other insurance be purchased. Without the written permission the farmowners coverage is suspended.

Farm Buildings The coverage for buildings other than the dwelling is provided in Coverage F (FR-8). Protection is on a scheduled basis for the perils of fire, lightning, extended coverage, and V&MM. The definitions of the perils insured against in the FR-8 are the same as in the FR-6, already discussed. However, there are not as many perils, since theft and electrocution of livestock are not insured against. Structures, such as garages, barns, cribs, silos, hog houses, henhouses, outdoor radio and television equipment, and implement sheds may be insured in this form. However, the list of structures is not limited to these. Any building an underwriter will accept can be scheduled on the form.

Property Covered. In the form, structures are divided into six different classes: (1) farm barns, buildings, and structures; (2) additional farm dwellings; (3) fences; (4) private power and light poles; (5) portable buildings and portable structures; and (6) improvements and betterments.

Farm Barns, Buildings, and Structures. When these items are scheduled, coverage applies to them and attached sheds and permanent fixtures. However, silos, whether attached to the structure or not, are not considered a part of the building. Silos must be separately scheduled and a specific premium paid on them. Included in this class are appurtenant structures normally insured in the homeowners. The dwelling coverage under the farmowners policy does not give automatic coverage on such items. Therefore, they must be scheduled on the FR-8.

Additional Farm Dwellings. This item includes building equipment, fixtures, and outdoor equipment pertaining to the service of the dwelling while such property is located on the described premises. Typically, these dwellings will be occupied by employees of the insured but owned by the insured. Often they may be mobile homes or house trailers.

Included in the definition of additional dwellings, barns, and structures are building materials and supplies intended for use in their construction, alteration, or repair. If these materials are to be used with a noninsured structure, there is no coverage.

FENCES. When scheduled on the form, this item includes fences, corrals, pens, chutes, and feed racks on the described premises, but it does not include field or pasture fences. It is the insurer's intent to cover fences around and used with insured buildings. In many cases, the fences are attached to the insured structures.

When fences are covered, the insurance company requires 100 percent insurance to value. The form states, "The Company shall not be liable for a greater portion of any loss than the amount of insurance applying to this coverage bears to the total value of such property at the time of the loss."

PRIVATE POWER AND LIGHT POLES. In FR-8, private power and light poles may be insured. When this is done, outdoor wiring and attachments also are covered. Attachments are defined as including switch boxes, fuse boxes, and other electrical equipment mounted on the poles.

PORTABLE BUILDINGS AND PORTABLE STRUCTURES. As often written, this clause insures on a blanket basis. When this is done, a 100 percent insurance-to-value requirement exists, and consequently, great care should be taken to include all items. As an alternative, those buildings and structures which are capable of separate and distinct identification may be scheduled to avoid having to insure all the items.

These pieces of property may also be insured in FR-6, if the insured wishes. The rate is about the same, and more perils are insured.

IMPROVEMENTS AND BETTERMENTS. This coverage is the standard for such exposures. It is used in the FR program by an insured tenant to protect the insured's interest in such improvements and betterments.

Exclusions and Conditions. The exclusions and conditions in FR-8 are the same as those in FR-6. Also, the deductible in the dwelling coverage (FR-1, 2, and 4) applies to FR-8.

Endorsements to the Farmowners and Ranchowners Policy
There are numerous endorsements available under this program. Some of them are designed just for the FR program and others are homeowners endorsements that can be used because they pertain to dwelling coverage. The present analysis is basically concerned with farm property protection and not the dwelling.

Earthquake. The perils insured against can be extended to cover earthquake. The policy limits are not affected by the endorsement, and the standard definition of earthquake is used.

A 2 percent deductible, subject to a minimum of $250, applies separately to each building and each item of scheduled personal property.

Flood and tidal wave losses are excluded, as is loss to exterior masonry veneer. Stucco is not considered masonry veneer.

Replacement Cost Endorsement. This endorsement may be attached to the dwelling, barns, buildings, structures, and additional dwellings in FR-8. The property insured under FR-8 must be of type 1 construction (superior). Roof surfacing, outdoor radio and television antennas and aerials, carpeting, awnings, domestic appliances, and outdoor equipment are excluded from replacement cost protection. An 80 percent coinsurance clause is mandatory.

Money and Securities. Coverage for money and securities is provided under the dwelling forms, but since they have business uses, they are discussed here also. Limits for these types of property may be increased. Basic coverage is $100 on money and $500 on securities. The limits may be raised to $500 on money and $1,000 on securities.

Peak Season. In FR-7, blanket farm personal property, a peak season endorsement may be attached to cover increased exposures after the harvest and before the crop is sold.

Accidental Shooting and Drowning. The perils insured against may be extended to cover accidental shooting and drowning of livestock other than poultry. The shooting cannot be by the insured, the insured's family, employee, or tenants. Swine under the age of thirty days are not covered. When this endorsement is attached, the broad water exclusion in FR-6 and FR-7 does not apply to loss of these animals by drowning.

Extra Expense. When damage occurs to property insured under Coverages D, E, or F (FR-6, 7, and 8) or to a building or structure containing property insured in these forms, extra expense insurance may be purchased. The limit is an aggregate amount, and there is no monthly limit.

Glass. The homeowners scheduled glass endorsement amounts to plate glass insurance. Usually this endorsement is used on the dwelling, but in big commercial cattle farms, it might be used to insure glass in show areas.

Inflation Guard. Coverages A, B, C and barns, buildings, structures, and additional dwellings in FR-8 may be modified with this endorsement. Normally, the policy limits are increased 1.5 percent per quarter.

Supplemental Floater. Inland marine coverages on farm personal property, agricultural machinery, livestock, and other property may be purchased. This coverage is subject to the rules and forms of the insurance company providing the protection. The insured must be sure not to violate any of the rules of the FR program when this coverage is purchased and should notify the insurer of its purchase.

The Electronic Data Processing Exposure

The last combination policy that will be examined is the electronic data processing (EDP) policy. It is often a single-line policy in that only direct and indirect property coverages are provided, but it can be multiple-line, since it sometimes has an errors and omissions liability form attached. However, the errors and omissions policy is usually separate.

The EDP policy is designed to meet the needs of insureds who own or lease EDP equipment. These machines are very valuable, must be maintained in a closely controlled environment, and can be easily damaged. In addition, standard property policies really do not meet the needs of insuring EDP equipment. Consequently, a special policy has evolved to cover the exposure. Actually there is no standard EDP policy—each insurer designs its own. Since there is no standard form, this discussion will review some representative approaches to EDP coverage but not all EDP policies are written like those analyzed here.

Typically, the EDP policy will contain coverage on the data processing equipment. Such equipment includes computers, card and tape readers, high speed printers, and card and tape coding devices. Of course, in larger installations there would be many kinds of tape drives, disc pacs, and even some graphing and charting devices.

Media containing data also can be quite valuable. The term *media* refers to the computer tapes, discs, and cards that are used to communicate with the computer. All of a firm's computer programs are usually contained on these media, as are its data files. Destruction of media would create a huge loss with respect to both direct and indirect losses. In terms of direct losses, it would take many people many hours just to recode the data. If original computer programs were destroyed, it could take months to bring the EDP operation back on line. Actually, in terms of indirect losses, the computer media are usually more important than the computer equipment. Often, replacement equipment can be obtained quickly from manufacturers or equipment leasing firms; also, it is very common for two or more large users of EDP equipment to have mutual aid agreements, whereby one organization can use the equipment of another organization in case of emergency; however, programs unique to the insured must be rewritten, and that takes time.

Since it may take time to restore operations or because it will be expensive to maintain operations, EDP policies contain extra expense protection and frequently business interruption coverage. The standard fire business interruption policy gives only thirty days coverage for losses resulting from damage to EDP equipment. Also, in the EDP policy "all-risks" coverage is provided and the exclusions are few.

In addition to these coverages, valuable papers and accounts receivable endorsements are available with the EDP policy. These items could be purchased separately from the EDP policy, but because of its nature its availability in the EDP policy is logical.

Finally, many insureds have need for an additional policy closely related to the EDP property coverage. This policy is the data processing errors and omissions policy. It is a liability policy that protects insureds who do data processing for others. Both firms who perform service work as a primary occupation and those that do it to utilize slack computer time need the coverage. Usually, it is the firm for which contract data processing is a sideline which has the greatest problem in this area, since it often does not realize that the liability exposure exists. Consequently, protection is not obtained until after the first claim is filed. There is a Minnesota case that follows this pattern and the plaintiff was awarded $480,000.[3] In a similar situation, a $160,000 claim was filed.[4] As can be seen, there is need for this special liability policy, but details of the coverage are beyond the scope of this text on property insurance.

Content of the EDP Policy   The EDP policy is divided in the same manner as the exposures just reviewed. Not all policies cover all the exposures, and the errors and omissions coverage is often a separate policy. However, this discussion will review all property coverages.

General Conditions and Exclusions.[5]   Each separate coverage has its own endorsement. Each endorsement includes terms and conditions particular to it. However, there is a set of conditions and exclusions that apply to all coverages, and these items are analyzed herein. It should be noted that these are common conditions and exclusions, but they are not necessarily found in all policies.

The territorial limit of the policy is the forty-eight contiguous states of the U.S., Canada, and the District of Columbia. When the insured property is in imminent danger of loss, damage or expense, coverage will follow it while it is moved to a place of safety and during the return trip to the insured's premises. Written notice of its removal must be given the insurer within ten days of its removal. Often, but not always, an other insurance clause is found in the conditions section. It states that the EDP policy is excess over other valid and collectible insurance. Situations where other insurance would apply are: (1) when the equipment is leased and the lessor's insurance will pay, or (2) where other property insurance carried by the insured would pay. For example, the insured's fire insurance policy would cover EDP equipment.

Other common provisions are a sue and labor clause like that found in marine contracts, a ten-day cancellation clause, an appraisal clause, a loss clause (losses do not reduce the policy limits), proof of loss to be given within ninety days, and all suits against the insurer to be brought within twelve months. There is a debris removal clause in the policy, but it does not affect the policy limits nor is there any restriction on how much is spent on debris removal. The policy also contains assignment, subrogation, and examination under oath clauses.

In the conditions section there are two standard exclusions, war and nuclear reaction and contamination. One policy also has the standard flood, surface water, and water below the surface exclusion. This exclusion would make that policy undesirable, since one of the most attractive features of the EDP policy is its broad "all-risks" coverage.

Data Processing Equipment. Coverage for this property is on a scheduled basis, and the equipment and its component parts may be insured. The equipment may be owned, leased, or under the control of the insured, but it must be on the schedule. There are three types of property specifically excluded: (1) accounts, bills, evidences of debt, valuable papers, records, abstracts, deeds, and manuscripts (these may be insured in another section of the policy); (2) property rented or leased to others while away from the premises of the insured; and (3) active data processing media. This last item is defined as "all forms of converted data and/or program and/or instruction vehicles employed in the insured's data processing operation." This type of property may be insured in the EDP media section of the policy.

The coverage is for all risks of direct physical loss except:

1. inherent vice, wear, tear, gradual deterioration, or depreciation;
2. dishonest act of insured or an officer, director, or trustee;
3. delay or loss of market;
4. actual work upon the covered property, unless fire or explosion ensues, and then only the damage caused by the fire or explosion;
5. dryness or dampness of atmosphere, extremes of temperature, corrosion, or rust unless directly resulting from physical damage to the data processing system's air conditioning facilities caused by an insured peril;
6. damage due to mechanical failure, faulty construction, error in design, unless fire or explosion ensue and then only the fire and explosion loss is covered; and
7. short circuit, blow-out, or other electrical disturbance, other than lightning, within apparatus, unless fire or explosion ensue and then only the fire or explosion loss is insured.

In some policies, these last three perils are covered, but subject to a $10,000 deductible. All of the exclusions in the conditions section apply, but this protection is still among the broadest available with respect to perils insured against.

Typically, the policy is written on an 80, 90, or 100 percent coinsurance basis when coverage is purchased on an ACV basis. When replacement cost coverage is purchased, a 100 percent coinsurance clause is often mandatory. Deductibles are available and may range up to $100,000 on larger EDP installations.

The equipment coverage includes a provision which states that the insured must file with the insurer a copy of any lease or rental agreement pertaining to the property insured under the policy insofar as it concerns the lessor's liability for loss or damage to the insured property, and coverage afforded under the policy will be only for the difference in conditions between those contained in the lease or rental agreement and the terms of the insuring agreement. The insured agrees to give the company thirty days notice of any alteration, cancellation or termination of the lease or rental agreement pertaining to the lessor's liability. This provision means that if the lessor is responsible for fire and EC losses, the EDP policy will not pay for fire and EC loss, but if a flood loss occurred, it would pay.

This provision is important to the underwriter. If the underwriter knows most of the physical damage will be paid by the lessor, a much lower rate can be charged. If the lease agreement changes and the underwriter does not know it, the insurer may be providing primary coverage on all perils but only charging a rate based on a much smaller exposure.

In one case, a business firm did not purchase an EDP policy because they believed the lessor was responsible for physical loss to the equipment. The lessor was liable, but only for fire and EC and certain listed perils. A V&MM loss occurred and V&MM was not one of the listed perils—the lessee had no V&MM coverage.[6] If an EDP policy had been in force, it would have paid.

Data Processing Media. In this coverage the active data processing media owned by the insured or for which the insured is responsible is protected. The term "active data processing media" is defined as "all forms of converted data and/or program and/or instruction vehicles employed in the insured's data processing operations, except all such unused property." In addition to this definition, the insured may, by schedule, delete any data processing media for which insurance protection is not wanted. Converted data means data on a punched card, tape, or disc. If data from an accounts receivable voucher is key punched onto a card, the card is converted data. The voucher is not. Excluded from this term are accounts, bills, valuable papers, and similar property, and any data processing media which cannot be replaced with other of like kind and quality. In some policies, the insured is required to maintain in a fireproof safe or vault in another building a separate copy of each master program or instruction tape insured. However, even this procedure may fail if the second copy is on tape and the climate control in the second location is poor. In one such situation the original tape was damaged, and when the copy was taken from its off-site location, it was severely damaged due to lack of temperature and humidity control.

The insured has two options from which to determine the basis of recovery. Valuation can be either on an actual reproduction cost basis or on a valued basis. When the valued approach is taken, a given value is placed on each item, $100 per reel of tape or $.10 per punch card. If five reels are damaged, the insured receives $500 regardless of reproduction cost.

In the media section there is no coinsurance clause, so the insured does not have to insure to value. With regard to deductibles, the insured can choose any reasonable deductible amount. The perils excluded in the media section are the same as in the equipment section, and, of course, coverage is "all-risks."

Extra Expense. Since the insured will probably want to maintain operations if the EDP equipment is damaged, extra expense coverage is provided in the policy on an optional basis. The term "extra expense" is defined as "the excess (if any) of the total cost during the period of restoration of the operation of the business over and above the total cost of such operation that would *normally* have been incurred during the same time period had no loss occurred; the cost in each case to include expense of using other property or facilities of other concerns or other necessary emergency expenses." The term "normal" means, "the condition that would have existed had no loss occurred."

Protection is on an "all-risks" basis. Direct loss to the EDP equipment or media or to the climate control system causes the extra expense coverage to become operable.

The extra expense coverage has several additional exclusions which are not found in the media or equipment coverage. All the exclusions of the media and equipment coverage are included except the one pertaining to the air conditioning system. In addition, there are exclusions for loss resulting from: (1) enforcement of building laws, (2) suspension, lapse or cancellation of leases, (3) on-site strikes, and (4) errors in programming. Also excluded are bills, valuable papers, and similar property.

Coverage is on an actual loss sustained basis, and the time period of recovery is limited to that required with the exercise of due diligence and dispatch to repair, rebuild, or replace such part of said property that is destroyed or damaged. Interruption by order of civil authority resulting from damage by an insured peril to adjacent property is covered for a period not to exceed two weeks. Funds may be spent to purchase replacement equipment and media but only for the purpose of reducing the loss, and the amount payable under the policy cannot exceed the amount by which the loss is reduced.

Unlike some extra expense coverages, there is no limitation on how much of the policy limits can be spent in any one month. A deductible may be included at the option of the insured.

Valuable Papers and Records. Valuable papers insurance may be written under the EDP policy, or it can be written separately. In the EDP policy the valuable papers insured must be listed on the declaration page, and the policy defines the term to mean, "written, printed or otherwise inscribed documents and records, including books, maps, films, drawings, abstracts, deeds, mortgages and manuscripts, but it does not mean money or securities, or electronic data control tapes." This last category would be insured in the media section of the policy. The insured must own the valuable papers or be liable for them.

The coverage is for all direct physical loss except for: (1) wear and tear, (2) dishonest acts of the insured or executives and directors of the insured, (3) war and nuclear risks, (4) loss to property held as samples for delivery or sale, (5) loss due to electrical or magnetic injury, disturbance or erasure of electronic recordings, except by lightning, (6) loss resulting directly from errors or omissions in processing or copying unless fire or explosion ensues, and (7) loss to scheduled property that cannot be replaced with other of like kind and quality.

Recovery cannot exceed the lesser of the actual cash value of the property at time of loss or the cost to repair or replace. However, if the insured places a value by certain items on the declarations page, then that value applies.

Accounts Receivable. As was the case with valuable papers, accounts receivable insurance can be purchased in the EDP policy or separately. Coverage is for all risk of loss or damage to the records of accounts receivable subject to six exclusions: (1) war; (2) accounting errors; (3) loss proven only by inventory computation; (4) dishonest acts of insured or insured's officers, directors, or trustees; (5) loss due to electrical or magnetic injury, disturbance, or erasure of electronic recordings, except by lightning; and (6) loss due to destruction or falsification of records to conceal wrongful taking. Even with these exclusions, almost all types of loss are covered.

The amount recoverable is similar to normal accounts receivable insurance. The insurance company will pay:

1. all sums due the insured from customers, provided the insured is unable to effect collection thereof solely because of loss or damage to records of accounts receivable;

2. interest charges on any loan to offset impaired collections pending repayment of such sums made uncollectible by such loss or damage;
3. collection expense in excess of normal collection cost and made necessary because of such loss or damage; and
4. other expenses, when reasonably incurred by the insured in reestablishing records of accounts receivable following such loss.

These items represent both direct and indirect losses, and the definition of peril insured against does not require direct physical loss. It covers all risk of loss subject to certain exclusions.

In such contracts, the insured typically must maintain proper storage facilities so the probability of loss will be minimized. In the declarations the insured must state the type of receptacle (if any) in which the records are kept when the premises are not open for business. If a loss occurs when the premises are closed and the records are not in the declared receptacle, the insured cannot collect.

Business Interruption. As was stated previously, not all EDP policies have the business interruption option. One of the major advantages of purchasing business interruption insurance in an EDP policy is the broad perils insured against. While standard business interruption insurance can be purchased, it is usually a named peril contract; even if it is "all-risks," there are numerous exclusions. The EDP policy covers interruption of business as a direct result of physical loss or damage from any peril (except those excluded) to insured property owned, leased, rented or under the control of the insured.

The excluded perils and events are the same as for the extra expense endorsement. However, only the EDP equipment and media are protected. If the air conditioner is damaged and interruption occurs, recovery may not be allowed because no direct loss occurred to the insured property.

As is standard with business interruption insurance, the insured must use due diligence and dispatch to restore operations. Expenses incurred to reduce the loss are recoverable to the extent that the loss is reduced. Unlike many forms of business interruption insurance, this form is a valued form. The insured receives a stated dollar amount for each work day on which total or partial interruption occurs. Partial interruptions are settled on the basis of the amount of production lost and not down time. The term work day means, "a period of twenty-four hours and shall mean a day on which the operations of the insured are usually performed."

MULTI-COVERAGE ACCOUNT RATING

The multi-coverage account rating program is relatively new. It allows a firm to purchase an integrated program of fire, inland marine, and liability coverages, and can be made flexible enough to meet individual needs. However, it is not a manuscript policy or, for that matter, a package policy like the SMP. The fire and allied lines and boiler forms are particular to the program, but the other forms used are the regular insurance contracts offered by the insurer. Examples of such additional contracts include inland marine, liability, burglary and automobile physical damage.

The multi-coverage account program (MAP) is not available for all firms. A minimum premium of $5,000 is required, and the program is not available in all states. In some cases, the minimum premium may be $10,000 if expense modifications (primarily lower commissions) are made. Actually, this minimum premium is not a very high hurdle, since it can be a three-year premium and all lines except workers' compensation, surety, automobile, ocean marine, and accident and health are involved. Automobile coverages can be written in the MAP, but their premiums are not included in meeting minimum premium requirements. The minimum does eliminate many small mercantile establishments; however, the businessowners policy was developed especially to meet their needs.

The term *"account"* is basic to an understanding of the program, since it determines how coverages from more than one insurer can be combined. "Account" is defined as: "such insurance as is written under this program for an insured when afforded by one insurance company or two or more insurance companies under common management."[7] Exceptions to this rule include:

1. Contributing insurance for property coverages with other companies under identical forms. On the larger risk of this program, this sharing of the property exposure may be necessary.
2. Boiler and machinery or fidelity coverages with other companies when written as a combination policy in accordance with the rules of the multi-coverage account program.

An important attribute of the program is its account rating plan. Through the recognition of the specific loss characteristics, using a system of debits and credits similar to other risk modification plans, manual rates are modified to reflect the loss exposure of the insured. The details of the rating plan are beyond the scope of this chapter. For the present, it is enough to know that such plans allow superior loss exposures to obtain better rates, and vice versa.

Coverages Available

In the multi-coverage account rating plan, the insured must purchase fire and allied lines coverage on buildings and personal property in one of several forms available. There is a full range of fire and allied line coverages available, and the insured may add other forms in the areas of liability, inland marine, glass, automobile physical damage, and crime.

MAP Forms There are seventeen MAP forms from which an insured can choose. No one insured would use all of them since some are mutually exclusive. The following discussion will identify each form, and, if warranted, give a brief description of each.

General Property Form (MAP-1). Buildings, personal property, and improvements and betterments are insured in this form. The perils insured against are fire, lightning, and the extended coverage perils. It also has a number of extensions of coverage like those found in the SMP general building form. A mandatory $250 deductible is included in this form, and, in fact, applies to all fire and allied line direct property loss coverages and to boiler and machinery coverage.

Boiler and Machinery (MAP-2). The MAP has its own boiler and machinery form, which insures loss to property of the insured and property of others in the insured's care, custody, or control. If the insured does not want coverage under form MAP-2, a separate boiler and machinery policy may be attached to the MAP policy.

Institutional Form (MAP-3). In place of the MAP general property form, this form is used to insure public and institutional properties. In the MAP institutional program, optional "all-risks" coverage is available under form MAP-3B. This form is the special institutional extended coverage endorsement.

Commercial Forms (MAP-4). In the case of certain commercial personal property, this form is used to replace personal property coverage in MAP-1. Coverage can be written on a nonreporting form (MAP-4) or a reporting form (MAP-4A) basis. The perils insured against are all direct physical losses except those specifically excluded.

Office Form (MAP-5). Eligible office risks can insure their personal property on an "all-risks" basis in this form. When this form is used, it replaces personal property coverage in the MAP-1 form.

Additional Perils Insured Against. Two endorsements can be added to increase the perils insured against on a named peril basis. These are MAP-7 for V&MM and MAP-8 for sprinkler leakage. The sprinkler leakage coverage can be written on a flat or coinsurance basis.

Indirect Loss Forms. In the MAP there are three forms that can be used to insure indirect losses. These endorsements are business interruption (MAP-9), loss of rents (MAP-10), and extra expense (MAP-11). All three pay when a covered loss occurs, but boiler and machinery losses are not covered. The business interruption coverage is on a gross earnings form and the extra expense form has a monthly limitation.

Reporting Forms. There are two general reporting forms available in this program. Both are used to insure personal property in conjunction with the general property form (MAP-1). The form MAP-12 uses specific rates for each location, and form MAP-13 uses average rates for the account and is only used with loss exposures rated in accordance with the multiple location rating plan.

Clauses Restricting Recovery. There is an 80 percent coinsurance clause in MAP-1, 3, 4, 5, 6, and 7, and, if the insured desires or if the rating bureau requires, a higher percentage can be used. Forms MAP-1, 2, 3, 4, 4A, 5 and 16 contain a mandatory $250 deductible. Where allowed, higher deductibles may be used and rate credits are given for them.

CASE STUDIES IN PROPERTY EXPOSURES AND THEIR TREATMENT

As a review of the material in this text, this section provides two case studies in property risk management. Following a description of each operation is a brief analysis of that operation's property loss exposures and a discussion of ways in which these exposures might be treated. Recognize that the techniques discussed for handling each exposure are not exhaustive, since exhaustive treatment would be beyond the scope of this text.

The Sheltering Arms Case

Sheltering Arms Hospital is an 800-bed general hospital located in a mid-western metropolitan area. The hospital's main building is a ten-story fire-resistive building, adjacent to the intersection of the two major expressways in the downtown area of the city. The actual cash value of the main building is estimated at $10 million. Replacement cost is approximately $15 million.

Steam to heat the hospital buildings and for other uses is furnished by the hospital power plant, located approximately 250 feet from the main building. The power plant contains four large steam boilers with maximum operating pressure of 130 pounds per square inch. Any three of the four boilers can supply all the steam needed for the hospital. The power plant is connected to the hospital facilities by underground steam lines which pass under a public thoroughfare. The power plant also is connected to the nearby steam plant of the local public utility. Steam can be purchased at an increased cost from the utility in an emergency. The actual cash value of the hospital power plant is estimated at $300,000 and its replacement cost at $340,000. It is fire-resistive and approximately three years old. Gas and electricity are purchased from public utilities.

The hospital laundry is located in a new, fire-resistive building adjacent to the power plant. The laundry building, which is less than a year old, was constructed at a cost of $250,000.

An additional building owned by Sheltering Arms is a three-story nurses' home of ordinary masonry construction with an actual cash value of $200,000. The cost to rebuild it in its present form would be $300,000. If this building should suffer damage to the extent of 50 percent or more of its value, it would be necessary to demolish it and replace it with a fire-resistive structure to comply with present building codes. The cost of such a structure would be approximately $400,000.

A dormitory building is presently under construction. The Brick Construction Company is the general contractor, and the building is scheduled for completion in eight months. Its cost when completed is estimated to be $1 million.

Five years ago the hospital rented, under a fifteen-year lease, one floor of a nearby office building to house some of its research activities. The monthly rental for the term of the lease is $5,000. The current rental for similar facilities is $8,000 per month.

Sheltering Arms has the usual facilities of a general hospital. There are operating rooms, dietary facilities, laboratories, and a pharmacy which furnishes drugs to hospital patients and to welfare patients at the outpatient clinics. There is a complete radiology laboratory. Radioactive cobalt is used. In addition, Sheltering Arms recently leased from another hospital for its temporary use advanced equipment for treating kidney diseases.

Many of the physicians who practice at Sheltering Arms rent office space in its main building. These physicians often keep their own equipment at the hospital.

Sheltering Arms is the principal emergency hospital of the city and operates ten ambulances for emergency calls. It recently received a grant from the federal government to test the feasibility of using a helicopter for emergency evacuation of automobile accident victims. A helicopter has been purchased and a landing pad constructed on the hospital roof.

The medical histories of all patients are stored on open filing shelves in a large room on the second floor of the main building. The room contains approximately 200,000 files.

All billing records, payroll records, and purchase records are maintained by computer. The computer equipment is leased from the manufacturer. Computer tapes are stored in a room adjacent to the computer room on the first floor of the main hospital building.

The hospital operates two cafeterias in the main building. The hospital also owns three parking lots. Two of them are used for employee parking. The third is leased to a private operator and is open to the general public. A gift shop in the main building also is leased to a private operator. (The charitable immunity doctrine has recently been struck down by the courts of the state in which the hospital is located.)

Total annual income of Sheltering Arms is $10 million. Approximately half of this amount is received from the city and adjacent counties for medical services to welfare patients. The balance comes mainly from other patients. About $800,000 per year is required to pay interest and principal on the bonded indebtedness of the hospital. Sheltering Arms has 800 full-time employees and 200 part-time employees.

The trustees of Sheltering Arms have requested an evaluation of the hospital's property loss exposures and recommendations for a suitable property risk management program.

Sheltering Arms Hospital—Evaluation The principal direct property loss exposures to which Sheltering Arms is subject are:

1. damage to buildings or contents by fire, wind, boiler explosion, radioactive contamination, or many other perils;
2. damage to or destruction of medical records;
3. damage to data processing media, such as punch cards or magnetic tape;
4. damage to ambulances and equipment therein;
5. damage to helicopter; and
6. loss of money, drugs, or other property through criminal acts of employees or others.

The principal exposures to indirect loss are:

1. loss of earnings (including rental income) following damage to or destruction of hospital property;

2. extra expenses incurred to continue hospital services following damage to or destruction of hospital property;
3. spoilage of food or drugs resulting from damage to or failure of refrigeration equipment;
4. loss of favorable lease on the research facility resulting from damage to the building;
5. demolition cost and increased cost of construction resulting from damage to nurses' home;
6. loss from inability to collect accounts receivable because of destruction of data processing media;
7. extra expense to buy steam if power plant is unable to operate; and
8. extra expense to provide data processing service if the leased computer is damaged.

Sheltering Arms Hospital—Recommendations The exposure to damage to buildings and contents is too great for Sheltering Arms to retain, so it should be insured. A substantial deductible may be provided if the premium credit is commensurate with the losses assumed under it.

The perils for which the buildings and contents are insured should include at least fire and the extended coverage perils. Broader perils or "all-risks" coverage may be considered if the cost is appropriate.

Coverage for radioactive contamination is available in two forms. The limited form covers radioactive contamination resulting from a named peril, such as windstorm, fire, and so forth. The broad form covers radioactive contamination as a named peril, without requiring the intervention of any other named peril. The principal exposure to radioactive contamination losses at Sheltering Arms arises from the use of radioactive cobalt in the radiology department. It is likely that the potential loss from this exposure is within Sheltering Arms' ability to retain, since the principal loss would be decontamination expenses. However, if a large deductible is provided in the fire coverages, the limited form coverage may be desirable in order to avoid superimposing a contamination loss on top of the deductible amount if radioactive material is released by a named peril.

The property insurance should be written blanket on buildings and contents. Buildings should be insured for replacement cost.

Consideration should be given to the installation of automatic sprinkler systems in the owned buildings. Such installations would not only reduce insurance costs but would also reduce uninsured losses. Most importantly, they would reduce the probability of loss of life, a very important consideration in a hospital because of the number of patients who cannot escape a fire without substantial help.

A boiler and machinery policy is needed to cover damage from explosion of steam boilers and steam pipes. Such explosions are excluded from coverage under the extended coverage endorsement. The boiler policy should be written to provide replacement cost coverage.

Medical records are covered under the contents policy, but the coverage is limited to the cost of blank forms plus the cost of transcribing the records. There would be no coverage for the cost of research to reconstruct the information on the records if they were damaged to the extent that they could not be copied. A valuable papers policy can be written to cover the cost of research to replace destroyed records. It is an "all-risks" policy. As an alternative to insurance, or possibly in conjunction with it, Sheltering Arms could establish a procedure for frequent microfilming of medical records, with the microfilm copies stored in a separate building from the originals.

Damage to data processing media is covered under the contents insurance, but the coverage is limited to the cost of new blank media. Neither the cost of transcription nor the cost of research to construct information on the records is covered. These costs can be covered under the valuable papers policy discussed above or under a special data processing policy. Both policies provide "all-risks" coverage. To avoid the delays that are inevitable in reconstructing computer records, Sheltering Arms should keep duplicate tapes, updated daily, in a building separate from the main media storage area. This procedure will not only minimize delays of reconstruction, but will also reduce insurance costs. Of course, the potential loss may be so small that insurance will not be necessary if duplicate tapes are kept.

Because of the high values involved, Sheltering Arms probably would want to insure the ambulances against physical damage, but a deductible of $1,000 or more should apply to each loss. If the ambulances contain valuable medical equipment which would not be considered a part of the vehicle for insurance purposes, such equipment can be insured under an inland marine form.

Physical damage coverage on the helicopter also should be carried. The extended coverage endorsement on buildings and contents would cover any damage to them by the helicopter.

Employee dishonesty losses can be insured under a commercial blanket fidelity bond, a blanket position bond, or the employee dishonesty insuring agreement of a comprehensive 3-D or blanket crime policy. This coverage is essential for Sheltering Arms.

If substantial amounts of cash are handled, Sheltering Arms also should carry money and securities broad form coverage, both on and off premises. It seems likely that other crime losses would be within the amount that Sheltering Arms can afford to retain.

Business interruption coverage should be carried on the hospital building only. Damage to the other buildings would not result in an interruption of business. Ordinary payroll coverage would seem to be desirable because of the training required in most of the positions. The amount of insurance and the coinsurance percentage would be determined with due consideration for the time required to restore the building after a loss.

Extra expense coverage would be needed for the other buildings (other than the hospital building) to cover the extra cost of steam, laundry, and housing for nurses if those buildings are damaged. Outage coverage should be added to the policy covering steam boilers to cover extra expenses resulting from an accident as defined in the policy.

Coverage for loss from spoilage of food or drugs as a result of damage to refrigeration equipment by an insured peril can be provided by adding a consequential loss endorsement to the contents policy. Spoilage resulting from the breakdown of refrigeration equipment or from power failure can be insured under a boiler and machinery policy.

The exposure to loss from cancellation of the favorable lease on the research facility resulting from damage to the building from an insured peril can be covered by attaching a leasehold interest endorsement to a fire insurance policy. The amount of insurance would be the present value on the effective date of the endorsement of $3,000 per month (the rent for other comparable quarters minus the rent required under the lease) for the remaining term of the lease.

Three endorsements must be added to the building fire policy to cover the additional loss to Sheltering Arms if the nurses' home must be torn down and rebuilt because of a partial loss. The first of these endorsements requires the insurer to pay a total loss under those circumstances. The second pays for the cost of demolishing the remainder of the building and removing the debris. The third pays the difference in cost between: (1) building a new building identical to the old one; and (2) building a new building which complies with existing building codes.

The loss from inability to collect accounts receivable because of destruction of data processing media seems to be within the amount that Sheltering Arms can retain, especially if duplicate computer tapes are maintained as indicated above.

Insurance is available under data processing policies to cover the extra expenses incurred to provide data processing services following damage to the insured's computer. However, a better approach would be for Sheltering Arms to enter into an agreement with one or more other users of similar equipment so that each party could use equipment belonging to the others in emergency situations.

The White Lightning Case

The White Lightning Corporation is a wholesale distributor of alcoholic beverages with its main office in Atlanta, Georgia. In addition to the main office which is in a two-story building, it also has a large warehouse located in Atlanta and five other branch offices and warehouses in Georgia. In addition to its Georgia locations, it has three locations in Florida and two in California. In all locations the warehouse and the office of the branch are at the same premises. Of the eleven locations, seven qualify as highly protected risks and four do not. All of the buildings are owned by White Lightning.

Most of the accounting and recordkeeping is done at the Atlanta office, but each branch has a set of books for its operations. The main office has a computer, owned by the company, to aid in recordkeeping.

At the various locations the firm has an inventory of beverages plus office furniture, lift trucks, delivery trucks, office supplies, and warehouse equipment. In addition, company cars are furnished to five of the top executives.

Since some of the firm's business is on a cash basis, truck drivers carry money and sizable amounts of money have been known to accumulate at branch locations but no longer than overnight. Given the nature of the product sold, robbery of delivery vehicles does occur.

Besides selling domestic goods, the firm imports wine from Europe and some tequila from Mexico. The wine is shipped across the Atlantic FOB shipping point, and the tequila is carried in trucks FOB buyer's dock.

Given the fact that it has five branch locations in Georgia and a large warehouse in Atlanta, management believes that any loss at a Georgia branch would not cause a loss of service to that area. Replacement merchandise could be transported to the branch location and substitute warehouse space rented. However, damage to the Atlanta warehouse or any of the Florida or California locations would cause an interruption in business.

In the liquor business, brand identification is very important and 75 percent of White Lightning's sales result from products sold by two manufacturers. If for some reason these products were not available, a substantial reduction in sales would occur since White Lightning would have little to sell. Since the two manufacturers have international operations and are quite large, the possibility of this occurring is not great, but it is possible.

At the Atlanta office, the firm has a steam boiler used to generate heat for the office and warehouse. There also is a large air conditioning facility at that location. The other locations use small air conditioners and forced air heating.

White Lightning has requested an evaluation of their property, loss exposures, and a suggested property risk management program.

White Lightning—Evaluation The direct property loss exposures to which White Lightning is subject are:

1. damage to or destruction of buildings and their contents by fire, lightning, wind, boiler explosion, and many other perils;
2. damage to or destruction of property in transit;
3. loss of money and other property by criminal activity or government confiscation; and
4. damage to or destruction of owned cars and trucks by collision, fire, and many other perils.

The indirect property loss exposures are:

1. loss of earnings resulting from damage to the main warehouse or one or more of the California or Florida branches;
2. extra expenses to maintain operations following damage to one or more of the Georgia branches;
3. loss due to inability to collect accounts receivable as a result of damage to accounts receivable records, including data processing media, or the expenses incurred to reconstruct such records;
4. loss of earnings due to inability to obtain merchandise following an interruption of production at distilleries; and
5. loss of use of vehicles resulting from physical damage to them.

White Lightning—Recommendations The building loss exposure is potentially too severe for White Lightning to retain in its entirety. However, a substantial deductible may be attractive if: (1) the rate credit granted for it is adequate; and (2) White Lightning is financially able to bear it. The buildings and contents should be insured on a blanket basis for at least fire, the extended coverage perils, and sprinkler leakage (at the seven locations with automatic sprinkler systems). Broader perils or "all-risks" coverage may be considered if the price is reasonable. Coverage for the buildings should be on the basis of replacement cost. Multiple location forms may be used to gain the advantage of rate credits for dispersion of values, number of locations, and loss frequency. Consideration should be given to the installation of automatic sprinkler systems at the remaining four locations. Such installations would reduce insurance costs and reduce the probable severity of uninsured losses.

Boiler coverage should be provided on the steam boiler and steam pipes at the main office and warehouse, since the explosion of steam boilers and steam pipes is excluded under the extended coverage endorsement. Depending on the size of the air conditioning system, it may be desirable to provide coverage under the boiler policy for mechanical breakdown of the compressor and electrical failure in the motor and other electrical equipment. The potential losses from air conditioner failure at the other locations seem to be sufficiently small for White Lightning to retain them.

Earthquake coverage should be provided for both buildings and contents, especially at the California locations. It can be provided either as a separate policy or as an endorsement to the fire policy.

Although the computer and data processing media (punch cards, magnetic tape, etc.) are covered for their intrinsic value under the contents fire insurance policy, it may be desirable to insure them specifically. This is especially true if the contents policy is not "all-risks," since special "all-risks" data processing policies are readily available at reasonable cost. "All-risks" coverage is desirable for computers because of their high value and high damageability.

The contents policy would cover data processing media only to the extent of the cost to replace new blank cards or tape. The data processing policy would cover the cost to reconstruct the media.

It is possible that White Lightning may prefer to maintain duplicate media at another location, rather than insure the media. Or it may be desirable to do both, depending on the costs involved.

Extra expense coverage also is available to cover the cost of renting computer time elsewhere following damage to the insured's computer. As an alternative to this coverage, White Lightning may be able to work out an arrangement with another computer owner so that each will provide computer time to the other in emergency situations.

The wine is shipped from Europe, F.O.B. shipping point, so losses in transit would appear to fall on White Lightning. If the potential losses are greater than the company can retain, they should be insured under an ocean marine cargo policy with a warehouse-to-warehouse clause. Tequila is shipped F.O.B. buyer's dock, placing the burden of transit losses on the Mexican shipper. Substantial amounts of merchandise are shipped by White Lightning's owned vehicles. Insurance for this exposure should be provided under an owners' form motor truck transit policy, an inland marine coverage. Deductibles should be considered under both the ocean marine and inland marine forms provided the rate credits are sufficiently large to justify the exposure. Because of the nature of the cargoes, company trucks should be equipped with alarm systems to discourage theft and hijacking.

The exposure to loss of property by government confiscation is not insurable, so the only option open to White Lightning is to retain the exposure. Most criminal loss exposures can be insured and should be insured to the extent that the potential losses exceed the amount which White Lightning is willing to bear. Criminal losses to goods in transit could be covered under the ocean marine and inland marine policies mentioned above. Other crime coverages needed by White Lightning are:

1. blanket fidelity coverage to protect against crime losses caused by one or more employees;
2. broad form money and securities coverage, providing virtually "all-risks" protection on money and securities, and robbery and safe burglary coverage on other property, both on and off the insured's premises; and
3. open stock burglary coverage, providing insurance against theft of merchandise and office equipment through forcible entry into or exit from the insured's premises while the premises are not open for business.

All of the required crime coverages could be provided under a comprehensive 3-D policy or under blanket crime and open stock burglary policies.

White Lightning should institute some measures to control crime losses. Large sums of money should not be left in offices overnight. Arrangements should be made for a late pickup by an armored car company or bank night depository facilities should be used. Trucks should be equipped with safes that are firmly attached to the vehicle and of a type that the driver can put money in but not get it out. The amount of money carried by drivers should be minimized, possibly by requiring customers to pay by check. Burglary alarms, and possibly robbery alarms, should be installed at all locations.

White Lightning may want to retain the automobile physical damage loss exposure, but the decision to do so would depend on the value of the most expensive unit and the possibility of damage to more than one unit in a single occurrence, such as fire, tornado, or flood. Collision losses may be retained even if losses from other perils are not. If collision losses are insured, a substantial deductible should be provided.

The exposure to loss of earnings following damage to or destruction of company property is too great for White Lightning to retain in full. The exposure to loss of earnings should be insured under a gross earnings business interruption policy. The insured perils should be at least fire and the extended coverage perils, and broader perils or "all-risks" coverage may be considered if the cost is commensurate with the exposure. The policy limit and the coinsurance percentage should be determined with due regard to the probable restoration period and seasonal fluctuations in White Lightning's business. The business interruption coverage should be written on the main warehouse since the branches are supplied from the main warehouse and their business would be interrupted by a major loss at the main warehouse. The business interruption loss resulting from a loss at a branch warehouse would be minor, affecting the firm only until a temporary location could be secured and supplies shipped in. Such a small loss amount could easily be retained. The boiler policy at the main warehouse also should provide business interruption coverage, since loss caused by steam boiler explosion is excluded under fire and extended coverage.

Extra expense coverage may be needed at the Georgia branches, since property damage at those locations would not cause an interruption of business. The extra expense coverage would indemnify White Lightning for additional transportation costs, additional rent expense for substitute quarters, and other additional expenses (in excess of normal expenses) incurred to maintain service following damage to a branch. The business interruption coverage would pay such additional expenses to the extent that the business interruption loss is reduced, but that may not be adequate to cover all of the expenses incurred to maintain normal service. It is possible, of course, that the extra expenses which would not be covered by the business interruption policy are within the amount that White Lightning is willing to bear. In that case, the extra expense coverage would not be necessary.

Each branch has its own accounting records. If these records include up-to-date accounts receivable records, it would seem to be relatively simple for White Lightning to reconstruct its accounts receivable records. In that case, accounts receivable coverage would not be necessary. If branch records are not adequate to reconstruct accounts receivable, White Lightning should explore the feasibility and cost of: (1) maintaining a duplicate set of records at another location; or (2) insuring the records. Cost would be the determining factor in the choice between them. If the accounts receivable records are computerized, this coverage could be provided under a data processing policy, rather than under a separate policy.

The exposure to loss of earnings because of inability to get merchandise following damage to a supplier's factory may be sufficiently small for White Lightning to retain. This is especially possible because of the large size of the two principal suppliers, indicating that they probably have more than one factory.

If the potential loss is too great for White Lightning to bear, coverage can be provided under a contingent business interruption policy. Perils insured should be at least fire and the extended coverage perils. The amount of insurance should be determined with due regard for the time required to restore the destroyed factory and any seasonal variation in White Lightning's business. Also, if any of the liquor is aged for a prolonged period, allowance should be made for the longer interruption resulting from the aging period.

Since White Lightning does not seem to have any exceptionally valuable or unusual vehicles, the loss-of-use exposure for motor vehicles should be retained. Retention of the loss-of-use exposure would be especially attractive if the physical damage exposure is insured. However, it seems like a good exposure for retention even if the physical damage exposure also is retained.

Chapter Notes

1. *FC&S Bulletins*, Fire and Marine, Commercial Multi-Peril Mer 9.
2. *FC&S Bulletins*, Fire and Marine, Commercial Multi-Peril Pb-1.
3. *FC&S Bulletins, Companies and Coverages*, Specialty Lines, Dp-7.
4. *Insurance Buyer's Guide*, Joe T. Parrett, editor, Miscellaneous exposures, p. 1.11.
5. The information on the EDP policy is taken from FC&S Bulletins and the EDP policies used by The Home Insurance Company, The Continental Insurance Companies, and Wm. H. McGee and Co. Inc.
6. *Insurance Buyer's Guide*, p. 1.10.
7. *Multi-Coverage Account Program Manual*, New York, Insurance Services Office, p. 2.

Bibliography

Aetna Life and Casualty. *Commercial Lines Casualty & Surety Division Educational Course.*

Algermissen, S. T. "Seismic Risk Studies in the United States." Fourth World Conference on Earthquake Engineering, 1969.

Anderson, Ronald A. and Kumpf, Walter A. *Business Law.* 9th ed. Cincinnati: South-Western Publishing Co., 1973.

Bardwell, E. C. *New Profits—Business Interruption.* Indianapolis: The Rough Notes Co., 1973.

Black, Henry Campbell. *Black's Law Dictionary.* 4th ed. St. Paul: West Publishing Co., 1968.

The Cost of Crimes Against Business. Washington, DC: United States Department of Commerce, November 1974.

Criddle, A. Hawthorne. "How Can the Part Time Insurance Manager Know His Risks?" Address to the Delaware Valley Chapter of RIMS (formerly ASIM), 8 Oct. 1958.

Crime in the United States. Washington, DC: Federal Bureau of Investigation.

Daigle, Paul N. "Third Party Liability under 1972 LSHWCA Amendments." *For the Defense,* Vol. 17, July 1976.

Encyclopaedia Britannica. *1977 Book of the Year.*

F.C.&S. Bulletins. Cincinnati: The National Underwriter Co.

Fire Protection Handbook. 13th ed. Boston, MA: National Fire Protection Association, 1969.

——————. 14th ed. Boston, MA: National Fire Protection Association, 1976.

Georgia Rule Book. Insurance Services Office of Georgia.

Glendenning, G. William and Holtom, Robert B. *Personal Lines Underwriting.* Malvern, PA: Insurance Institute of America, 1977.

Gordis, Philip. *Property and Casualty Insurance.* 23rd ed. Indianapolis: The Rough Notes Co., June 1974.

"A Guide to Consumer Markets 1975-76." New York: The Conference Board.

Hershbarger, Robert A. and Miller, Ronald K. "Difference in Conditions: The Coverage and the Market." *The CPCU Annals,* Vol. 29, No. 1, March 1976.

"Highly Protected Risks." *Practical Risk Management,* B-5, July 1975.

Horn, Ronald C. *Subrogation in Insurance Theory and Practice.* Published for the S. S. Huebner Foundation for Insurance Education, Univ. of Pennsylvania. Homewood, IL: Richard D. Irwin, 1964.

How Much Honesty Insurance? Surety Association of America.

Huebner, S. S. *Property Insurance.* New York: Appleton-Century-Crofts, 1938.

Huebner, S. S.; Black, J. Kenneth; and Cline, Robert S. *Property and Liability Insurance.* New York: Appleton-Century-Crofts, 1968.

Insurance Buyer's Guide. Ed. Joe T. Parrett. Chicago: Cudahy Publishing Co.

Insurance Facts. New York: Insurance Information Institute, 1977.

Insurance Services Office Fire Class Rate Manual. 4th ed. New York: Insurance Services Office, 1975.

Launie, J. J.; Lee, Finley J.; and Baglini, Norman A. *Principles of Property and Liability Underwriting.* Malvern, PA: Insurance Institute of America, 1976.

Lincoln, N. O. and Tisdale, G. W. *Insurance Inspection and Underwriting.* 8th ed. Philadelphia: Chilton Co., 1965.

Long, John C. and Gregg, Davis W. *Property and Liability Insurance Handbook.* Homewood, IL: Richard D. Irwin, 1965.

Mehr, Robert I. and Hedges, Bob A. *Risk Management Concepts and Applications.* Homewood, IL: Richard D. Irwin, 1974.

Multi-Coverage Account Program Manual. New York: Insurance Services Office.

NFPA Inspection Manual. 4th ed. Boston, MA: National Fire Protection Association, 1976.

P.F.&M. Analyses. Property Manual. Indianapolis, IN: Rough Notes Co. Riegel, Robert; Miller, Jerome S.; and Williams, C. Arthur Jr. *Insurance Principles and Practices: Property and Liability.* 6th ed. Englewood Cliffs, NJ: Prentice-Hall Publishing Co., 1976.

Rodda, William H. *Marine Insurance: Ocean and Inland.* 3rd ed. Englewood Cliffs, NJ: Prentice-Hall Publishing Co., 1970.

Santa Clara Valley Chapter, Society of CPCU. *The Insuring of Condominiums and Cooperatives.* Indianapolis: The Rough Notes Company, 1976.

Tipton, Howard D. "Require Sprinklers in Public Buildings, NFPCA Official Urges." *The National Underwriter* (Property/Casualty), 11 Nov. 1977, pp. 56-57.

U.S. Department of Commerce. *Crime in Retailing.* Washington, DC: GPO, 1974.

——————. *Crime in Retailing.* Washington, DC: GPO, 1975.

Vaughan, Emmett J. and Elliot, C. H. *Fundamentals of Risk and Insurance.* Santa Barbara: Wiley-Hamilton, 1972.

Werbel's General Insurance Guide. Ed. Bernard G. Werbel. New York: Insurance Educational Publications, 1972.

Winter, William D. *Marine Insurance.* 3rd ed. New York: McGraw-Hill Book Co., 1952.

1978 Year Book Covering the Year 1977, Annual Supplement to Collier's Encyclopedia and Merit Students Encyclopedia. New York: Macmillan Educational Corp., 1977.

Index

A

Abandonment, 44
Accident, 210
Accidental shooting and drowning, 341
Account rating, multi-coverage, 349
Accounts receivable, 94, 347
Accounts receivable endorsement (MP-175), 265
Acts of God, 6
Acts of the public enemy, 6
Actual cash value, 37
Advantages, of combination, 248
Agreement, insuring, 173, 211
Agreements, general, 173, 181
    side track, 10
Air conditioning equipment, and boiler pressure vessels, 325
Alarms, central station, 143
    local, 143
Alarm systems, 142
    deficiencies of, 143
    selection of, 143
"All-risks" coverage, and business personal property, 131
    deductibles in, 133
"All-risks" crop coverage, 229
"All-risks" policies, crime losses covered by, 134
Alteration of forgery, 180
Alternatives, risk management, 201
Amounts covered, 167

Animal floaters, 74
Animal mortality insurance, 225
Annual transit policies, 52
Apartment building, 317
Association, condominium, 280
Assumption, earthquake, 324
Automatic cancellation, 168
Automatic coverage, 212

B

Bailee, no benefit to, 41
Bailee coverage for miscellaneous situations, 68
Bailees, commercial, 16
    indirect loss exposures of, 17
    liability of, 15
Bailees' customers insurance, 62
Bailees' customers policies, other, 67
Bailment loss exposures, 14
Bankers blanket bond, 177
Bankers bonds, other, 185
Banks, excess and catastrophe coverages for, 185
Barewall concept, 279
Bill of lading, mistake on, 9
    order, 8
    released, 8
    straight, 8
Bills of lading, 7
Blackmail or extortion, 104

367

C

D

M

R